Life Is Sweeter with a *Taste of Home!*

Here are the dishes we love and the meals we remember.

64

90

219

For decades, *Taste of Home* has meant good, honest home cooking, the kinds of memorable dishes we pass from one generation to the next. These are the recipes that great home cooks share with their own families, and we're sure that you'll love them, too!

As you page through *Taste of Home Annual Recipes*, you'll find 470 delectable dishes, plus a heartwarming note about what makes each recipe special. You'll discover dozens of Test Kitchen tips, tricks, serving ideas and more. Soon these specialties will find their way onto your table...and into your family's hearts.

This cookbook includes an entire year's worth of recipes from the magazine, plus hundreds of bonus dishes never before seen in *Taste of Home.* Featured chapters include:

- **Quick Fixes**
  Thirty entrees are table-ready in 30 minutes or less.

- **Cook It Fast or Slow**
  Each recipe includes cooking instructions for both the Instant Pot® and slow cooker.

- **Meal Planner**
  Save money and time with amazing uses for Thanksgiving turkey, a summer garden's bounty, and more.

Five icons help you make the most of kitchen time:

- = Finished in 30 minutes or less
- = Lower in calories, fat and sodium
- = Pressure-cooked recipe
- = Made in a slow cooker
- = Uses 5 or fewer ingredients
(excluding water, salt, pepper, and canola/olive oil)
- = Includes freezing/reheating instructions

Find new classics to flip for when you cook with *Taste of Home!*

MODERN COMFORT

Fresh takes on comfort-food classics are moments away when you thumb through *Taste of Home Annual Recipes.* Everybody loves handy sheet-pan meals, and Rosemary Salmon & Veggies (top) is quick and healthy, plus it packs in a serving of veggies. If you've never tasted Cincinnati Chili (center), see what you've been missing with a choice recipe from an Ohio native! Finally, get ready for exclamations of glee when Raspberry Moscow Mule Cake (bottom) lands on the table.

SUPREME PIZZA QUINOA BOWL
PAGE 119

Taste of Home

Executive Editor: Mark Hagen
Senior Art Director:
Raeann Thompson
Editors: Christine Rukavena,
Amy Glander, Hazel Wheaton
Art Director: Maggie Conners
Graphic Designers:
Arielle Jardine, Jazmin Delgado
Deputy Editor, Copy Desk:
Dulcie Shoener

Cover Photographer:
Dan Roberts
Set Stylist: Stacey Genaw
Food Stylist: Josh Rink

Pictured on front cover:
Herbed Rib Roast, p. 288;
Grandma's Yeast Rolls, p. 291;
Dutch Cran-Apple Pie, p. 214
Pictured on back cover: Broccoli
with Garlic, Bacon & Parmesan,
p. 155; Mashed Potatoes with
Horseradish, p. 288.

**International Standard
Book Number:**
D 978-1-61765-987-4
U 978-1-61765-988-1
**International Standard Serial
Number:**
1094-3463

Component Number:
D 117400100H
U 117400102H

Printed in U.S.A.
1 3 5 7 9 10 8 6 4 2

Contents

Get Social with Us!

 Like Us:
facebook.com/tasteofhome

 Pin Us:
pinterest.com/taste_of_home

To find a recipe: tasteofhome.com

To submit a recipe: tasteofhome.com/submit

 Follow Us:
@tasteofhome

Tweet Us:
twitter.com/tasteofhome

To find out about other *Taste of Home* **products:**
shoptasteofhome.com

CHICKEN PICCATA MEATBALLS
PAGE 14

Appetizers & Beverages

Here you'll find more than two dozen tasty twists on nachos, hot wings, meatballs and other fun bites that people crave. Get refreshing sippers, too! Good food makes a gathering great, so let's get the party started.

STICKY MAPLE PEPPER GLAZED CHICKEN WINGS

2. Using a sharp knife, cut through the 2 wing joints; discard wing tips. In a shallow bowl, combine flour, baking powder, pepper, salt and garlic powder. Add wing pieces, a few at a time, and toss to coat; shake off excess.

3. Place on prepared baking sheets. Bake until no longer pink, 40-50 minutes, turning once. Meanwhile, in a small saucepan, combine glaze ingredients. Bring to a boil. Reduce heat; simmer until thickened, 5-7 minutes, stirring frequently. Drizzle over wings; toss to coat. If desired, top with chopped green onions.

1 PIECE: *66 cal., 3g fat (1g sat. fat), 14mg chol., 63mg sod., 4g carb. (3g sugars, 0 fiber), 5g pro.*

MARGARITA ICE CREAM FLOATS

On a hot afternoon, what could be better than a cold margarita? The addition of creamy ice cream really takes this treat to the next level.
—Teri Rasey, Cadillac, MI

TAKES: 5 min. • **MAKES:** 6 servings

    Lime wedges
    Sugar
- 2 cups vanilla ice cream
- 2 cups lime sherbet
- 6 cups lemon-lime soda, chilled
- ¾ cup lime juice
- 9 oz. silver tequila

1. Using lime wedges, moisten the rims of 6 margarita or cocktail glasses. Set aside lime wedges for garnish. Sprinkle sugar on a plate; hold each glass upside down and dip rim into sugar. Set aside. Discard remaining sugar on plate.

2. Scoop ice cream and sherbet into prepared glasses. Combine soda, lime juice and tequila; pour into glasses. Garnish with reserved lime wedges. Serve immediately.

1 MARGARITA: *372 cal., 6g fat (4g sat. fat), 20mg chol., 83mg sod., 55g carb. (46g sugars, 1g fiber), 2g pro.*

STICKY MAPLE PEPPER GLAZED CHICKEN WINGS

This is one of my favorite appetizers to make over the holidays! The coarse ground pepper cuts the sweetness of the maple syrup by adding just the right amount of heat. These chicken wings are best fresh out of the oven (they are nice and crispy), but they are also delicious if made ahead and kept warm in a slow cooker.
—Shannon Dobos, Calgary, AB

PREP: 25 min. • **BAKE:** 40 min.
MAKES: about 40 pieces

- 4 lbs. chicken wings
- ¼ cup all-purpose flour
- ½ Tbsp. baking powder
- 1 tsp. coarsely ground pepper
- 1 tsp. kosher salt
- ½ tsp. garlic powder

GLAZE
- ⅔ cup maple syrup
- 2 tsp. coarsely ground pepper
- 2 tsp. soy sauce
- 1 garlic clove, minced
    Chopped green onions, optional

1. Preheat the oven to 425°. Line two 15x10x1-in. baking pans with foil and coat with cooking spray; set aside.

CHERRY LIMEADE SWEET TEA

Sweet tea and cherry limeade are two of my favorite summer libations. So I decided to combine them—the results are wonderful.
—Renee Page, Rochelle, IL

PREP: 10 min. • **COOK:** 10 min. + cooling
MAKES: 14 servings (about 2½ qt.)

8   cups water
6   tea bags
¼   cup sugar
1   can (12 oz.) frozen limeade concentrate, thawed
1   cup chilled cherry juice blend
    Ice cubes
    Lime wedges and pitted dark sweet cherries

1. In a Dutch oven, bring water to a boil; remove from heat. Add tea bags; steep, covered, 10 minutes. Discard tea bags. Stir in sugar until dissolved; cool slightly. Transfer to a pitcher; cool completely.
2. Add limeade concentrate and cherry juice to tea. Serve over ice with lime wedges and cherries.
¾ CUP: 71 cal., 0 fat (0 sat. fat), 0 chol., 6mg sod., 18g carb. (16g sugars, 0 fiber), 0 pro.

CHERRY LIMEADE SWEET TEA

5i MINI CHEESE BALLS

These mini cheese balls are the perfect quick appetizer for any party. Roll them in toasted sesame seeds, fresh rosemary and/or paprika to add even more flavor.
—Judy Spivey, Ennice, NC

PREP: 30 min. + chilling • **MAKES:** 36 cheese balls

1   pkg. (8 oz.) cream cheese, softened
2   cups shredded sharp cheddar cheese
    Optional toppings: Toasted sesame seeds, minced fresh rosemary and paprika
    Optional garnishes: Halved rye crisps and rolled tortilla chips

In a large bowl, combine cheeses. Shape into 36 balls; roll balls in toppings as desired. Cover and refrigerate 8 hours or overnight. To serve, if desired, press a rye crisp or rolled corn chip into the top of each cheese ball.
1 CHEESE BALL: 47 cal., 4g fat (2g sat. fat), 13mg chol., 61mg sod., 1g carb. (0 sugars, 0 fiber), 2g pro.

BUFFALO CHICKEN CRESCENT ROLLS

PEACHES & CREAM FIZZ

This recipe came about when I was a child living in peach country in eastern Washington. There were fresh peaches everywhere, so my mom and I came up with this refreshing beverage. We called it a fizz because there's a bit of bubbling from the ginger ale. This recipe says summer to my family and me. Add more ginger ale to make it thinner, more ice cream to make it thicker. By the way, there is no need to peel the peaches.
—Teresa Jarnot, Monroe, WA

TAKES: 10 min. • **MAKES:** 6 servings

- 3 medium peaches, pitted
- ⅓ cup ginger ale, chilled, plus additional for topping if desired
- 2 Tbsp. honey
- 1 qt. vanilla ice cream
  Optional: Whipped cream and peach slices

Place peaches, ginger ale and honey in a blender; cover and process until smooth. Add ice cream; cover and process until combined. Pour into serving glasses. If desired, top with whipped cream or additional ginger ale and garnish with peach slices. Serve immediately.
¾ CUP: 237 cal., 10g fat (6g sat. fat), 39mg chol., 72mg sod., 35g carb. (32g sugars, 2g fiber), 4g pro.

BUFFALO CHICKEN CRESCENT ROLLS

My husband loves Buffalo wings, but they are so messy! These Buffalo chicken rolls are mess-free and always go fast at parties— and they're much tastier than regular Buffalo wings, if you ask me.
—Tiffinie Cichon, Gulfport, MS

PREP: 20 min. • **BAKE:** 15 min. • **MAKES:** 16 rolls

- 1 cup shredded cooked chicken
- 4 oz. cream cheese, cubed
- ½ cup shredded cheddar cheese
- 2 Tbsp. prepared ranch salad dressing
- 2 Tbsp. Buffalo wing sauce
- 2 tubes (8 oz. each) refrigerated crescent rolls
- ⅓ cup crumbled blue cheese

1. Preheat oven to 375°. In a small saucepan, combine chicken, cream cheese, cheddar cheese, ranch dressing and wing sauce. Cook and stir over low heat until cheeses are melted, about 5 minutes. Remove from the heat.
2. Unroll tubes of crescent dough; separate into 16 triangles. Place 1 Tbsp. chicken mixture in the center of each triangle; sprinkle with 1 tsp. blue cheese. Bring corners of dough over the filling and twist; pinch seams to seal (filling will not be completely enclosed). Place on ungreased baking sheets.
3. Bake until golden brown, 15-20 minutes. Serve warm.
1 APPETIZER: 175 cal., 11g fat (3g sat. fat), 21mg chol., 372mg sod., 13g carb. (3g sugars, 0 fiber), 6g pro.

PEACHES & CREAM FIZZ

MARINATED OLIVES

These olives are nice to have for get-togethers because they're simple to make and they add a little zest to the other offerings on the buffet.
—Marguerite Shaeffer, Sewell, NJ

PREP: 10 min. + marinating • **MAKES:** 4 cups

- 2 cups large pimiento-stuffed olives, drained
- 1 cup pitted kalamata olives, drained
- 1 cup pitted medium ripe olives, drained
- ¼ cup olive oil
- 2 Tbsp. lemon juice
- 1 Tbsp. minced fresh thyme or 1 tsp. dried thyme
- 2 tsp. minced fresh rosemary or ½ tsp. dried rosemary, crushed
- 2 tsp. grated lemon zest
- 4 garlic cloves, slivered
   Pepper to taste

1. Place olives in a bowl. Combine remaining ingredients; pour over olives and stir. Cover and refrigerate for 1-2 days before serving, stirring several times each day.

2. Olives may be refrigerated for 2 weeks. Serve with a slotted spoon.

¼ **CUP:** 98 cal., 10g fat (1g sat. fat), 0 chol., 572mg sod., 3g carb. (0 sugars, 0 fiber), 0 pro.

CRANBERRY & BACON SWISS CHEESE DIP

This warm, rich and creamy Swiss dip is guaranteed to please family and friends alike. Served with thin, crunchy slices of French bread, it makes the perfect appetizer— especially because it can be prepared ahead, put in the fridge, and then baked just before you want to serve it.
—Jeanne Holt, Mendota Heights, MN

PREP: 20 min. • **BAKE:** 25 min. • **MAKES:** 3 cups

- ⅔ cup mayonnaise
- ⅓ cup spreadable chive and onion cream cheese
- 1 Tbsp. stone-ground mustard
- ¼ tsp. garlic pepper blend
- 3 cups shredded Swiss cheese
- 1 pkg. (10 oz.) frozen chopped onions, thawed and patted dry

CRANBERRY & BACON SWISS CHEESE DIP

- 8 pieces ready-to-serve fully cooked bacon, chopped
- ½ cup sliced almonds, divided
- ⅓ cup dried cranberries, chopped
   Slices French bread baguette (¼ in. thick), toasted

1. Preheat oven to 325°. In a large bowl, combine the mayonnaise, cream cheese, mustard and garlic pepper blend. Add Swiss cheese; mix well. Stir in the onions, bacon, ¼ cup almonds and cranberries. Spread into a greased 3-cup baking dish. Sprinkle with remaining ¼ cup almonds. Place on a baking sheet.

2. Bake, uncovered, until bubbly, 25-30 minutes. Serve warm with baguette slices.

¼ **CUP:** 266 cal., 22g fat (8g sat. fat), 30mg chol., 222mg sod., 8g carb. (5g sugars, 1g fiber), 10g pro.

BUFFALO WING NACHOS
I like using spicy Buffalo sauce, shredded chicken and celery. I finish it all off with a drizzle of ranch dressing and some blue cheese crumbles.
—Marina Castle Kelley, Canyon Country, CA

A little squeeze of lime brightens up almost any kind of nachos.

NACHO AVERAGE
NACHOS

Pile your plate with these loaded-up twists on a game-day classic.

BLACK BEAN NACHOS
We use corn, black beans, sliced green onions, black olives and shredded cheddar cheese on our nachos.
—Becky Carver, North Royalton, OH

APPLE NACHOS
Slice up apples, then add a drizzle of caramel and a sauce made of marshmallows melted with butter. Sprinkle peanuts and chocolate chips on top.
—RaeAnn Gnatkowski, Carrolton, MI

NACHO TOTS
We make nachos using Tater Tots! Top with chorizo, black beans, jalapenos, cilantro, green onions, avocado, tomato and a little sour cream.
—Connie Krupp, Racine, WI

CHORIZO NACHOS
We love the spicy-cool combo, so our nachos are topped with chorizo, queso, jalapenos and guacamole.
—Angela Lively, Conroe, TX

GRINDER NACHOS

In our house, we add Italian sausage, mushrooms, onions, pizza sauce, scamorza cheese and pickled pepper rings.
—*Barbara Rankin, Des Moines, IA*

PULLED PORK NACHOS

Our go-to nachos are Tex-Mex style, with barbecued pulled pork, coleslaw, BBQ sauce, pickled red onions, nacho cheese and sour cream.
—*Dave Reed III, Charlotte, NC*

NACHO PIE

Crush 4 cups **nacho-flavored tortilla chips;** put in a greased 9-in. pie plate. Cook 1 lb. **ground beef** and ½ cup chopped **onion** until beef is no longer pink; drain. Spoon over chips; top with a 16-oz. can **chili beans,** an 8-oz. can **tomato sauce** and 1 cup **shredded mozzarella.** Bake at 375° 7-8 minutes.
—*LaVerna Mjones, Moorhead, MN*

SLOPPY JOE NACHOS

Turn a sandwich classic into nachos. Top tortilla chips with sloppy joe mix, shredded cheddar cheese and a scattering of sliced black olives.
—*Janet Rhoden, Hortonville, WI*

NACHO POPCORN

Make nacho-flavored popcorn! Combine ½ cup melted **butter,** 2 Tbsp. **grated Parmesan,** 2 Tbsp. **dried parsley,** 1 tsp. **garlic salt,** 1 tsp. **chili powder** and a few drops of **hot sauce,** then toss with **popcorn.**
—*Linda Boehme, Fairmont, MN*

FLORENTINE CIABATTA

PEPPY PEACH SALSA

Garden-fresh salsas are one of my favorite condiments. So when I saw a recipe for peach salsa in the newspaper, I couldn't think of anything that sounded better.
—Jennifer Abbott, Moraga, CA

TAKES: 20 min. • **MAKES:** 1¼ cups

- 2 Tbsp. lime juice
- 1 Tbsp. honey
- ½ tsp. minced garlic
- ⅛ tsp. ground ginger
- 2 fresh peaches, peeled and diced
- ½ green serrano chile pepper, seeded and minced
- ½ red serrano chile pepper, seeded and minced
- ½ small yellow chile pepper, seeded and minced
- 2 tsp. minced fresh cilantro
   Tortilla chips

In a small bowl, combine the lime juice, honey, garlic and ginger; let stand for 5 minutes. Stir in the peaches, peppers and cilantro. Serve with chips. Refrigerate leftovers.

¼ CUP: *30 cal., 0 fat (0 sat. fat), 0 chol., 1mg sod., 8g carb. (6g sugars, 1g fiber), 0 pro.*

FLORENTINE CIABATTA

I came up with this appetizer because of my love for white pizza. I've served my ciabatta pizza at many holiday parties, and it's always a big hit with both the children and the adults.
—Noreen McCormick Danek, Cromwell, CT

PREP: 20 min. + cooling • **BAKE:** 15 min. • **MAKES:** 16 servings

- ½ cup olive oil
- 2 garlic cloves, minced
- ¾ tsp. dried basil
- ¼ tsp. kosher salt
- ¼ tsp. dried oregano
   Dash crushed red pepper flakes
- 1 loaf (16 oz.) ciabatta bread, cut into 16 slices
- ⅓ cup chopped oil-packed sun-dried tomatoes
- ⅓ cup chopped roasted sweet red peppers
- ¼ cup frozen chopped spinach, thawed and squeezed dry
- 1½ cups shredded mozzarella cheese
- ⅓ cup pine nuts, toasted

1. In a small saucepan, heat oil over medium heat. Add garlic; cook 1 minute. Remove from heat: stir in seasonings. Cool completely.
2. Preheat oven to 400°. Place bread on ungreased baking sheets. Bake until golden brown, 5-7 minutes on each side. Spread with garlic oil. Top with sun-dried tomatoes, roasted peppers and spinach; sprinkle with cheese. Bake until cheese is melted, 3-5 minutes longer. Sprinkle with pine nuts. Serve immediately.
1 SLICE: *200 cal., 12g fat (3g sat. fat), 8mg chol., 258mg sod., 19g carb. (1g sugars, 1g fiber), 5g pro.*

PEPPY PEACH SALSA

CREAMY PUMPKIN HUMMUS

CHIA SEED PROTEIN BITES

I keep these little bites on hand in my refrigerator and grab them for breakfast or a snack when I'm in a hurry. We have a lot of food allergies in our family, and I like to keep healthy snacks around that everyone can eat. This recipe has no gluten, eggs, dairy or corn, so it's the perfect go-to treat in our house.
—*Tanja Miller, Peoria, AZ*

PREP: 15 min. + chilling • **MAKES:** about 2½ dozen

- 1½ cups quick-cooking oats
- ½ cup almond butter or creamy peanut butter
- ½ cup chia seeds
- ½ cup honey
- ¼ cup vanilla or chocolate protein powder
- ¼ cup unsweetened shredded coconut
   Additional unsweetened shredded coconut, optional

In a large bowl, combine the first 6 ingredients. Refrigerate for 1 hour or until firm enough to roll. Shape into 1½-in. balls. Roll in additional coconut if desired. Store in the refrigerator.
1 PIECE: *72 cal., 4g fat (1g sat. fat), 0 chol., 14mg sod., 9g carb. (5g sugars, 2g fiber), 2g pro.*

CHIA SEED PROTEIN BITES

CREAMY PUMPKIN HUMMUS

I love to serve this pumpkin hummus with sliced apples, pears and pita chips. Top it with toasted pumpkin seeds, a drizzle of pumpkin seed oil and even fried sage leaves.
—*James Schend, Pleasant Prairie, WI*

TAKES: 25 min. • **MAKES:** 3 cups

- 1 can (15 oz.) garbanzo beans, rinsed and drained
- 1 cup canned pumpkin
- ⅓ cup tahini
- ¼ cup olive oil or pumpkin seed oil
- 3 Tbsp. orange juice
- 1 Tbsp. toasted sesame oil
- 1 tsp. ground cumin
- 1 tsp. minced garlic
- ¼ tsp. salt
- 2 Tbsp. pumpkin seed oil or olive oil, optional
- ¼ cup salted pumpkin seeds or pepitas
- ¼ cup pomegranate seeds
   Baked pita chips and sliced apples and pears

In a food processor, combine the first 9 ingredients; cover and process until smooth. Transfer to a serving platter or bowl. Garnish with oil if desired; top with pumpkin seeds and pomegranate seeds. Serve with pita chips, apples and pears.
¼ CUP: *153 cal., 12g fat (2g sat. fat), 0 chol., 104mg sod., 9g carb. (2g sugars, 3g fiber), 4g pro.* **Diabetic exchanges:** *2½ fat, ½ starch.*

**ST. LOUIS
TOASTED RAVIOLI**

ST. LOUIS
TOASTED RAVIOLI

*While visiting a friend who had just moved
to St. Louis, Missouri, I tried these toasted
ravioli at almost every restaurant! When I
got home, I had to try to replicate them, and
this recipe comes pretty close.*
—Cristina Carrera, Kenosha, WI

- -

PREP: 15 min. • **COOK:** 20 min.
MAKES: about 1½ dozen

- 1 cup seasoned bread crumbs
- ¼ cup shredded Parmesan cheese
- 2 tsp. dried basil
- 1 cup all-purpose flour
- 2 large eggs, lightly beaten
- 1 pkg. (9 oz.) frozen beef ravioli, thawed
  Oil for deep-fat frying
  Fresh minced basil and additional
  shredded Parmesan cheese, optional
- 1 cup marinara sauce

1. In a shallow bowl, mix bread crumbs,
Parmesan cheese and basil. Place flour and
eggs in separate shallow bowls. Dip ravioli
in flour to coat both sides; shake off excess.
Dip in egg, then in crumb mixture, patting
to help coating adhere.

2. In a deep cast-iron or electric skillet, heat
½ in. of oil to 375°. Fry ravioli, a few at a
time, until golden brown, 1-2 minutes on
each side. Drain on paper towels. If desired,
immediately sprinkle with basil and cheese.
Serve warm with marinara sauce.
1 PIECE: *73 cal., 5g fat (1g sat. fat), 6mg chol.,
117mg sod., 6g carb. (1g sugars, 1g fiber),
2g pro.*

CHICKEN
PICCATA
MEATBALLS
(SHOWN ON PAGE 4)

*The classic chicken piccata entree is my
favorite dish, but I wanted another way
to have all the same flavors. These chicken
piccata meatballs are the perfect solution,
whether served alone or with a sauce like
marinara or Buffalo! Serve over buttered
noodles if you'd like, or stick toothpicks in
them for appetizers.*
—Dawn Collins, Rowley, MA

- -

PREP: 20 min. • **COOK:** 25 min.
MAKES: 2 dozen

- ½ cup dry bread crumbs
- ⅓ cup grated Parmesan cheese

- 1 large egg, lightly beaten
- 1 tsp. garlic powder
- ¼ tsp. salt
- ⅛ tsp. pepper
- 1 lb. ground chicken
- 2 Tbsp. canola oil, divided
- 2 garlic cloves, minced
- ⅓ cup chicken broth
- ¼ cup white wine
- 1 jar (3½ oz.) capers, drained
- 1 Tbsp. lemon juice
- 2 Tbsp. butter
  Shredded Parmesan cheese and
  lemon wedges

1. In a large bowl, combine the first
6 ingredients. Add chicken; mix lightly
but thoroughly. With wet hands, shape
into 1-in. balls.

2. In a large skillet, heat 1 Tbsp. oil over
medium heat. Brown meatballs in batches;
drain. Remove and keep warm. In the same
skillet, heat remaining 1 Tbsp. oil over
medium heat. Add garlic; cook 1 minute.

3. Add broth and wine to pan; increase
heat to medium-high. Cook 1 minute,
stirring to loosen browned bits from pan.
Add capers and lemon juice; bring to a boil.
Add meatballs. Reduce heat; simmer,
uncovered, until meatballs are cooked
through, 5-7 minutes, stirring occasionally.
Remove from heat; stir in butter until
melted. Sprinkle with Parmesan cheese
and serve with lemon wedges.
1 MEATBALL: *63 cal., 4g fat (1g sat. fat), 24mg
chol., 193mg sod., 2g carb. (0 sugars, 0 fiber),
4g pro.*

🕐 5️⃣

HIBISCUS ICED TEA
*This calorie- and caffeine-free tea has a
delightful rosy color.*
—Taste of Home *Test Kitchen*

- -

TAKES: 10 min. • **MAKES:** 1 serving

- 1 cup water
- 5 dried hibiscus flowers or 1 tsp.
  crushed dried hibiscus flowers
  Ice cubes

In a saucepan, bring water to a boil. Remove
from the heat. Add hibiscus flowers and let
stand 5 minutes. Strain tea. Serve in chilled
glasses over ice.

DAIRY-FREE QUESO

🕐 🍎 ⑤ ROSEMARY WALNUTS

My Aunt Mary started making this recipe years ago, and each time we visited her she would have a batch ready for us. The use of cayenne adds an unexpected zing to the savory combo of rosemary and walnuts. When you need a good housewarming or hostess gift, double the batch and save one for yourself.
—*Renee Ciancio, New Bern, NC*

- -

TAKES: 20 min. • **MAKES:** 2 cups

- 2 **cups walnut halves**
    Cooking spray
- 2 **tsp. dried rosemary, crushed**
- ½ **tsp. kosher salt**
- ¼ **to ½ tsp. cayenne pepper**

1. Place walnuts in a small bowl. Spritz with cooking spray. Add the seasonings; toss to coat. Place in a single layer on a baking sheet.
2. Bake at 350° for 10 minutes. Serve warm, or cool completely and store in an airtight container.
¼ **CUP:** *166 cal., 17g fat (2g sat. fat), 0 chol., 118mg sod., 4g carb. (1g sugars, 2g fiber), 4g pro.* **Diabetic exchanges:** *3 fat.*

ROSEMARY WALNUTS

🍎 DAIRY-FREE QUESO

This healthy queso is our household's newest obsession. It's so shockingly delicious, you have to try it to believe it!
—*Becky Hardin, St. Peters, MO*

- -

PREP: 20 min. + standing • **COOK:** 5 min. • **MAKES:** 3 cups

- 2 **cups raw cashews**
- 1 **cup water or unsweetened almond milk**
- ⅓ **cup nutritional yeast**
- ¼ **cup chopped fresh cilantro**
- 1 **Tbsp. lime juice**
- 1 **tsp. salt**
- ½ **tsp. chili powder**
- 1 **can (10 oz.) diced tomatoes and green chiles, drained**
    Tortilla chips and assorted vegetables

1. Rinse cashews in cold water. Place in a large bowl; add water to cover by 3 in. Cover and let stand overnight.
2. Drain and rinse cashews, discarding liquid. Transfer to a food processor. Add 1 cup water, nutritional yeast, cilantro, lime juice, salt and chili powder; cover and process until pureed, 3-4 minutes, scraping down sides as needed.
3. Transfer to a small saucepan. Stir in tomatoes; heat through. Serve with tortilla chips and vegetables.
¼ **CUP:** *117 cal., 8g fat (1g sat. fat), 0 chol., 301mg sod., 7g carb. (1g sugars, 1g fiber), 4g pro.*

TEST KITCHEN TIP

Cashews give this queso a rich and creamy texture but only if they're soaked long enough. It's best to start the night before and let them soak at least 8 hours.

FROZEN BRANDY OLD-FASHIONEDS

Both sides of my family are midwestern, so our strong brandy tradition is evident in the slush we make for the holidays and in the Wisconsin old-fashioned cocktails we enjoy year-round. I decided to combine those recipes into something completely new. The drinks go very quickly at gatherings!
—Stephanie Vaughan, Madison, WI

- -

PREP: 15 min. + freezing
MAKES: 12 servings (about 2½ qt. slush mix)

- 6   cups water
- 1   cup sugar
- 2   cups brandy
- 1   can (12 oz.) frozen orange juice concentrate, thawed
- ¼   cup maraschino cherry juice
- ¼   cup bitters

EACH SERVING
- ¼   cup lemon-lime soda, chilled
     Optional: Maraschino cherries and orange wedges

1. In a large saucepan, bring water and sugar to a boil. Cook and stir until sugar is dissolved; cool completely. Stir in brandy, orange juice concentrate, juice and bitters. Pour into a 3-qt. freezer container. Freeze overnight or until set.

2. For each serving, scoop ¾ cup slush into a rocks glass. Pour lemon-lime soda into the glass; serve with fruit as desired.

1 SERVING: *246 cal., 0 fat (0 sat. fat), 0 chol., 9mg sod., 38g carb. (32g sugars, 0 fiber), 1g pro.*

KICKIN' CAULIFLOWER

KICKIN' CAULIFLOWER

Try these savory bites for a zippy appetizer that's healthy, too!
—Emily Tyra, Traverse City, MI

- -

TAKES: 25 min. • **MAKES:** 8 servings

- 1   medium head cauliflower (about 2¼ lbs.), cut into florets
- 1   Tbsp. canola oil
- ½   cup Buffalo wing sauce
     Blue cheese salad dressing

1. Preheat oven to 400°. Toss cauliflower with oil; spread in a 15x10x1-in. pan. Roast until tender and lightly browned, 20-25 minutes, stirring once.

2. Transfer to a bowl; toss with wing sauce. Serve with dressing.
⅓ CUP: *39 cal., 2g fat (0 sat. fat), 0 chol., 474mg sod., 5g carb. (2g sugars, 2g fiber), 2g pro.*

FROZEN BRANDY OLD-FASHIONEDS

CHILEAN MONKEY TAIL PUNCH

Stories vary surrounding the origins of this punch's unique name. Some say it was initially served in a bottle depicting a monkey with a long tail, but others suggest that it was named after a funny incident with a Chilean president in the early 1900s. Whatever the origin, this sweet chilled drink made with coffee and spirits will warm you right up during the holiday season.
—Taste of Home *Test Kitchen*

PREP: 5 min. • **COOK:** 10 min. + chilling
MAKES: 16 servings

- 4 cups 2% milk
- 1 cup sugar
- 3 cinnamon sticks (3 in.)
- 3 whole cloves
- 2 cups strong brewed coffee
- 1½ cups pisco, aguardiente, grappa or brandy
- 2 tsp. vanilla extract

1. In a large saucepan, combine the milk, sugar, cinnamon sticks and cloves. Bring to a boil. Reduce heat; simmer, uncovered, 5 minutes. Remove from heat and cool to room temperature.
2. Strain into a large pitcher, discarding spices. Stir in coffee, pisco and vanilla. Cover and refrigerate until chilled. Serve over ice.

½ CUP: 129 cal., 1g fat (1g sat. fat), 5mg chol., 29mg sod., 16g carb. (16g sugars, 0 fiber), 2g pro.

NACHO TRIANGLES WITH SALSA-RANCH DIPPING SAUCE

These nacho bites are a fun fusion of Greek appetizers and flavors of the American Southwest. The simple dipping sauce is a perfect match—the ranch balances out the heat of the jalapeno and chipotle peppers—and takes the recipe to the next level.
—Angela Spengler, Niceville, FL

PREP: 45 min. • **BAKE:** 15 min./batch
MAKES: 4 dozen

- ½ lb. ground beef
- ¼ cup finely chopped onion
- ½ cup shredded pepper jack cheese

NACHO TRIANGLES WITH SALSA-RANCH DIPPING SAUCE

- ½ cup shredded cheddar cheese
- ¼ cup frozen corn, thawed
- ¼ cup canned diced tomatoes
- 2 Tbsp. taco seasoning
- 2 Tbsp. finely chopped seeded jalapeno pepper
- 1 Tbsp. finely chopped chipotle peppers in adobo sauce
- 32 sheets phyllo dough (14x9-in. size)
- ¾ cup butter, melted
- ½ cup ranch salad dressing
- ½ cup salsa

1. Preheat oven to 375°. In a small skillet, cook beef and onion over medium heat until beef is no longer pink and onion is tender, 5-7 minutes, breaking up beef into crumbles; drain. Stir in cheeses, corn, diced tomatoes, taco seasoning, and the jalapeno and chipotle peppers; set aside.
2. Place 1 sheet phyllo dough on a work surface; brush lightly with butter. Cover with another sheet of phyllo; brush with butter. (Keep remaining phyllo covered with plastic wrap and a damp towel to prevent it from drying out.)
3. Cut the 2 layered sheets into three 14x3-in. strips. Place 1 Tbsp. filling about 1 in. from the corner of each strip. Fold 1 corner of dough over filling, forming a triangle. Fold triangle over, forming another triangle. Continue folding, like a flag, until you reach the end of the strip. Brush end with butter and press onto triangle to seal. Turn triangle and brush top with butter. Repeat with remaining phyllo and filling.
4. Place triangles on greased baking sheets. Bake until golden brown, 12-15 minutes. Combine ranch dressing and salsa; serve with triangles.
FREEZE OPTION: Freeze cooled triangles in freezer containers. To use, reheat triangles on a greased baking sheet in a preheated 375° oven until crisp and heated through.

1 APPETIZER: 77 cal., 5g fat (3g sat. fat), 13mg chol., 143mg sod., 5g carb. (1g sugars, 0 fiber), 2g pro.

**GRILLED JERK
SHRIMP ORZO SALAD
PAGE 21**

Salads & Dressings

Nothing packs in nutrition, crunch and flavor like a colorful salad. Turn here for light lunch ideas, pleasing picnic sides, and every kind of delightful salad in between.

BACON & PEAR SALAD WITH PARMESAN GARLIC DRESSING

BACON & PEAR SALAD WITH PARMESAN GARLIC DRESSING

This simple salad is an elegant side dish for any menu. With a blend of fresh pears and warm, comforting flavors, it's perfect for special meals.
—Rachel Lewis, Danville, VA

TAKES: 15 min. • **MAKES:** 6 servings

- 2 cups chopped leaf lettuce
- 2 cups chopped fresh kale
- 2 medium pears, thinly sliced
- 1 cup shredded pepper jack cheese
- 4 bacon strips, cooked and crumbled

PARMESAN GARLIC DRESSING

- ¼ cup mayonnaise
- 1 Tbsp. Dijon mustard
- 2 tsp. grated Parmesan cheese
- ½ tsp. garlic powder
- ⅛ tsp. pepper
- 2 to 3 Tbsp. 2% milk

In a large bowl, combine lettuce and kale. Top with pears, pepper jack cheese and bacon. In a small bowl, whisk the mayonnaise, mustard, Parmesan cheese, garlic powder and pepper. Gradually whisk in enough milk to reach desired consistency. Drizzle over salad; toss to coat.

1 CUP: *206 cal., 15g fat (5g sat. fat), 27mg chol., 335mg sod., 11g carb. (6g sugars, 2g fiber), 7g pro.*

GRANDMA'S POTATO SALAD

This salad is a must for picnics. The red potatoes hold their shape and texture even after they are boiled. It's Grandma's treasured recipe.
—Sue Gronholz, Beaver Dam, WI

PREP: 1 hour + chilling • **MAKES:** 24 servings

- 6 lbs. medium red potatoes
  Water

DRESSING

- 1 cup water
- ½ cup butter, cubed
- ¼ cup white vinegar
- 2 large eggs
- ½ cup sugar
- 4½ tsp. cornstarch
- ¾ cup heavy whipping cream
- ¾ cup Miracle Whip

SALAD

- 1 small onion, finely chopped
- 2 green onions, sliced
- 1 tsp. salt
- ½ tsp. pepper
- 3 hard-boiled large eggs, sliced
  Paprika

1. Place potatoes in a stockpot and cover with water. Bring to a boil. Reduce heat; cover and cook until tender, 15-20 minutes. Drain. When cool enough to handle, peel and slice potatoes; cool completely.

2. For the dressing, in the top of a double boiler or metal bowl over barely simmering water, heat 1 cup water, butter and vinegar until butter is melted. In a small bowl, beat eggs; add sugar and cornstarch. Add to butter mixture; cook and stir until thickened, 5-7 minutes. Transfer to a large bowl; cool completely.

3. In a small bowl, beat cream until stiff peaks form. Stir Miracle Whip into cooled dressing mixture; fold in whipped cream. Stir in onion, green onions, salt and pepper. Add potatoes; toss lightly to combine. Refrigerate, covered, until chilled.

4. To serve, top with hard-boiled eggs; sprinkle with paprika.

¾ CUP: *197 cal., 10g fat (5g sat. fat), 58mg chol., 202mg sod., 24g carb. (6g sugars, 2g fiber), 4g pro.*

GRANDMA'S POTATO SALAD

GRILLED JERK SHRIMP ORZO SALAD

(SHOWN ON PAGE 18)

It doesn't matter what the temperature outside is—you'll feel as if you're in the Caribbean when you take your first bite of this tropical salad.
—Eileen Budnyk, Palm Beach Gardens, FL

- -

PREP: 25 min. • **GRILL:** 10 min.
MAKES: 2 servings

- ⅓ cup uncooked whole wheat orzo pasta
- ½ lb. uncooked shrimp (31-40 per lb.), peeled and deveined
- 1 Tbsp. Caribbean jerk seasoning
- 1 medium ear sweet corn, husked
- 1 tsp. olive oil
- 6 fresh asparagus spears, trimmed
- 1 small sweet red pepper, chopped

DRESSING
- 3 Tbsp. lime juice
- 1 Tbsp. water
- 1 Tbsp. olive oil
- ⅛ tsp. salt
- ⅛ tsp. pepper

1. Cook orzo according to the package directions. Drain and rinse with cold water; drain well. Meanwhile, toss shrimp with jerk seasoning; thread onto metal or soaked wooden skewers. Brush corn with oil.
2. On a covered grill over medium heat, cook corn until tender and lightly browned, 10-12 minutes, turning occasionally; cook asparagus until crisp-tender, 5-7 minutes, turning occasionally. Grill shrimp until they turn pink, 1-2 minutes per side.
3. Cut corn from cob; cut asparagus into 1-in. pieces. Remove shrimp from skewers. In a large bowl, combine orzo, grilled vegetables, shrimp and red pepper. Whisk together the dressing ingredients; toss with salad.
2 CUPS: *340 cal., 12g fat (2g sat. fat), 138mg chol., 716mg sod., 35g carb. (6g sugars, 7g fiber), 25g pro.* **Diabetic exchanges:** *2 starch, 3 lean meat, 1 vegetable, 1 fat.*

ROAST BEETS WITH ORANGE GREMOLATA & GOAT CHEESE

My grandma always grew beets then pickled or canned them, but I prefer to prepare them a little bit differently.
—Courtney Archibeque, Greeley, CO

- -

PREP: 25 min. • **BAKE:** 55 min. + cooling
MAKES: 12 servings

- 3 medium fresh golden beets (about 1 lb.)
- 3 medium fresh beets (about 1 lb.)
- 2 Tbsp. lime juice
- 2 Tbsp. orange juice
- ½ tsp. fine sea salt
- 1 Tbsp. minced fresh parsley
- 1 Tbsp. minced fresh sage
- 1 garlic clove, minced
- 1 tsp. grated orange zest
- 3 Tbsp. crumbled goat cheese
- 2 Tbsp. sunflower kernels

1. Preheat oven to 400°. Scrub beets and trim tops by 1 in. Place beets on a double thickness of heavy-duty foil (about 24x12 in.). Fold foil around beets, sealing tightly. Place on a baking sheet. Roast until tender, 55-65 minutes. Open foil carefully to allow steam to escape.
2. When cool enough to handle, peel, halve and slice beets; place in a serving bowl. Add lime juice, orange juice and salt; toss to coat. Combine parsley, sage, garlic and orange zest; sprinkle over beets. Top with goat cheese and sunflower kernels. Serve warm or chilled.
¾ CUP: *49 cal., 1g fat (0 sat. fat), 2mg chol., 157mg sod., 9g carb. (6g sugars, 2g fiber), 2g pro.* **Diabetic exchanges:** *1 vegetable.*

ROAST BEETS WITH ORANGE GREMOLATA & GOAT CHEESE

LEMON VINAIGRETTE

COOL COUSCOUS SALAD

Here's a refreshing side dish for hot summer days or any time you want to eat light. I combine hearty couscous and tangy feta cheese for Mediterranean flair, and then I top it off with my favorite balsamic vinaigrette for a punch of flavor.
—*Tiffany Blepp, Olathe, KS*

PREP: 15 min. + chilling • **MAKES:** 2 servings

- ⅓ cup water
- ¼ cup uncooked couscous
- ⅓ cup garbanzo beans or chickpeas, rinsed and drained
- ¼ cup seeded chopped cucumber
- 1 small plum tomato, seeded and chopped
- ¼ cup prepared balsamic vinaigrette
- 2 lettuce leaves
- 2 Tbsp. crumbled feta cheese

1. In a small saucepan, bring water to a boil. Stir in couscous. Cover and remove from the heat; let stand for 5-10 minutes or until water is absorbed. Fluff with a fork; cover and refrigerate for at least 1 hour.
2. In a small bowl, combine the garbanzo beans, cucumber, tomato and couscous. Pour dressing over couscous mixture; toss to coat. Place lettuce leaves on 2 individual serving plates. Top with couscous mixture; sprinkle with cheese.
¾ CUP: *212 cal., 7g fat (1g sat. fat), 4mg chol., 484mg sod., 29g carb. (5g sugars, 3g fiber), 7g pro.* **Diabetic exchanges:** *2 starch, 1½ fat.*

LEMON VINAIGRETTE

The fresh lemon flavor brightens up simple green salads but is also a lively addition to fresh steamed vegetables, such as broccoli, cauliflower or green beans.
—*Sarah Farmer, Waukesha, WI*

TAKES: 5 min. • **MAKES:** ½ cup

- 2 Tbsp. fresh lemon juice
- 2 tsp. Dijon mustard
- ¼ tsp. salt
- ⅛ tsp. coarsely ground pepper
- 6 Tbsp. extra virgin olive oil

In a large bowl, whisk together first 4 ingredients. Slowly add olive oil while whisking constantly.
2 TBSP.: *183 cal., 20g fat (3g sat. fat), 0 chol., 208mg sod., 1g carb. (0 sugars, 0 fiber), 0 pro.*

TEST KITCHEN TIP

Success with Homemade Vinaigrette

For the best results, start with all the ingredients at room temperature. If the oil is cool or cold, it is much more difficult to form the emulsion. To get the most flavor out of these simple ingredients, mix up the vinaigrette and let it sit at room temperature 1-3 hours before serving. Refrigerate any leftovers; bring cold vinaigrette to room temperature before shaking to combine.

COOL COUSCOUS SALAD

SUNFLOWER BROCCOLI SALAD

SUNFLOWER BROCCOLI SALAD

This salad is so refreshing—we always make sure to get every last bit from the bowl.
—*Marilyn Newcomer, Sun City, CA*

PREP: 20 min. + chilling • **MAKES:** 2 servings

- 2 cups fresh broccoli florets
- 2 bacon strips, cooked and crumbled
- 1 green onion, chopped
- 3 Tbsp. raisins
- 1 Tbsp. sunflower kernels

DRESSING
- ⅓ cup mayonnaise
- 4 tsp. sugar
- 2 tsp. white vinegar

In a bowl, combine the broccoli, bacon, onion, raisins and sunflower kernels. In another bowl, combine dressing ingredients; stir until smooth. Pour over broccoli mixture and toss gently. Cover and refrigerate for at least 2 hours before serving, stirring occasionally.

1 CUP: *290 cal., 19g fat (3g sat. fat), 19mg chol., 464mg sod., 27g carb. (21g sugars, 3g fiber), 6g pro.*

CUCUMBER CRUNCH COLESLAW

This recipe came about as a way to use a julienne peeler that I received as a gift. Leftover sparkling wine was my other inspiration, and I combined it with cucumbers to create a refreshing slaw. It's a nice way to round out a brunch or picnic.
—*Merry Graham, Newhall, CA*

TAKES: 30 min. • **MAKES:** 8 servings

- ⅓ cup olive oil
- ¼ cup sparkling or dry white wine
- 1 Tbsp. minced fresh basil
- 1 Tbsp. Key lime juice
- 1 serrano pepper, seeded and minced
- 1½ tsp. minced fresh mint
- 1½ tsp. molasses
- 1 tsp. sugar
- 1 garlic clove, minced
- ¾ tsp. salt
- ¾ tsp. grated lime zest
- ½ tsp. pepper

COLESLAW
- 3 English cucumbers, julienned
- 2 cups fresh arugula or baby spinach, coarsely chopped
- 1 cup fresh snow peas, cut into ½-in. pieces
- ½ cup sliced almonds, toasted
- 1 cup dried cranberries

1. In a small bowl, combine the first 12 ingredients. In a large bowl, combine cucumbers, arugula, peas, almonds and cranberries.
2. Just before serving, pour dressing over salad; toss to coat.
NOTE: Wear disposable gloves when cutting hot peppers; the oils can burn skin. Avoid touching your face.
¾ CUP: *178 cal., 12g fat (2g sat. fat), 0 chol., 227mg sod., 16g carb. (11g sugars, 2g fiber), 2g pro.* **Diabetic exchanges:** *2 fat, 1 vegetable, ½ starch.*

CUCUMBER CRUNCH COLESLAW

CUCUMBERS WITH DILL

SOUTHWESTERN SPIRAL PASTA

A friend who has a catering business asked me to create a dish with pasta for a southwestern-themed event. This is the recipe I dreamed up for her. I was told it was a hit and is now one of the caterer's most-requested dishes.
—Valonda Seward, Coarsegold, CA

TAKES: 30 min. • **MAKES:** 16 servings

- ½ cup fresh lime juice
- ¼ cup olive oil
- 2 tsp. ground cumin
- 2 garlic cloves, minced
- 1 Tbsp. salsa
- 1 Tbsp. white wine vinegar
- ¾ tsp. cayenne pepper
- ½ tsp. salt
- 1 pkg. (16 oz.) uncooked spiral or cavatappi pasta
- 1½ cups fresh or frozen whole kernel corn, thawed
- 1 can (15 oz.) black beans, rinsed and drained
- 1 cup cherry tomatoes, halved
- 2 cans (2¼ oz. each) sliced ripe olives, drained
- 1 small green pepper, finely chopped
- 1 small sweet red pepper, finely chopped
- 1 small red onion, finely chopped
- ½ cup coarsely chopped fresh cilantro, divided
- 1 medium ripe avocado, peeled and sliced

1. In a small bowl, whisk the first 8 ingredients until blended. Cook pasta according to package directions. Drain pasta; rinse with cold water.
2. In a large bowl, mix pasta, corn, beans, tomatoes, olives, peppers, onion and ¼ cup cilantro. Pour dressing over salad; toss to coat. Refrigerate until serving.
3. Just before serving, top with avocado and the remaining cilantro.
¾ CUP: *203 cal., 6g fat (1g sat. fat), 0 chol., 191mg sod., 32g carb. (3g sugars, 4g fiber), 6g pro.* **Diabetic exchanges:** *2 starch, 1 fat.*

CUCUMBERS WITH DILL

Sprinkling cucumber slices with salt and letting them stand in a colander draws out excess water so they stay crisp when set on a barbecue buffet. Try them alongside any grilled entree.
—Taste of Home *Test Kitchen*

PREP: 20 min. + chilling • **MAKES:** 6 servings

- 2 medium cucumbers, sliced ⅛ in. thick
- 1 Tbsp. kosher salt
- ½ cup white vinegar
- ¼ cup snipped fresh dill
- 3 Tbsp. sugar
- ½ tsp. coarsely ground pepper

1. Place cucumber slices in a colander over a plate; sprinkle with salt and toss. Let stand for 15 minutes, stirring once. Rinse and drain well.
2. In a large bowl, combine the vinegar, dill, sugar and pepper. Add cucumbers; toss to coat. Cover and refrigerate for at least 15 minutes before serving.
⅔ CUP: *35 cal., 0 fat (0 sat. fat), 0 chol., 480mg sod., 8g carb. (7g sugars, 1g fiber), 1g pro.*
Diabetic exchanges: *1 vegetable, ½ starch.*

SOUTHWESTERN
SPIRAL PASTA

RUSSIAN POTATO SALAD

RUSSIAN POTATO SALAD

This Russian potato salad recipe comes from my grandmother, who had written it down in Russian before she translated it for me when I was a teen. We made this every Easter, or for any event where family and friends gathered together.
—Gala McGaughey, Berryville, VA

PREP: 40 min. + chilling • **MAKES:** 16 servings

- 5 lbs. potatoes, peeled and cubed (about 8 cups)
- ⅓ cup sugar
- ⅓ cup cider vinegar
- ¼ cup canola oil
- 1 can (14½ oz.) sliced carrots, drained
- 1 medium onion, chopped
- 2 jars (16 oz. each) pickled whole beets, drained and chopped
- 1 cup chopped celery
- ½ cup chopped sweet pickles
- ½ cup chopped dill pickles
- 1 cup mayonnaise
- 1 tsp. salt
- ½ tsp. pepper

1. Place potatoes in a Dutch oven; cover with water. Bring to a boil. Reduce heat; cover and simmer until tender, 10-15 minutes. Drain and transfer to a large bowl.

2. Meanwhile, combine sugar and vinegar in a small saucepan. Cook and stir over medium heat until sugar is dissolved; pour over hot potatoes. Cool to room temperature.

3. In a large skillet, heat oil over medium-high heat. Add carrots and onion; cook and stir until crisp-tender, 6-8 minutes. Add to potatoes. Stir in beets, celery and pickles. Combine mayonnaise, salt and pepper; gently stir into potato mixture. Refrigerate, covered, until chilled.

¾ CUP: 269 cal., 14g fat (2g sat. fat), 1mg chol., 455mg sod., 35g carb. (15g sugars, 3g fiber), 2g pro.

TEST KITCHEN TIP

Make sugar-free by using Splenda and no-sugar-added sweet gherkins and beets.

EASY BREEZY BAHAMAS SEAFOOD SALAD

This super simple, deceptively delicious recipe was inspired by a seafood salad I had in the Bahamas that featured conch. I substitute crab and shrimp and like it even more!
—Cindy Heyd, Edmond, OK

TAKES: 15 min. • **MAKES:** 4 servings

- 1 medium orange
- 1 medium lemon
- 1 medium lime
- ½ lb. peeled and deveined cooked shrimp, coarsely chopped
- ½ lb. refrigerated fresh or imitation crabmeat, coarsely chopped
- 2 Tbsp. finely chopped sweet onion
- 2 Tbsp. finely chopped sweet red pepper
  Shredded lettuce
  Assorted crackers

Finely grate zest from orange. Cut orange crosswise in half; squeeze juice from orange. Transfer zest and juice to a large bowl. Repeat with lemon and lime. Add shrimp, crab, onion and pepper; toss to coat. Serve on lettuce with crackers.

¾ CUP: 128 cal., 2g fat (0 sat. fat), 141mg chol., 103mg sod., 2g carb. (1g sugars, 0 fiber), 7g pro.

EASY BREEZY BAHAMAS SEAFOOD SALAD

**APPLE-CARROT SLAW
WITH PISTACHIOS**

HONEY-MUSTARD BRUSSELS SPROUTS SALAD

Even if you dislike Brussels sprouts salad, you just might love this dish. The dressing is truly tasty, and it pairs so nicely with the apples, grapes and walnuts. You can also add whatever cheese, nuts or fruit you prefer.
—*Sheila Sturrock, Coldwater, ON*

TAKES: 25 min. • **MAKES:** 10 servings

1	lb. fresh Brussels sprouts, trimmed and shredded
2	medium tart apples, chopped
1	medium red onion, chopped
1	small sweet orange pepper, chopped
½	cup chopped walnuts
½	cup green grapes, sliced
½	cup shredded cheddar cheese
3	bacon strips, cooked and crumbled
¼	cup olive oil
2	Tbsp. red wine vinegar
2	Tbsp. honey mustard
1	garlic clove, minced
¼	tsp. salt
¼	tsp. pepper

In a large bowl, combine the first 8 ingredients. In a small bowl, whisk remaining ingredients. Pour over salad; toss to coat.
1 CUP: *170 cal., 12g fat (3g sat. fat), 8mg chol., 177mg sod., 13g carb. (7g sugars, 3g fiber), 5g pro.* **DIABETIC EXCHANGES:** *2 fat, 1 starch.*

**HONEY-MUSTARD
BRUSSELS SPROUTS SALAD**

APPLE-CARROT SLAW WITH PISTACHIOS

Sweet, crunchy and colorful, a vibrant slaw like this will be an all-star at your next potluck spread. I prefer to use freshly julienned carrots and apples because I love their sunny flavors.
—*Linda Schend, Kenosha, WI*

TAKES: 20 min. • **MAKES:** 8 servings (1 cup each)

6	cups julienned carrots (about 9 oz.)
4	medium Fuji, Gala or other sweet apples, julienned
¼	cup lemon juice
2	Tbsp. sugar
1½	tsp. ground cinnamon
1	cup chopped pistachios, divided
	Dash salt

In a large bowl, combine the first five ingredients. Add ½ cup pistachios; toss to combine. Season with salt to taste. Refrigerate, covered, until serving. Just before serving, sprinkle with remaining ½ cup pistachios.
1 CUP: *171 cal., 8g fat (1g sat. fat), 0 chol., 140mg sod., 24g carb. (15g sugars, 5g fiber), 4g pro..*

GRILLED CHICKEN RAMEN SALAD

165°, 8-10 minutes on each side. Cool slightly and chop into ½-in. pieces.

4. In a large bowl, combine coleslaw mix and cilantro. Layer coleslaw mixture, peas, chicken, carrots, salad greens, noodles and green onions in an 8- to 10-qt. dish. Sprinkle with bacon; serve with vinaigrette.

1 SERVING: *458 cal., 29g fat (4g sat. fat), 47mg chol., 738mg sod., 28g carb. (10g sugars, 4g fiber), 22g pro.*

SOUTHWESTERN BEAN & RICE SALAD

We enjoy fajitas and tacos, but finding a good side dish to go with them wasn't easy—until this recipe came along.
—Stephanie Liston, Ankeny, IA

- -

PREP: 10 min. + chilling • **MAKES:** 8 servings

- 3 cups cooked long grain rice, cooled
- 1 can (16 oz.) kidney beans, rinsed and drained
- 1 medium green pepper, diced
- 1 can (2¼ oz.) sliced ripe olives, drained
- ⅓ cup lime juice
- ¼ cup chopped green onions
- 2 Tbsp. canola oil
- 1 Tbsp. minced fresh cilantro
- 2 garlic cloves, minced
- ½ tsp. salt
- ½ tsp. ground cumin

In a large bowl, combine the rice, beans, green pepper and olives. In a jar with a tight-fitting lid, combine the remaining ingredients; shake well. Pour over the rice mixture; toss to coat. Cover and refrigerate for 1 hour or until chilled. Toss the salad before serving.

¾ CUP: *154 cal., 5g fat (0 sat. fat), 0 chol., 404mg sod., 24g carb. (0 sugars, 3g fiber), 4g pro.* **Diabetic exchanges:** *1½ starch, 1 fat.*

READER REVIEW

"I was looking for a quick side dish to make for my cousin's cookout, and I stumbled upon this little gem. It was incredibly quick and easy, and the best part is that it's a low-calorie recipe!"

— HALI86, TASTEOFHOME.COM

GRILLED CHICKEN RAMEN SALAD

This is one of those recipes that I love because it's pretty much a complete meal in one bowl, and when it goes on the table, everyone says, "Yeah!"
—Karen Carlson, San Luis Obispo, CA

- -

TAKES: 30 min. • **MAKES:** 8 servings

- 2 Tbsp. canola oil
- 2 pkg. (3 oz. each) ramen noodles, crumbled
- ⅔ cup canola oil
- 2 tsp. sesame oil
- ⅓ cup seasoned rice vinegar
- 1 Tbsp. sugar
- 2 Tbsp. reduced-sodium soy sauce
- 1½ lbs. boneless skinless chicken breast halves

- ½ tsp. pepper
- ¼ tsp. salt
- 1 pkg. (14 oz.) coleslaw mix
- ½ cup minced fresh cilantro
- 3 cups fresh snow peas, thinly sliced lengthwise
- 2 cups shredded carrots
- 4 cups torn mixed salad greens
- 3 thinly sliced green onions
- ⅓ cup crumbled cooked bacon, optional

1. In a large saucepan, heat oil over medium-low heat. Add ramen noodles; cook and stir until toasted, 5-8 minutes. Remove from pan; set aside.

2. In a small bowl, whisk oils, vinegar, sugar and soy sauce until blended; set aside.

3. Sprinkle chicken with pepper and salt. Place chicken on a lightly oiled grill rack. Grill, covered, over medium heat or broil 4-5 in. from heat until a thermometer reads

GRILLED STEAK BRUSCHETTA SALAD FOR 2

Fire up the grill for this tasty salad. The meat will be done in a snap, leaving you time to enjoy the summer evening. Sometimes I add crumbled blue cheese.
—Devon Delaney, Westport, CT

TAKES: 25 min. • **MAKES:** 2 servings

- ½ lb. beef tenderloin steaks (1 in. thick)
- ¼ tsp. salt
- ⅛ tsp. pepper
- 2 slices Italian bread (½ in. thick)
- 1 cup fresh arugula or fresh baby spinach
- ⅓ cup jarred or prepared bruschetta topping
- ⅓ cup blue cheese salad dressing

1. Sprinkle steaks with salt and pepper. Grill, covered, over medium heat until meat reaches desired doneness (for medium-rare, a thermometer should read 135°; medium, 140°; medium-well, 145°), 6-8 minutes on each side. Let stand for 5 minutes.
2. Grill bread, covered, until toasted, 1-2 minutes on each side; place on salad plates.
3. Thinly slice steak; arrange over toast. Top with arugula and bruschetta topping. Drizzle with salad dressing.
1 SERVING: *460 cal., 31g fat (7g sat. fat), 57mg chol., 1183mg sod., 17g carb. (3g sugars, 1g fiber), 28g pro.*

NICOISE SALAD

GRILLED STEAK BRUSCHETTA SALAD FOR 2

NICOISE SALAD

This garden-fresh Nicoise is a feast for the eyes as well as the palate. Add some crusty bread and you have a mouthwatering meal.
—Marla Fogderud, Mason, MI

PREP: 40 min. + cooling • **MAKES:** 2 servings

- ⅓ cup olive oil
- 3 Tbsp. white wine vinegar
- 1½ tsp. Dijon mustard
- ⅛ tsp. each salt, onion powder and pepper

SALAD
- 2 small red potatoes
- ½ cup cut fresh green beans
- 3½ cups torn Bibb lettuce
- ½ cup cherry tomatoes, halved
- 10 Greek olives, pitted and halved
- 2 hard-boiled large eggs, quartered
- 1 can (5 oz.) albacore white tuna in water, drained and flaked

1. In a small bowl, whisk the oil, vinegar, mustard, salt, onion powder and pepper; set aside.
2. Place potatoes in a small saucepan and cover with water. Bring to a boil. Reduce heat; cover and simmer until tender, 15-20 minutes. Drain and cool; cut into quarters.
3. Place beans in another saucepan and cover with water. Bring to a boil. Cover and cook until crisp-tender, 3-5 minutes; drain and rinse in cold water.
4. Divide lettuce between 2 salad plates; top with potatoes, beans, tomatoes, olives, eggs and tuna. Drizzle with dressing.
1 SERVING: *613 cal., 49g fat (8g sat. fat), 242mg chol., 886mg sod., 18g carb. (3g sugars, 3g fiber), 26g pro.*

QUICK MACARONI SALAD

You can't go wrong with this time-tested winner. Here it is pared down for two.
—Carma Blosser, Livermore, CO

TAKES: 20 min. • **MAKES:** 2 servings

- ¾ cup uncooked elbow macaroni
- ⅓ cup frozen peas
- ⅓ cup cubed cheddar cheese
- ¼ cup mayonnaise
- 3 Tbsp. chopped celery
- 1 tsp. finely chopped onion
- 1 tsp. diced pimientos
- 1 tsp. finely chopped green pepper
- ⅛ tsp. salt

1. Cook macaroni according to package directions, adding peas during the last 2 minutes of cooking. Drain and rinse in cold water.
2. In a small bowl, combine the remaining ingredients. Stir in macaroni and peas. Chill until serving.

1 CUP: *276 cal., 15g fat (4g sat. fat), 24mg chol., 544mg sod., 28g carb. (4g sugars, 2g fiber), 10g pro.*

PEA & CHEESE SALAD

QUICK MACARONI SALAD

PEA & CHEESE SALAD

Radish slices add color and crunch to this fresh-tasting potluck favorite. I often serve it in a bowl lined with romaine leaves.
—Inez Orsburn, DeMotte, IN

PREP: 10 min. + chilling • **MAKES:** 8 servings

- 4 cups frozen peas (about 16 oz.), thawed
- 1 cup chopped celery
- 2 hard-boiled large eggs, chopped
- ¼ cup chopped green onions
- 1 cup cubed cheddar cheese
- ½ cup thinly sliced radishes or 1 jar (2 oz.) pimientos, drained
- 1 cup mayonnaise
- 3 Tbsp. sweet pickle relish
- 1 tsp. sugar
- 1 tsp. seasoned salt
- 1 tsp. ground mustard

In a large bowl, combine the first 6 ingredients. In a small bowl, combine mayonnaise, relish and seasonings. Stir into pea mixture. Cover and refrigerate until serving.

¾ CUP: *325 cal., 27g fat (7g sat. fat), 65mg chol., 574mg sod., 12g carb. (6g sugars, 3g fiber), 9g pro.*

AIR-FRYER CRISPY SHRIMP CAESAR SALAD

My friend and I have a favorite lunch spot that serves a fantastic salad on Wednesdays. I made my own version so I can share it with family whenever I want.
—Marla Clark, Albuquerque, NM

PREP: 15 min. • **COOK:** 5 min./batch • **MAKES:** 4 servings

- 2 romaine hearts, coarsely chopped
- 1 cup cherry tomatoes, halved
- ¼ cup shredded Parmesan cheese
- ½ cup all-purpose flour
- ¾ tsp. salt
- ½ tsp. pepper
- 1 lb. uncooked shrimp (26-30 per lb.), peeled and deveined
  Cooking spray
- ½ cup creamy Caesar salad dressing
  Optional: Additional shredded Parmesan cheese and pepper

1. Preheat air fryer to 375°. In a large bowl, combine romaine, tomatoes and cheese; refrigerate until serving. In a shallow bowl, mix flour, salt and pepper. Add shrimp, a few pieces at a time, and toss to coat; shake off excess.
2. In batches, place shrimp in a single layer on greased tray in air-fryer basket; spritz with cooking spray. Cook until lightly browned, 2-3 minutes. Turn; spritz with cooking spray. Cook until lightly browned and shrimp turn pink, 2-3 minutes longer. Remove and keep warm.
3. Drizzle dressing over romaine mixture and toss to coat. Top with shrimp. If desired, sprinkle with additional cheese and pepper; serve immediately.
1 SERVING: *313 cal., 21g fat (4g sat. fat), 153mg chol., 680mg sod., 8g carb. (2g sugars, 2g fiber), 23g pro.*

AIR-FRYER CRISPY SHRIMP CAESAR SALAD

STRAWBERRY TARRAGON CHICKEN SALAD

STRAWBERRY TARRAGON CHICKEN SALAD

After thinking about creating this salad for some time, one spring I used my homegrown strawberries and fresh tarragon to do a little experimenting. It didn't take me very long to come up with a winner! My husband enjoyed my creation as much as I did, and now we can't wait for strawberry season to come around again each year.
—Sue Gronholz, Beaver Dam, WI

TAKES: 30 min. • **MAKES:** 5 servings

- ½ cup mayonnaise
- 2 tsp. sugar
- 2 tsp. minced fresh tarragon or 1 tsp. dried tarragon
- ¼ tsp. salt
- ⅛ tsp. pepper
- 2½ cups cubed cooked chicken breast
- 2 cups quartered fresh strawberries
- 1 cup fresh shelled peas or frozen peas, thawed
- ½ cup chopped celery
- 2 Tbsp. chopped sweet onion
  Torn mixed salad greens
- ½ cup chopped pecans, toasted

In a large bowl, whisk the first 5 ingredients until blended. Stir in the chicken, strawberries, peas, celery and onion. Serve over salad greens; sprinkle with pecans.
1 CUP: *378 cal., 26g fat (4g sat. fat), 56mg chol., 285mg sod., 13g carb. (7g sugars, 4g fiber), 23g pro.*

> **TEST KITCHEN TIP**
>
> This salad is better when made ahead of time so the flavors can blend. But don't add the strawberries until you're ready to serve the salad, as they tend to turn the salad pink when they sit!

HEARTY PORK
BEAN SOUP
PAGE 37

Soups & Sandwiches

Featuring the convenience busy cooks crave along with the familiarity everyone adores, the classic combo of soup and sammie can't be beat! Create your own pairing today.

KUNG PAO SLOPPY JOES

KUNG PAO SLOPPY JOES

What happens when you combine two favorites into one easy dish? Clean plates, that's what! My family loves Chinese food, but takeout can be expensive and it's not always the healthiest. This colorful stovetop kung pao sloppy joe recipe will please everyone at dinnertime, including the kids. My husband prefers to skip the bun and eat it over brown rice or rolled in lettuce wrap.
—Julie Peterson, Crofton, MD

- -

TAKES: 30 min. • **MAKES:** 6 servings

- 1 lb. lean ground beef (90% lean)
- 1 small sweet red pepper, chopped
- 4 green onions, chopped, divided
- 2 garlic cloves, minced
- 2 tsp. minced fresh gingerroot
- 1 to 1½ tsp. Sriracha chili sauce
- ½ cup reduced-sodium soy sauce
- 6 Tbsp. rice vinegar, divided
- ¼ cup water
- 3 Tbsp. sesame oil, divided
- 2 Tbsp. cornstarch
- 2 Tbsp. brown sugar
- 1 pkg. (12 oz.) broccoli coleslaw mix
- ½ cup chopped unsalted peanuts
- 6 hamburger buns, split, or flour tortillas (8 in.)
  Fresh cilantro leaves, optional

1. In a large cast-iron or other heavy skillet, cook the beef, red pepper and 2 green onions over medium-high heat until the beef is no longer pink and the vegetables are tender, 6-8 minutes, breaking up beef into crumbles; drain. Add garlic, ginger and chili sauce; cook 1 minute longer.

2. In a small bowl, mix soy sauce, 4 Tbsp. vinegar, water, 1 Tbsp. oil, cornstarch and brown sugar until smooth; stir into beef mixture. Bring to a boil, stirring constantly; cook and stir until thickened, 1-2 minutes.

3. For the slaw, in a large bowl, combine coleslaw mix, remaining 2 green onions, 2 Tbsp. vinegar and 2 Tbsp. oil; toss to coat. Spoon ½ cup of the beef mixture onto bun bottoms. Top with ½ cup slaw and peanuts. If desired, top with cilantro leaves. Serve remaining slaw on the side.

FREEZE OPTION: Freeze the cooled meat mixture in freezer containers. To use, partially thaw in refrigerator overnight. Heat through in a saucepan, stirring occasionally; add water if necessary.

1 SANDWICH: *461 cal., 21g fat (5g sat. fat), 47mg chol., 1299mg sod., 44g carb. (16g sugars, 4g fiber), 25g pro.*

SOPA DE CAMARONES (SHRIMP SOUP)

GINGER CHICKEN NOODLE SOUP

This is one of my favorite soup recipes to serve in the wintertime because it's easy and comforting, and it fills the entire house with a wonderful aroma. My whole family loves it!
—Brandy Stansbury, Edna, TX

PREP: 15 min. • **COOK:** 3½ hours • **MAKES:** 8 servings (2½ qt.)

- 1 lb. boneless skinless chicken breasts, cubed
- 2 medium carrots, shredded
- 3 Tbsp. sherry or reduced-sodium chicken broth
- 2 Tbsp. rice vinegar
- 1 Tbsp. reduced-sodium soy sauce
- 2 to 3 tsp. minced fresh gingerroot
- ¼ tsp. pepper
- 6 cups reduced-sodium chicken broth
- 1 cup water
- 2 cups fresh snow peas, halved
- 2 oz. uncooked angel hair pasta, broken into thirds

1. In a 5-qt. slow cooker, combine the first 9 ingredients. Cook, covered, on low 3-4 hours or until chicken is tender.
2. Stir in snow peas and pasta. Cook, covered, on low about 30 minutes longer, until snow peas and pasta are tender.
1¼ CUPS: *126 cal., 2g fat (0 sat. fat), 31mg chol., 543mg sod., 11g carb. (3g sugars, 2g fiber), 16g pro.* **Diabetic exchanges:** *2 lean meat, 1 starch.*

SOPA DE CAMARONES (SHRIMP SOUP)

My daughter and I came up with this soup recipe when she was younger, and it's been a favorite with family and friends ever since. And it may even be tastier as leftovers the next day!
—Patti Fair, Valdosta, GA

PREP: 20 min. • **COOK:** 2 hours • **MAKES:** 6 cups (1½ qt.)

- 3 Tbsp. butter
- 3 celery ribs, sliced
- 1 small onion, chopped
- ⅓ cup lemon juice
- 6 garlic cloves, minced
- 1 to 2 Tbsp. sugar
- 2 cans (14½ oz. each) Mexican petite diced tomatoes, undrained
- 1 lb. peeled and deveined cooked shrimp (61-70 per lb.)
- 1 can (6 oz.) tomato paste
  Hot cooked rice
  Optional: Lime wedges and chopped cilantro

In a large skillet, heat butter over medium heat. Add celery and onion; cook and stir until crisp-tender, 3-4 minutes. Add lemon juice, garlic and sugar; cook 1 minute longer. Transfer to a 3- or 4-qt. slow cooker. Add tomatoes with juices, shrimp and tomato paste. Cook, covered, on low 2-3 hours or until heated through . Serve with hot rice and, if desired, lime wedges and cilantro.
1½ CUPS: *313 cal., 11g fat (6g sat. fat), 195mg chol., 712mg sod., 26g carb. (16g sugars, 4g fiber), 28g pro.*

GINGER CHICKEN NOODLE SOUP

GARBANZO BEAN BURGERS

These meatless burgers are totally awesome. I think I'd rather have one than any cheeseburger at a restaurant. They really rock!
—Berea Rider, East Point, KY

PREP: 25 min. • **COOK:** 10 min. • **MAKES:** 4 servings

- 1 can (15 oz.) garbanzo beans or chickpeas, rinsed and drained
- 3 Tbsp. water
- 1 tsp. lemon juice
- 1 cup dry bread crumbs
- 1 large egg
- 1 tsp. Italian seasoning
- ½ tsp. garlic powder
- ½ tsp. onion powder
  Dash crushed red pepper flakes
- 2 Tbsp. canola oil
- 4 whole wheat or whole grain hamburger buns, split and toasted
- 4 slices reduced-fat American cheese
  Optional toppings: Dill pickle slices, fat-free mayonnaise, ketchup, sliced red onion, lettuce and sliced tomato

1. Place the beans, water and lemon juice in a food processor; cover and process until blended. Transfer to a large bowl. Add the bread crumbs, egg and seasonings; mix well. Shape into 4 patties.
2. In a large cast-iron or other heavy skillet, cook patties in oil in batches until lightly browned, 3-4 minutes on each side. Serve on buns with cheese. Top as desired.
1 BURGER: *447 cal., 16g fat (3g sat. fat), 50mg chol., 807mg sod., 60g carb. (10g sugars, 9g fiber), 17g pro.*

GARBANZO BEAN BURGERS

CHILI CONEY DOGS

CHILI CONEY DOGS

From the youngest kids to the oldest adults, everyone in our family loves these hot dogs. They're so easy to throw together in the slow cooker. They're delicious any time of year.
—Michele Harris, Vicksburg, MI

PREP: 20 min. • **COOK:** 4 hours • **MAKES:** 8 servings

- 1 lb. lean ground beef (90% lean)
- 1 can (15 oz.) tomato sauce
- ½ cup water
- 2 Tbsp. Worcestershire sauce
- 1 Tbsp. dried minced onion
- ½ tsp. garlic powder
- ½ tsp. ground mustard
- ½ tsp. chili powder
- ½ tsp. pepper
  Dash cayenne pepper
- 8 hot dogs
- 8 hot dog buns, split
  Optional toppings: Shredded cheddar cheese, relish and chopped onion

1. In a large skillet, cook beef over medium heat until no longer pink, 6-8 minutes, breaking into crumbles; drain. Stir in tomato sauce, water, Worcestershire sauce, onion and seasonings.
2. Place hot dogs in a 3-qt. slow cooker; top with beef mixture. Cook, covered, on low 4-5 hours or until heated through. Serve on buns with toppings as desired.
1 CHILI DOG: *371 cal., 20g fat (8g sat. fat), 53mg chol., 992mg sod., 26g carb. (5g sugars, 2g fiber), 21g pro.*

HEARTY PORK BEAN SOUP

(*SHOWN ON PAGE 32*)

It's wonderful to come home to this pretty soup simmering to perfection in the slow cooker, especially on a busy weeknight. With a little planning, you can get it all started in the morning before work. Then, when you get home, just add a few more ingredients, and soon dinner will be ready!
—*Colleen Delawder, Herndon, VA*

PREP: 20 min. + soaking
COOK: 6 hours 20 min.
MAKES: 12 servings (4 qt.)

- 1 pkg. (16 oz.) dried great northern beans, rinsed and drained
- 1 large sweet onion, chopped
- 3 medium carrots, chopped
- 3 celery ribs, chopped
- 1 pork tenderloin (1 lb.)
- 1 tsp. garlic powder
- 1 Tbsp. fresh minced chives or 1 tsp. dried chives
- 1 tsp. dried oregano
- ½ tsp. dried thyme
- 1 tsp. pepper
- 1 carton (32 oz.) reduced-sodium chicken broth
- 1 can (14½ oz.) reduced-sodium chicken broth
- 1 bottle (12 oz.) extra pale ale
- 1 can (14½ oz.) diced tomatoes, drained
- 5 oz. fresh spinach
- 1½ to 2 tsp. salt

1. Place beans in a large bowl; add cool water to cover. Soak 5 hours or overnight. Drain beans, discarding water; rinse with cool water.

2. In a 6-qt. slow cooker, layer the beans, vegetables and pork. Add seasonings, broth and ale. Cook, covered, on low 6-8 hours or until beans and pork are tender.

3. Remove pork; shred with 2 forks. Stir in the tomatoes, spinach and salt. Return pork to slow cooker. Cook, covered, low about 20 minutes or until heated through.

1⅓ CUPS: *207 cal., 2g fat (1g sat. fat), 21mg chol., 695mg sod., 30g carb. (5g sugars, 9g fiber), 18g pro.* **Diabetic exchanges:** *2 starch, 2 lean meat.*

QUICK & HEALTHY TURKEY VEGGIE SOUP

I freeze our leftover turkey at the holidays so we can enjoy meals like this whenever we want. This colorful soup is especially delicious on a chilly fall or winter day. If you're looking for a dish that's more filling, add some cooked pasta.
—*Joan Hallford, North Richland Hills, TX*

TAKES: 30 min. • **MAKES:** 9 servings (3 qt.)

- 2 Tbsp. butter
- 1 medium onion, chopped
- 1 celery rib, chopped
- 2 garlic cloves, minced
- 5 cups reduced-sodium chicken broth
- 3 medium carrots, julienned
- ¼ tsp. pepper
- 1 lb. zucchini or yellow summer squash, julienned (about 6 cups)
- 3 medium tomatoes, chopped
- 1 can (15½ oz.) hominy, rinsed and drained
- 2½ cups frozen lima beans (about 12 oz.), thawed
- 2 cups cubed cooked turkey
- 1½ tsp. minced fresh basil or ½ tsp. dried basil
  Shredded Parmesan cheese

In a Dutch oven, heat butter over medium-high heat. Add onion, celery and garlic; cook and stir until tender, 5-8 minutes. Add the broth, carrots, and pepper. Bring to a boil; reduce heat. Simmer, uncovered, 5 minutes. Add zucchini, tomatoes, hominy, lima beans and turkey. Cook until zucchini is tender, 5-8 minutes. Top with basil; serve with Parmesan cheese.

1¼ CUPS: *187 cal., 4g fat (2g sat. fat), 38mg chol., 614mg sod., 22g carb. (5g sugars, 5g fiber), 16g pro.* **Diabetic exchanges:** *2 lean meat, 1½ starch, ½ fat.*

QUICK & HEALTHY TURKEY VEGGIE SOUP

CALIFORNIA ROLL WRAPS

CHEESY ROAST BEEF PINWHEELS

Take your lunches to the next level with these warm pinwheels. Rolled in crescent dough, cut into spirals and baked, they're a tasty twist on the traditional roast beef sandwich. Best of all, you can stash a few in the freezer for quick bites and no-fuss meals.
—Holley Grainger, Brimingham, AL

TAKES: 30 min. • **MAKES:** 8 servings

- 1 tube (8 oz.) refrigerated crescent rolls
- 2 Tbsp. honey mustard or Dijon mustard
- 8 slices provolone cheese
- 8 slices deli roast beef
- ½ cup finely chopped sweet red pepper, optional

1. Preheat oven to 375°. Unroll crescent dough and separate into 2 rectangles; press perforations to seal.
2. Spread rectangles with mustard. Top with cheese and roast beef, overlapping if needed, and, if desired, red pepper. Roll up jelly-roll style, starting with a short side; pinch seam to seal. Cut each roll crosswise into 4 slices; place on parchment-lined baking sheets, cut side down. Bake until pinwheels are golden brown and cheese is melted, 15-18 minutes. Serve warm.
FREEZE OPTION: Cover and freeze cooled pinwheels on parchment-lined baking sheets until firm. Transfer to freezer containers; return to freezer. To use, bake at 375° until heated through.
1 PINWHEEL: *203 cal., 12g fat (4g sat. fat), 27mg chol., 502mg sod., 14g carb. (4g sugars, 0 fiber), 11g pro.*

CALIFORNIA ROLL WRAPS

I love California rolls I get at sushi restaurants, and I wanted to capture those flavors in a sandwich that I could take to work. I started with the standard ingredients, added a few others and came up with a hit.
—Mary Pax-Shipley, Bend, OR

TAKES: 20 min. • **MAKES:** 6 wraps

- ½ cup wasabi mayonnaise
- 6 whole wheat tortillas (8 in.)
- 2 pkg. (8 oz. each) imitation crabmeat
- 1 medium ripe avocado, peeled and thinly sliced
- 1½ cups julienned peeled jicama
- 1 medium sweet red pepper, julienned
- 1 small cucumber, seeded and julienned
- ¾ cup bean sprouts

Divide wasabi mayonnaise evenly among the 6 tortillas and spread to within ½ in. of edges. Layer with crabmeat, avocado, jicama, red peppers, cucumber and bean sprouts. Roll up tightly.
1 WRAP: *365 cal., 18g fat (3g sat. fat), 10mg chol., 647mg sod., 39g carb. (2g sugars, 7g fiber), 13g pro.* **Diabetic exchanges:** *2 starch, 2 fat, 1 lean meat, 1 vegetable.*

TEST KITCHEN TIP

This wrap lends itself to many substitutions. Toss in your favorite raw veggies, substitute smoked salmon or tuna for the crab, or use half a pita instead of the tortilla. If you can't find wasabi mayo, or don't like the spicy kick, simply use regular mayo instead.

GOLDEN BUTTERNUT SQUASH SOUP

I created this soup for my vegan relatives, but everyone else ended up loving it, too! It's so creamy and delicious.
—*Susan Sabia, Windsor, CA*

- -

PREP: 20 min. • **COOK:** 20 min. • **MAKES:** 6 servings

- 2 Tbsp. olive oil
- 2 cups cubed peeled butternut squash
- 2 medium carrots, chopped
- 1 medium sweet red or yellow pepper, chopped
- 1 medium Gala apple, peeled and chopped
- 1 small onion, chopped
- 2 cups water
- 2 tsp. vegetable base
- ½ tsp. salt
- ½ tsp. dried oregano
- ¼ tsp. ground nutmeg
- ¼ tsp. pepper
- 1½ cups unsweetened almond milk

1. In a large saucepan, heat oil over medium heat. Add squash, carrots, red pepper, apple and onion; cook and stir until crisp-tender, 8-10 minutes. Stir in water, vegetable base and seasonings. Bring to a boil; reduce heat. Simmer, uncovered, until vegetables are tender, 8-10 minutes. Stir in almond milk.

2. Puree soup using an immersion blender. Or, cool soup slightly and puree in batches in a blender; return to pan and heat through.

1 CUP: *110 cal., 6g fat (1g sat. fat), 0 chol., 486mg sod., 15g carb. (6g sugars, 3g fiber), 2g pro.* **Diabetic exchanges:** *1 starch, 1 fat.*

AVOCADO EGG SALAD TOAST

AVOCADO EGG SALAD TOAST

After purchasing far too many unripe avocados for an event, I had a surplus of ripe ones each day in my kitchen for a week after! I was making some egg salad sandwiches for lunch on one of these avocado surplus days, and had the great idea to use avocado to bind it together instead of traditional mayo. Not only was this version unbelievably delicious, the healthy fats in the avocado make it a much better option than the traditional mayo-laden version.
—*Shannon Dobos, Calgary, AB*

- -

TAKES: 20 min. • **MAKES:** 4 servings

- 1 medium ripe avocado, peeled and cubed
- 6 hard-boiled large eggs, chopped
- 1 green onion, finely chopped
- 1 tsp. lemon juice
- ¼ tsp. salt
- ⅛ tsp. pepper
- 4 large slices sourdough bread, halved and toasted

In a large bowl, mash avocado to desired consistency. Gently stir in eggs, green onion, lemon juice, salt and pepper. Spread over toast. Serve immediately.

2 PIECES: *367 cal., 15g fat (4g sat. fat), 280mg chol., 671mg sod., 41g carb. (4g sugars, 4g fiber), 18g pro.*

GOLDEN BUTTERNUT SQUASH SOUP

SLOW-COOKER MINESTRONE

FREEZE OPTION: Freeze cooled soup in freezer containers. To use, partially thaw in refrigerator overnight. Heat through in a saucepan, stirring occasionally; add water if necessary.

1⅓ CUPS: 165 cal., 1g fat (0 sat. fat), 0 chol., 813mg sod., 33g carb. (6g sugars, 6g fiber), 7g pro.

BUFFALO CHICKEN SLIDERS

I came up with the idea for these sliders from my mom and dad, who'd made a similar recipe for a family get-together. To make it special, I sometimes use several different styles of Buffalo sauce and let guests mix and match their favorites.
—Christina Addison, Blanchester, OH

PREP: 20 min. • **COOK:** 3 hours
MAKES: 6 servings

- 1 lb. boneless skinless chicken breasts
- 2 Tbsp. plus ⅓ cup Louisiana-style hot sauce, divided
- ¼ tsp. pepper
- ¼ cup butter, cubed
- ¼ cup honey
- 12 Hawaiian sweet rolls, warmed
  Optional ingredients: Lettuce leaves, sliced tomato, thinly sliced red onion and crumbled blue cheese

1. Place chicken in a 3-qt. slow cooker. Toss with 2 Tbsp. hot sauce and pepper; cook, covered, on low 3-4 hours or until tender.
2. Remove chicken; discard cooking juices. In a small saucepan, combine butter, honey and remaining hot sauce; cook and stir over medium heat until blended. Shred the chicken with 2 forks; stir into the sauce and heat through. Serve on rolls with desired optional ingredients.
FREEZE OPTION: Freeze cooled chicken mixture in freezer containers. To use, partially thaw chicken in refrigerator overnight. Microwave, covered, on high in a microwave-safe dish until heated through, stirring occasionally; add a little water or broth if necessary.
2 SLIDERS: 396 cal., 15g fat (8g sat. fat), 92mg chol., 873mg sod., 44g carb. (24g sugars, 2g fiber), 24g pro.

SLOW-COOKER MINESTRONE

There's nothing quite like the comfort of warm homemade soup, and it's even better when your slow cooker does most of the work for you! This hearty minestrone is easy to put together, but has all the flavor of a high-effort dish.
—Erin Raatjes, New Lenox, IL

PREP: 20 min. • **COOK:** 6½ hours
MAKES: 12 servings (4 qt.)

- 1 carton (32 oz.) vegetable or chicken stock
- 3 cups V8 or tomato juice
- 2 cups water
- 2 medium potatoes, peeled and chopped
- 2 celery ribs, chopped
- 2 medium carrots, chopped
- 1 can (14½ oz.) diced tomatoes, undrained
- 1 medium onion, chopped
- 3 garlic cloves, minced
- 2 bay leaves
- 1 Tbsp. Italian seasoning
- 1 tsp. salt
- ½ tsp. pepper
- 1 can (16 oz.) kidney beans, rinsed and drained
- 1 can (15 oz.) cannellini beans, rinsed and drained
- 1 can (14½ oz.) cut green beans, drained
- 1 small zucchini, chopped
- 1 cup uncooked ditalini or other small pasta
  Grated Parmesan cheese, optional

Combine the first 13 ingredients in a 5- or 6-qt. slow cooker. Cook, covered, on low 6-8 hours or until vegetables are tender. Stir in the remaining ingredients. Cook, covered, on high about 30 minutes longer, until pasta is tender. Discard bay leaves. If desired, top with grated Parmesan cheese.

BUFFALO CHICKEN SLIDERS

LENTIL SLOPPY JOES

LENTIL SLOPPY JOES

When I experimented with making more vegetarian-friendly recipes, this was one of my biggest hits—we still eat it weekly! My preschooler will finish every bite of these tangy sandwiches.
—*Christina Rock, Covington, WA*

PREP: 30 min. • **COOK:** 35 min. • **MAKES:** 14 servings

2	Tbsp. olive oil
1	large sweet onion, chopped
1	medium green pepper, chopped
½	medium sweet red pepper, chopped
1	medium carrot, shredded
6	garlic cloves, minced
2½	cups reduced-sodium vegetable broth
1	cup dried red lentils, rinsed
5	plum tomatoes, chopped
1	can (8 oz.) tomato sauce
2	Tbsp. chili powder
2	Tbsp. yellow mustard
4½	tsp. cider vinegar
2	tsp. vegan Worcestershire sauce
2	tsp. honey
1½	tsp. tomato paste
¼	tsp. salt
⅛	tsp. pepper
14	whole wheat hamburger buns, split and toasted

1. In a large skillet, heat oil over medium-high heat. Add onion, peppers and carrot; cook and stir until crisp-tender, 6-8 minutes. Add garlic; cook 1 minute longer.
2. Add broth and lentils; bring to a boil. Reduce heat; simmer, uncovered, until lentils are tender, about 15 minutes, stirring occasionally. Stir in chopped tomatoes, tomato sauce, chili powder, mustard, vinegar, Worcestershire sauce, honey, tomato paste, salt and pepper. Bring to a boil. Reduce heat; simmer until thickened, about 10 minutes. Serve on buns.
1 SANDWICH: *215 cal., 5g fat (1g sat. fat), 0 chol., 438mg sod., 38g carb. (8g sugars, 7g fiber), 8g pro.* **Diabetic exchanges:** *2½ starch, 1 fat.*

FRUITY CHICKEN SALAD PITAS

I found this handwritten recipe tucked into an old community cookbook I bought at a garage sale more than 40 years ago. I made a few changes over the years to suit my family's tastes, and we still enjoy the refreshing sandwiches to this day. What a great, easy and fast way to use up leftover chicken.
—*Kristine Chayes, Smithtown, NY*

TAKES: 15 min. • **MAKES:** 2 servings

1	cup cubed rotisserie chicken
½	cup chopped apple
½	cup chopped celery
½	cup unsweetened crushed pineapple, well drained
¼	cup dried cranberries
¼	cup mayonnaise
1	tsp. lemon juice
¼	tsp. onion powder
⅛	tsp. salt
4	pita pocket halves

Combine the first 9 ingredients. Fill pita halves with chicken mixture.
2 FILLED PITA HALVES: *588 cal., 26g fat (5g sat. fat), 64mg chol., 670mg sod., 63g carb. (28g sugars, 4g fiber), 26g pro.*

FRUITY CHICKEN SALAD PITAS

STEAKHOUSE SOUP

Enjoy a steak dinner in a bowl with this easy yet hearty steak soup. Because of the chili powder and cayenne pepper, it packs a little heat, but the recipe can easily be adjusted if you're cooking for kids.
—Erica Schmidt, Kansas City, KS

PREP: 20 min. • **COOK:** 8 hours
MAKES: 10 servings (3¾ qt.)

- 1 carton (32 oz.) beef broth
- 1½ lbs. red potatoes, cubed
- 1½ lbs. beef stew meat, cut into ½-in. pieces
- 1 pkg. (16 oz.) frozen vegetables of your choice, thawed
- 2 cups water
- 1 medium onion, chopped
- 1 cup steak sauce
- 2 Tbsp. minced fresh parsley or 2 tsp. dried parsley flakes
- 1 Tbsp. chili powder
- 1 tsp. ground cumin
- ¼ tsp. cayenne pepper

Combine all ingredients in a 5- or 6-qt. slow cooker. Cook, covered, on low 8-10 hours or until steak and potatoes are tender.

FREEZE OPTION: Freeze cooled soup in freezer containers. To use, partially thaw in the refrigerator overnight. Heat through in a saucepan, stirring occasionally; add water if necessary.

1½ CUPS: 198 cal., 5g fat (2g sat. fat), 42mg chol., 874mg sod., 20g carb. (5g sugars, 3g fiber), 16g pro.

VIETNAMESE CHICKEN MEATBALL SOUP WITH BOK CHOY

Throughout Vietnam there are many kinds of soups served all year long. I particularly love enjoying this warm, flavorful bowl of chicken soup on laid-back weekends, but it's also great packed in a thermos for lunch. It's the perfect way to use bok choy.
—Brenda Watts, Gaffney, SC

PREP: 45 min. • **COOK:** 6 hours
MAKES: 8 servings (about 2½ qt.)

- ¼ cup panko bread crumbs
- ¼ cup finely chopped onion
- 1 large egg, lightly beaten
- 2 serrano peppers, seeded and minced

VIETNAMESE CHICKEN MEATBALL SOUP WITH BOK CHOY

- 1 garlic clove, minced
- ½ lb. ground chicken
- 2 Tbsp. peanut oil

SOUP
- 6 cups chicken or vegetable stock
- 1 can (14½ oz.) fire-roasted diced tomatoes, undrained
- 1 small onion, cut into thin strips
- 1 cup bok choy leaves, cut into 1-in. strips
- 1 cup fresh baby carrots, julienned
- 1 cup julienned roasted sweet red peppers
- 3 serrano peppers, julienned
- 2 garlic cloves, minced
- ½ tsp. salt
- ¼ cup panko bread crumbs, optional
- 1 large egg, beaten

1. In a large bowl, combine the first 5 ingredients. Add chicken; mix lightly but thoroughly. Shape into ¾-in. balls. In a large skillet, heat oil over medium heat. Brown meatballs in batches; drain. Transfer to a 4- or 5-qt. slow cooker.

2. Add stock, tomatoes, onion, bok choy, carrots, red peppers, julienned serrano peppers, garlic and salt. Cook, covered, on low 6-8 hours or until the meatballs are cooked through and vegetables are tender. If desired, stir in panko. Without stirring, drizzle beaten egg into slow cooker. Let stand until egg is set, 2-3 minutes.

FREEZE OPTION: Before adding egg, cool soup. Freeze in freezer containers. To use, partially thaw in refrigerator overnight. Heat through in a saucepan, stirring occasionally; add broth if necessary. Without stirring, drizzle beaten egg into soup. Let stand until egg is set, 2-3 minutes.

NOTE: Wear disposable gloves when cutting hot peppers; the oils can burn skin. Avoid touching your face.

1⅓ CUPS: 147 cal., 7g fat (2g sat. fat), 65mg chol., 836mg sod., 9g carb. (5g sugars, 1g fiber), 10g pro.

GREEN CHILE CHEESEBURGERS

A diner outside of Albuquerque, New Mexico, served the most amazing burgers topped with freshly roasted green chiles. They have a smoky flavor and a bit of a bite—perfect after a long day.
—James Schend, Pleasant Prairie, WI

- -

PREP: 20 min. • **GRILL:** 15 min.
MAKES: 6 servings

- 3   whole green chiles, such as Anaheim or Hatch
- 2   lbs. ground beef
- 1   tsp. salt
- ½   tsp. pepper
- 6   slices slices sharp cheddar cheese
- 6   hamburger buns, split and toasted
    Optional toppings: Lettuce leaves, sliced tomato, sliced onion, bacon and mayonnaise

1. Grill peppers, covered, over high heat until all sides are blistered and blackened, 8-10 minutes, carefully turning as needed. Immediately place peppers in a small bowl; let stand, covered, 20 minutes. Reduce grill temperature to medium heat.
2. Meanwhile, in a large bowl, combine beef, salt and pepper; mix lightly but thoroughly. Shape into six ¾-in.-thick patties.
3. Peel off and discard charred skin from peppers. Cut peppers lengthwise in half; carefully remove stems and seeds. Cut into slices or coarsely chop.
4. Grill burgers, covered, over medium heat until a thermometer reads 160°, 5-7 minutes on each side. Top with cheese and chiles; grill, covered, until cheese is melted, 1-2 minutes longer. Top bun bottoms with burgers. If desired, serve wth lettuce, tomato, onion, bacon and mayonnaise.
1 BURGER: 482 cal., 26g fat (11g sat. fat), 116mg chol., 552mg sod., 23g carb. (4g sugars, 1g fiber), 36g pro.

EASY WHITE CHICKEN CHILI

Chili is one of our best cold-weather strategies. We use chicken and white beans for a twist on the traditional variety. To us, it's soothing comfort food.
—Rachel Lewis, Danville, VA

- -

TAKES: 30 min. • **MAKES:** 6 servings

- 1   lb. lean ground chicken
- 1   medium onion, chopped
- 2   cans (15 oz. each) cannellini beans, rinsed and drained
- 1   can (4 oz.) chopped green chiles
- 1   tsp. ground cumin
- ½   tsp. dried oregano
- ¼   tsp. pepper
- 1   can (14½ oz.) reduced-sodium chicken broth
    Optional toppings: Reduced-fat sour cream, shredded cheddar cheese and chopped fresh cilantro

1. In a large saucepan, cook chicken and onion over medium-high heat until chicken is no longer pink, 6-8 minutes, breaking chicken into crumbles.
2. Pour 1 can of beans in a small bowl; mash slightly. Stir mashed beans, remaining can of beans, chiles, seasonings and broth into chicken mixture; bring to a boil. Reduce heat; simmer, covered, until flavors are blended, 12-15 minutes. Serve with toppings as desired.
FREEZE OPTION: Freeze cooled chili in freezer containers. To use, partially thaw chili in refrigerator overnight. Heat through in a saucepan, stirring occasionally; add broth if necessary.
1 CUP: 228 cal., 5g fat (1g sat. fat), 54mg chol., 504mg sod., 23g carb. (1g sugars, 6g fiber), 22g pro. **Diabetic exchanges:** 3 lean meat, 1½ starch.

GREEN CHILE CHEESEBURGERS

TURKEY SWEET
POTATO CHILI

SLOW-COOKER HOMEMADE CHICKEN & RICE SOUP

Using the slow cooker takes some of the effort out of making from-scratch chicken soup. The long cook time helps develop great homemade flavor.
—*Kevin Bruckerhoff, Columbia, MO*

PREP: 15 min. • **COOK:** 8 hours • **MAKES:** 16 servings (4 qt.)

- 3 qt. water
- 4 bone-in chicken breast halves (about 3 lbs.)
- 1½ tsp. salt
- ¼ tsp. pepper
- ¼ tsp. poultry seasoning
- 1 tsp. chicken bouillon granules
- 3 medium carrots, chopped
- 2 celery ribs, chopped
- 1 small onion, chopped
- ½ cup uncooked converted rice
  Minced fresh parsley, optional

1. In a 6-qt. slow cooker, place water, chicken, salt, pepper and poultry seasoning. Cover and cook on low 6-7 hours or until chicken is tender.

2. With a slotted spoon, remove chicken from broth. When cool enough to handle, remove meat from bones; discard skin and bones. Cut chicken into bite-sized pieces. Skim fat from broth; add chicken and remaining ingredients. Cover and cook on high 1-2 hours or until vegetables and rice are tender. If desired, sprinkle with parsley.

1 CUP: *202 cal., 6g fat (2g sat. fat), 66mg chol., 513mg sod., 10g carb. (1g sugars, 1g fiber), 25g pro.*

TURKEY SWEET POTATO CHILI

My slow-cooker specialty is packed with flavor. Swapping ground turkey for ground beef lightens it up, and sweet potato puree sneaks in a healthy dose of vitamin A.
—*Rachel Lewis, Danville, VA*

PREP: 20 min. • **COOK:** 5 hours • **MAKES:** 6 servings (2¼ qt.)

- 1 lb. ground turkey
- 1 small onion, chopped
- 2 cups chicken broth
- 1 can (15 oz.) sweet potato puree or canned pumpkin
- 1 can (4 oz.) chopped green chiles
- 1 Tbsp. chili powder
- 1 tsp. garlic powder
- 1 tsp. ground cumin
- 1 tsp. curry powder
- ½ tsp. dried oregano
- ½ tsp. salt
- 1 can (15½ oz.) great northern beans, rinsed and drained
  Optional: Sour cream, fresh cilantro and sliced red onions

1. In a large skillet, cook the turkey and onion over medium heat until turkey is no longer pink and onion is tender, 5-7 minutes, breaking up turkey into crumbles; drain. Transfer to a 3- or 4-qt. slow cooker.

2. Stir in broth, sweet potato puree, chiles and seasonings. Cook, covered, on low 4-5 hours. Stir in the beans; cook until heated through, about 1 hour. If desired, top with sour cream, cilantro and red onions.

FREEZE OPTION: Freeze cooled chili in freezer containers. To use, partially thaw in refrigerator overnight. Heat through in a saucepan, stirring occasionally; add broth if necessary.

1½ CUPS: *243 cal., 6g fat (1g sat. fat), 52mg chol., 606mg sod., 27g carb. (5g sugars, 7g fiber), 20g pro.* **Diabetic exchanges:** *2 starch, 2 lean meat.*

SLOW-COOKER HOMEMADE
CHICKEN & RICE SOUP

CHUNKY CHIPOTLE PORK CHILI

CHUNKY CHIPOTLE PORK CHILI

Perfect for using leftover shredded pork, this tasty recipe can be made ahead, frozen and reheated. To me, it tastes even better the second day.
—Peter Halferty, Corpus Christi, TX

PREP: 15 min. • **COOK:** 20 min. • **MAKES:** 4 servings

- 1 medium green pepper, chopped
- 1 small onion, chopped
- 1 chipotle pepper in adobo sauce, finely chopped
- 1 Tbsp. canola oil
- 3 garlic cloves, minced
- 1 can (16 oz.) red beans, rinsed and drained
- 1 cup beef broth
- ½ cup salsa
- 2 tsp. ground cumin
- 2 tsp. chili powder
- 2 cups shredded cooked pork
- ¼ cup sour cream
   Sliced jalapeno pepper, optional

1. In a large saucepan, saute the green pepper, onion and chipotle pepper in oil until tender. Add garlic; cook 1 minute longer.
2. Add beans, broth, salsa, cumin and chili powder. Bring to a boil. Reduce the heat; simmer, uncovered, until thickened, about 10 minutes. Add the pork; heat through. Serve with sour cream and, if desired, jalapeno slices.
FREEZE OPTION: Cool chili and transfer to freezer containers. Freeze for up to 3 months. To use, thaw in refrigerator. Transfer chili to a large saucepan; heat through, adding water to thin if desired. Serve with sour cream and, if desired, jalapeno slices.
1 CUP: *340 cal., 14g fat (4g sat. fat), 73mg chol., 834mg sod., 24g carb. (3g sugars, 7g fiber), 27g pro.*

SWISS CHICKEN SLIDERS

Friends came over for a spur-of-the-moment bonfire, and I dreamed up these quick chicken sliders so we'd have something to eat. Bake them till the cheese is nice and gooey. Wrapped individually in foil and stashed in the refrigerator, they make wonderful grab-and-go lunches for the week. Give 'em a try and see!
—Sara Martin, Whitefish, MT

TAKES: 25 min. • **MAKES:** 6 servings

- ½ cup mayonnaise
- 3 Tbsp. yellow mustard
- 12 mini buns, split
- 12 slices deli ham
- 3 cups shredded rotisserie chicken
- 6 slices Swiss cheese, cut in half

1. Preheat oven to 350°. In a small bowl, mix mayonnaise and mustard. Spread bun bottoms and tops with mayonnaise mixture. Layer bottoms with ham, chicken and cheese; replace tops. Arrange in a single layer in a 15x10x1-in. baking pan.
2. Bake, covered, until sandwiches are heated through and cheese is melted, 10-15 minutes.
2 SLIDERS: *508 cal., 27g fat (6g sat. fat), 100mg chol., 894mg sod., 28g carb. (4g sugars, 1g fiber), 37g pro.*

SWISS CHICKEN SLIDERS

BRATWURST BURGERS WITH BRAISED ONIONS

This burger is a fun mashup of a bratwurst with onion and peppers, chicken-fried steak and a beef burger. What a surprising change of pace this will be for all the burger lovers at your table.
—Priscilla Yee, Concord, CA

- -

TAKES: 30 min. • **MAKES:** 4 servings

- 1 Tbsp. canola oil
- 1 large onion, sliced
- 1 medium sweet red pepper, sliced
- 1 medium sweet yellow pepper, sliced
- 1 cup dark beer or chicken broth

BURGERS

- ½ lb. ground beef
- ½ lb. uncooked bratwurst links, casings removed
- 1 large egg, lightly beaten
- 1 Tbsp. 2% milk
- ¾ cup seasoned bread crumbs
- 4 slices Muenster cheese
- 4 hamburger buns, split and toasted
- 8 tsp. spicy brown mustard

1. In a large skillet, heat oil over medium heat. Add onion and peppers; cook and stir for 5 minutes. Stir in beer. Bring to a boil. Reduce heat; simmer, uncovered, until vegetables are tender and liquid is almost evaporated, 15-20 minutes . Remove and keep warm.

2. In a small bowl, combine the beef and bratwurst, mixing lightly but thoroughly. Shape into four ¾-in.-thick patties.

3. In a shallow bowl, mix egg and milk. Place bread crumbs in a separate shallow bowl. Dip patties in egg mixture, then roll in the crumb mixture to coat.

4. In the same skillet over medium heat, cook burgers until a thermometer reads 160° for medium doneness and juices run clear, 3-4 minutes on each side; top with cheese during the last 1-2 minutes of cooking. Serve burgers on buns with mustard and onion mixture.

1 BURGER: *659 cal., 36g fat (13g sat. fat), 145mg chol., 1409mg sod., 41g carb. (10g sugars, 3g fiber), 32g pro.*

ITALIAN BEEF VEGETABLE SOUP

ITALIAN BEEF VEGETABLE SOUP

This hearty vegetable beef soup features a ton of fresh vegetables, making it the perfect dish to use up all that summer produce. It's also great during cooler weather! Make sure you serve this Italian soup with some rolls, breadsticks or flaky biscuits.
—Courtney Stultz, Weir, KS

- -

PREP: 20 min. • **COOK:** 5 hours
MAKES: 6 servings (1½ qt.)

- ½ lb. lean ground beef (90% lean)
- ¼ cup chopped onion
- 2 cups chopped cabbage
- 2 medium carrots, chopped
- 1 cup fresh Brussels sprouts, quartered
- 1 cup chopped fresh kale
- 1 celery rib, chopped
- 1 Tbsp. minced fresh parsley
- ½ tsp. pepper
- ½ tsp. dried basil
- ¼ tsp. salt
- 3 cups beef stock
- 1 can (14½ oz.) Italian diced tomatoes, undrained

1. In a large skillet, cook and crumble beef with onion over medium-high heat until browned, 4-5 minutes. Transfer to a 3- or 4-qt. slow cooker. Stir in the remaining ingredients.

2. Cook, covered, on low 5-6 hours or until carrots are tender.

FREEZE OPTION: Freeze cooled soup in freezer containers. To use, partially thaw in refrigerator overnight. Heat through in a saucepan, stirring occasionally.

1 CUP: *127 cal., 3g fat (1g sat. fat), 24mg chol., 617mg sod., 14g carb. (9g sugars, 3g fiber), 11g pro.* **Diabetic exchanges:** *1 starch, 1 lean meat.*

TEST KITCHEN TIP

Our tasting panel thought the flavor was like an Italian cabbage roll and suggested adding more ground beef for an even thicker, heartier entree.

SLOW-COOKED CHICKEN CAESAR WRAPS

MEXICAN STREET CORN CHOWDER

Summer sweet corn is one of my favorite vegetables, so when it's in season I always make this super easy soup in the slow cooker.
—*Rashanda Cobbins, Milwaukee, WI*

PREP: 35 min. • **COOK:** 3½ hrs.
MAKES: 8 servings (2¼ qt.)

- 10 ears fresh corn (about 5½ cups)
- 1¼ to 2 cups water
- 6 bacon strips, chopped
- 2 small onions, chopped
- 2 small green peppers, chopped
- 1 jalapeno pepper, seeded and finely chopped
- 1 tsp. ground chipotle pepper
- 2 tsp. salt
- ¾ tsp. ground cumin
- ¼ tsp. pepper
- 1 cup heavy whipping cream
- 1 medium lime, zested and juiced
  Optional: Fresh cilantro, lime wedges, sliced jalapeno, chopped bell pepper and crumbled cotija cheese

1. Cut corn off cobs. Rub edge of a knife over each cob to "milk" it; add enough water to cob juice to equal 2 cups. Add corn and liquid to a 5-qt. slow cooker.
2. In a large skillet, cook bacon over medium heat until crisp, 5-7 minutes. Remove with a slotted spoon; drain on paper towels; discard drippings, reserving 2 Tbsp. in pan.
3. Add the onion, green pepper and jalapeno to drippings; cook and stir over medium-high heat until soft, 3-4 minutes. Add seasonings and cook 1 minute more; transfer to slow cooker. Cook on low for 3½-4 hours or until corn is tender and mixture has thickened slightly, .
4. Stir in the cream and lime zest and juice. Puree mixture with an immersion blender to desired consistency. Garnish with the reserved bacon. If desired, sprinkle with cilantro and serve with lime wedges, jalapeno, bell pepper and cojita cheese.
NOTE: Wear disposable gloves when cutting hot peppers; the oils can burn skin. Avoid touching your face.
1 CUP: *287 cal., 18g fat (9g sat. fat), 43mg chol., 743mg sod., 29g carb. (10g sugars, 4g fiber), 8g pro.*

SLOW-COOKED CHICKEN CAESAR WRAPS

I created this recipe for our daughter who loves Caesar salads, but came to rely on it during a vacation with extended family. It's such an easy meal—perfect when you'd rather be outside than inside cooking all day.
—*Christine Hadden, Whitman, MA*

PREP: 10 min. • **COOK:** 3 hours
MAKES: 6 servings

- 1½ lbs. boneless skinless chicken breast halves
- 2 cups chicken broth
- ¾ cup creamy Caesar salad dressing
- ½ cup shredded Parmesan cheese
- ¼ cup minced fresh parsley
- ½ tsp. pepper
- 6 flour tortillas (8 in.)
- 2 cups shredded lettuce
  Optional: Salad croutons and cooked crumbled bacon

1. Place chicken and broth in a 1½- or 3-qt. slow cooker. Cook, covered, on low for 3-4 hours or until a thermometer inserted in chicken reads 165°. Remove chicken and discard cooking juices. Shred chicken with 2 forks; return to slow cooker.
2. Stir in dressing, Parmesan, parsley and pepper; heat through. Serve in tortillas with lettuce and, if desired, salad croutons, crumbled bacon and additional shredded Parmesan cheese.
1 WRAP: *476 cal., 25g fat (5g sat. fat), 81mg chol., 1089mg sod., 29g carb. (1g sugars, 2g fiber), 31g pro.*

CASHEW CHICKEN SALAD SANDWICHES

I think this is the best chicken salad recipe around! You can make it quickly, and cucumber and cashews amp up the flavor and texture. Be sure to try the peanut version, too.
—*Peggi Kelly, Fairbury, NE*

TAKES: 15 min. • **MAKES:** 6 servings

2   **cups diced cooked chicken**
½   **cup chopped salted cashews**
½   **cup chopped red apple**
½   **cup chopped peeled cucumber**
½   **cup mayonnaise**
½   **tsp. sugar**
½   **tsp. salt**
   Dash pepper
6   **kaiser rolls or croissants, split**
6   **lettuce leaves, optional**

In a large bowl, combine chicken, cashews, apple and cucumber. In a small bowl, combine mayonnaise, sugar, salt and pepper. Stir into chicken mixture. Serve on rolls, with lettuce if desired.
1 SANDWICH: *463 cal., 26g fat (4g sat. fat), 48mg chol., 720mg sod., 36g carb. (3g sugars, 2g fiber), 21g pro.*
PEANUT CHICKEN SALAD SANDWICHES: Substitute ½ chopped salted peanuts for the cashews.

CASHEW CHICKEN SALAD SANDWICHES

DAIRY-FREE CREAM OF MUSHROOM SOUP

This homemade version of the canned standard has no dairy or preservatives. Try it in your favorite green bean casserole recipe!
—*Courtney Stultz, Weir, KS*

PREP: 15 min. • **COOK:** 20 min. • **MAKES:** 5 servings

2   **Tbsp. olive oil**
1   **lb. sliced fresh mushrooms**
1   **large onion, finely chopped**
2   **garlic cloves, minced**
1   **tsp. salt**
1   **tsp. white wine vinegar**
½   **tsp. dried thyme**
½   **tsp. pepper**
4   **Tbsp. cornstarch**
4   **cups unsweetened almond milk**

In a large saucepan, heat oil over medium-high heat. Add mushrooms and onion; cook and stir until tender, 8-10 minutes. Add garlic, salt, vinegar, thyme and pepper; cook 1 minute longer. Mix cornstarch and almond milk until smooth; stir into saucepan. Bring to a boil; cook and stir until thickened, 3-4 minutes.
1 CUP: *139 cal., 8g fat (1g sat. fat), 0 chol., 623mg sod., 14g carb. (3g sugars, 2g fiber), 4g pro.* **Diabetic exchanges:** *1 vegetable, 1 fat, ½ starch.*

TEST KITCHEN TIP

You are in full control of how intensely flavored this soup will be. If you like it mellow or are going to be using it in another recipe, simply keep the mushrooms and veggies from getting too browned.

VEGETARIAN SKILLET
ENCHILADAS
PAGE 65

Quick Fixes

Busy weekdays mean crunch time, come dinner. We have your back—all 30 of the recipes here are ready to eat in 30 minutes or less. Make these simple dinners your go-tos!

BACON-CHICKEN CLUB PIZZA

BACON-CHICKEN CLUB PIZZA

I've combined a sandwich classic and a quick pizza into a delicious new dinner idea. The cream cheese and shallot sauce is such a fun twist, and the vegetables on top add a crisp, cool crunch to the cheesy crust.
—Debbie Reid, Clearwater, FL

TAKES: 25 min. • **MAKES:** 8 servings

- 1   prebaked 12-in. pizza crust
- 4   oz. cream cheese, softened
- 1   shallot, minced
- 2   cups shredded rotisserie chicken
- 1½ cups shredded Monterey Jack cheese
- 1   cup shredded sharp cheddar cheese
- 8   slices ready-to-serve fully cooked bacon, cut into 1-in. pieces
- ¼   cup sour cream
- 3   Tbsp. 2% milk
- 2   tsp. ranch salad dressing mix
- 1   cup shredded lettuce
- 1   plum tomato, seeded and chopped

1. Place crust on an ungreased pizza pan. Combine cream cheese and shallot; spread over crust. Top with chicken, cheeses and bacon.
2. Bake at 425° until edges are lightly browned and cheese is melted, 12-15 minutes .
3. Meanwhile, in a small bowl, combine the sour cream, milk and dressing mix. Sprinkle lettuce and tomato over pizza; drizzle with dressing.
1 SLICE: *444 cal., 25g fat (13g sat. fat), 84mg chol., 939mg sod., 26g carb. (1g sugars, 0 fiber), 28g pro.*

CRISPY ORANGE CHICKEN

These tangy chicken nuggets go a long way. We eat them over noodles or rice, in sandwiches, and even on top of lettuce and cabbage.
—Darlene Brenden, Salem, OR

TAKES: 30 min. • **MAKES:** 4 servings

- 16   oz. frozen popcorn chicken (about 4 cups)
- 1   Tbsp. canola oil
- 2   medium carrots, thinly sliced
- 1   garlic clove, minced
- 1½ tsp. grated orange zest
- 1   cup orange juice
- ⅓   cup hoisin sauce
- 3   Tbsp. sugar
- ¼   tsp. salt
- ¼   tsp. pepper
       Dash cayenne pepper
       Hot cooked rice

1. Bake popcorn chicken according to package directions.
2. Meanwhile, in a large skillet, heat oil over medium-high heat. Add carrots; cook and stir until tender, 3-5 minutes. Add garlic; cook 1 minute longer. Stir in orange zest, juice, hoisin sauce, sugar and seasonings; bring to a boil. Reduce heat; simmer, uncovered, until thickened, 4-6 minutes, stirring constantly.
3. Add chicken to skillet; toss to coat. Serve with rice.
1 CUP: *450 cal., 20g fat (3g sat. fat), 35mg chol., 1294mg sod., 56g carb. (25g sugars, 3g fiber), 14g pro.*

CRISPY ORANGE CHICKEN

GROUNDNUT STEW

My Aunt Linda was a missionary in Africa for more than 40 years and gave me the recipe for this cozy stew with a hint of peanut butter.
—Heather Ewald, Bothell, WA

TAKES: 30 min. • **MAKES:** 7 servings

- 6 oz. lamb stew meat, cut into ½-in. pieces
- 6 oz. pork stew meat, cut into ½-in. pieces
- 2 Tbsp. peanut oil
- 1 large onion, cut into wedges
- 1 large green pepper, cut into wedges
- 1 cup chopped tomatoes
- 4 cups cubed eggplant
- 2 cups water
- ½ cup fresh or frozen sliced okra
- ½ cup creamy peanut butter
- 1 tsp. salt
- ½ tsp. pepper
  Hot cooked rice
  Chopped green onions, optional

1. In a large skillet, brown meat in oil; set aside. In a food processor, combine the onion, green pepper and tomatoes; cover and process until blended.

2. In a large saucepan, combine the cubed eggplant, water, okra and onion mixture. Bring to a boil. Reduce the heat; cook, uncovered, until vegetables are tender, 7-9 minutes.

3. Stir in the peanut butter, salt, pepper and browned meat. Cook, uncovered, until heated through, about 10 minutes. Serve with rice. If desired, top with chopped green onions.

FREEZE OPTION: Freeze cooled stew in freezer containers. To use, partially thaw in refrigerator overnight. Heat through in a saucepan, stirring occasionally; add a little broth or water if necessary.

1 CUP: 230 cal., 13g fat (3g sat. fat), 31mg chol., 470mg sod., 14g carb. (7g sugars, 4g fiber), 16g pro. **Diabetic exchanges:** *2 lean meat, 1 starch, 1 fat.*

GORGONZOLA SHRIMP PASTA

GORGONZOLA SHRIMP PASTA

This creamy pasta dish is so quick and easy. It's perfect for weeknights, but feels special enough for company.
—Robin Haas, Hyde Park, MA

TAKES: 30 min. • **MAKES:** 6 servings

- 12 oz. uncooked penne pasta
- 2 Tbsp. olive oil
- 1 lb. uncooked shrimp (31-40 per lb.), peeled and deveined
- 3 garlic cloves, minced
- ½ cup dried cranberries
- ½ cup dry white wine or reduced-sodium chicken broth
- 6 oz. fresh baby spinach (about 3 cups)
- 4 oz. reduced-fat cream cheese, cubed
- ½ cup crumbled Gorgonzola cheese
- 3 Tbsp. minced fresh parsley
- ¼ tsp. salt
- ⅓ cup chopped walnuts

1. Cook penne according to package directions for al dente. Meanwhile, in a large cast-iron skillet or Dutch oven, heat oil over medium heat. Add shrimp and minced garlic; cook until the shrimp are pink, 5-10 minutes. Remove from pan and keep warm.

2. Stir cranberries and wine into same pan. Bring to a boil; cook until liquid is almost evaporated, 5 minutes.

3. Drain penne, reserving 1 cup of pasta water; add penne to pan. Stir in spinach, cream cheese, Gorgonzola cheese, parsley, salt and the reserved shrimp. Cook and stir until mixture is heated through and cheeses are melted, about 5 minutes, adding enough reserved pasta water to reach desired consistency. Top with chopped walnuts.

2 CUPS: 486 cal., 18g fat (6g sat. fat), 114mg chol., 422mg sod., 57g carb. (13g sugars, 4g fiber), 26g pro.

GREEK CHICKEN & RICE

A fresh take on comfort food, this dish is my go-to on busy weeknights and when unexpected company stops by. Boost the health benefits and toss in chopped spinach, too.
—Savannah Lay, Baker City, OR

TAKES: 30 min. • **MAKES:** 4 servings

1   lb. boneless skinless chicken breasts, cut into 1-in. cubes
¼   tsp. garlic powder
¼   tsp. pepper
2   tsp. olive oil
1   jar (12 oz.) marinated quartered artichoke hearts, drained and chopped
1   jar (12 oz.) roasted sweet red peppers, drained and chopped
⅓   cup oil-packed sun-dried tomatoes, chopped
⅓   cup Greek olives, sliced
1   pkg. (8.8 oz.) ready-to-serve brown rice
1   Tbsp. minced fresh parsley

1. Sprinkle chicken with garlic powder and pepper. In a large skillet, heat oil over medium heat. Add chicken; cook and stir until no longer pink, 8-10 minutes. Stir in artichokes, roasted peppers, tomatoes and olives. Cook and stir until heated through, 3-5 minutes.
2. Meanwhile, prepare rice according to package directions. Serve with chicken. Sprinkle with parsley.
1¼ CUPS: *436 cal., 21g fat (4g sat. fat), 63mg chol., 1008mg sod., 29g carb. (3g sugars, 7g fiber), 26g pro.*

GREEK CHICKEN & RICE

ROAST LEMON BUTTER SHRIMP

ROAST LEMON BUTTER SHRIMP

This baked shrimp is a quick and easy weeknight meal that has lots of great flavor!
—Anne Ormond, Dover, NH

TAKES: 30 min. • **MAKES:** 4 servings

6   Tbsp. unsalted butter, cubed
¼   cup Worcestershire sauce
2   garlic cloves, minced
3   Tbsp. lemon juice
1   fresh rosemary sprig
½   tsp. salt
¼   tsp. pepper
1   lb. uncooked shrimp (26-30 per lb.), peeled and deveined, tails removed
1   pkg. (8½ oz.) ready-to-serve jasmine rice
3   Tbsp. heavy whipping cream
     Hot pepper sauce, optional

1. Preheat oven to 400°. Place the first 7 ingredients in a 13x9-in. baking dish. Place dish in oven until butter is melted, 3-5 minutes. Add shrimp. Bake, uncovered, until shrimp turn pink, 12-15 minutes, stirring halfway through cooking. Meanwhile, cook rice according to package directions.
2. Discard rosemary; stir in cream. Serve shrimp mixture with rice and, if desired, hot pepper sauce.
1 SERVING: *431 cal., 24g fat (14g sat. fat), 196mg chol., 607mg sod., 32g carb. (2g sugars, 1g fiber), 22g pro.*

EASY CHICKEN PESTO STUFFED PEPPERS

On weekdays, I don't want to spend more than 30 minutes preparing dinner, nor do I want to wash a towering pile of dishes. This recipe delivers without having to sacrifice flavor!
—Olivia Cruz, Greenville, SC

- -

TAKES: 25 min. • **MAKES:** 4 servings

- 4 medium sweet yellow or orange peppers
- 1½ cups shredded rotisserie chicken
- 1½ cups cooked brown rice
- 1 cup prepared pesto
- ½ cup shredded Havarti cheese
  Fresh basil leaves, optional

1. Cut peppers lengthwise in half; remove stems and seeds. Place peppers on a baking sheet, skin side up. Broil 4 in. from heat until skins blister, about 5 minutes. Reduce oven temperature to 350°.
2. Meanwhile, in a large bowl, combine chicken, rice and pesto. When cool enough to handle, fill peppers with chicken mixture; return to baking sheet. Bake until filling is heated through, about 5 minutes. Sprinkle with cheese; bake until cheese is melted, 3-5 minutes. If desired, sprinkle with basil.
2 STUFFED PEPPER HALVES: *521 cal., 31g fat (7g sat. fat), 62mg chol., 865mg sod., 33g carb. (7g sugars, 5g fiber), 25g pro.*

EASY CHICKEN PESTO STUFFED PEPPERS

CHILI-TOPPED CORNBREAD WAFFLES

CHILI-TOPPED CORNBREAD WAFFLES

Everyone in my family loves chili except my daughter, but she loves cornbread. One day she asked if she could have mostly cornbread, with just a little chili. Then we had an idea—cornbread waffles topped with chili and all the fixings! It was a hit. If you're going gluten-free, make sure your chili is also free of gluten.
—Courtney Stultz, Weir, KS

- -

TAKES: 20 min. • **MAKES:** 8 servings

- 1½ cups gluten-free all-purpose baking flour
- 1½ cups cornmeal
- 2 tsp. baking powder
- 1 tsp. sea salt
- 2 large eggs, room temperature
- 2 cups 2% milk
- ½ cup olive oil
- 2 cans (15 oz.) chili with beans or 4 cups leftover chili, warmed
  Jalapeno slices, shredded cheddar cheese, sour cream, cubed avocado and minced fresh cilantro

1. Preheat waffle maker. In a large bowl, whisk flour, cornmeal, baking powder and salt. In another bowl, whisk eggs, milk and oil until blended. Add to dry ingredients; stir just until moistened.
2. Bake waffles according to manufacturer's directions until golden brown. Serve with chili and toppings of your choice.
1 SERVING: *464 cal., 20g fat (4g sat. fat), 64mg chol., 796mg sod., 57g carb. (6g sugars, 6g fiber), 15g pro.*

SUMMER GARDEN PASTA WITH CHICKEN SAUSAGE

SUMMER GARDEN PASTA WITH CHICKEN SAUSAGE

Here's a great 30-minute meal for everyone at the table! If you don't feel like grilling, you can prepare the chicken sausages under the broiler or on the stovetop.
—Karie Houghton, Lynnwood, WA

- -

TAKES: 30 min. • **MAKES:** 8 servings

3¼	cups uncooked mini penne pasta
1	pkg. (12 oz.) fully cooked roasted garlic chicken sausage links or flavor of your choice
4	medium tomatoes, chopped (about 3 cups)
1	round (8 oz.) Brie cheese, cubed
1	cup shredded Parmesan cheese
1	cup loosely packed basil leaves, thinly sliced
3	garlic cloves, minced
½	tsp. salt
½	tsp. pepper
¼	cup olive oil

1. Cook the pasta according to package directions. Meanwhile, grill sausages, covered, over medium heat or broil 4 in. from heat until a thermometer reads 165°, 7-9 minutes, turning occasionally. Remove sausages from grill; cut into slices.

2. Drain pasta; transfer to a large bowl. Stir in sausage, chopped tomatoes, cheeses, basil, garlic, salt and pepper. Drizzle with oil; toss to coat.

1½ CUPS: *445 cal., 22g fat (9g sat. fat), 71mg chol., 739mg sod., 40g carb. (3g sugars, 3g fiber), 24g pro.*

PORK CHOPS WITH RHUBARB

A quick rhubarb sauce makes these tender chops extra special. I like it on the tangy side, but you can always add more honey to sweeten up the sauce a bit if it's too puckery for your family.
—Bonnie Bufford, Nicholson, PA

- -

TAKES: 25 min. • **MAKES:** 2 servings

1	Tbsp. all-purpose flour
	Salt and pepper to taste
2	bone-in pork loin chops (½ to ¾ in. thick)
2	Tbsp. butter
½	lb. fresh or frozen rhubarb, chopped
1	Tbsp. honey
⅛	tsp. ground cinnamon
1½	tsp. minced fresh parsley

1. In a shallow dish, combine the flour, salt and pepper; add pork chops and turn to coat. In a skillet, melt butter over medium heat. Add the pork chops; cook until a thermometer reads 145°, 4-5 minutes on each side. Remove and keep warm.

2. Add the rhubarb, honey and cinnamon to the skillet; cook until rhubarb is tender, about 5 minutes. Serve sauce over pork chops. Sprinkle with parsley.

1 PORK CHOP: *390 cal., 19g fat (7g sat. fat), 111mg chol., 82mg sod., 17g carb. (10g sugars, 2g fiber), 38g pro.*

TURKEY ALFREDO PIZZA

A longtime family favorite, this thin-crust pizza is both tasty and nutritious. It's an excellent way to use up leftover turkey, too.
—Edie DeSpain, Logan, UT

TAKES: 25 min. • **MAKES:** 6 servings

1	prebaked 12-in. thin pizza crust
1	garlic clove, peeled and halved
¾	cup reduced-fat Alfredo sauce, divided
1	pkg. (10 oz.) frozen chopped spinach, thawed and squeezed dry
2	tsp. lemon juice
¼	tsp. salt
⅛	tsp. pepper
2	cups shredded cooked turkey breast
¾	cup shredded Parmesan cheese
½	tsp. crushed red pepper flakes

1. Place the crust on a baking sheet; rub with cut sides of garlic. Discard garlic. Spread ½ cup Alfredo sauce over crust.
2. In a small bowl, combine the spinach, lemon juice, salt and pepper; spoon evenly over sauce. Top with turkey; drizzle with remaining Alfredo sauce. Sprinkle with Parmesan cheese and pepper flakes.
3. Bake at 425° until ingredients are heated through and cheese is melted, 11-13 minutes.
1 PIECE: *300 cal., 9g fat (4g sat. fat), 60mg chol., 823mg sod., 27g carb. (2g sugars, 2g fiber), 25g pro.* **Diabetic exchanges:** *3 lean meat, 2 starch, ½ fat.*

TURKEY ALFREDO PIZZA

STEAK STIR-FRY

STEAK STIR-FRY

No one would guess this elegant entree is a snap to prepare at the last minute. To save even more prep time, use frozen mixed veggies instead of fresh. Sometimes I substitute chicken, chicken bouillon and curry for the beef, beef bouillon and ginger.
—Janis Plourde, Smooth Rock Falls, ON

TAKES: 25 min. • **MAKES:** 4 servings

1	tsp. beef bouillon granules
1	cup boiling water
2	Tbsp. cornstarch
⅓	cup soy sauce
1	lb. beef top sirloin steak, cut into thin strips
1	garlic clove, minced
1	tsp. ground ginger
¼	tsp. pepper
2	Tbsp. canola oil, divided
1	large green pepper, julienned
1	cup julienned carrots or sliced celery
5	green onions, cut into 1-in. pieces
	Hot cooked rice

1. Dissolve bouillon in water. Combine the cornstarch and soy sauce until smooth; add to bouillon. Set aside. Toss beef with garlic, ginger and pepper. In a large skillet or wok over medium-high heat, stir-fry beef in 1 Tbsp. oil until meat is no longer pink; remove and keep warm.
2. Heat remaining 1 Tbsp. oil; stir-fry vegetables until crisp-tender. Stir soy sauce mixture and add to the skillet; bring to a boil. Cook and stir for 2 minutes. Return meat to skillet and heat through. Serve with rice.
1 CUP: *266 cal., 13g fat (3g sat. fat), 63mg chol., 1484mg sod., 12g carb. (4g sugars, 2g fiber), 25g pro.*

SOUTHWEST SWEET
POTATO SKILLET

MUGHALI CHICKEN

I enjoy cooking for my family and try to incorporate healthy new foods into our menus. This authentic Indian dish is a favorite.
—*Aruna Kancharla, Bentonville, AR*

TAKES: 30 min. • **MAKES:** 6 servings

- 4 cardamom pods
- 10 garlic cloves, peeled
- 6 whole cloves
- 4½ tsp. chopped fresh gingerroot
- 1 Tbsp. unblanched almonds
- 1 Tbsp. salted cashews
- 1 tsp. ground cinnamon
- 6 small red onions, halved and sliced
- 4 jalapeno peppers, seeded and finely chopped
- ¼ cup canola oil
- 3 Tbsp. water
- 1½ lbs. boneless skinless chicken breasts, cut into ½-in. cubes
- 1 cup coconut milk
- 1 cup plain yogurt
- 1 tsp. ground turmeric
  Fresh cilantro leaves
  Hot cooked basmati rice, optional

1. Remove seeds from cardamom pods; place in a food processor. Add the garlic, cloves, ginger, almonds, cashews and cinnamon; cover and process until blended. Set aside.
2. In a large skillet, saute red onions and jalapenos in oil until tender. Stir in water and the garlic mixture. Add the chicken, coconut milk, yogurt and turmeric. Bring to a boil. Reduce heat; simmer, uncovered, until chicken juices run clear, 8-10 minutes. Sprinkle with cilantro. Serve with basmati rice if desired.
NOTE: Wear disposable gloves when cutting hot peppers; the oils can burn skin. Avoid touching your face.
1 CUP: *367 cal., 23g fat (10g sat. fat), 68mg chol., 93mg sod., 14g carb. (5g sugars, 3g fiber), 27g pro.*

SOUTHWEST SWEET POTATO SKILLET

One of the first things my husband made for me was a variation of this sweet potato skillet. Over the years, it's become a family favorite. Top with cheese, sour cream, avocado, lettuce or anything else your family likes.
—*MacKenzie Wright, Lebanon, OR*

TAKES: 30 min. • **MAKES:** 4 servings

- 1 Tbsp. olive oil
- 2 medium sweet potatoes, cubed (about ½-in. cubes)
- ½ medium onion, finely chopped
- 1 garlic clove, minced
- 2 cups cubed cooked chicken
- 1 can (15 oz.) black beans, rinsed and drained
- 1 medium zucchini, chopped
- 1 cup reduced-sodium chicken broth
- 1 cup salsa
- ½ large sweet red pepper, chopped
- 1 tsp. ground cumin
- 1 tsp. chili powder
- ¼ tsp. salt
- ¼ tsp. pepper
  Optional: Sour cream and minced fresh cilantro

1. In a large skillet, heat oil over medium-high heat. Add the sweet potatoes and onion; cook and stir until lightly browned, 5-8 minutes. Add garlic; cook 1 minute longer. Stir in chicken, black beans, zucchini, broth, salsa, red pepper and seasonings.
2. Bring to a boil; reduce heat. Simmer, covered, until sweet potatoes are tender, 10-12 minutes. If desired, serve with sour cream and cilantro.
1½ CUPS: *392 cal., 9g fat (2g sat. fat), 62mg chol., 826mg sod., 47g carb. (15g sugars, 9g fiber), 29g pro.*

SOUTHWEST SWEET
POTATO SKILLET

MUGHALI CHICKEN

MEDITERRANEAN SOLE

HASH BROWN PORK SKILLET

When you have leftover pork, add it to potatoes and veggies to make this easy and satisfying weeknight supper.
—Taste of Home *Test Kitchen*

TAKES: 25 min. • **MAKES:** 6 servings

- 4 cups frozen O'Brien potatoes, thawed
- 1 cup chopped onion
- 1 cup chopped green pepper
- 2 Tbsp. butter
- 2 cups shredded cooked pork
- 2 tsp. chicken bouillon granules
- ¼ tsp. pepper
- 2 tsp. all-purpose flour
- ½ cup 2% milk
- ¾ cup shredded cheddar cheese

1. In a large cast-iron or other heavy skillet, cook the potatoes, onion and green pepper in butter over medium heat until almost tender. Stir in the pork, bouillon and pepper; heat through.
2. In a small bowl, combine flour and milk until smooth; add to skillet. Cook on medium-low heat until mixture is thickened, stirring frequently, 4-5 minutes.
3. Sprinkle with cheese. Remove from the heat; cover and let stand until cheese is melted.
1 CUP: *286 cal., 13g fat (7g sat. fat), 70mg chol., 449mg sod., 22g carb. (4g sugars, 3g fiber), 19g pro.*

MEDITERRANEAN SOLE

Steaming in parchment is an easy and healthy way to cook fish and vegetables. This is a simple recipe, but it's elegant and incredibly flavorful. Any white fish will work in place of the sole.
—Andrea Potischman, Menlo Park, CA

TAKES: 25 min. • **MAKES:** 4 servings

- 1 lb. sole fillets, cut into 4 portions
- ¼ tsp. pepper
- 1 medium lemon, sliced
- 2 Tbsp. dry white wine or chicken broth
- 2 Tbsp. olive oil, divided
- 2 cups cherry tomatoes, halved
- ½ cup Greek olives, halved
- 1 Tbsp. capers, drained
- 1 Tbsp. lemon juice
- 2 garlic cloves, minced
- 2 Tbsp. minced fresh parsley

1. Preheat oven to 400°. Place each fillet on a piece of heavy-duty foil or parchment (about 12 in. square). Sprinkle the fillets with pepper; top with lemon slices. Drizzle with wine and 1 Tbsp. oil.
2. In a small bowl, combine tomatoes, olives, capers, lemon juice, garlic and remaining 1 Tbsp. oil; spoon over fillets. Fold foil or parchment around fish, sealing tightly.
3. Place packets on a baking sheet. Bake until fish just begins to flake easily with a fork, 10-12 minutes. Open packets carefully to allow steam to escape. Sprinkle with parsley.
1 PACKET: *211 cal., 14g fat (2g sat. fat), 51mg chol., 669mg sod., 7g carb. (2g sugars, 2g fiber), 15g pro.* **Diabetic exchanges:** *3 lean meat, 3 fat, 1 vegetable.*

HASH BROWN PORK SKILLET

ONE-PAN SWEET CHILI SHRIMP & VEGGIES

ONE-PAN SWEET CHILI SHRIMP & VEGGIES

This recipe has everything I'm looking for in a weeknight family dinner: quick, flavorful, nutritious and all three of my kids will eat it! My oldest son loves shrimp and I thought it could work really well as a sheet-pan supper.
—Elisabeth Larsen, Pleasant Grove, UT

- -

TAKES: 30 min. • **MAKES:** 4 servings

1 lb. uncooked shrimp (16-20 per lb.), peeled and deveined
2 medium zucchini, halved and sliced
½ lb. sliced fresh mushrooms
1 medium sweet orange pepper, julienned
3 Tbsp. sweet chili sauce
1 Tbsp. canola oil
1 Tbsp. lime juice
1 Tbsp. reduced-sodium soy sauce
3 green onions, chopped
¼ cup minced fresh cilantro

1. Preheat oven to 400°. Place shrimp, zucchini, mushrooms and orange pepper in a greased 15x10x1-in. baking pan. Combine chili sauce, oil, lime juice and soy sauce. Pour over shrimp mixture and toss to coat.
2. Bake until shrimp turn pink and the vegetables are tender, 12-15 minutes. Sprinkle with green onions and cilantro.
1 SERVING: *199 cal., 6g fat (1g sat. fat), 138mg chol., 483mg sod., 15g carb. (11g sugars, 3g fiber), 22g pro.* **Diabetic exchanges:** *3 lean meat, 2 vegetable, 1 fat.*

CORN DOGS

It's super easy to make homemade corn dogs, and they taste just like the ones sold at carnivals and fairs.
—Ruby Williams, Bogalusa, LA

- -

TAKES: 25 min. • **MAKES:** 10 servings

¾ cup yellow cornmeal
¾ cup self-rising flour
1 large egg, lightly beaten
⅔ cup 2% milk
10 pop sticks
10 hot dogs
Oil for deep-fat frying

1. In a large bowl, combine cornmeal, flour and egg. Stir in milk to make a thick batter; let stand 4 minutes. Insert sticks into hot dogs; dip into batter.
2. In an electric skillet or deep-fat fryer, heat oil to 375°. Fry corn dogs, a few at a time, until golden brown, 6-8 minutes, turning occasionally. Drain on paper towels.
NOTE: As a substitute for self-rising flour, place 1 tsp. baking powder and ¼ tsp. salt in a measuring cup. Add all-purpose flour to measure ¾ cup.
1 CORN DOG: *316 cal., 23g fat (7g sat. fat), 45mg chol., 588mg sod., 18g carb. (2g sugars, 1g fiber), 8g pro.*

TEST KITCHEN TIP

To help the batter stick to the hot dog, make sure the dogs are thoroughly dry before dipping them. The batter won't adhere to any part that's wet.

CORN DOGS

GRILLED SAUSAGE-BASIL PIZZAS

These little pizzas are a wonderful change of pace from the classic cookout menu. They're easy to customize by adding your family's favorite toppings.
—Lisa Speer, Palm Beach, FL

- -

TAKES: 30 min. • **MAKES:** 4 servings

- 4 Italian sausage links (4 oz. each)
- 4 naan flatbreads or whole pita breads
- ¼ cup olive oil
- 1 cup tomato basil pasta sauce
- 2 cups shredded part-skim mozzarella cheese
- ½ cup grated Parmesan cheese
- ½ cup thinly sliced fresh basil

1. Grill sausages, covered, over medium heat until a thermometer reads 160°, 10-12 minutes, turning occasionally. Cut into ¼-in. slices.
2. Brush both sides of flatbreads with oil. Grill flatbreads, covered, over medium heat until bottoms are lightly browned, 2-3 minutes.
3. Remove from grill. Layer grilled sides with sauce, sausage, cheeses and basil. Return to grill; cook, covered, until cheese is melted, 2-3 minutes longer.
1 PIZZA: *808 cal., 56g fat (19g sat. fat), 112mg chol., 1996mg sod., 41g carb. (9g sugars, 3g fiber), 34g pro.*

POPCORN SHRIMP TACOS WITH CABBAGE SLAW

I love combining classic flavors in new ways. This healthy recipe puts crispy popcorn shrimp into tacos! It's one of my family's favorites. To make them lower in carbs, use lettuce instead of tortillas.
—Julie Peterson, Crofton, MD

- -

TAKES: 30 min. • **MAKES:** 4 servings

- 2 cups coleslaw mix
- ¼ cup minced fresh cilantro
- 2 Tbsp. lime juice
- 2 Tbsp. honey
- ¼ tsp. salt
- 1 jalapeno pepper, seeded and minced, optional
- 2 large eggs
- 2 Tbsp. 2% milk
- ½ cup all-purpose flour
- 1½ cups panko bread crumbs
- 1 Tbsp. ground cumin
- 1 Tbsp. garlic powder
- 1 lb. uncooked shrimp (41-50 per lb.), peeled and deveined
  Cooking spray
- 8 corn tortillas (6 in.), warmed
- 1 medium ripe avocado, peeled and sliced

1. In a small bowl, combine coleslaw mix, cilantro, lime juice, honey, salt and, if desired, jalapeno; toss to coat. Set aside.
2. Preheat air fryer to 375°. In a shallow bowl, whisk the eggs and milk. Place the flour in a separate shallow bowl. In a third shallow bowl, mix panko, cumin and garlic powder. Dip shrimp in flour to coat both sides; shake off excess. Dip in the egg mixture, then in panko mixture, patting to help coating adhere.
3. In batches, arrange shrimp in a single layer in greased air-fryer basket; spritz with cooking spray. Cook until golden brown, 2-3 minutes. Turn; spritz with cooking spray. Cook until golden brown and shrimp turn pink, 2-3 minutes longer.
4. Serve shrimp in tortillas with coleslaw mix and avocado.
NOTE: Wear disposable gloves when cutting hot peppers; the oils can burn skin. Avoid touching your face.
2 TACOS: *456 cal., 12g fat (2g sat. fat), 213mg chol., 414mg sod., 58g carb. (11g sugars, 8g fiber), 29g pro.*

GRILLED SAUSAGE-BASIL PIZZAS

PORK GRAPEFRUIT STIR-FRY

SHRIMP & SPAGHETTI SKILLET

I enjoy developing quick, easy recipes that are both nutritious and delicious. This one-pan meal features two family favorites: shrimp and spaghetti.
—Roxanne Chan, Albany, CA

TAKES: 30 min. • **MAKES:** 4 servings

1	can (15 oz.) cannellini beans, rinsed and drained
1	can (14½ oz.) diced tomatoes, undrained
1	can (14½ oz.) chicken broth
1	can (14 oz.) water-packed artichoke hearts, drained and halved
1	can (6½ oz.) chopped clams, drained
4	oz. thin spaghetti, broken in half
1	tsp. Italian seasoning
½	tsp. salt
½	lb. peeled and deveined cooked shrimp (31-40 per lb.)
¼	cup minced fresh parsley
	Grated lemon zest

In a large skillet, combine the first 8 ingredients. Bring to a boil; reduce heat. Cook and stir over medium heat until spaghetti is tender, 12-15 minutes. Add shrimp and parsley; heat through. Sprinkle servings with lemon zest.
1½ CUPS: *334 cal., 2g fat (0 sat. fat), 105mg chol., 1492mg sod., 49g carb. (5g sugars, 7g fiber), 27g pro.*

PORK GRAPEFRUIT STIR-FRY

For a refreshing change of pace, try this easy sweet-and-sour stir-fry.
—Edie DeSpain, Logan, UT

TAKES: 25 min. • **MAKES:** 6 servings

3	Tbsp. cornstarch
¾	cup thawed grapefruit juice concentrate
¾	cup water
3	Tbsp. soy sauce
1	Tbsp. honey
½	tsp. ground ginger
3	cups sliced zucchini
1	medium sweet red or green pepper, julienned
1	Tbsp. canola oil
1½	lbs. pork tenderloin, cut into thin strips
3	medium grapefruit, peeled and sectioned
1	Tbsp. sesame seeds, toasted
	Hot cooked rice, optional

1. In a small bowl, combine the cornstarch, grapefruit juice concentrate, water, soy sauce, honey and ginger; set aside. In a skillet or wok, stir-fry zucchini and red pepper in oil over medium-high heat until crisp-tender, 3-4 minutes. Remove and keep warm. Add half of the pork; stir-fry until no longer pink, about 4 minutes. Remove and keep warm. Repeat with remaining pork.
2. Add reserved sauce to skillet; bring to a boil. Cook and stir until thickened, about 2 minutes. Return pork and vegetables to pan; stir until coated. Gently stir in grapefruit. Sprinkle with sesame seeds. Serve over rice if desired.
1¼ CUPS: *320 cal., 7g fat (2g sat. fat), 74mg chol., 364mg sod., 39g carb. (0 sugars, 7g fiber), 27g pro.* **Diabetic exchanges:** *3 lean meat, 2 fruit, 1 vegetable.*

SHRIMP & SPAGHETTI SKILLET

HONEY BALSAMIC CHICKEN

ROSEMARY SALMON & VEGGIES

My husband and I eat a lot of salmon. One night, while in a rush to get dinner on the table, I created this meal. It's a keeper! You can also include sliced zucchini, small cauliflower florets or fresh green beans.
—Elizabeth Bramkamp, Gig Harbor, WA

TAKES: 30 min. • **MAKES:** 4 servings

- 1½ lbs. salmon fillets, cut into 4 portions
- 2 Tbsp. melted coconut oil or olive oil
- 2 Tbsp. balsamic vinegar
- 2 tsp. minced fresh rosemary or ¾ tsp. dried rosemary, crushed
- 1 garlic clove, minced
- ½ tsp. salt
- 1 lb. fresh asparagus, trimmed
- 1 medium sweet red pepper, cut into 1-in. pieces
- ¼ tsp. pepper
-    Lemon wedges

1. Preheat oven to 400°. Place salmon in a greased 15x10x1-in. baking pan. Combine oil, vinegar, rosemary, garlic and salt. Pour half over salmon. Place asparagus and red pepper in a large bowl; drizzle with remaining oil mixture and toss to coat. Arrange around salmon in pan; sprinkle with pepper.
2. Bake until salmon flakes easily with a fork and vegetables are tender, 12-15 minutes. Serve with lemon wedges.
1 SERVING: *357 cal., 23g fat (9g sat. fat), 85mg chol., 388mg sod., 7g carb. (4g sugars, 2g fiber), 31g pro.* **Diabetic exchanges:** *4 lean meat, 1½ fat, 1 vegetable.*

HONEY BALSAMIC CHICKEN

I adapted this dish from a cookbook that featured quick and easy recipes. I adjusted the seasonings and added a bit more honey to better suit my tastes.
—Lisa Varner, El Paso, TX

TAKES: 20 min. • **MAKES:** 2 servings

- 2 boneless skinless chicken breast halves (5 oz. each)
- ½ tsp. garlic salt
- ⅛ tsp. coarsely ground pepper
- 2 tsp. canola oil
- 1 Tbsp. balsamic vinegar
- 1 Tbsp. honey
- ½ tsp. dried basil

1. Sprinkle chicken with garlic salt and pepper. In a large skillet over medium heat, cook chicken in oil until juices run clear, 4-7 minutes on each side. Remove and keep warm.
2. Add the vinegar, honey and basil to the pan; cook and stir 1 minute. Return chicken to the pan; heat through, turning to coat with glaze.
1 CHICKEN BREAST HALF: *233 cal., 8g fat (1g sat. fat), 78mg chol., 559mg sod., 11g carb. (11g sugars, 0 fiber), 29g pro.* **Diabetic exchanges:** *4 lean meat, 1 fat, ½ starch.*

ROSEMARY SALMON & VEGGIES

VEGETARIAN SKILLET ENCHILADAS

(SHOWN ON PAGE 50)

Whether it's meatless Monday or your family eats vegetarian every day, everyone will be satisfied with these unconventional enchiladas. Garnish with the optional toppings or other favorites like tortilla chips and extra shredded cheese.
—Taste of Home *Test Kitchen*

- -

TAKES: 25 min. • **MAKES:** 4 servings

- 1   Tbsp. canola oil
- 1   medium onion, chopped
- 1   medium sweet red pepper, chopped
- 2   garlic cloves, minced
- 1   can (15 oz.) black beans, rinsed and drained
- 1   can (10 oz.) enchilada sauce
- 1   cup frozen corn
- 2   tsp. chili powder
- ½   tsp. ground cumin
- ⅛   tsp. pepper
- 8   corn tortillas (6 in.), cut into ½-in. strips
- 1   cup shredded Mexican cheese blend
     Optional: Chopped fresh cilantro, sliced avocado, sliced radishes, sour cream and lime wedges

1. Preheat oven to 400°. Heat oil a 10-in. cast-iron or other ovenproof skillet over medium-high heat. Add onion and pepper; cook and stir until tender, 2-3 minutes. Add garlic; cook 1 minute longer. Stir in beans, enchilada sauce, corn, chili powder, cumin and pepper. Stir in tortillas.

2. Bring to a boil. Reduce heat; simmer, uncovered, until tortillas are softened, 3-5 minutes. Sprinkle with cheese. Bake, uncovered, until mixture is bubbly and cheese is melted, 3-5 minutes. If desired, garnish with optional ingredients.

1½ CUPS: 307 cal., 14g fat (5g sat. fat), 25mg chol., 839mg sod., 33g carb. (5g sugars, 7g fiber), 14g pro.

ONE-POT RED BEANS & RICE

ONE-POT RED BEANS & RICE

Here's a great one-pot meal that's ready in just 30 minutes. It's one of my husband's favorites and uses simple ingredients, so it's been a go-to recipe in our house for years.
—Janice Conklin, Stevensville, MT

- -

TAKES: 30 min. • **MAKES:** 6 servings

- 1   Tbsp. olive oil
- 2   celery ribs, sliced
- 1   medium onion, chopped
- 1   medium green pepper, chopped
- 1   pkg. (14 oz.) smoked turkey sausage, sliced
- 1   carton (32 oz.) reduced-sodium chicken broth
- 1   can (16 oz.) kidney beans, rinsed and drained
- 1¼ cups uncooked converted rice
- ⅓   cup tomato paste
- 1   bay leaf
- 1½ tsp. Cajun seasoning
- ¼   tsp. cayenne pepper
      Hot pepper sauce, optional

1. In a Dutch oven, heat oil over medium-high heat. Add celery, onion and green pepper; cook and stir until crisp-tender, 3-4 minutes. Add sausage; cook until browned, 2-3 minutes.

2. Stir in broth, beans, rice, tomato paste, bay leaf, Cajun seasoning and cayenne pepper. Bring to a boil; reduce the heat. Simmer, uncovered, until rice is tender and liquid is absorbed, 15-20 minutes, stirring occasionally. Discard bay leaf. If desired, serve with pepper sauce.

1⅓ CUPS: 347 cal., 6g fat (2g sat. fat), 41mg chol., 1272mg sod., 50g carb. (6g sugars, 5g fiber), 22g pro.

TEST KITCHEN TIP

Also called parboiled rice, converted rice is the unhulled grain that has been steam-pressured before milling. This process retains nutrients and makes fluffy separated grains of cooked rice. Converted rice takes slightly longer to cook than regular long grain rice.

PINEAPPLE SHRIMP FRIED RICE

HERB CHICKEN WITH HONEY BUTTER

When the whole crowd could use a heartwarming meal, this one fits the bill! You'll love how the honey's sweetness mixes perfectly with the herbs' salty flavor. It's a wonderful combination!
—Taste of Home *Test Kitchen*

TAKES: 25 min. • **MAKES:** 4 servings

- 1 large egg, lightly beaten
- ¾ cup seasoned bread crumbs
- 2 Tbsp. dried parsley flakes
- 1 tsp. Italian seasoning
- ¾ tsp. garlic salt
- ½ tsp. poultry seasoning
- 4 boneless skinless chicken breast halves (6 oz. each)
- 3 Tbsp. butter

HONEY BUTTER

- ¼ cup butter, softened
- ¼ cup honey

1. Place egg in a shallow bowl. In another shallow bowl, combine bread crumbs and seasonings. Dip chicken in egg, then coat with bread crumb mixture.
2. In a large skillet over medium heat, cook chicken in butter until a thermometer reads 165°, 4-5 minutes on each side. Combine the softened butter and honey; serve with chicken.

1 CHICKEN BREAST HALF WITH 2 TBSP. HONEY BUTTER: *485 cal., 25g fat (14g sat. fat), 171mg chol., 709mg sod., 27g carb. (18g sugars, 1g fiber), 38g pro.*

Chicken with Sun-Dried Tomato Butter: Combine ⅓ cup butter, ¼ cup Parmesan cheese, 2 Tbsp. sun-dried tomato pesto and ¼ tsp. pepper. Substitute for the honey butter.

PINEAPPLE SHRIMP FRIED RICE

My husband often ordered pineapple fried rice at Thai restaurants, so I surprised him by tweaking some similar recipes to come up with a version that's both simple and delicious.
—Bonnie Brien, Pacific Grove, CA

TAKES: 30 min. • **MAKES:** 4 servings

- 2 Tbsp. reduced-sodium soy sauce
- 1 tsp. curry powder
- ½ tsp. sugar
- 2 Tbsp. peanut or canola oil, divided
- 1 lb. uncooked shrimp (31-40 per lb.), peeled and deveined
- 2 tsp. minced fresh gingerroot
- 1 garlic clove, minced
- 1 medium sweet red pepper, chopped
- 1 medium carrot, finely chopped
- ½ cup chopped onion
- 1 can (20 oz.) unsweetened pineapple tidbits, drained
- 2 cups cooked rice, room temperature
- 6 green onions, chopped
- ½ cup finely chopped salted peanuts
  Lime wedges

1. Mix soy sauce, curry powder and sugar. In a large skillet, heat 1 Tbsp. oil over medium-high heat; stir-fry shrimp until they turn pink, 2-3 minutes. Remove from pan.
2. In same pan, heat remaining oil over medium-high heat. Add ginger and garlic; cook just until fragrant, about 10 seconds. Add pepper, carrot and onion; stir-fry for 2 minutes. Stir in pineapple and shrimp. Add the rice and soy sauce mixture; heat through over medium heat, tossing to combine and break up any clumps of rice. Stir in green onions. Sprinkle with peanuts; serve with lime wedges.

1½ CUPS: *491 cal., 18g fat (3g sat. fat), 138mg chol., 513mg sod., 54g carb. (22g sugars, 5g fiber), 28g pro.*

WALNUT & OAT-CRUSTED SALMON

This recipe gives the most omega-3 fatty acid bang for your buck!
—*Cristen Dutcher, Marietta, GA*

TAKES: 30 min. • **MAKES:** 2 servings

- 2 salmon fillets (6 oz. each), skin removed
- ¼ tsp. salt
- ¼ tsp. pepper
- 3 Tbsp. quick-cooking oats, crushed
- 3 Tbsp. finely chopped walnuts
- 2 Tbsp. olive oil

Preheat oven to 400°. Place salmon on a baking sheet; sprinkle with salt and pepper. Combine remaining ingredients; press onto salmon. Bake until fish just begins to flake easily with a fork, 12-15 minutes.

1 FILLET: *484 cal., 37g fat (6g sat. fat), 85mg chol., 381mg sod., 7g carb. (0 sugars, 2g fiber), 32g pro.* **Diabetic exchanges:** *5 lean meat, 3 fat, ½ starch.*

> **TEST KITCHEN TIP**
>
> Just 3 oz. of salmon packs more than 100% of the vitamin D you need daily. Salmon is also loaded with omega-3 fatty acids, which can help reduce your risk of depression.

WALNUT & OAT-CRUSTED SALMON

EDAMAME & SOBA NOODLE BOWL

EDAMAME & SOBA NOODLE BOWL

Toothsome soba noodles are made from buckwheat flour.
—*Matthew Hass, Ellison Bay, WI*

TAKES: 30 min. • **MAKES:** 6 servings

- 1 pkg. (12 oz.) uncooked Japanese soba noodles or whole wheat spaghetti
- 2 Tbsp. sesame oil
- 2 cups fresh small broccoli florets
- 1 medium onion, halved and thinly sliced
- 3 cups frozen shelled edamame, thawed
- 2 large carrots, cut into ribbons with a vegetable peeler
- 4 garlic cloves, minced
- 1 cup reduced-fat Asian toasted sesame salad dressing
- ¼ tsp. pepper
   Sesame seeds, toasted, optional

1. In a 6 qt. stockpot, cook noodles according to package directions; drain and return to pan.

2. Meanwhile, in a large skillet, heat oil over medium heat. Add broccoli and onion; cook and stir until crisp-tender, 4-6 minutes. Add edamame and carrots; cook and stir until tender, 6-8 minutes. Add garlic; cook 1 minute longer. Add vegetable mixture, dressing and pepper to noodles; toss to combine. Sprinkle with sesame seeds if desired.

1⅓ CUPS: *414 cal., 12g fat (1g sat. fat), 0 chol., 867mg sod., 64g carb. (12g sugars, 4g fiber), 18g pro.*

**CHEDDAR-TOPPED
BARBECUE MEAT LOAF
PAGE 71**

Main Dishes

Get excited. Here are the special dinners families love: comfort-food classics like meat loaf and potpie. Also find cook-all-day faves from the slow cooker, amazing casseroles and easy sheet-pan meals.

CAULIFLOWER ALFREDO

My family loves this quick and healthy cauliflower Alfredo sauce served over hot pasta.
—Shelly Bevington, Hermiston, OR

PREP: 20 min. • **COOK:** 20 min. • **MAKES:** 6 servings

- 2 Tbsp. extra virgin olive oil
- 3 garlic cloves, minced
- 1 shallot, minced
- 1 medium head cauliflower, chopped
- 4 cups water
- 2 vegetable bouillon cubes
- ⅔ cup shredded Parmesan cheese plus additional for garnish
- ¼ tsp. crushed red pepper flakes
- 1 pkg. (16 oz.) fettuccine
   Chopped fresh parsley

1. In a Dutch oven, heat oil over medium-high heat. Add garlic and shallot; cook and stir until fragrant, 1-2 minutes. Add cauliflower, water and bouillon; bring to a boil. Cook, covered, until tender, 5-6 minutes. Drain; cool slightly. Transfer to a food processor; add ⅔ cup Parmesan and pepper flakes. Process until pureed smooth.
2. Meanwhile, cook the fettuccine according to package directions for al dente. Drain the fettuccine; place in a large bowl. Add the cauliflower mixture; toss to coat. Sprinkle with chopped parsley and additional Parmesan.
1⅓ CUPS: *371 cal., 9g fat (3g sat. fat), 6mg chol., 533mg sod., 60g carb. (5g sugars, 5g fiber), 16g pro.*

CAULIFLOWER ALFREDO

**PORTOBELLO & CHICKPEA
SHEET-PAN SUPPER**

PORTOBELLO & CHICKPEA
SHEET-PAN SUPPER

This is a fantastic meatless dinner or an amazing side dish. It works well with a variety of roasted vegetables. We enjoy using zucchini or summer squash in the summer. You can also change up the herbs in the dressing to include your favorites.
—Elisabeth Larsen, Pleasant Grove, UT

PREP: 15 min. • **BAKE:** 35 min. • **MAKES:** 4 servings

- ¼ cup olive oil
- 2 Tbsp. balsamic vinegar
- 1 Tbsp. minced fresh oregano
- ¾ tsp. garlic powder
- ½ tsp. salt
- ¼ tsp. pepper
- 1 can (15 oz.) chickpeas or garbanzo beans, rinsed and drained
- 4 large portobello mushrooms (4 to 4½ in.), stems removed
- 1 lb. fresh asparagus, trimmed and cut into 2-in. pieces
- 8 oz. cherry tomatoes

1. Preheat oven to 400°. In a small bowl, combine the first 6 ingredients. Toss chickpeas with 2 Tbsp. oil mixture. Transfer to a 15x10x1-in. baking pan. Bake 20 minutes.
2. Brush mushrooms with 1 Tbsp. oil mixture; add to pan. Toss asparagus and tomatoes with remaining oil mixture; arrange around the mushrooms. Bake until the vegetables are tender, 15-20 minutes longer.
1 MUSHROOM WITH 1 CUP VEGETABLES: *279 cal., 16g fat (2g sat. fat), 0 chol., 448mg sod., 28g carb. (8g sugars, 7g fiber), 8g pro.* **Diabetic exchanges:** *3 fat, 2 starch.*

CHEDDAR-TOPPED BARBECUE MEAT LOAF

(SHOWN ON PAGE 68)

My family loves the bold barbecue flavor of this tender meat loaf. I love that it's such an easy recipe to prepare in the slow cooker.
—David Snodgrass, Columbia, MO

PREP: 20 min. • **COOK:** 3¼ hours
MAKES: 8 servings

- 3 large eggs, lightly beaten
- ¾ cup old-fashioned oats
- 1 large green or sweet red pepper, chopped (about 1½ cups)
- 1 small onion, finely chopped
- 1 envelope onion soup mix
- 3 garlic cloves, minced
- ½ tsp. salt
- ¼ tsp. pepper
- 2 lbs. lean ground beef (90% lean)
- 1 cup ketchup
- 2 Tbsp. brown sugar
- 1 Tbsp. barbecue seasoning
- 1 tsp. ground mustard
- 1 cup shredded cheddar cheese

1. Cut three 18x3-in. strips of heavy-duty foil; crisscross so they resemble spokes of a wheel. Place strips on bottom and up sides of a 3-qt. slow cooker. Coat strips with cooking spray.

2. In a large bowl, combine eggs, oats, chopped pepper, onion, soup mix, garlic, salt and pepper. Add beef; mix lightly but thoroughly. Shape into a 7-in. round loaf. Place loaf in center of strips in slow cooker. Cook, covered, on low 3-4 hours or until a thermometer reads at least 160°.

3. In a small bowl, mix ketchup, brown sugar, barbecue seasoning and mustard; pour over meat loaf and sprinkle with cheese. Cook, covered, on low until cheese is melted, about 15 minutes longer. Let stand 5 minutes. Using the foil strips as handles, remove meat loaf to a platter.

1 SLICE: *356 cal., 17g fat (7g sat. fat), 154mg chol., 1358mg sod., 22g carb. (13g sugars, 2g fiber), 29g pro.*

SLOW-COOKER SALSA CHICKEN

This is a go-to recipe when I know I'll be having a busy day. My family loves salsa, so I came up with this recipe for something to throw into a slow cooker and simmer on low. We love it served over rice or noodles and topped with tortilla chips and sour cream.
—Deborah Pennington, Cullman, AL

PREP: 15 min. • **COOK:** 3 hours
MAKES: 4 servings

- 4 boneless skinless chicken breast halves (6 oz. each)
- 1 jar (16 oz.) salsa
- 1¾ cups frozen corn, thawed
- 1 can (15 oz.) pinto beans, rinsed and drained
- 1 can (15 oz.) no-salt-added black beans, rinsed and drained
- 1 can (10 oz.) diced tomatoes and green chiles, undrained
- 1 tsp. sugar
- ½ tsp. salt
- ¼ tsp. pepper
  Optional: Hot cooked rice, cubed avocado, chopped fresh tomato, sliced green onions and lime wedges

Place chicken in a 4- or 5-qt. slow cooker. Add salsa, corn, beans, tomatoes, sugar, salt and pepper. Cook, covered, on low 3-4 hours or until a thermometer in chicken reads 165°. Serve with toppings as desired.

1 CHICKEN BREAST HALF WITH 1½ CUPS BEAN MIXTURE: *470 cal., 6g fat (1g sat. fat), 94mg chol., 1270mg sod., 55g carb. (8g sugars, 11g fiber), 47g pro.*

SLOW-COOKER SALSA CHICKEN

SMOKY SWEET POTATO & BLACK BEAN ENCHILADAS

SMOKY SWEET POTATO & BLACK BEAN ENCHILADAS

My hearty, delicious, nutrient-packed vegetarian dish is amazingly healthy for you. Everyone I've made it for has loved it—even carnivores! I always make two batches and freeze one. You'll want to eat this every week!
—Elizabeth Lindemann, Salem, MA

PRE: 40 min. • **BAKE:** 20 min.
MAKES: 6 servings

- 1 large sweet potato, cubed
- 1 small onion, chopped
- 1 small sweet red pepper, chopped
- ½ cup minced fresh cilantro
- 1 tsp. smoked paprika
- ½ tsp. garlic powder
- ½ tsp. ground cumin
- ½ tsp. ground coriander
- ½ tsp. pepper
- 1 can (15 oz.) black beans, rinsed and drained
- 1 can (15 oz.) enchilada sauce
- 12 corn tortillas (6 in.), warmed
- 2 cups shredded Monterey Jack cheese, divided
  Optional: Cubed avocado, sour cream, salsa, minced fresh cilantro and hot sauce

1. Preheat oven to 375°. In a large saucepan, place steamer basket over 1 in. of water. Place sweet potato, onion and red pepper in basket. Bring water to a boil. Reduce heat to maintain a simmer; steam, covered, until tender, 15-20 minutes.

2. Transfer vegetables to a large bowl. Mash vegetables, gradually adding cilantro, spices and pepper to reach desired consistency. Stir in black beans.

3. Spread ⅓ cup enchilada sauce into a greased 13x9-in. baking dish. Place ⅓ cup vegetable mixture in center on each tortilla; sprinkle with 4 tsp. cheese. Roll up and place in prepared dish, seam side down. Top with remaining enchilada sauce; sprinkle with remaining cheese.

4. Bake, uncovered, until heated through and cheese is melted, 20-25 minutes. If desired, serve with optional toppings.

FREEZE OPTION: Cover and freeze unbaked enchiladas. To use, partially thaw in the refrigerator overnight. Remove from refrigerator 30 minutes before baking. Preheat oven to 375°. Cover casserole with foil; bake until casserole is heated through, sauce is bubbling and cheese is melted, 30-35 minutes. Serve as directed.

2 ENCHILADAS: *399 cal., 14g fat (7g sat. fat), 34mg chol., 843mg sod., 52g carb. (9g sugars, 8g fiber), 18g pro.*

TEST KITCHEN TIP

Short on time? This recipe can be made ahead of time. Just refrigerate the assembled (and unbaked) enchiladas for up to a week, and bake when ready. You can also freeze them for up to 6 months, then defrost and bake when ready.

EASY JAMBALAYA

I brought this simple jambalaya to a Sunday potluck, and everyone quickly gobbled it up. When friends asked me for the recipe, they could not believe how easy it was!
—Tami Kuehl, Loup City, NE

PREP: 15 min. • **COOK:** 25 min. • **MAKES:** 4 servings

- 1 pkg. (8 oz.) jambalaya mix
- 1 pkg. (14 oz.) hot smoked sausage, cut into ½-in. slices
- 1 cup uncooked shrimp (16-20 per lb.), peeled and deveined, cut into ¾-in. pieces
- 3 green onions, thinly sliced
- ½ cup shredded cheddar cheese
- ½ cup pico de gallo

Prepare jambalaya mix according to package directions, adding sausage and shrimp during the last 5 minutes of cooking. Remove from the heat. Stir in cheddar cheese, pico de gallo and green onions; heat through.

1½ CUPS: *601 cal., 32g fat (14g sat. fat), 127mg chol., 2159mg sod., 48g carb. (3g sugars, 1g fiber), 28g pro.*

PARMESAN PORK TENDERLOIN

EASY JAMBALAYA

PARMESAN PORK TENDERLOIN

I am of Danish descent and love all things pork, both old recipes and new. Here's a dish I came up with myself.
—John Hansen, Marstons Mills, MA

PREP: 25 min. • **COOK:** 25 min. • **MAKES:** 2 servings

- 1 pork tenderloin (¾ lb.)
- 6 Tbsp. grated Parmesan cheese
- 1 small sweet onion, sliced and separated into rings
- 1½ cups sliced fresh mushrooms
- 1 garlic clove, minced
- 2 tsp. butter, divided
- 2 tsp. olive oil, divided
- ¼ cup reduced-sodium beef broth
- 2 Tbsp. port wine or additional beef broth
- ⅛ tsp. salt, optional
- ⅛ tsp. each dried basil, thyme and rosemary, crushed
  Dash pepper
- ½ tsp. cornstarch
- 3 Tbsp. water

1. Cut pork into ½-in. slices; flatten to ⅛-in. thickness. Coat with Parmesan cheese; set aside.
2. In a large skillet, saute the onion, mushrooms and garlic in 1 tsp. butter and 1 tsp. oil until tender; remove and keep warm. In the same skillet, cook pork in remaining 1 tsp. butter and 1 tsp. oil in batches over medium heat until juices run clear, about 2 minutes on each side. Remove and keep warm.
3. Add broth to pan, scraping to loosen browned bits. Stir in wine or additional broth; add seasonings. Bring to a boil. Reduce heat; simmer, uncovered, for 5 minutes. Combine cornstarch and water until smooth; stir into pan juices. Bring to a boil; cook and stir until thickened, about 2 minutes. Serve sauce with the pork and the onion mixture.

1 SERVING: *388 cal., 19g fat (8g sat. fat), 118mg chol., 472mg sod., 11g carb., 2g fiber, 43g pro.*

YOU SAY POTATO...

Load those taters with outrageous toppings when just a pat of butter won't do. Oh yeah, this spud's for you.

Bake these beauties!
Preheat the oven to 400°. Scrub the spuds. Pierce 'em several times with a fork. Bake until tender, 50-75 minutes. Cut an "X" in each potato. Fluff the pulp with a fork, then top away!

BUENOS DIAS BAKED POTATOES
Top with sauteed bell pepper and onion slices, cooked Southwestern chicken strips, chopped green chiles and minced chipotle in adobo sauce. Drizzle with salsa con queso, then add fresh salsa, avocado slices and french-fried onion strings.
—Taste of Home
Test Kitchen

THAT'S AMORE BAKED POTATOES
Cook up ground beef with green pepper, shredded carrot, onion and a little minced garlic; drain. Mix in spaghetti sauce, chopped pepperoni, a splash of red wine, oregano and salt. Spoon mixture over potato. Sprinkle with Colby-Monterey Jack cheese.
—Taste of Home
Test Kitchen

STEAKHOUSE BAKED POTATOES
Stack up steak slices and fresh arugula. Drizzle with blue cheese salad dressing, dollop a spoonful of sour cream and sprinkle with crumbled blue cheese.
—Debbie Glasscock, Conway, AR

EGGS BENEDICT BAKED POTATOES
Top with sliced Canadian bacon and a poached egg. Slather it all in hollandaise sauce and sprinkle with minced parsley.
—Becky Carver, North Royalton, OH

HAM & BROCCOLI BAKED POTATOES

Make a sauce of 1 can cream of mushroom soup, ¼ cup milk, 2 cups chopped ham, 1½ cups shredded cheddar, ½ cup sour cream and 1 cup broccoli. Spoon mixture onto 4 potatoes. Top with cheddar and buttery bread crumbs; bake 5-7 minutes. Sprinkle with chives.

—Patricia Prescott, Manchester, NH

CHILI DOG BAKED POTATOES

Top each baked potato with a cooked hot dog, your favorite chili and shredded cheddar. Bake until the cheese melts, 3-5 minute. Sprinkle with chopped onion and crushed corn chips.

—Anna Miller, Churdan, IA

HUNGRY MAN'S BAKED POTATOES

Saute onion slices and corn in bacon drippings. Layer each potato with shredded barbecued pork, corn mixture, bacon pieces, goat cheese and fresh minced cilantro.

—Taste of Home
Test Kitchen

CORNED BEEF BAKED POTATOES

Heat sauteed onion slices, chopped cooked corned beef, salt, pepper and mustard. Spoon over potato. Top with shredded Swiss cheese, Thousand Island dressing and sliced green onions.

—Kallee Krong-McCreery, Escondido, CA

VERY VEGGIE BAKED POTATOES

Toss sliced summer squash, zucchini, eggplant and leeks in a little Italian dressing. Grill 8-12 minutes. Sprinkle with salt. Combine garlic-herb spreadable cheese with a dollop of sour cream. Top potato with veggies and cheese mixture. Sprinkle with sliced basil.

—Taste of Home
Test Kitchen

TACO BAKED POTATOES

Pile on ground beef taco meat, salsa and sour cream. Sprinkle with Cotija cheese, then add avocado and green onions.

—Anne Ormond, Dover, NH

CHICKEN & FALAFEL WAFFLES

MODERN TUNA CASSEROLE

I loved tuna casserole as a kid and found myself craving it as an adult. However, the massive amounts of fat and salt in the traditional recipe were a turnoff healthwise, and it didn't taste as good as I remembered. I reconfigured the recipe to include more vegetables, and the result was delicious.
—Rebecca Blanton, St. Helena, CA

PREP: 20 min. • **COOK:** 20 min.
MAKES: 6 servings

- 3 Tbsp. butter, divided
- 4 medium carrots, chopped
- 1 medium onion, chopped
- 1 medium sweet red pepper, chopped
- 1 cup sliced baby portobello mushrooms
- 2 cans (5 oz. each) albacore white tuna in water, drained and flaked
- 2 cups fresh baby spinach
- 1 cup frozen peas
- 3 cups uncooked spiral pasta
- 1 Tbsp. all-purpose flour
- ⅔ cup reduced-sodium chicken broth
- ⅓ cup half-and-half cream
- ½ cup shredded Parmesan cheese
- ¾ tsp. salt
- ¼ tsp. pepper

1. In a large skillet, heat 1 Tbsp. butter over medium-high heat. Add carrots, onion, red pepper and mushrooms. Cook and stir until tender, 8-10 minutes. Add tuna, spinach and peas; cook until spinach is just wilted, 2-3 minutes.
2. Meanwhile, cook pasta according to package directions for al dente. Drain pasta, reserving 1 cup pasta water. In a large bowl, place pasta and tuna mixture; toss to combine. Wipe skillet clean.
3. In the same skillet, melt the remaining butter over medium heat. Stir in flour until smooth; gradually whisk in the broth and cream. Bring to a boil, stirring constantly; cook and stir until thickened, 1-2 minutes, adding some reserved pasta water if needed. Stir in cheese, salt and pepper. Pour over pasta; toss to coat.

1¾ CUPS: 372 cal., 11g fat (6g sat. fat), 47mg chol., 767mg sod., 44g carb. (7g sugars, 5g fiber), 23g pro. **Diabetic exchanges:** 3 lean meat, 2½ starch, 1½ fat, 1 vegetable.

CHICKEN & FALAFEL WAFFLES

These gluten-free waffles made from garbanzo beans perfectly complement Moroccan-spiced chicken with cucumber relish.
They're a savory, low-carb spin on a classic comfort dish.
—Arlene Erlbach, Morton Grove, IL

PREP: 30 min. • **COOK:** 10 min.
MAKES: 4 servings

- ¾ cup plain Greek yogurt
- ¾ cup chopped peeled cucumber
- 1 cup chopped green onions, divided
- 2 Tbsp. minced fresh mint plus additional for garnish
- ¼ tsp. salt
- ⅛ tsp. pepper
- 1 can (15 oz.) no-salt-added garbanzo beans or chickpeas, rinsed and drained
- 1 large egg, room temperature
- ⅓ cup fresh parsley leaves
- 4½ tsp. gluten-free all-purpose baking flour
- 2 Tbsp. Moroccan seasoning (ras el hanout), divided
- 1½ cups shredded cooked chicken
- 1½ cups reduced-sugar apricot preserves
- ¾ cup chili sauce

1. Preheat waffle iron. In a small bowl, combine yogurt, cucumber, ½ cup green onions, 2 Tbsp. mint, salt and pepper. Cover and refrigerate until serving.
2. Place the garbanzo beans, egg, parsley, gluten-free flour, 1 Tbsp. Moroccan seasoning and remaining green onions in a blender. Cover and pulse until blended (batter with be thick). Bake waffles according to manufacturer's directions until golden brown.
3. Meanwhile, in a small skillet, mix the chicken, preserves, chili sauce and remaining Moroccan seasoning; heat through. Serve with waffles. Top with yogurt mixture and additional mint.

1 WAFFLE WITH ⅔ CUP CHICKEN MIXTURE AND ⅓ CUP SAUCE: 491 cal., 10g fat (4g sat. fat), 104mg chol., 959mg sod., 72g carb. (43g sugars, 5g fiber), 25g pro.

HONEY-RHUBARB CHICKEN

The sauce on this honey chicken is like a sweet-tart spin on teriyaki. Everyone who's tried it raves about it—even my husband, who's not usually a rhubarb lover.
—*Rachel Beach, Whitley City, KY*

PREP: 30 min. • **BAKE:** 35 min.
MAKES: 6 servings

- 1¼ cups all-purpose flour
- 1 Tbsp. poultry seasoning
- 1 large egg
- 1 cup 2% milk
- 1 broiler/fryer chicken (3 to 4 lbs.), cut up
- ¼ cup canola oil

HONEY-RHUBARB SAUCE
- ¼ cup cornstarch
- 1¾ cups cold water, divided
- ½ cup packed brown sugar
- ½ cup honey
- 3 Tbsp. soy sauce
- 1½ cups chopped fresh or frozen rhubarb
- 2 Tbsp. chopped onion
- 2 garlic cloves, peeled

1. Preheat oven to 400°. Combine flour and poultry seasoning. In another bowl, whisk egg and milk. Dip chicken, 1 piece at a time, into flour mixture, then into egg mixture; coat again with flour mixture.
2. In a large skillet, heat oil over medium-high heat. Brown chicken on both sides. Place in a greased 13x9-in. baking dish.
3. For sauce, combine cornstarch and 1½ cups cold water in a large saucepan until smooth; stir in brown sugar, honey and soy sauce. Pulse rhubarb, onion, garlic and remaining water in a food processor until blended. Stir into the cornstarch mixture. Bring to a boil over medium heat; cook and stir until thickened, 2-3 minutes. Pour over the chicken.
4. Bake, uncovered, until a thermometer inserted into a chicken thigh reads 170°, 35-40 minutes.
1 SERVING: *639 cal., 25g fat (5g sat. fat), 114mg chol., 565mg sod., 70g carb. (43g sugars, 2g fiber), 34g pro.*

VEGGIE-CASHEW STIR-FRY

Getting my meat-loving husband and two sons, ages 5 and 7, to eat more veggies had always been a struggle until I whipped up this stir-fry one night. I was shocked when they cleaned their plates and asked for seconds.
—*Abbey Hoffman, Ashland, OH*

PREP: 20 min. • **COOK:** 15 min.
MAKES: 4 servings

- ¼ cup reduced-sodium soy sauce
- ¼ cup water
- 2 Tbsp. brown sugar
- 2 Tbsp. lemon juice
- 2 Tbsp. olive oil
- 1 garlic clove, minced
- 2 cups sliced fresh mushrooms
- 1 cup coarsely chopped fresh baby carrots
- 1 small zucchini, cut into ¼-in. slices
- 1 small sweet red pepper, coarsely chopped
- 1 small green pepper, coarsely chopped
- 4 green onions, sliced
- 2 cups cooked brown rice
- 1 can (8 oz.) sliced water chestnuts, drained
- ½ cup honey-roasted cashews

1. In a small bowl, mix soy sauce, water, brown sugar and lemon juice until smooth; set aside.
2. In a large skillet, heat oil over medium-high heat. Stir-fry garlic for 1 minute. Add vegetables; cook until vegetables are crisp-tender, 6-8 minutes.
3. Stir soy sauce mixture and add to pan. Bring to a boil. Add brown rice and water chestnuts; heat through. Top with cashews.
1½ CUPS: *385 cal., 16g fat (3g sat. fat), 0 chol., 671mg sod., 56g carb. (15g sugars, 6g fiber), 9g pro.*

VEGGIE-CASHEW STIR-FRY

**THE BEST
BABY BACK RIBS**

THE BEST BABY BACK RIBS

*I like to marinate racks of ribs before adding
my zesty spice rub. Then I grill them to
perfection. They always turn out juicy and
loaded with flavor.*
—Iola Egle, Bella Vista, AR

- -

PREP: 10 min. + marinating • **GRILL:** 80 min.
MAKES: 6 servings

    2   racks baby back ribs (about 4½ lbs.)
    ¾   cup chicken broth
    ¾   cup soy sauce
    1   cup sugar, divided
    6   Tbsp. cider vinegar
    6   Tbsp. olive oil
    3   garlic cloves, minced
    2   tsp. salt
    1   Tbsp. paprika
    ½   tsp. chili powder
    ½   tsp. pepper
    ¼   tsp. garlic powder
        Dash cayenne pepper
        Barbecue sauce, optional

1. If necessary, remove thin membrane
from ribs and discard. Combine broth, soy
sauce, ½ cup sugar, vinegar, olive oil and
garlic. Place ribs in a shallow baking dish;
pour two-thirds of the marinade over ribs.
Turn to coat; refrigerate overnight, turning
occasionally. Cover and refrigerate the
remaining marinade.
2. Drain ribs, discarding marinade. Combine
remaining sugar, salt and seasonings; rub
over both sides of ribs.
3. Grill ribs, covered, on an oiled rack over
indirect medium heat for 30 minutes on
each side.
4. Baste with reserved marinade, or, if
desired, barbecue sauce. Move ribs to
direct medium heat and cook until pork is
tender, turning and basting occasionally,
20-40 minutes longer.
1 SERVING: *647 cal., 41g fat (13g sat. fat),
123mg chol., 2345mg sod., 30g carb. (29g
sugars, 1g fiber), 37g pro.*

CHILI MAC

*This recipe has regularly appeared on my
family menus for more than 40 years, and
it's never failed to please at potlucks and
bring-a-dish gatherings. Sometimes I turn it
into soup by adding a can of beef broth.*
—Marie Posavec, Berwyn, IL

- -

PREP: 15 min. • **COOK:** 6 hours
MAKES: 6 servings

    1   lb. lean ground beef (90% lean),
        cooked and drained
    2   cans (16 oz. each) hot chili beans,
        undrained
    2   large green peppers, chopped
    1   large onion, chopped
    4   celery ribs, chopped
    1   can (8 oz.) no-salt-added
        tomato sauce
    2   Tbsp. chili seasoning mix
    2   garlic cloves, minced
    1   pkg. (7 oz.) elbow macaroni,
        cooked and drained
        Salt and pepper to taste
        Optional: Shredded pepper jack
        cheese and sliced jalapeno pepper

In a 5-qt. slow cooker, combine the first
8 ingredients. Cover and cook on low for
6 hours or until heated through. Stir in
macaroni. Season with salt and pepper.
If desired, top servings with pepper jack
cheese and sliced jalapenos.
1 SERVING: *348 cal., 8g fat (3g sat. fat), 47mg
chol., 713mg sod., 49g carb. (8g sugars,
12g fiber), 27g pro.* **Diabetic exchanges:**
3 starch, 3 lean meat.

CHILI MAC

MARTHA'S FISH TACOS

We can't get enough barbecued fish at our house. This recipe can be made ahead and served cold, or you can eat it hot off the grill. It's fantastic either way!

—Martha Benoit, Proctorsville, VT

PREP: 25 min. • GRILL: 10 min.
MAKES: 6 servings

- 2 large ears sweet corn, husked
- 1 tsp. butter, softened
- ⅛ tsp. salt
- ⅛ tsp. pepper
- 1 haddock fillet (8 oz.)
- 2 tsp. chili powder, divided
- 2 cups shredded lettuce
- 2 medium tomatoes, seeded and chopped
- 1 medium sweet red pepper, chopped
- 1 medium ripe avocado, cubed
- 3 Tbsp. taco sauce
- 2 Tbsp. lime juice, divided
- 1 Tbsp. minced fresh cilantro
- 1½ tsp. grated lime zest
- 12 flour tortillas (8 in.)

1. Spread corn with butter and sprinkle with salt and pepper. Grill, covered, over medium heat until tender, 10-12 minutes, turning occasionally.
2. Meanwhile, sprinkle fish with 1 tsp. chili powder. On a lightly oiled grill rack, grill fish, covered, over medium heat until fish flakes easily with a fork, 7-9 minutes.
3. Cool corn slightly; remove kernels from cobs. Place in a large bowl. Add the lettuce, tomatoes, red pepper, avocado, taco sauce, 1 Tbsp. lime juice, cilantro, lime zest and the remaining chili powder.
4. Drizzle remaining lime juice over fish; cut into ½-in. cubes. Add to corn mixture. Spoon ½ cup mixture over each tortilla. Serve immediately.

2 TACOS: 446 cal., 12g fat (2g sat. fat), 23mg chol., 650mg sod., 68g carb. (5g sugars, 5g fiber), 19g pro.

ITALIAN STUFFED BEEF ROLLS

The combination of spinach, artichoke and cream cheese is always a crowd pleaser. Add basil and a roasted red pepper sauce, and you have perfection on a fork! To save time, the filling can be made ahead and chilled. You can also make the sauce ahead and reheat it when you are ready to serve.

—Noelle Myers, Grand Forks, ND

PREP: 30 min. • BAKE: 20 min.
MAKES: 6 servings

- 1 beef top sirloin steak (2 lbs.)
- 2 jars (8 oz. each) roasted sweet red peppers, drained and chopped, divided
- 1 pkg. (10 oz.) frozen chopped spinach, thawed and squeezed dry
- 1 carton (8 oz.) spreadable chive and onion cream cheese
- 1 jar (7½ oz.) marinated quartered artichoke hearts, drained and finely chopped
- 2 Tbsp. minced fresh basil or 2 tsp. dried basil
- ¼ tsp. salt
- ¼ tsp. pepper
- 1 jar (24 oz.) pasta sauce
- 1 Tbsp. tomato paste

1. Preheat oven to 425°. Cut steak into 6 serving-size pieces; pound with a meat mallet to ¼-in. thickness. In a large bowl, combine ¼ cup roasted peppers, spinach, cream cheese, artichokes and basil; spread over steaks. Roll up jelly-roll style, starting with a short side. Place seam side down in a greased 13x9-in. baking dish; sprinkle with salt and pepper.
2. Bake until the meat reaches desired doneness (for medium-rare, a thermometer should read 135°; medium, 140°; medium-well, 145°), 30-35 minutes.
3. Meanwhile, place the pasta sauce and remaining roasted peppers in a blender; cover and process until smooth. Transfer to a large saucepan; stir in tomato paste. Bring to a boil; reduce heat. Simmer, uncovered, until slightly thickened, 15-20 minutes. Let steaks stand 5 minutes before cutting into 1-in.-thick slices. Serve with sauce.

1 BEEF ROLL: 438 cal., 21g fat (9g sat. fat), 86mg chol., 1326mg sod., 21g carb. (13g sugars, 6g fiber), 38g pro.

MARTHA'S FISH TACOS

SAUSAGE MANICOTTI WITH
PUMPKIN SAUCE

SAUSAGE MANICOTTI WITH PUMPKIN SAUCE

This from-scratch manicotti is a wonderful change from typical pumpkin dishes in the fall.
—*Barry Dale, Puyallup, WA*

PREP: 25 min. • **BAKE:** 30 min. + standing **MAKES:** 5 servings

- 1 lb. bulk pork sausage
- 1 celery rib, chopped
- 1 medium carrot, chopped
- ½ medium onion, chopped
- 1 can (15 oz.) pumpkin
- 1 cup heavy whipping cream
- ½ cup dry white wine
- ¼ tsp. each ground ginger, cinnamon and nutmeg
- ⅛ tsp. cayenne pepper
- 20 wonton wrappers

1. In a large skillet, cook sausage, celery, carrot and onion over medium heat until meat is no longer pink and vegetables are tender, 10-12 minutes, breaking up sausage into crumbles; drain.
2. Meanwhile, in a large saucepan, combine pumpkin, cream, wine and spices. Heat through (do not allow to boil).
3. Preheat oven to 350°. Spread 1 cup of the pumpkin sauce into a greased 13x9-in. baking dish. Place 2 Tbsp. sausage filling in center of a wonton wrapper. (Cover remaining wrappers with a damp paper towel until ready to use.) Moisten wrapper edges with water. Roll up. Place in prepared dish, seam side down. Repeat.
4. Top with remaining sauce. Bake, uncovered, until bubbly, 30-35 minutes. Let stand 10 minutes before serving.
4 STUFFED MANICOTTI: *627 cal., 38g fat (18g sat. fat), 109mg chol., 974mg sod., 52g carb. (5g sugars, 4g fiber), 19g pro.*

MOROCCAN CHICKEN THIGHS

My husband and I love Mediterranean and Middle Eastern food. This flavorful recipe has quickly become one of our favorites.
—*Susan Mills, Three Rivers, CA*

PREP: 25 min. • **COOK:** 40 min. • **MAKES:** 2 servings

- ½ tsp. brown sugar
- ½ tsp. ground coriander
- ½ tsp. ground cumin
- ½ tsp. paprika
- ¼ tsp. ground cinnamon
- ⅛ tsp. garlic powder
- ⅛ tsp. salt
- ⅛ tsp. pepper
- 2 tsp. all-purpose flour
- 4 bone-in chicken thighs (about 1½ lbs.), skin removed
- 1 Tbsp. olive oil

SAUCE
- 3 shallots, chopped
- ½ cup plus 2 Tbsp. reduced-sodium chicken broth, divided
- 4 pitted dates, chopped
- 1 tsp. all-purpose flour
- 1½ tsp. minced fresh cilantro

COUSCOUS
- ¼ cup water
- 3 Tbsp. reduced-sodium chicken broth
- ⅛ tsp. salt
    Dash ground cumin
- ⅓ cup uncooked couscous
- 1½ tsp. slivered almonds, toasted

1. In a small bowl, combine the first 8 ingredients. Set aside 1 tsp. spice mixture; add flour to remaining mixture and sprinkle over chicken.
2. In a large nonstick skillet, brown chicken in oil on both sides. Remove and keep warm. Add shallots to pan; cook and stir over medium heat 3 minutes. Stir in ½ cup broth and dates. Bring mixture to a boil.
3. Reduce heat; return chicken to pan. Cover and simmer until chicken juices run clear, 20-25 minutes. Remove chicken and keep warm. Combine the flour with reserved 1 tsp. spice mixture and remaining 2 Tbsp. broth until smooth; gradually stir into the pan. Bring to a boil; cook and stir until thickened, about 2 minutes. Stir in minced cilantro.
4. For couscous, in a small saucepan, bring water, broth, salt and cumin to a boil. Stir in couscous. Cover and remove from heat; let stand until water is absorbed, 5-10 minutes. Fluff with a fork; stir in almonds. Serve with chicken and sauce.
1 SERVING: *644 cal., 24g fat (6g sat. fat), 174mg chol., 685mg sod., 51g carb. (15g sugars, 4g fiber), 57g pro.*

MOROCCAN
CHICKEN THIGHS

**QUICK & EASY
VEGETABLE POTPIE**

QUICK & EASY VEGETABLE POTPIE

This meatless Monday superstar comes together quickly and is inexpensive as well. My 4-year-old always asks for seconds! You can substitute any canned or frozen beans for the canned lentils in this easy vegetable potpie. We also like using frozen edamame.
—Maggie Torsney-Weir, Los Angeles, CA

PREP: 30 min. • **BAKE:** 30 min. • **MAKES:** 6 servings

- 2 Tbsp. butter
- 3 cups frozen mixed vegetables, thawed
- 1 can (15 oz.) lentils, drained
- 2 Tbsp. all-purpose flour
- 1 cup vegetable or chicken broth
- 1 Tbsp. Dijon mustard
- 1 tsp. quatre epices (French four spice)
- ½ tsp. salt
- 1 sheet refrigerated pie crust
- 1 Tbsp. olive oil
- ¼ cup grated Parmesan cheese

1. Preheat oven to 375°. In a large skillet, melt butter over medium heat. Add mixed vegetables and lentils; cook and stir until heated through, 3-5 minutes. Stir in flour until blended; gradually whisk in broth. Bring to a boil, stirring constantly; cook and stir until thickened, 1-2 minutes. Stir in mustard, quatre epices and salt.
2. Transfer to a greased 9-in. pie plate. Place pie crust over filling. Trim; cut slits in top. Brush with oil; sprinkle with Parmesan. Bake until golden brown, 30-35 minutes. Cool 5 minutes before serving.
1 SERVING: *356 cal., 17g fat (7g sat. fat), 20mg chol., 705mg sod., 41g carb. (5g sugars, 9g fiber), 10g pro.*

TEST KITCHEN TIP

For a smoky Spanish flavor, use lemon-pepper seasoning and smoked paprika instead of the quatre epices.

RHUBARB BEEF

My daughter made a trip around the world and brought home this recipe from Iran. I've served it often to many of my friends, and they always seem to savor its different, zingy taste.
—Bertha Davis, Springfield, MO

PREP: 10 min. • **COOK:** 2¼ hours • **MAKES:** 6 servings

- 2 to 2½ lbs. beef stew meat, cut into 1-in. cubes
- 2 Tbsp. butter
- 2 large onions, chopped
- 1 tsp. saffron
- 1 can (10½ oz.) beef broth
- 1 cup water
- ¼ cup lemon juice
- ¼ cup chopped fresh parsley
- 1½ tsp. dried mint
- 2 tsp. salt
- ¼ tsp. pepper
- 2 to 3 cups sliced fresh or frozen rhubarb
  Hot cooked rice
  Fresh mint leaves, torn

In a Dutch oven, brown beef in butter. Remove meat from pan; drain all but 2 Tbsp. drippings. Saute onions until lightly browned. Return meat to pan. Add saffron, beef broth, water, lemon juice, parsley, mint, salt and pepper; cover and simmer until meat is tender, about 2 hours. Add more water as needed. Add rhubarb during the last 15 minutes of cooking. Serve over rice; top with fresh mint.
1 CUP: *287 cal., 15g fat (6g sat. fat), 104mg chol., 1072mg sod., 8g carb. (5g sugars, 2g fiber), 30g pro.*

RHUBARB BEEF

SKILLET PASTA FLORENTINE

Here's a great weeknight supper that's budget-friendly, healthy and a hit with children. With such a thick, cheesy topping, who'd ever guess that it's lighter?
—Kelly Turnbull, Jupiter, FL

PREP: 20 min. • **COOK:** 35 min.
MAKES: 6 servings

- 3 cups uncooked spiral pasta
- 1 large egg, lightly beaten
- 2 cups 2% cottage cheese
- 1½ cups reduced-fat ricotta cheese
- 1 pkg. (10 oz.) frozen chopped spinach, thawed and squeezed dry
- 1 cup shredded part-skim mozzarella cheese, divided
- 1 tsp. each dried parsley flakes, oregano and basil
- 1 jar (14 oz.) meatless spaghetti sauce
- 2 Tbsp. grated Parmesan cheese

1. Cook pasta according to package directions. Meanwhile, in a large bowl, combine the egg, cottage cheese, ricotta, spinach, ½ cup mozzarella and herbs.
2. Drain pasta. Place half the sauce in a large skillet; layer with pasta and remaining sauce. Top with cheese mixture.
3. Bring to a boil. Reduce heat; cover and cook until a thermometer reads 160°, 25-30 minutes.
4. Sprinkle with Parmesan cheese and remaining mozzarella cheese; cover and cook until cheese melts, about 5 minutes longer. Let the pasta stand for 5 minutes before serving.
1 SERVING: *383 cal., 9g fat (5g sat. fat), 73mg chol., 775mg sod., 47g carb. (12g sugars, 4g fiber), 27g pro.*

TURKEY CREPES

This savory crepe recipe has been passed down through many generations in my family. You can also use the turkey filling to make a potpie.
—Andrea Price, Grafton, WI

PREP: 30 min. + chilling • **COOK:** 50 min.
MAKES: 6 servings

- 3 large eggs, room temperature
- 3¼ cups 2% milk
- 2 cups all-purpose flour
- 1 tsp. salt
- 1 tsp. baking powder

TURKEY CREPES

FILLING

- 3 Tbsp. butter, divided
- 1 cup frozen peas and carrots (about 5 oz.), thawed
- ½ cup chopped onion
- 3 Tbsp. all-purpose flour
- 1 cup 2% milk
- 1 cup chicken broth
- 2 cups chopped cooked turkey
- ½ tsp. salt
- ½ tsp. minced fresh thyme or ¼ tsp. dried thyme
- ⅛ tsp. pepper

1. In a large bowl, whisk eggs and milk. In another bowl, mix flour, salt and baking powder; add to egg mixture and mix well. Refrigerate, covered, 1 hour.
2. Heat a lightly greased 8-in. nonstick skillet over medium heat. Stir batter. Fill a ¼-cup measure with batter; pour into center of pan. Quickly lift and tilt pan to coat bottom evenly. Cook until top appears dry; turn crepe over and cook until bottom is cooked, 15-20 seconds longer. Remove to a wire rack. Repeat with remaining batter, greasing pan as needed. When cool, stack crepes between pieces of waxed paper or paper towels.
3. For filling, in a large saucepan, heat 2 Tbsp. butter over medium heat. Add peas and carrots and onion; cook and stir until onion is tender, 8-10 minutes. Stir in flour until blended; gradually whisk in milk and broth. Bring to a boil, stirring constantly; cook and stir until thickened, 5-8 minutes. Stir in remaining ingredients; heat through.
4. Spread ¼ cup filling down the center of each crepe; fold sides and ends over filling and roll up. Wipe out skillet. In batches, heat remaining 1 Tbsp. butter over medium heat. Cook the crepes until golden brown, 2-4 minutes on each side.
2 FILLED CREPES: *434 cal., 14g fat (7g sat. fat), 170mg chol., 1063mg sod., 47g carb. (9g sugars, 2g fiber), 28g pro.*

❄️
CORNISH PASTIES

My Great-Aunt Gladys was from a small mining town in England where pasties were popular. I loved to watch her craft each Cornish pasty, as she made them in different sizes depending on who was eating. Serve with a green salad to make a wonderful meal.
—Verna Hainer, Pueblo, CO

PREP: 30 min. + chilling • **BAKE:** 50 min.
MAKES: 8 servings

- 3 cups all-purpose flour
- 1½ tsp. salt
- ¾ tsp. baking powder
- 1 cup shortening
- 8 to 10 Tbsp. ice water

FILLING
- 1 lb. beef top round steak, cut into ½-in. pieces
- 1½ cups finely chopped onion
- 1½ cups cubed peeled potatoes (½-in. cubes)
- 1½ cups chopped peeled turnips (½-in. cubes)
- 1 tsp. salt
- ¼ tsp. pepper
- 4 Tbsp. butter
- ½ cup evaporated milk, optional
  Ketchup

1. In a large bowl, mix flour, salt and baking powder; cut in shortening until crumbly. Gradually add water, tossing with a fork until dough forms a ball. Cover and refrigerate for 30 minutes.

2. Preheat oven to 375°. In another large bowl, combine the beef, onion, potatoes, turnips, salt and pepper. Divide dough into 4 equal portions. On a lightly floured surface, roll 1 portion into a 9-in. circle. Mound 1½ cups filling on half of circle; dot with 1 Tbsp. butter. Moisten edges with water; fold dough over filling and press edges with a fork to seal.

3. Place on a parchment-lined rimmed 15x10x1-in. baking pan. Repeat with remaining dough, filling and butter. Cut slits in tops of pasties. Bake 30 minutes. If desired, pour milk into slits. Bake until golden brown, 20-30 minutes longer. Serve with ketchup.

FREEZE OPTION: Freeze cooled pasties in a freezer container. To use, reheat the pasties on a parchment-lined baking sheet in a preheated 375° oven until heated through.

½ **PASTY:** 556 cal., 32g fat (10g sat. fat), 47mg chol., 864mg sod., 46g carb. (3g sugars, 3g fiber), 19g pro.

APPLE CIDER CHICKEN QUINOA SKILLET

Since I'm especially busy with three active teenagers, I don't have much time to get dinner on the table in the evening. Instead, I rely on quick options, like this one-skillet dish that boasts essential proteins, veggies and good carbohydrates.
—Julie Peterson, Crofton, MD

PREP: 15 min. • **COOK:** 25 min.
MAKES: 4 servings

- 1 Tbsp. olive oil
- 1 pkg. (12 oz.) fully cooked apple chicken sausage links or flavor of your choice, cut into ½-in.-thick slices
- 1 small onion, chopped
- 1 cup chicken broth
- 1 cup apple cider or juice
- ¼ tsp. salt
- 4 cups chopped fresh kale
- 1 cup quinoa, rinsed
- 1 medium apple, chopped
- ¼ cup chopped pecans
- ¼ cup dried cranberries
- 2 Tbsp. chopped fresh sage or 1 tsp. dried sage leaves

1. In a large skillet, heat oil over medium heat. Add sausage and onion; cook and stir until sausage is golden brown, 8-10 minutes. Add broth, cider and salt; bring to a boil. Stir in kale and quinoa.

2. Reduce heat; simmer, covered, until liquid is absorbed, 15-20 minutes. Remove from heat; stir in remaining ingredients. Cover skillet and let stand for 5 minutes before serving.

1½ **CUPS:** 492 cal., 18g fat (3g sat. fat), 61mg chol., 888mg sod., 62g carb. (29g sugars, 6g fiber), 22g pro.

CORNISH PASTIES

TUSCAN
PORTOBELLO
STEW

SPICY LEMON CHICKEN KABOBS

When I see Meyer lemons in the store, I can't resist grabbing a few. I like using them for these easy chicken kabobs, but regular grilled lemons also add a signature smoky tang.
—Terri Crandall, Gardnerville, NV

PREP: 15 min. + marinating • **GRILL:** 10 min. • **MAKES:** 6 servings

- ¼ cup lemon juice
- 4 Tbsp. olive oil, divided
- 3 Tbsp. white wine
- 1½ tsp. crushed red pepper flakes
- 1 tsp. minced fresh rosemary or ¼ tsp. dried rosemary, crushed
- 1½ lbs. boneless skinless chicken breasts, cut into 1-in. cubes
- 2 medium lemons, halved
  Minced chives

1. In a large shallow dish, combine lemon juice, 3 Tbsp. oil, wine, pepper flakes and rosemary. Add the chicken and turn to coat. Refrigerate up to 3 hours.
2. Drain chicken, discarding marinade. Thread chicken onto 6 metal or soaked wooden skewers. Grill, covered, over medium heat until no longer pink, turning once, 10-12 minutes.
3. Meanwhile, place lemons on grill, cut side down. Grill until lightly browned, 8-10 minutes. Squeeze the lemon halves over chicken. Drizzle with remaining oil; sprinkle with chives.
1 KABOB: *182 cal., 8g fat (2g sat. fat), 63mg chol., 55mg sod., 2g carb. (1g sugars, 1g fiber), 23g pro.* **Diabetic exchanges:** *3 lean meat, 1 fat.*

TUSCAN PORTOBELLO STEW

Here's a healthy one-skillet meal that's quick and easy to prepare, yet elegant enough for company. I often take this stew to my school's potlucks, where it is devoured by vegetarian teachers and students.
—Jane Siemon, Viroqua, WI

PREP: 20 min. • **COOK:** 20 min. • **MAKES:** 4 servings (1¼ qt.)

- 2 large portobello mushrooms, coarsely chopped
- 1 medium onion, chopped
- 3 garlic cloves, minced
- 2 Tbsp. olive oil
- ½ cup white wine or vegetable broth
- 1 can (28 oz.) diced tomatoes, undrained
- 2 cups chopped fresh kale
- 1 bay leaf
- 1 tsp. dried thyme
- ½ tsp. dried basil
- ½ tsp. dried rosemary, crushed
- ¼ tsp. salt
- ¼ tsp. pepper
- 2 cans (15 oz. each) cannellini beans, rinsed and drained

1. In a large skillet, saute mushrooms, onion and garlic in oil until tender. Add the wine. Bring to a boil; cook until liquid is reduced by half. Stir in the tomatoes, kale and seasonings. Bring to a boil. Reduce heat; cover and simmer for 8-10 minutes.
2. Add beans; heat through. Discard bay leaf.
1¼ CUPS: *309 cal., 8g fat (1g sat. fat), 0 chol., 672mg sod., 46g carb. (9g sugars, 13g fiber), 12g pro.* **Diabetic exchanges:** *2 starch, 2 vegetable, 1½ fat, 1 lean meat.*

**SPICY LEMON
CHICKEN KABOBS**

BUFFALO CHICKEN STUFFED POBLANO PEPPERS

BUFFALO CHICKEN STUFFED POBLANO PEPPERS

Since I do not care for green bell peppers, I decided to create a filling that would go well with my favorite pepper, the poblano. After a few taste tests with my family, this stuffed poblano peppers recipe is now one of our favorites. I have also added black beans, used Cubanelle peppers, and served cilantro lime rice on the side.

—Lorri Stout, Gaithersburg, MD

PREP: 15 min. • **BAKE:** 30 min.
MAKES: 8 servings

- 4   poblano peppers
- 2   Tbsp. butter
- 4   green onions, thinly sliced, divided
- 3   cups shredded cooked chicken breast
- 1   cup frozen corn (about 5 oz.), thawed
- 4   oz. cream cheese, cubed
- ¾   cup shredded Mexican cheese blend, divided
- ½   cup Buffalo wing sauce
- ¼   cup crumbled blue cheese
- 1   tsp. granulated garlic

1. Preheat oven to 350°. Cut peppers lengthwise in half; remove seeds. Place in a greased 13x9-in. baking dish. In a large skillet, heat butter over medium-high heat. Add 3 green onions; cook and stir until tender, about 5 minutes. Add chicken, corn, cream cheese, ½ cup shredded cheese, wing sauce, blue cheese and garlic; cook and stir until cheeses are melted.
2. Fill pepper halves with chicken mixture. Bake, covered, 25-30 minutes. Sprinkle with the remaining ¼ cup shredded cheese and green onion; bake, uncovered, until cheese is melted, about 5 minutes.

1 STUFFED PEPPER HALF: *246 cal., 14g fat (8g sat. fat), 75mg chol., 668mg sod., 9g carb. (3g sugars, 2g fiber), 21g pro.*

DID YOU KNOW?

Many people agree that Teressa Bellissimo first tossed chicken wings in a mixture of cayenne pepper, hot sauce and butter at her family's Anchor Bar in Buffalo, New York, in 1964. Others say John Young created the combo, called "mambo sauce," at his restaurant, Wings 'n Things. Either way, the sauce is definitely from Buffalo.

COMFORTING TUNA PATTIES

❄ COMFORTING TUNA PATTIES

My grandmother and mother made these tuna patties on Fridays during Lent. I'm not the biggest fan of tuna, but it's perfect in this dish. These patties are even good served cold the next day, if there are any leftovers.

—Ann Marie Eberhart, Gig Harbor, WA

PREP: 25 min. + chilling • **COOK:** 5 min./batch
MAKES: 6 servings

- 2   Tbsp. butter
- 3   Tbsp. all-purpose flour
- 1   cup evaporated milk
- 1   pouch (6.4 oz.) light tuna in water
- ⅓   cup plus ½ cup dry bread crumbs, divided
- 1   green onion, finely chopped
- 2   Tbsp. lemon juice
- ½   tsp. salt
- ¼   tsp. pepper
      Oil for frying

1. In a small saucepan, melt butter over medium heat. Stir in flour until smooth; gradually whisk in milk. Bring to a boil, stirring constantly; cook and stir until thickened, 2-3 minutes. Remove from heat. Transfer to a small bowl; cool.
2. Stir in tuna, ⅓ cup bread crumbs, green onion, the lemon juice, salt and pepper. Refrigerate, covered, at least 30 minutes.
3. Place remaining ½ cup bread crumbs in a shallow bowl. Drop ⅓ cup tuna mixture into crumbs. Gently coat and shape into a ½-in.-thick patty. Repeat.
4. In a large skillet, heat oil over medium heat. Add tuna patties in batches; cook until golden brown, 2-3 minutes on each side. Drain on paper towels.

FREEZE OPTION: Freeze cooled tuna patties in freezer containers, separating layers with waxed paper. To use, reheat tuna patties on a baking sheet in a preheated 325° oven until heated through.

1 TUNA PATTY: *255 cal., 17g fat (5g sat. fat), 34mg chol., 419mg sod., 15g carb. (5g sugars, 1g fiber), 10g pro.*

WEEKNIGHT GOULASH

With this recipe, you can put in a full day's work, run some errands and still get dinner on the table in hardly any time. Make it extra special by serving the meat sauce over spaetzle.
—*Cyndy Gerken, Naples, FL*

PREP: 25 min. • **COOK:** 8½ hours • **MAKES:** 2 servings

- 1 lb. beef stew meat
- 1 Tbsp. olive oil
- 1 cup beef broth
- 1 small onion, chopped
- ¼ cup ketchup
- 1 Tbsp. Worcestershire sauce
- 1½ tsp. brown sugar
- 1½ tsp. paprika
- ¼ tsp. ground mustard
- 1 Tbsp. all-purpose flour
- 2 Tbsp. water
  Hot cooked egg noodles or spaetzle

1. In a large skillet, brown beef in oil; drain. Transfer to a 1½-qt. slow cooker. Combine the broth, onion, ketchup, Worcestershire sauce, brown sugar, paprika and mustard. Pour over beef. Cover and cook on low 8-10 hours or until meat is tender.
2. In a small bowl, combine flour and water until smooth. Gradually stir into the beef mixture. Cover and cook on high until thickened, about 30 minutes longer. Serve with noodles.
1 CUP: *478 cal., 23g fat (7g sat. fat), 141mg chol., 1005mg sod., 20g carb. (14g sugars, 1g fiber), 45g pro.*

WEEKNIGHT GOULASH

TANGY PORK CHOPS

TANGY PORK CHOPS

When my husband and I had our first child, we found this recipe so convenient. I could start it during nap time and we'd enjoy an easy, satisfying dinner that night.
—*Karol Hines, Kitty Hawk, NC*

PREP: 15 min. • **COOK:** 5½ hours • **MAKES:** 4 servings

- 4 bone-in pork loin chops
- ⅛ tsp. pepper
- 2 medium onions, chopped
- 2 celery ribs, chopped
- 1 large green pepper, sliced
- 1 can (14½ oz.) no-salt-added stewed tomatoes
- ½ cup ketchup
- 2 Tbsp. cider vinegar
- 2 Tbsp. brown sugar
- 2 Tbsp. Worcestershire sauce
- 1 Tbsp. lemon juice
- 1 tsp. beef bouillon granules
- 3 Tbsp. cornstarch
- 2 Tbsp. cold water
  Hot cooked rice or mashed potatoes, optional

1. Place chops in a 3-qt. slow cooker; sprinkle with pepper. Add the onions, celery, green pepper and tomatoes. Combine the ketchup, cider vinegar, brown sugar, Worcestershire sauce, lemon juice and bouillon; pour over vegetables. Cover and cook on low 5-6 hours or until meat is tender.
2. Mix cornstarch and water until smooth; stir into liquid in slow cooker. Cover and cook on high for about 30 minutes or until thickened. If desired, serve with rice or mashed potatoes.
1 PORK CHOP: *349 cal., 9g fat (3g sat. fat), 86mg chol., 757mg sod., 34g carb. (24g sugars, 4g fiber), 32g pro.*

SHEET-PAN HONEY MUSTARD CHICKEN

This sheet-pan chicken is an easy gluten-free, low-carb meal ideal for busy weekdays. The chicken is tender, juicy and so delicious! It is now on the list of our favorite meals. If you don't have green beans on hand, you can substitute any low-carb vegetable.
—Denise Browning, San Antonio, TX

PREP: 20 min. • **BAKE:** 45 min.
MAKES: 6 servings

- 6 bone-in chicken thighs (about 2¼ lbs.)
- ¾ tsp. salt, divided
- ½ tsp. pepper, divided
- 2 medium lemons
- ⅓ cup olive oil
- ⅓ cup honey
- 3 Tbsp. Dijon mustard
- 4 garlic cloves, minced
- 1 tsp. paprika
- ½ cup water
- ½ lb. fresh green beans, trimmed
- 6 miniature sweet peppers, sliced into rings
- ¼ cup pomegranate seeds, optional

1. Preheat oven to 425°. Place chicken in a greased 15x10x1-in. baking pan. Sprinkle with ½ tsp. salt and ¼ tsp. pepper. Thinly slice 1 lemon; place over chicken. Cut the remaining lemon crosswise in half; squeeze juice into a small bowl. Whisk in oil, honey, mustard, garlic and paprika. Pour half of the mixture over chicken; reserve the remainder for beans. Pour water into pan. Bake 25 minutes.

2. Meanwhile, combine green beans, sweet peppers, remaining sauce, ¼ tsp. salt and ¼ tsp. pepper; toss to coat. Arrange the vegetables around chicken in pan. Bake until a thermometer inserted in chicken reads 170°-175° and beans are tender, 15-20 minutes. If desired, sprinkle with pomegranate seeds.

1 SERVING: *419 cal., 26g fat (6g sat. fat), 81mg chol., 548mg sod., 22g carb. (17g sugars, 2g fiber), 24g pro.*

SHEET-PAN HONEY MUSTARD CHICKEN

CINCINNATI CHILI

BLACK BEAN TORTILLA PIE

I found this entree a while ago but decreased the cheese and increased the herbs originally called for. It's one of my toddler's favorite meals. She always smiles when she sees it on the table.
—Wendy Kelly, Petersburg, NY

- -

PREP: 50 min. • **BAKE:** 15 min.
MAKES: 6 servings

1	Tbsp. olive oil
1	medium green pepper, chopped
1	medium onion, chopped
1	tsp. ground cumin
¼	tsp. pepper
3	garlic cloves, minced
2	cans (15 oz. each) black beans, rinsed and drained
1	can (14½ oz.) vegetable broth
1	pkg. (10 oz.) frozen corn, thawed
4	green onions, sliced
4	flour tortillas (8 in.)
1	cup shredded reduced-fat cheddar cheese, divided

1. Preheat oven to 400°. In a large skillet, heat oil over medium-high heat. Add green pepper, onion, cumin and pepper; cook and stir until vegetables are tender. Add garlic; cook 1 minute longer.
2. Stir in beans and broth. Bring to a boil; cook until liquid is reduced to about ⅓ cup, stirring occasionally. Stir in corn and green onions; remove from heat.
3. Place 1 tortilla in a 9-in. springform pan coated with cooking spray. Layer with 1½ cups bean mixture and ¼ cup cheese. Repeat layers twice. Top with remaining tortilla. Place pan on a baking sheet.
4. Bake, uncovered, until heated through, 15-20 minutes. Sprinkle with remaining cheese. Loosen sides from pan with a knife; remove rim from pan. Cut into 6 wedges.
1 SLICE: *353 cal., 9g fat (3g sat. fat), 14mg chol., 842mg sod., 53g carb. (6g sugars, 8g fiber), 17g pro.* **Diabetic exchanges:** *3 starch, 1 lean meat, 1 very lean meat, 1 vegetable, 1 fat.*

CINCINNATI CHILI

Cinnamon and cocoa give a rich brown color to hearty Cincinnati chili. This dish will warm you up on a cold day.
—Edith Joyce, Parkman, OH

- -

PREP: 20 min. • **COOK:** 1¾ hours
MAKES: 8 servings

1	lb. ground beef
1	lb. ground pork
4	medium onions, chopped
6	garlic cloves, minced
2	cans (16 oz. each) kidney beans, rinsed and drained
1	can (28 oz.) crushed tomatoes
¼	cup white vinegar
¼	cup baking cocoa
2	Tbsp. Worcestershire sauce
2	tsp. hot pepper sauce
1	tsp. sugar
2	Tbsp. chili powder
4	tsp. ground cinnamon
3	tsp. dried oregano
2	tsp. ground cumin
2	tsp. ground allspice
3	bay leaves
	Salt and pepper to taste
	Hot cooked spaghetti
	Optional: Shredded cheddar cheese, sour cream, chopped tomatoes and green onions

1. In a Dutch oven, cook the beef, pork and onions over medium heat until meat is no longer pink, breaking meat into crumbles. Add garlic; cook 1 minute longer. Drain. Add the beans, tomatoes, vinegar, cocoa, sauces, sugar and seasonings; bring to a boil. Reduce heat; cover and simmer for 1½ hours.
2. Discard bay leaves. Serve with spaghetti. If desired, garnish with cheese, sour cream, tomatoes and onions.
1 CUP: *421 cal., 16g fat (6g sat. fat), 75mg chol., 443mg sod., 38g carb. (7g sugars, 11g fiber), 32g pro.*

AIR-FRYER GROUND BEEF WELLINGTON

Trying new recipes—like this air-fryer Wellington—is one of my favorite hobbies. I replaced the filet mignon with ground beef to make it easier, while still keeping the dish's beefy goodness.
—Julie Frankamp, Nicollet, MN

PREP: 30 min. • **COOK:** 20 min.
MAKES: 2 servings

- 1 Tbsp. butter
- ½ cup chopped fresh mushrooms
- 2 tsp. all-purpose flour
- ¼ tsp. pepper, divided
- ½ cup half-and-half cream
- 1 large egg yolk
- 2 Tbsp. finely chopped onion
- ¼ tsp. salt
- ½ lb. ground beef
- 1 tube (4 oz.) refrigerated crescent rolls
- 1 large egg, lightly beaten, optional
- 1 tsp. dried parsley flakes

1. Preheat air fryer to 300°. In a saucepan, heat butter over medium-high heat. Add mushrooms; cook and stir until tender, 5-6 minutes. Stir in flour and ⅛ tsp. pepper until blended. Gradually add cream. Bring to a boil; cook and stir for 2 minutes or until thickened. Remove from the heat and set aside.
2. In a bowl, combine egg yolk, onion, 2 Tbsp. mushroom sauce, salt and the remaining ⅛ tsp. pepper. Crumble beef over mixture and mix well. Shape into 2 loaves. Unroll crescent dough and separate into 2 rectangles; press the perforations to seal. Place meat loaf on each rectangle. Bring edges together and pinch to seal. If desired, brush with some beaten egg.
3. Place Wellingtons in a single layer on greased tray in air-fryer basket. Cook until golden brown and a thermometer inserted into meat loaf reads 160°, 18-22 minutes.
4. Meanwhile, warm the remaining sauce over low heat; stir in parsley. Serve sauce with Wellingtons.
1 SERVING: 585 cal., 38g fat (14g sat. fat), 208mg chol., 865mg sod., 30g carb. (9g sugars, 1g fiber), 29g pro.

ONE-SKILLET CHICKEN FAJITA PASTA

You can have this quick, easy fajita pasta on the table in no time. We love the spicy southwestern flavor, and I like being able to make the whole meal in my cast-iron skillet. I sometimes garnish it with crushed corn chips.
—Joan Hallford, North Richland Hills, TX

PREP: 25 min. • **COOK:** 20 min.
MAKES: 6 servings

- 3 cups uncooked elbow macaroni
- 2 Tbsp. olive oil, divided
- 1 lb. boneless skinless chicken breasts, cut into 1-in. cubes
- 1 envelope fajita seasoning mix, divided
- 1 large onion, chopped
- 1 large green pepper, chopped
- 3 garlic cloves, minced
- 2 cups reduced-sodium chicken broth
- 1 can (10 oz.) diced tomatoes and green chiles, drained
- 1 can (4 oz.) chopped green chiles, drained
- ½ cup heavy whipping cream
- ½ tsp. salt
- 1 cup shredded sharp cheddar cheese

1. Cook macaroni according to package directions for al dente.
2. Meanwhile, heat 1 Tbsp. oil in a large skillet oven over medium-high heat. Add chicken and 4½ tsp. fajita seasoning; cook and stir until no longer pink, 5-7 minutes. Remove chicken and keep warm.
3. Heat remaining 1 Tbsp. oil in skillet. Add onion, green pepper and the remaining 4½ tsp. fajita seasoning. Cook and stir until crisp-tender, 5-7 minutes. Add garlic; cook 1 minute longer. Remove from pan.
4. In the same skillet, add chicken broth, diced tomatoes, green chiles, whipping cream and salt. Bring to a boil. Reduce heat; simmer, uncovered, until thickened, about 10 minutes. Return macaroni, chicken and vegetables to skillet; heat through. Sprinkle with cheese.
1⅓ CUPS: 448 cal., 21g fat (10g sat. fat), 83mg chol., 1304mg sod., 38g carb. (4g sugars, 3g fiber), 27g pro.

ONE-SKILLET CHICKEN FAJITA PASTA

CREAMY PESTO CHICKEN

Basil usually takes over our garden in the middle of June, but we don't mind because we love this pesto! It's a dairy-free version but tastes so good. We love this mixture over cauliflower rice or gluten-free pasta.
—Courtney Stultz, Weir, KS

PREP: 20 min. • **BAKE:** 20 min.
MAKES: 2 servings

- 1 Tbsp. balsamic vinegar
- 1 tsp. olive oil
- 1 tsp. dried oregano
- ½ tsp. minced garlic
- ¼ tsp. salt
- 2 boneless skinless chicken breast halves (6 oz. each)

PESTO
- ¼ cup loosely packed basil leaves
- ¼ cup packed fresh parsley leaves
- ¼ tsp. salt
- ¼ cup canned coconut milk

1. Preheat oven to 350°. Combine the first 5 ingredients; brush over chicken. Place in a greased 8-in. square baking dish. Bake until a thermometer reads 165°, 20-25 minutes.
2. Meanwhile, place basil, parsley and salt in a small food processor; pulse until chopped. While processing, gradually add coconut milk in a steady stream until the mixture is pureed. Serve with chicken.

1 CHICKEN BREAST HALF WITH 2 TBSP. PESTO: *261 cal., 11g fat (6g sat. fat), 94mg chol., 684mg sod., 4g carb. (3g sugars, 1g fiber), 35g pro.* **Diabetic exchanges:** *5 lean meat, 1½ fat.*

TEST KITCHEN TIP

It's important to get the correct coconut milk. The ones in the refrigerated dairy case have a tendency to curdle in this recipe, so be sure to grab the canned variety.

GREEK SHRIMP ORZO

This is one of our favorite dishes. It's delicious and satisfying, and it reheats so well. My husband would rather have "the orzo dish" than go out to a restaurant to eat. Serve it with crusty bread and salad.
—Molly Seidel, Edgewood, NM

PREP: 45 min. • **COOK:** 2 hours
MAKES: 6 servings

- 2 cups uncooked orzo pasta
- 2 Tbsp. minced fresh basil or 2 tsp. dried basil
- 3 Tbsp. olive oil, divided
- 1½ Tbsp. chopped shallot
- 2 Tbsp. butter
- 1 can (14½ oz.) diced tomatoes, drained
- 2 Tbsp. minced fresh oregano or 2 tsp. dried oregano
- 3 garlic cloves, minced
- 1 lb. uncooked large shrimp, peeled and deveined
- 1 cup oil-packed sun-dried tomatoes, chopped
- 2½ cups (10 oz.) crumbled feta cheese
- 1½ cups pitted Greek olives

1. Cook the orzo according to package directions; rinse in cold water and drain. Transfer to a large bowl. Add basil and 1 Tbsp. oil; toss to coat and set aside.
2. In a large skillet, saute shallot in butter and remaining oil until tender. Add the diced tomatoes, oregano and garlic; cook and stir for 1-2 minutes. Add shrimp and sun-dried tomatoes; cook and stir until shrimp turn pink, 2-3 minutes.
3. Transfer to a greased 5-qt. slow cooker. Stir in the orzo mixture, cheese and olives. Cover and cook on low for 2-3 hours or until heated through.

1½ CUPS: *673 cal., 32g fat (10g sat. fat), 127mg chol., 1262mg sod., 63g carb. (5g sugars, 6g fiber), 31g pro.*

CREAMY PESTO CHICKEN

CURRY SHRIMP & RICE

CURRY SHRIMP & RICE

My family and I absolutely love curry shrimp and rice. I created this version so I can make it in a hurry. Except for the butter and shrimp, all the ingredients are right in my pantry. To add a little heat, we like to stir in a tablespoon of fresh ground chili paste.
—Angela Spengler, Niceville, FL

PREP: 10 min. • **COOK:** 25 min. • **MAKES:** 8 servings

- 2 Tbsp. butter
- ½ medium onion, chopped
- 1 carton (32 oz.) chicken broth
- 2 cans (14½ oz. each) diced potatoes, drained
- 2 cans (7 oz. each) white or shoepeg corn, drained
- 1 can (13.66 oz.) coconut milk
- 1 can (8 oz.) bamboo shoots, drained
- 1 Tbsp. curry powder
- 1 to 3 tsp. Thai red chili paste, optional
- ½ tsp. salt
- ½ tsp. pepper
- 12 oz. peeled and deveined cooked shrimp (61-70 per lb.)
- 2 pkg. (8.8 oz. each) ready-to-serve long grain rice
  Optional: Lime wedges and fresh basil

1. In a Dutch oven, heat butter over medium-high heat. Add onion; cook and stir until tender, 4-5 minutes. Add broth, potatoes, corn, coconut milk, bamboo shoots, curry powder, chili paste if desired, salt and pepper. Bring to a boil; reduce heat. Simmer, uncovered, until flavors have blended, 12-15 minutes, stirring occasionally.
2. Add shrimp; heat through. Prepare rice according to the package directions; serve with curry. Sprinkle with additional curry powder. If desired, serve with lime wedges and basil.
1 SERVING: *354 cal., 13g fat (10g sat. fat), 75mg chol., 1112mg sod., 42g carb. (3g sugars, 3g fiber), 14g pro.*

BUFFALO CHICKEN MEAT LOAF

Here's a great way to spice up a plain chicken meat loaf. It combines two of my favorite Sunday afternoon foods into one easy-to-make meal. It's a huge hit with my family.
—Holly Jones, Kennesaw, GA

PREP: 25 min. • **BAKE:** 45 min. + standing • **MAKES:** 4 servings

- 1 cup dry whole wheat bread crumbs
- 2 celery ribs, chopped
- 1 small onion, chopped
- 2 large eggs, lightly beaten
- ½ cup Buffalo wing sauce
- 3 garlic cloves, minced
- 1 tsp. pepper
- 1 cup crumbled blue cheese, divided
- 1 lb. ground chicken
- 6 bacon strips

GLAZE
- ¼ cup Buffalo wing sauce
- 4 tsp. prepared mustard
- 4 tsp. honey
  Additional chopped celery, optional

1. Preheat oven to 350°. In a large bowl, combine the first 7 ingredients; stir in ¾ cup cheese. Add chicken; mix lightly but thoroughly. Shape into an 8x4-in. loaf on a greased 15x10x1-in. baking pan. Arrange bacon over top.
2. For glaze, in a small bowl, mix the wing sauce, mustard and honey; spoon over meat loaf. Bake until a thermometer reads 165°, 45-50 minutes. Sprinkle with remaining blue cheese and, if desired, additional celery. Let stand 10 minutes before slicing.
1 SLICE: *621 cal., 38g fat (15g sat. fat), 229mg chol., 2445mg sod., 37g carb. (9g sugars, 4g fiber), 36g pro.*

BUFFALO CHICKEN MEAT LOAF

THE BEST BEEF STEW

4. Discard bay leaves. In a small bowl, combine remaining ½ tsp. rosemary, remaining ¼ tsp. salt and remaining 2 Tbsp. flour. Add cold water and vinegar; stir until smooth. Stir into stew. Bring to a boil; add peas. Cook, stirring, until thickened, about 2 minutes. If desired, top with additional fresh rosemary.

1½ CUPS: 366 cal., 11g fat (3g sat. fat), 71mg chol., 605mg sod., 40g carb. (9g sugars, 6g fiber), 28g pro. Diabetic exchanges: 3 lean meat, 2½ starch, ½ fat.

SLOW-COOKER CHICKEN PARMESAN

I love making this satisfying dish—it's easy and elegant, and the slow cooker minimizes my time in the kitchen. I make this during football season, too. For game days, I skip the pasta and serve the chicken on submarine rolls with a bit of the sauce and some chopped lettuce. It's also good cut in half and served on smaller buns as sliders.
—Bonnie Hawkins, Elkhorn, WI

- -

PREP: 25 min. • **COOK:** 4 hours • **MAKES:** 4 servings

½	cup seasoned bread crumbs
½	cup grated Parmesan cheese
½	tsp. Italian seasoning
½	tsp. pepper
¼	tsp. salt
1	large egg, lightly beaten
1	Tbsp. water
4	(6 oz. each) boneless skinless chicken breast halves
1	jar (24 oz.) marinara sauce
4	slices part-skim mozzarella cheese
	Hot cooked pasta, optional

1. In a shallow bowl, combine bread crumbs, Parmesan cheese, Italian seasoning, pepper and salt. In another bowl, combine egg and water. Dip chicken in egg mixture, then in crumb mixture to coat both sides, patting to help coating adhere.

2. Transfer chicken to a 4- or 5-qt. slow cooker. Pour sauce over chicken. Cook, covered, on low 4-6 hours or until a thermometer inserted in chicken reads 165°. Top with cheese, re-cover, and cook for 10-15 minutes or until cheese is melted. If desired, serve chicken and sauce with pasta.

1 SERVING: 475 cal., 17g fat (7g sat. fat), 171mg chol., 1689mg sod., 27g carb. (11g sugars, 4g fiber), 50g pro.

SLOW-COOKER CHICKEN PARMESAN

THE BEST BEEF STEW

Our best beef stew recipe has tons of flavor, thanks to its blend of herbs and the addition of red wine and balsamic vinegar. Learn how to make this comforting classic and take it to the next level.
—James Schend, Pleasant Prairie, WI

- -

PREP: 30 min. • **COOK:** 2 hours • **MAKES:** 6 servings (2¼ qt.)

1½	lbs. beef stew meat, cut into 1-in. cubes
½	tsp. salt, divided
6	Tbsp. all-purpose flour, divided
½	tsp. smoked paprika
1	Tbsp. canola oil
3	Tbsp. tomato paste
2	tsp. herbes de Provence
2	garlic cloves, minced
2	cups dry red wine
2	cups beef broth
1½	tsp. minced fresh rosemary, divided
2	bay leaves
3	cups cubed peeled potatoes
3	cups coarsely chopped onions (about 2 large)
2	cups sliced carrots
2	Tbsp. cold water
2	Tbsp. balsamic or red wine vinegar
1	cup fresh or frozen peas
	Additional fresh rosemary, optional

1. In a small bowl, toss beef and ¼ tsp. salt. In a large bowl, combine 4 Tbsp. flour and paprika. Add beef, a few pieces at a time, and toss to coat.

2. In a Dutch oven, brown beef in oil over medium heat. Stir in the tomato paste, herbes de Provence and garlic; cook until fragrant and color starts to darken slightly. Add wine; cook until mixture just comes to a boil. Simmer until reduced by half, about 5 minutes. Stir in broth, 1 tsp. rosemary and bay leaves. Bring to a boil. Reduce heat; cover and simmer until meat is almost tender, about 1½ hours.

3. Add potatoes, onions and carrots. Cover; simmer until meat and vegetables are tender, about 30 minutes longer.

AIR-FRYER GINGERED HONEY SALMON

The ginger, garlic and green onion marinade give this air-fryer salmon recipe a pleasant flavor. We've found it tastes even better when marinated in the fridge overnight.
—Dan Strumberger, Farmington, MN

PREP: 10 min. + marinating • **COOK:** 15 min.
MAKES: 6 servings

⅓	cup orange juice
⅓	cup reduced-sodium soy sauce
¼	cup honey
1	green onion, chopped
1	tsp. ground ginger
1	tsp. garlic powder
1	salmon fillet (1½ lbs. and ¾ in. thick)

1. For marinade, mix first 6 ingredients. In a shallow bowl, combine salmon and ⅔ cup marinade; chill 30 minutes, turning occasionally. Reserve remaining mixture for basting.

2. Preheat air fryer to 325°. Drain fish and discard marinade; place fillet on greased tray in air-fryer basket. Cook until fish just begins to flake easily with a fork, 15-18 minutes, basting with reserved marinade during the last 5 minutes.

3 OZ. COOKED FISH: *237 cal., 10g fat (2g sat. fat), 57mg chol., 569mg sod., 15g carb. (13g sugars, 0 fiber), 20g pro.* **Diabetic exchanges:** *3 lean meat, 1 starch.*

HOW-TO

Clean the Coil

If you detect smoking or an off odor when using the air fryer, there may be oil or residue on the heating coil. To clean, simply unplug the machine, let cool, then wipe the coil with a damp cloth—just like the heating element on an electric stove.

FLAVORFUL CHICKEN FAJITAS

FLAVORFUL CHICKEN FAJITAS

This chicken fajita recipe is a regular in my weeknight dinner rotation. The marinated chicken in these wraps is mouthwatering.
—Julie Sterchi, Campbellsville, KY

PREP: 20 min. + marinating • **COOK:** 10 min.
MAKES: 6 servings

4	Tbsp. canola oil, divided
2	Tbsp. lemon juice
1½	tsp. seasoned salt
1½	tsp. dried oregano
1½	tsp. ground cumin
1	tsp. garlic powder
½	tsp. chili powder
½	tsp. paprika
½	tsp. crushed red pepper flakes, optional
1½	lbs. boneless skinless chicken breast, cut into thin strips
½	medium sweet red pepper, julienned
½	medium green pepper, julienned
4	green onions, thinly sliced
½	cup chopped onion
6	flour tortillas (8 in.), warmed
	Optional: Shredded cheddar cheese, taco sauce, salsa, guacamole, sliced red onions and sour cream

1. In a large bowl, combine 2 Tbsp. oil, lemon juice and seasonings; add the chicken. Turn to coat; cover. Refrigerate for 1-4 hours.

2. In a large cast-iron or other heavy skillet, saute peppers and onions in remaining oil until crisp-tender. Remove and keep warm.

3. Drain chicken, discarding marinade. In the same skillet, cook the chicken over medium-high heat until no longer pink, 5-6 minutes. Return pepper mixture to pan; heat through.

4. Spoon filling down the center of tortillas; fold in half. Serve with desired toppings.

1 FAJITA: *369 cal., 15g fat (2g sat. fat), 63mg chol., 689mg sod., 30g carb. (2g sugars, 1g fiber), 28g pro.* **Diabetic exchanges:** *3 lean meat, 2 starch, 2 fat.*

ZIPPY TURKEY ZOODLES

LOW COUNTRY BOIL

Ideal for camping and relaxing trips to the beach, this crowd-pleasing recipe makes an appetizing presentation of perfectly seasoned meats, veggies and seafood.
—Mageswari Elagupillai, Victorville, CA

PREP: 20 min. • **COOK:** 40 min.
MAKES: 4 servings

- 2 qt. water
- 1 bottle (12 oz.) beer
- 2 Tbsp. seafood seasoning
- 1½ tsp. salt
- 4 medium red potatoes, cut into wedges
- 1 medium sweet onion, cut into wedges
- 4 medium ears sweet corn, cut in half
- ⅓ lb. smoked chorizo or kielbasa, cut into 1-in. slices
- 3 Tbsp. olive oil
- 6 large garlic cloves, minced
- 1 Tbsp. ground cumin
- 1 Tbsp. minced fresh cilantro
- ½ tsp. paprika
- ½ tsp. pepper
- 1 lb. uncooked large shrimp, deveined
- 1 lb. uncooked snow crab legs
  Optional: Seafood cocktail sauce, lemon wedges and melted butter

1. In a Dutch oven, combine the water, beer, seafood seasoning and salt; add potatoes and onion. Bring to a boil. Reduce heat; simmer, uncovered, for 10 minutes. Add corn and chorizo; simmer until potatoes and corn are tender, 10-12 minutes longer.
2. Meanwhile, in a small skillet, heat oil. Add the garlic, cumin, cilantro, paprika and pepper. Cook and stir over medium heat for 1 minute.
3. Stir the shrimp, crab legs and garlic mixture into the stockpot; cook until shrimp and crab turn pink, 4-6 minutes. Drain; transfer seafood mixture to a large serving bowl. Serve with the condiments of your choice.
1 SERVING: *500 cal., 20g fat (5g sat. fat), 212mg chol., 1318mg sod., 41g carb. (6g sugars, 5g fiber), 40g pro.*

ZIPPY TURKEY ZOODLES

Eating healthy doesn't have to mean you're sacrificing flavor—and these spiced-up zoodles prove it. If you don't have a spiralizer, simply slice the zucchini julienne-style.
—Elizabeth Bramkamp, Gig Harbor, WA

PREP: 25 min. • **COOK:** 20 min.
MAKES: 4 servings

- 4 tsp. olive oil, divided
- 1 lb. ground turkey
- 1 small onion, finely chopped
- 1 jalapeno pepper, seeded and chopped
- 2 garlic cloves, minced
- ¾ tsp. ground cumin
- ½ tsp. salt
- ¼ tsp. chili powder
- ¼ tsp. crushed red pepper flakes
- ¼ tsp. pepper
- 3 medium zucchini, spiralized
- 4 plum tomatoes, chopped
- 1 cup frozen corn, thawed
- 1 cup black beans, rinsed and drained
  Optional: Chopped fresh cilantro and shredded cheddar cheese

1. In a large nonstick skillet, heat 2 tsp. olive oil over medium heat. Add turkey, onion, jalapeno and garlic; cook until turkey is no longer pink and the vegetables are tender, breaking up turkey into crumbles, 8-10 minutes; drain. Stir in seasonings; remove and keep warm. Wipe out pan.
2. In the same pan, heat remaining olive oil and cook zucchini over medium heat until crisp-tender, 3-5 minutes. Stir in tomatoes, corn, beans and reserved turkey mixture; heat through. Serve with fresh cilantro and cheese, if desired.
NOTE: Wear disposable gloves when cutting hot peppers; the oils can burn skin. Avoid touching your face.
1¾ CUPS: *332 cal., 14g fat (3g sat. fat), 75mg chol., 500mg sod., 26g carb. (7g sugars, 6g fiber), 29g pro.* **Diabetic exchanges:** *3 medium-fat meat, 2 vegetable, 1 starch, 1 fat.*

**SHEPHERD'S PIE
TWICE-BAKED POTATOES
PAGE 105**

Meal Planner

The key to saving time and money for today's busy cooks is planning ahead—and these recipes are just the thing to help you do it! When buying ingredients or pulling together a big meal tonight, think about the delicious dishes you can make tomorrow!

Roast Pork Redux

One savory slow-cooked pork roast makes for three delectable dinners so satisfying you'll swoon.

ROAST PORK SOUP

This well-seasoned, sure-to-please soup has a rich, full-bodied broth brimming with tender chunks of pork, potatoes and navy beans. It has been a family favorite for years. Served with cornbread, it's one of our comfort foods in winter.
—*Sue Gulledge, Springville, AL*

- -

PREP: 15 min. • **COOK:** 55 min. • **MAKES:** 9 servings (2¼ qt.)

  3 cups cubed cooked pork roast
  2 medium potatoes, peeled and chopped
  1 large onion, chopped
  1 can (15 oz.) navy beans, rinsed and drained
  1 can (14½ oz.) Italian diced tomatoes, undrained
  4 cups water
  ½ cup unsweetened apple juice
  ½ tsp. salt
  ½ tsp. pepper
    Minced fresh basil

In a soup kettle or Dutch oven, combine the first 9 ingredients. Bring to a boil. Reduce heat; cover and simmer until vegetables are crisp-tender, about 45 minutes. Sprinkle with basil.

1 CUP: *206 cal., 5g fat (2g sat. fat), 42mg chol., 435mg sod., 23g carb. (6g sugars, 4g fiber), 18g pro.* **Diabetic exchanges:** *1 starch, 1 meat, 1 vegetable.*

PORK SPANISH RICE

PORK SPANISH RICE

My family wasn't fond of pork roast until I used it in this yummy casserole. Now they can't get enough!
—*Betty Unrau, MacGregor, MB*

- -

PREP: 20 min. • **BAKE:** 20 min. • **MAKES:** 4 servings

  1 medium green pepper, chopped
  1 small onion, chopped
  2 Tbsp. butter
  1 can (14½ oz.) diced tomatoes, drained
  1 cup chicken broth
  ½ tsp. salt
  ¼ tsp. pepper
1¾ cups cubed cooked pork
  1 cup uncooked instant rice
    Optional: Lime wedges and minced cilantro

1. Preheat oven to 350°. In a large skillet, saute green pepper and onion in butter until tender. Stir in the tomatoes, broth, salt and pepper. Bring to a boil; stir in pork and rice.
2. Transfer to a greased 2-qt. baking dish. Cover and bake until the rice is tender and the liquid is absorbed, 20-25 minutes. Stir before serving. If desired, serve with lime wedges and top with minced cilantro.

1 CUP: *304 cal., 12g fat (6g sat. fat), 71mg chol., 756mg sod., 29g carb. (5g sugars, 3g fiber), 21g pro.* **Diabetic exchanges:** *3 lean meat, 2 starch, 1½ fat.*

ROAST PORK SOUP

GARLIC-APPLE PORK ROAST

This is the meal I have become famous for, and it's so simple to prepare in the slow cooker. The garlic and apple flavors really complement the pork. It's especially good with steamed fresh asparagus and roasted red potatoes.

—*Jennifer Loos, Washington Boro, PA*

- -

PREP: 10 min. • **COOK:** 8 hours + standing
MAKES: 12 servings

- 1   boneless pork loin roast (3½ to 4 lbs.)
- 1   jar (12 oz.) apple jelly
- ½   cup water
- 2½ tsp. minced garlic
- 1   Tbsp. dried parsley flakes
- 1   to 1½ tsp. seasoned salt
- 1   to 1½ tsp. pepper

1. Cut the roast in half; place in a 5-qt. slow cooker. In a small bowl, combine the jelly, water and garlic; pour over roast. Sprinkle with parsley, salt and pepper.
2. Cover and cook on low until the meat is tender, 8-10 hours. Let stand for 15 minutes before slicing. Serve with the cooking juices if desired.

4 OZ. COOKED PORK: 237 cal., 6g fat (2g sat. fat), 66mg chol., 165mg sod., 19g carb. (17g sugars, 0 fiber), 26g pro.

READER REVIEW

"You can't really miss with a simple recipe like this, and cooked in a slow cooker to boot! Other jellies could be substituted for the apple jelly, if you don't have any on hand. Try peeling and dicing some Granny Smith or other cooking apples to cook along with the roast. Delicious!"

—NH-RESCUE, TASTEOFHOME.COM

GARLIC-APPLE
PORK ROAST

Ham It Up

Prep a slow-cooked Sunday ham in just five minutes, then transform it into two more weeknight dishes that are ready in about half an hour.

SLOW-COOKED HAM

Entertaining doesn't get much easier than when you serve this tasty five-ingredient ham from the slow cooker. Plus, the leftovers are delicious in casseroles!
—Heather Spring, Sheppard Air Force Base, TX

- -

PREP: 5 min. • **COOK:** 6 hours • **MAKES:** 20 servings

- ½ cup packed brown sugar
- 1 tsp. ground mustard
- 1 tsp. prepared horseradish
- 2 Tbsp. plus ¼ cup cola, divided
- 1 fully cooked boneless ham (5 to 6 lbs.), cut in half

In a small bowl, combine the brown sugar, mustard, horseradish and 2 Tbsp. cola. Rub over ham. Transfer to a 5-qt. slow cooker; add remaining cola to slow cooker. Cover and cook on low until a thermometer reads 140°, 6-8 hours.

3 OZ. COOKED HAM: *143 cal., 4g fat (1g sat. fat), 58mg chol., 1180mg sod., 6g carb. (6g sugars, 0 fiber), 21g pro.*

CREAMY NOODLE CASSEROLE

CREAMY NOODLE CASSEROLE

My husband, Ronald, works long hours and frequently doesn't arrive home until past 7 p.m. This casserole is a smart choice for those late nights—it's just as tasty after it's been warmed in the microwave.
—Barb Marshall, Pickerington, OH

- -

TAKES: 25 min. • **MAKES:** 8 servings

- 1 pkg. (12 oz.) egg noodles
- 1 pkg. (16 oz.) frozen broccoli cuts
- 3 cups cubed fully cooked ham
- 1 cup shredded part-skim mozzarella cheese
- 1 cup shredded Parmesan cheese
- ⅓ cup butter, cubed
- ½ cup half-and-half cream
- ¼ tsp. each garlic powder, salt and pepper

1. In a Dutch oven, cook noodles in boiling water for 5 minutes. Add the broccoli and ham; cook until the noodles are tender, 5-10 minutes longer.
2. Drain; return to pan. Stir in remaining ingredients. Cook and stir over low heat until butter is melted and mixture is heated through.
FREEZE OPTION: Freeze cooled noodle mixture in freezer containers. To use, partially thaw in refrigerator overnight. Microwave, covered, on high in a microwave-safe dish until heated through, gently stirring; add broth or milk if necessary.
1 SERVING: *428 cal., 20g fat (11g sat. fat), 112mg chol., 1087mg sod., 35g carb. (3g sugars, 3g fiber), 25g pro.*

SLOW-COOKED HAM

CHEDDAR HAM SOUP

I knew this recipe was a keeper when my mother-in-law asked for it! The filling soup, rich with loads of leftover ham, veggies and cheese, is creamy and comforting. Although the recipe makes enough to feed a crowd, don't expect any leftovers!
—*Marty Matthews, Clarksville, TN*

TAKES: 30 min. • **MAKES:** 7 servings

- 2 **cups diced peeled potatoes**
- 2 **cups water**
- ½ **cup sliced carrot**
- ¼ **cup chopped onion**
- ¼ **cup butter, cubed**
- ¼ **cup all-purpose flour**
- 2 **cups 2% milk**
- ¼ **to ½ tsp. salt**
- ¼ **tsp. pepper**
- 2 **cups shredded cheddar cheese**
- 1½ **cups cubed fully cooked ham**
- 1 **cup frozen peas**

1. In a large saucepan, combine the potatoes, water, carrot and onion. Bring to a boil. Reduce heat; cover and cook until tender, 10-15 minutes.

2. Meanwhile, in another saucepan, melt butter. Stir in flour until smooth. Gradually add the milk, salt and pepper. Bring to a boil; cook and stir until thickened, about 2 minutes. Stir in cheese until melted. Stir into undrained potato mixture. Add ham and peas; heat through.

1 CUP: *331 cal., 20g fat (12g sat. fat), 73mg chol., 772mg sod., 19g carb. (5g sugars, 2g fiber), 19g pro.*

READER REVIEW

"If I could, I would give this 7 stars! First time I made this (tonight) it came out fantastic. My husband thinks I am a great cook now."
—MOLLYSISK, TASTEOFHOME.COM

Endless Summer

These veggie-packed recipes are twice as nice. Serve them up tonight, or freeze for garden-fresh flavor long after temps fall.

CARNITAS WITH ORZO & PEPPERS IN RED MOLE SAUCE

For a tasty way to stretch my grocery dollars, I combine pork shoulder roast with orzo, peppers and mole for this spicy comfort food.
—Kari Wheaton, South Beloit, IL

PREP: 1 hour 35 min. • **BAKE:** 40 min.
MAKES: 5 servings

- 1 boneless pork shoulder butt roast (1½ to 2 lbs.), cut into ½-in. cubes
- 1½ tsp. salt, divided
- ½ tsp. pepper
- 1 cup uncooked orzo pasta
- 1 each medium green, sweet red and yellow peppers, chopped
- 2 jalapeno peppers, seeded and chopped
- 1 medium onion, chopped
- 1 Tbsp. olive oil
- 1 cup chicken broth
- ¼ cup red mole sauce
- 2 Tbsp. tomato paste
- 1 cup quesadilla or Monterey Jack cheese, shredded
- Optional: Chopped cilantro and sour cream

1. Place pork in a 15x10x1-in. baking pan; sprinkle with 1 tsp. salt and ½ tsp. pepper. Bake at 325° until tender, about 1½ hours. Remove pork from oven. Increase oven setting to 350°.

2. Meanwhile, cook pasta according to package directions; drain and set aside. In a large skillet, saute peppers and onion in oil until crisp-tender. In a greased 13x9-in. baking pan, combine the orzo, peppers and onion.

3. In a small saucepan, whisk the chicken broth, mole sauce, tomato paste and remaining salt. Cook and stir until thickened and bubbly. Pour over orzo and vegetables. Stir in pork; sprinkle with cheese. Cover and bake until heated through, 35-40 minutes. Uncover; broil 3-4 in. from the heat until cheese is golden brown, 4-5 minutes. If desired, top with chopped cilantro and serve with sour cream.

FREEZE OPTION: Cool unbaked casserole; cover and freeze. To use, partially thaw in refrigerator overnight. Remove from the refrigerator 30 minutes before baking. Bake casserole as directed, increasing time as necessary to heat through.

NOTE: Wear disposable gloves when cutting hot peppers; the oils can burn skin. Avoid touching your face.

1⅓ **CUPS:** *559 cal., 26g fat (9g sat. fat), 105mg chol., 1509mg sod., 45g carb. (8g sugars, 5g fiber), 37g pro.*

CARNITAS WITH ORZO & PEPPERS IN RED MOLE SAUCE

SHEPHERD'S PIE TWICE-BAKED POTATOES

(SHOWN ON PAGE 98)

This recipe captures the best of two classics—baked potatoes and shepherd's pie. Serve with a green salad.
—Cyndy Gerken, Naples, FL

PREP: 1¾ hours • **BAKE:** 25 min.
MAKES: 6 servings

- 6 **large russet potatoes**
- 2 **Tbsp. olive oil**
- 1 **lb. ground beef**
- 1 **medium onion, chopped**
- 1 **medium green pepper, chopped**
- 1 **medium sweet red pepper, chopped**
- 4 **garlic cloves, minced**
- 1 **pkg. (16 oz.) frozen mixed vegetables**
- 3 **Tbsp. Worcestershire sauce**
- 1 **Tbsp. tomato paste**
- 1 **Tbsp. steak seasoning**
- ¼ **tsp. salt**
- ⅛ **tsp. pepper**
  Dash cayenne pepper
- 2 **tsp. paprika, divided**
- ½ **cup butter, cubed**
- ¾ **cup heavy whipping cream**
- ¼ **cup sour cream**
- 1 **cup shredded Monterey Jack cheese**
- 1 **cup shredded cheddar cheese**
- ¼ **cup shredded Parmesan cheese**
- 2 **Tbsp. minced chives**

TOPPINGS
- ½ **cup shredded cheddar cheese**
- 1 **Tbsp. minced chives**
- 1 **tsp. paprika**

1. Scrub and pierce potatoes; rub with oil. Bake at 375° until tender, about 1 hour.
2. In a large skillet, cook the beef, onion, peppers and garlic over medium heat until beef is no longer pink; drain. Add the mixed vegetables, Worcestershire sauce, tomato paste, steak seasoning, salt, pepper, cayenne and 1 tsp. paprika. Cook and stir until vegetables are tender.
3. Cut a thin slice off the top of each potato and discard. Scoop out the pulp, leaving thin shells; set shells aside. Mash the pulp with butter. Add whipping cream, sour cream, cheeses and minced chives. Mash until combined.
4. Spoon 1 cup meat mixture into each potato shell; top with ½ cup potato mixture. Sprinkle with remaining paprika.
5. Place on a baking sheet. Bake at 375° for 20 minutes. Sprinkle with cheese; bake until melted, about 5 minutes longer. Sprinkle with chives and paprika.

FREEZE OPTION: Wrap unbaked stuffed potatoes and freeze. To use, partially thaw in refrigerator overnight. Bake as directed; add time until heated through.

1 STUFFED POTATO: *986 cal., 56g fat (32g sat. fat), 183mg chol., 1066mg sod., 86g carb. (12g sugars, 11g fiber), 37g pro.*

ROASTED VEGETABLE SAUCE

ROASTED VEGETABLE SAUCE

I make this recipe regularly and store containers of it in my freezer. I use it with pasta and on pizza—the extra vegetables make it healthier than regular sauce.
—Ann Sheehy, Lawrence, MA

PREP: 35 min. • **BAKE:** 50 min.
MAKES: 16 servings (2 qt.)

- 2 **medium zucchini or yellow summer squash, chopped**
- 3 **medium carrots, chopped**
- 2 **medium onions, chopped**
- ¾ **lb. sliced fresh mushrooms**
- 1 **medium sweet red pepper, chopped**
- 1 **medium green pepper, chopped**
- 3 **Tbsp. olive oil**
- 5 **garlic cloves, minced**
- 3 **tsp. Italian seasoning**
- 1 **tsp. kosher salt**
- ½ **tsp. crushed red pepper flakes, optional**
- 2 **cans (28 oz. each) crushed tomatoes in puree, divided**
- ½ **cup dry red wine**

1. Preheat oven to 400°. Place the first 6 ingredients in a roasting pan; toss with oil, garlic and the seasonings. Roast until tender, 50-60 minutes, stirring occasionally. Cool slightly.
2. Transfer half of the vegetables to a food processor; add 1 can of tomatoes. Process until smooth; remove to a 6-qt. stockpot. Repeat with remaining roasted vegetables and tomatoes.
3. Add wine to sauce; bring to a boil. Simmer, uncovered, 10 minutes to allow flavors to blend, stirring occasionally.

FREEZE OPTION: Freeze cooled sauce in freezer containers. To use, partially thaw in refrigerator overnight. Heat through in a saucepan, stirring occasionally.

½ **CUP:** *81 cal., 3g fat (0 sat. fat), 0 chol., 317mg sod., 12g carb. (7g sugars, 3g fiber), 3g pro.* **Diabetic exchanges:** *2 vegetable, ½ fat.*

Have a Ball!

Need a crowd-pleasing dinner in a pinch? These quick-prep meatball recipes inspire you to think outside spaghetti.

TANGY SWEET-AND-SOUR MEATBALLS

Tangy sauce, a green pepper and pineapple chunks transform premade meatballs into something special. Serve them over rice for a satisfying main dish.
—*Ruth Andrewson, Leavenworth, WA*

TAKES: 30 min. • **MAKES:** 6 servings

- 1 can (20 oz.) pineapple chunks
- ⅓ cup water
- 3 Tbsp. vinegar
- 1 Tbsp. soy sauce
- ½ cup packed brown sugar
- 3 Tbsp. cornstarch
- 30 frozen fully cooked Italian meatballs (about 15 oz.)
- 1 large green pepper, cut into 1-in. pieces
  Hot cooked rice

1. Drain pineapple, reserving juice; set pineapple aside. Add water to juice if needed to measure 1 cup; pour into a large skillet. Add ⅓ cup water, vinegar, soy sauce, brown sugar and cornstarch; stir until smooth.
2. Cook over medium heat until thick, stirring constantly. Add the pineapple, meatballs and green pepper.
3. Simmer, uncovered, until heated through, about 20 minutes. Serve with rice.

5 MEATBALLS: *389 cal., 19g fat (8g sat. fat), 30mg chol., 682mg sod., 47g carb. (36g sugars, 2g fiber), 11g pro.*

TANGY SWEET-AND-SOUR MEATBALLS

SLOW-COOKER MEATBALL SANDWICHES

SLOW-COOKER MEATBALL SANDWICHES

Our approach to meatball sandwiches is a simple one: Cook the meatballs low and slow, load them into hoagie buns, and top with provolone and pepperoncini.
—*Stacie Nicholls, Spring Creek, NV*

PREP: 5 min. • **COOK:** 3 hours • **MAKES:** 8 servings

- 2 pkg. (12 oz. each) frozen fully cooked Italian meatballs, thawed
- 2 jars (24 oz. each) marinara sauce
- 8 hoagie buns, split
- 8 slices provolone cheese
  Sliced pepperoncini, optional

1. Place meatballs and sauce in a 3- or 4-qt. slow cooker. Cook, covered, on low 3-4 hours or until meatballs are heated through.
2. On each bun bottom, layer cheese, meatballs and, if desired, pepperoncini; replace tops.

1 SANDWICH: *526 cal., 20g fat (7g sat. fat), 93mg chol., 1674mg sod., 55g carb. (15g sugars, 4g fiber), 32g pro.*

MEATBALL FLATBREADS

Because these flatbreads taste so amazing, you would never guess how quickly they come together. A little hidden carrot, unnoticed by the kids, adds sweet texture. For a crispier crust, bake the flatbreads in the oven until they are slightly crispy on top before applying tomato sauce.
—Kimberly Berg, North Street, MI

- -

TAKES: 25 min. • **MAKES:** 4 flatbreads

1	can (15 oz.) Italian tomato sauce
1	medium carrot, coarsely chopped
3	fresh basil leaves
1	garlic clove, halved
4	naan flatbreads
2	cups shredded mozzarella cheese
14	frozen fully cooked Italian meatballs, thawed and halved
	Dash each salt, pepper, dried parsley flakes and dried oregano

1. Preheat oven to 400°. Place tomato sauce, carrot, basil and garlic in a food processor; cover and process until pureed.
2. Place flatbreads on an ungreased baking sheet. Spread with tomato sauce mixture; top with cheese and meatballs. Sprinkle with seasonings.
3. Bake on a lower oven rack until cheese is melted, 12-15 minutes.

½ **FLATBREAD:** 228 cal., 10g fat (5g sat. fat), 46mg chol., 835mg sod., 21g carb. (3g sugars, 2g fiber), 14g pro.

READER REVIEW

"Had my grandkids over last weekend and made these flatbreads for them. I ended up making around 20 of them! Easy and delicious."
—JELLYBUG, TASTEOFHOME.COM

MEATBALL FLATBREADS

Turkey Day, Take Two

Raid the fridge for these brilliant ideas that turn Thanksgiving extras into next-day deliciousness.

LOADED MASHED POTATO BITES

Put those leftover mashed potatoes to good use! Transform them into these delectable bites loaded with bacon, cheese and onions.
—Becky Hardin, St. Peters, MO

PREP: 15 min. + chilling • **COOK:** 10 min. • **MAKES:** 1½ dozen

- 3 cups mashed potatoes
- 1½ cups shredded sharp cheddar cheese
- ¾ cup crumbled cooked bacon
- ½ cup chopped green onions
- 2 oz. Colby-Monterey Jack cheese, cut into eighteen ½-in. cubes
- ½ cup panko bread crumbs
- ½ cup grated Parmesan cheese
- ½ tsp. salt
- ½ tsp. pepper
- 1 large egg, beaten
  Oil for deep-fat frying

1. In a large bowl, combine potatoes, shredded cheese, bacon and green onions. Divide into eighteen ¼-cup portions. Shape each portion around a cheese cube to cover completely, forming a ball. Refrigerate, covered, at least 30 minutes.
2. In a shallow bowl, mix bread crumbs, Parmesan cheese, salt and pepper. Place eggs in a separate shallow bowl. Dip potato balls in egg, then in crumb mixture, patting to help coating adhere.
3. In an electric skillet or deep-fat fryer, heat oil to 375°. Fry potato balls, a few at a time, until golden brown, for 2 minutes. Drain on paper towels.
1 PIECE: *227 cal., 19g fat (5g sat. fat), 30mg chol., 420mg sod., 8g carb. (1g sugars, 1g fiber), 7g pro.*

CREAM OF TURKEY & WILD RICE SOUP

CREAM OF TURKEY & WILD RICE SOUP

A dear friend brought me some of this soup when I was ill—and it instantly hit the spot. I asked her for the recipe and I've made it several times since, especially when I have leftover turkey. Now I take it to friends when they're not feeling well. It's filling, and it really warms you up on a wintry day!
—Doris Cox, New Freedom, PA

PREP: 15 min. • **COOK:** 20 min. • **MAKES:** 6 servings

- 1 medium onion, chopped
- 1 can (4 oz.) sliced mushrooms, drained
- 2 Tbsp. butter
- 3 cups water
- 2 cups chicken broth
- 1 pkg. (6 oz.) long grain and wild rice mix
- 2 cups diced cooked turkey
- 1 cup heavy whipping cream
  Minced fresh parsley

In a large saucepan, saute onion and mushrooms in butter until onion is tender. Add water, broth and rice mix with seasoning; bring to a boil. Reduce heat; simmer for 20-25 minutes or until the rice is tender. Stir in turkey and cream; heat through. Sprinkle with parsley.
1 CUP: *364 cal., 21g fat (12g sat. fat), 100mg chol., 857mg sod., 25g carb. (3g sugars, 1g fiber), 19g pro.*

LOADED MASHED POTATO BITES

BISTRO TURKEY CALZONE

Turkey, cheddar, bacon and apple harmonize well in this family-friendly sandwich that bakes to golden brown perfection.
—Donna-Marie Ryan, Topsfield, MA

PREP: 25 min. • **BAKE:** 20 min.
MAKES: 6 servings

- 1 Tbsp. cornmeal
- 1 loaf (1 lb.) frozen pizza dough, thawed
- ¾ lb. thinly sliced cooked turkey
- 8 slices cheddar cheese
- 5 bacon strips, cooked and crumbled
- 1 small tart apple, peeled and thinly sliced
- 1 large egg, beaten
- ½ tsp. Italian seasoning

1. Preheat oven to 400°. Sprinkle cornmeal over a greased baking sheet. On a lightly floured surface, roll dough into a 15-in. circle. Transfer to prepared pan. Arrange half of turkey over half of the dough; top with cheese, bacon, apple and remaining turkey. Fold dough over filling and pinch edges to seal.

2. With a sharp knife, cut 3 slashes in the top of dough. Brush with egg and sprinkle with Italian seasoning. Bake until golden brown, 20-25 minutes. Let stand 5 minutes before cutting into 6 wedges.

1 SLICE: 481 cal., 20g fat (10g sat. fat), 124mg chol., 756mg sod., 38g carb. (3g sugars, 0 fiber), 34g pro.

TEST KITCHEN TIP

Pinching the edges of the dough is sufficient to create a seal, but going just a little bit further makes your calzones pretty as well as leak-proof. Treat the edge as you would any pie crust, and create a pattern in the dough. For the calzones pictured, we pressed out the sealed edge, then rolled it over in a twisting motion.

BISTRO TURKEY CALZONE

Beefed-Up Weeknights

A tender, savory pot roast can't be beat—except maybe by the cozy, comforting meals you create with the leftovers!

ITALIAN POT ROAST

This delicious pot roast is a favorite of my husband's. You'll love the tender beef seasoned with Italian herbs. I'm always asked for the recipe.
—Debbie Daly, Buckingham, IL

- -

PREP: 20 min. • **COOK:** 5 hours • **MAKES:** 8 servings

- 1 boneless beef chuck roast (3 to 4 lbs.)
- 1 can (28 oz.) diced tomatoes, drained
- ¾ cup chopped onion
- ¾ cup Burgundy wine or beef broth
- 1½ tsp. salt
- 1 tsp. dried basil
- ½ tsp. dried oregano
- 1 garlic clove, minced
- ¼ tsp. pepper
- ¼ cup cornstarch
- ½ cup cold water

1. Cut roast in half. Place in a 5-qt. slow cooker. Add the tomatoes, onion, wine, salt, basil, oregano, garlic and pepper. Cover and cook on low for 5-6 hours or until meat is tender.

2. Remove meat to a serving platter; keep warm. Skim fat from cooking juices; transfer to a small saucepan. Combine cornstarch and water until smooth. Gradually stir into pan. Bring to a boil; cook and stir until thickened, about 2 minutes. Serve with meat.

5 OZ. COOKED BEEF: *345 cal., 16g fat (6g sat. fat), 111mg chol., 641mg sod., 10g carb. (4g sugars, 2g fiber), 34g pro.*

ROAST BEEF PASTA SKILLET

ITALIAN POT ROAST

ROAST BEEF PASTA SKILLET

Leftover beef is the star in a skillet dinner that's perfect for two. Chopped tomato adds a burst of fresh flavor, and Parmesan cheese is an enticing finishing touch .
—Bill Hilbrich, St. Cloud, MN

- -

TAKES: 20 min. • **MAKES:** 2 servings

- 1 cup uncooked spiral pasta
- ½ cup chopped onion
- 1 tsp. olive oil
- 1 tsp. butter
- 1 cup cubed cooked roast beef
- 1 tsp. pepper
- ½ cup chopped tomato
- ½ cup grated Parmesan cheese

Cook pasta according to package directions. Meanwhile, in a large skillet, saute onion in oil and butter until tender. Add roast beef and pepper; heat through. Drain pasta; add to beef mixture. Stir in tomato and cheese.

2 CUPS: *448 cal., 14g fat (6g sat. fat), 87mg chol., 358mg sod., 38g carb. (4g sugars, 3g fiber), 40g pro.*

ROAST BEEF WITH CHIVE ROASTED POTATOES

It's hard to believe that last night's beef roast could get any better, but it shines in this heartwarming dish.
—Taste of Home *Test Kitchen*

PREP: 20 min. • **BAKE:** 25 min.
MAKES: 6 servings

- 2 lbs. red potatoes, cut into 1-in. cubes
- 2 Tbsp. olive oil
- 2 tsp. minced chives
- ¾ tsp. salt, divided
- 2 medium onions, halved and thinly sliced
- 1 lb. sliced fresh mushrooms
- ¼ cup butter, cubed
- 1 garlic clove, minced
- 1 tsp. dried rosemary, crushed
- ¼ tsp. pepper
- ⅓ cup dry red wine or beef broth
- 2 cups cubed cooked roast beef
- 1 cup beef gravy

1. Preheat oven to 425°. Place potatoes in a greased 15x10x1-in. baking pan. Drizzle with oil and sprinkle with chives and ¼ tsp. salt; toss to coat. Bake, uncovered, until tender, 25-30 minutes, stirring occasionally.
2. Meanwhile, in a large skillet, saute onions and mushrooms in butter until tender. Add garlic, rosemary, pepper and the remaining ½ tsp. salt; cook 1 minute longer. Stir in wine. Add beef and gravy; heat through. Serve with potatoes.

1 SERVING: *379 cal., 15g fat (6g sat. fat), 66mg chol., 591mg sod., 35g carb. (6g sugars, 5g fiber), 24g pro.*

READER REVIEW

"Quick, simple, and easy—and a great way to use up leftover roast. It's also excellent with leftover roast pork!"
—SUSIE77, TASTEOFHOME.COM

ROAST BEEF WITH CHIVE ROASTED POTATOES

CURRIED PUMPKIN RISOTTO
PAGE 117

Cook It Fast or Slow

Need for speed? Or slow-cooked all day? You can prepare these dishes either way you want. Each recipe comes with instructions for both the pressure cooker and slow cooker. Let these dishes inspire riffs on your favorite meals!

COQ AU VIN

COQ AU VIN

Don't be intimidated by the elegant name. The classic French dish is now made easy in your favorite appliance! This lovely chicken has all the classic flavors of a rich red wine and mushroom sauce but is so simple to make. My family loves it with whole grain country bread or French bread for dipping into the extra sauce.
—*Julie Peterson, Crofton, MD*

- -

PREP: 25 min. • **MAKES:** 6 servings

3	thick-sliced bacon strips, chopped
1½	lbs. boneless skinless chicken thighs
1	medium onion, chopped
2	Tbsp. tomato paste
5	garlic cloves, minced
1½	cups dry red wine or reduced-sodium chicken broth
4	medium carrots, chopped
2	cups sliced baby portobello mushrooms
1	cup reduced-sodium chicken broth
4	fresh thyme sprigs
2	bay leaves
½	tsp. kosher salt
¼	tsp. pepper

Fast Cook: **15 MIN. + RELEASING**

1. Select saute setting on a 6-qt. electric pressure cooker. Adjust for medium heat; add bacon. Cook and stir until crisp. Remove with a slotted spoon; drain on paper towels. Discard drippings, reserving 1 Tbsp. in pressure cooker. Brown chicken on both sides in reserved drippings; remove and set aside.

2. Add onion, tomato paste and garlic to pressure cooker; cook and stir 5 minutes. Add wine; cook 2 minutes. Press cancel.

3. Add chicken, carrots, mushrooms, broth, thyme, bay leaves, salt and pepper to pressure cooker. Lock lid; close pressure-release valve. Adjust to pressure-cook on high for 5 minutes. Quick-release pressure. A thermometer inserted in chicken should read at least 170°.

4. Remove the chicken and vegetables to a serving platter; keep warm. Discard thyme and bay leaves. Select saute setting and adjust for low heat. Simmer cooking juices until reduced by half, 10-15 minutes. Stir in bacon. Serve with chicken and vegetables.

Slow Cook: **6 HOURS**

1. In a large skillet, cook bacon over medium heat until crisp, stirring occasionally. Remove with a slotted spoon; drain on paper towels. Discard drippings, reserving 1 Tbsp. in pan. Brown chicken on both sides in reserved drippings; remove and set aside. Add the onion, tomato paste and garlic to skillet; cook and stir over medium-high heat 5 minutes. Add wine; cook 2 minutes. Transfer to a 4- or 5-qt. slow cooker.

2. Add chicken, carrots, mushrooms, broth, thyme, bay leaves, salt and pepper. Cook, covered, on low 6-7 hours or until chicken is tender.

3. Remove chicken and vegetables to a serving platter; keep warm. Discard thyme and bay leaves. Transfer cooking juices to a large saucepan. Bring to a boil; cook until liquid is reduced by half, 10-15 minutes. Stir in bacon. Serve with chicken and vegetables.

1 SERVING: 244 cal., 11g fat (3g sat. fat), 78mg chol., 356mg sod., 9g carb. (4g sugars, 2g fiber), 23g pro. **Diabetic exchanges:** 3 lean meat, 1 vegetable, ½ fat.

HEARTY PORK & BLACK BEAN NACHOS

My husband and I are both graduate students right now, so we don't have a lot of time to cook dinner. Our family loves coming home to this incredible nacho platter, and I love how easy it is to prepare.
—Faith Stokes, Chickamauga, GA

PREP: 15 min. • **MAKES:** 10 servings

- 1   pkg. (4 oz.) beef jerky
- 3   lbs. pork spareribs, cut into 2-rib sections
- 4   cans (15 oz. each) black beans, rinsed and drained
- 4   cups beef broth
- 1   cup chopped onion
- 6   bacon strips, cooked and crumbled
- 4   tsp. minced garlic
- 1   tsp. crushed red pepper flakes
     Tortilla chips
     Optional: Shredded cheddar cheese, sour cream, thinly sliced green onions, pickled jalapenos and chopped tomatoes

HEARTY PORK & BLACK BEAN NACHOS

Fast Cook: **40 MIN./BATCH + RELEASING**

1. Pulse beef jerky in a food processor until finely ground. Working in batches, place 1½ lbs. ribs in a 6-qt. electric pressure cooker; top with half of the jerky, 2 cans beans, 2 cups broth, ½ cup onion, 3 bacon strips, 2 tsp. garlic and ½ tsp. red pepper flakes. Lock lid; close pressure-release valve. Adjust to pressure-cook on high for 40 minutes.

2. Allow pressure to naturally release for 10 minutes; quick-release any remaining pressure. Remove pork mixture from pressure cooker; make second batch by adding remaining ingredients to cooker. Repeat previous procedure.

3. When cool enough to handle, remove meat from bones; discard bones. Shred meat with 2 forks; return to pressure cooker. Select saute setting and adjust for high heat; heat through. Strain pork mixture; discard juices. Serve with chips and toppings as desired.

Slow Cook: **6 HOURS**

1. Place beef jerky in a food processor; pulse until finely ground. Place ribs in a 5- or 6-qt. slow cooker; top with jerky, beans, broth, onion, bacon, garlic and pepper flakes. Cook, covered, on low 6-8 hours or until meat is tender.

2. When cool enough to handle, remove meat from bones; discard bones. Shred meat with 2 forks; return to slow cooker. Strain pork mixture; discard juices. Serve with chips and toppings as desired.

FREEZE OPTION: Freeze cooled shredded meat mixture with juices in freezer containers. To use, partially thaw in refrigerator overnight. Heat through in a saucepan, stirring occasionally. Strain pork mixture; discard juices. Serve with chips and toppings as desired.

¾ **CUP MEAT MIXTURE:** *469 cal., 24g fat (9g sat. fat), 87mg chol., 1055mg sod., 27g carb. (3g sugars, 7g fiber), 33g pro.*

PHILLY CHEESESTEAK
SANDWICHES

PHILLY CHEESESTEAK SANDWICHES

Melt-in-your-mouth delicious! For this steak and cheese recipe, I like to saute extra onions and green pepper just until they are al dente to add to the top of the meat before melting the cheese.
—Kimberly Wallace, Dennison, OH

PREP: 15 min. • **MAKES:** 8 servings

- 1 beef top sirloin steak (3 lbs.), thinly sliced
- 2 large onions, cut into ½-in. strips
- 1 can (10½ oz.) condensed French onion soup, undiluted
- 2 garlic cloves, minced
- 1 pkg. Italian salad dressing mix
- 2 tsp. beef base
- ½ tsp. pepper
- 2 large red or green peppers, cut into ½-in. strips
- ½ cup pickled pepper rings
- 8 hoagie buns or French rolls, spllit
- 8 slices provolone cheese

Fast Cook: **15 MIN. + RELEASING**

1. Combine the first 7 ingredients in a 6-qt. electric pressure cooker. Lock lid; close pressure-release valve. Adjust to pressure-cook on high for 10 minutes. Quick-release pressure. Add peppers and pepper rings. Lock lid; close pressure-release valve. Adjust to pressure-cook on high for an additional 5 minutes. Let pressure release naturally for 10 minutes; quick-release any remaining pressure. Press cancel.

2. Place buns on ungreased baking sheets, cut sides up. Using tongs, place beef and vegetables on bun bottoms. Place cheese on bun tops. Broil 3-4 in. from heat until cheese is melted, 1-2 minutes. Close sandwiches; serve with cooking juices.

Slow Cook: **7 HOURS**

1. Combine the first 7 ingredients in a 4- or 5-qt. slow cooker. Cook, covered, on low 6 hours. Stir in peppers and pepper rings; cook, covered, 1-2 hours or until meat is tender.

2. Place buns on ungreased baking sheets, cut sides up. Using tongs, place beef and vegetables on bun bottoms. Place cheese on bun tops. Broil 3-4 in. from heat until cheese melts, 1-2 minutes. Close sandwiches; serve with cooking juices.

1 SANDWICH: *547 cal., 18g fat (7g sat. fat), 85mg chol., 1381mg sod., 45g carb. (10g sugars, 3g fiber), 51g pro.*

CURRIED PUMPKIN RISOTTO

This easy pumpkin risotto tastes like fall and gets a flavor boost from the curry.
—Andrea Reaves, Stephens City, VA

PREP: 10 min. • **MAKES:** 6 servings

- 1 Tbsp. olive oil
- 1 small onion, chopped
- 1 cup uncooked arborio rice
- 2 garlic cloves, minced
- 2 cups chicken stock
- ½ cup canned pumpkin
- 1 Tbsp. curry powder
- 1½ tsp. minced fresh rosemary or ¾ tsp. dried rosemary, crushed
- ½ tsp. salt
- ¼ tsp. pepper

CURRIED PUMPKIN RISOTTO

Fast Cook: **15 MIN.**

1. Select saute setting on a 6-qt. electric pressure cooker. Adjust for medium heat; add oil. When oil is hot, cook and stir onion until crisp-tender, 5-7 minutes. Add rice and garlic; cook and stir until rice is coated, 1-2 minutes. Add stock; cook 1 minute, stirring to loosen browned bits from pan. Press cancel.

2. Stir in pumpkin, curry powder, rosemary, salt and pepper. Lock lid; close pressure-release valve. Adjust to pressure-cook on high for 7 minutes. Quick-release pressure. If desired, serve with additional minced rosemary.

Slow Cook: **3 HOURS**

1. Heat oil in a 3- or 4-qt. slow cooker on high until hot. Add rice; stir to coat. Stir in remaining ingredients.

2. Cook, covered, on low for 3-4 hours or until rice is tender, stirring halfway through cooking.

½ CUP: 163 cal., 3g fat (0 sat. fat), 0 chol., 369mg sod., 30g carb. (2g sugars, 2g fiber), 4g pro. **Diabetic exchanges:** 2 starch, ½ fat.

BEEF SHORT RIBS WITH TOMATO FIG CHUTNEY

BEEF SHORT RIBS WITH TOMATO FIG CHUTNEY

Slow-roasted tender meats can happen in half the time if you have an electric pressure cooker—or go low and slow if you prefer the slow-cooker method. I like to serve these savory beef short ribs over mashed potatoes, egg noodles or rice.
—Caitlin Marcellino, Apopka, FL

PREP: 30 min. • **MAKES:** 4 servings

- 1 tsp. olive oil
- 3 bacon strips, chopped
- 1 lb. boneless beef short ribs
- ½ tsp. salt
- ¼ tsp. pepper
- 1 lb. grape tomatoes
- 1 medium onion, chopped
- 3 garlic cloves, minced
- 2 cups water
- 1 cup Marsala wine or beef broth
- ¼ cup fig preserves
- 3 Tbsp. minced fresh rosemary or 1 Tbsp. dried rosemary, crushed

Fast Cook: **35 MIN. + RELEASING**

1. Select saute setting on a 6-qt. electric pressure cooker. Adjust for medium heat; add oil. When oil is hot, cook and stir the bacon until crisp. Remove with a slotted spoon; drain on paper towels. Sprinkle ribs with salt and pepper. Brown on all sides in drippings. Remove from pressure cooker.

2. Add tomatoes, onion and garlic to drippings; cook and stir until crisp-tender, 3-5 minutes, mashing tomatoes lightly. Stir in water, Marsala, fig preserves and rosemary. Cook 1 minute, stirring to loosen browned bits from pan. Return ribs and bacon to pressure cooker. Press cancel. Lock lid; close pressure-release valve. Adjust to pressure-cook on high for 35 minutes. Let the pressure release naturally. Remove ribs; shred with 2 forks and serve with reserved cooking juices.

Slow Cook: **6 HOURS**

1. In a large skillet, heat oil over medium heat; cook and stir bacon until crisp. Remove with a slotted spoon; drain on paper towels. Sprinkle ribs with salt and pepper. Brown on all sides in drippings. Transfer to a 4-qt. slow cooker.

2. In same skillet, add tomatoes, onion and garlic to drippings; cook and stir until crisp-tender, 3-5 minutes, mashing tomatoes lightly. Add tomato mixture to slow cooker; stir in water, Marsala, fig preserves and rosemary.

3. Cook, covered, on low 6-8 hours or until ribs are tender. Remove ribs; shred with 2 forks and serve with reserved cooking juices.

1 SERVING: *368 cal., 19g fat (7g sat. fat), 60mg chol., 472mg sod., 25g carb. (18g sugars, 2g fiber), 19g pro.*

SUPREME PIZZA QUINOA BOWL

If you like pizza night, give this low-calorie quinoa casserole a try! It's a fun way to sneak veggies into a meal that's packed with the flavors you love.
—Julie Peterson, Crofton, MD

PREP: 15 min. • **MAKES:** 6 servings

- 1 Tbsp. olive oil
- ½ lb. Italian turkey sausage links, casings removed
- 1 small red onion, sliced
- 2 cups sliced fresh mushrooms
- 2 cups chicken broth
- 1 cup quinoa, rinsed
- 2 cups pizza sauce
- 1 pkg. (6 oz.) sliced turkey pepperoni
- 1 medium green pepper, chopped
- ½ cup shredded part-skim mozzarella cheese
- ½ cup shredded Parmesan cheese
  Optional: Minced fresh basil, sliced olives, oil-packed sun-dried tomatoes (drained), banana peppers and red pepper flakes

SUPREME PIZZA QUINOA BOWL

Fast Cook: **10 MIN.**

1. Select saute setting on a 6-qt. electric pressure cooker. Adjust for medium heat; add oil. When oil is hot, cook and stir sausage and onion until sausage is no longer pink and onion is tender, 5-7 minutes, breaking up sausage into crumbles; drain. Press cancel.
2. Stir in mushrooms and broth. Add quinoa (do not stir). Lock lid; close pressure-release valve. Adjust to pressure-cook on high for 2 minutes. Quick-release pressure. Press cancel.
3. Stir in pizza sauce, pepperoni and green pepper; cover and let stand until pepper softens slightly, 5-10 minutes. Sprinkle servings with cheeses. If desired, serve with optional toppings.

Slow Cook: **6 HOURS**

1. In a large skillet, heat oil over medium heat; cook sausage and onion until sausage is no longer pink, 5-7 minutes, breaking up sausage into large crumbles. Drain.
2. Transfer sausage and onion to a 4- or 5-qt. slow cooker. Stir in mushrooms, broth and quinoa. Cook, covered, 5 hours; stir in pizza sauce, pepperoni and green pepper.
3. Cook, covered, 1 hour or until pepper is tender. Sprinkle servings with cheeses. If desired, serve with optional toppings.

1¼ CUPS: *350 cal., 15g fat (5g sat. fat), 61mg chol., 1481mg sod., 30g carb. (6g sugars, 4g fiber), 25g pro.*

SPICY BEEF
VEGETABLE STEW

SPICY BEEF VEGETABLE STEW

This zesty ground beef and vegetable stew is flavorful and comes together so quickly. It makes a complete meal when served with warm cornbread, sourdough or French bread. And leftovers are wonderful for a hearty lunch.
—*Lynnette Davis, Tullahoma, TN*

PREP: 10 min. • **MAKES:** 8 servings (3 qt.)

- 1 lb. lean ground beef (90% lean)
- 3½ cups water
- 1 jar (24 oz.) meatless pasta sauce
- 1 pkg. (16 oz.) frozen mixed vegetables
- 1 can (10 oz.) diced tomatoes and green chiles, undrained
- 1 cup chopped onion
- 1 cup sliced celery
- 1 tsp. beef bouillon granules
- 1 tsp. pepper

Fast Cook: **5 MIN. + RELEASING**

Select saute setting on a 6-qt. electric pressure cooker; adjust for medium heat. Cook beef until no longer pink, 6-8 minutes, breaking into crumbles; drain. Press cancel. Stir in remaining ingredients. Lock lid; close pressure-release valve. Adjust to pressure-cook on high for 5 minutes. Let pressure release naturally.

Slow Cook: **8 HOURS**

1. In a large skillet, cook beef and onion over medium heat until meat is no longer pink; drain.
2. Transfer to a 5-qt. slow cooker. Stir in remaining ingredients. Cover and cook on low 8 hours or until vegetables are tender.

FREEZE OPTION: Freeze cooled stew in freezer containers. To use, partially thaw in refrigerator overnight. Heat through in a saucepan, stirring occasionally and adding a little water if necessary.

1½ CUPS: *177 cal., 5g fat (2g sat. fat), 35mg chol., 675mg sod., 19g carb. (8g sugars, 5g fiber), 15g pro.* **Diabetic exchanges:** *2 lean meat, 1 starch.*

BEEF BRISKET IN BEER

One bite of this tender brisket and your family will be hooked! The rich gravy is just perfect for spooning over a side of creamy mashed potatoes.
—Eunice Stoen, Decorah, IA

PREP: 15 min. • **MAKES:** 6 servings

- 1 fresh beef brisket (2½ to 3 lbs.)
- 2 tsp. liquid smoke, optional
- 1 tsp. celery salt
- ½ tsp. pepper
- ¼ tsp. salt
- 1 large onion, sliced
- 1 can (12 oz.) beer or nonalcoholic beer
- 2 tsp. Worcestershire sauce
- 2 Tbsp. cornstarch
- ¼ cup cold water

TEST KITCHEN TIP

Liquid smoke is a great addition to this recipe, as it adds depth of flavor. Be careful not to overdo it; a small amount goes a long way. Look for liquid smoke in your grocery store near the spices and marinades.

BEEF BRISKET IN BEER

Fast Cook: **70 MIN. + RELEASING**

1. Cut brisket in half; rub with liquid smoke, if desired, and celery salt, pepper and salt. Place brisket fatty side up in a 6-qt. electric pressure cooker. Top with sliced onion. Combine the beer and Worcestershire sauce; pour over meat.

2. Lock lid; close pressure-release valve. Adjust to pressure-cook on high for 70 minutes. Allow pressure to naturally release for 10 minutes; quick-release any remaining pressure. If the brisket isn't fork-tender, reseal pressure cooker and cook for an additional 10-15 minutes.

3. Remove brisket, cover with foil and keep warm. Strain cooking juices, then return juices to pressure cooker. Select saute setting and adjust for medium heat; bring liquid to a boil. In a small bowl, mix cornstarch and water until smooth; gradually stir into juices. Cook and stir until sauce is thickened, about 2 minutes. Serve sauce with beef.

Slow Cook: **8 HOURS**

1. Cut brisket in half; rub with liquid smoke, if desired, and celery salt, pepper and salt. Place in a 3-qt. slow cooker. Top with onion. Combine beer and Worcestershire sauce; pour over meat. Cover and cook on low for 8-9 hours or until tender.

2. Remove brisket and keep warm. Strain cooking juices; transfer to a small saucepan. In a small bowl, combine cornstarch and water until smooth; stir into juices. Bring to a boil; cook and stir until thickened, about 2 minutes. Serve sauce with beef.

5 OZ. BRISKET WITH ABOUT ⅓ CUP SAUCE: *285 cal., 8g fat (3g sat. fat), 80mg chol., 430mg sod., 7g carb. (3g sugars, 0 fiber), 39g pro.* **Diabetic exchanges:** *5 lean meat, ½ starch.*

CARROT CAKE OATMEAL

CARROT CAKE OATMEAL

This warm breakfast cereal is a great way to get your veggies in the morning and keep a healthy diet! For extra crunch, I garnish individual servings with ground walnuts or pecans.
—Debbie Kain, Colorado Springs, CO

- -

PREP: 10 min. • **MAKES:** 8 servings

4½ cups water
1 can (20 oz.) crushed pineapple, undrained
2 cups shredded carrots
1 cup steel-cut oats
1 cup raisins
2 tsp. ground cinnamon
1 tsp. pumpkin pie spice
Brown sugar, optional

HOW-TO

Safely Vent Your Pressure Cooker

Just pick up a pair of tongs for safe, easy venting of your electric pressure cooker. Use the tongs to carefully turn the release valve—and keep your hands and face clear of the steam vent.

Fast Cook: **10 MIN. + RELEASING**
In a 6-qt. electric pressure cooker coated with cooking spray, combine the first 7 ingredients. Lock lid; close pressure-release valve. Adjust to pressure-cook on high for 10 minutes. Let pressure release naturally for 10 minutes; quick-release any remaining pressure. If desired, sprinkle oatmeal with brown sugar.

Slow Cook: **6 HOURS**
In a 4-qt. slow cooker coated with cooking spray, combine the first 7 ingredients. Cover and cook on low for 6-8 hours or until oats are tender and liquid is absorbed. If desired, sprinkle with brown sugar.

1 CUP: *197 cal., 2g fat (0 sat. fat), 0 chol., 23mg sod., 46g carb. (26g sugars, 4g fiber), 4g pro.*

CUBAN PULLED PORK SANDWICHES

I lived in Florida for a while and loved the pork served there, so I went about making it for myself! The flavorful meat makes amazing Cuban sandwiches, but you can use it in traditional pulled pork sandwiches and tacos, too.
—Lacie Griffin, Austin, TX

PREP: 20 min. • **MAKES:** 16 servings

- 1 boneless pork shoulder butt roast (4 to 5 lbs.)
- 2 tsp. salt
- 2 tsp. pepper
- 1 Tbsp. olive oil
- 1 cup orange juice
- ½ cup lime juice
- 12 garlic cloves, minced
- 2 Tbsp. spiced rum, optional
- 2 Tbsp. ground coriander
- 2 tsp. white pepper
- 1 tsp. cayenne pepper

SANDWICHES

- 2 loaves (1 lb. each) French bread
  Yellow mustard, optional
- 16 dill pickle slices
- 1½ lbs. thinly sliced deli ham
- 1½ lbs. Swiss cheese, sliced

CUBAN PULLED PORK SANDWICHES

Fast Cook: **25 MIN. + RELEASING**

1. Cut pork into 2-in.-thick pieces; season with salt and pepper. Select saute setting on a 6-qt. electric pressure cooker. Adjust for medium heat; add oil. When oil is hot, brown pork in batches. Remove from pressure cooker.

2. Add orange and lime juices, stirring to scrape browned bits from bottom of cooker. Add garlic, rum if desired, coriander, white pepper and cayenne pepper. Return pork and any collected juices to cooker. Press cancel.

3. Lock lid; close pressure-release valve. Adjust to pressure-cook on high for 25 minutes. Let pressure release naturally for 10 minutes; quick-release any remaining pressure. Remove roast; when cool enough to handle, shred with 2 forks. Remove 1 cup cooking liquid from cooker; add to pork and toss together.

4. Cut each loaf of bread in half lengthwise. If desired, spread mustard over cut sides of bread. Layer bottom halves of bread with pickles, pork, ham and cheese. Replace tops. Cut each loaf into 8 slices.

Slow Cook: **8 HOURS**

1. Sprinkle roast with salt and pepper; place in a 6- or 7-qt. slow cooker. Combine oil, juices, garlic, rum if desired and spices; add to slow cooker. Cook, covered, on low 8-10 hours or until tender. Remove roast; shred with 2 forks.

2. Cut each loaf of bread in half lengthwise. If desired, spread mustard over cut sides of bread. Layer bottom halves of bread with pickles, pork, ham and cheese. Replace tops. Cut each loaf into 8 slices.

1 SANDWICH: *619 cal., 31g fat (13g sat. fat), 143mg chol., 1257mg sod., 35g carb. (5g sugars, 2g fiber), 50g pro.*

CHICKEN ENCHILADA SOUP

This soup delivers a big bowl of fresh comfort—just ask my husband. Toppings like avocado, sour cream and tortilla strips are a must.
—Heather Sewell, Harrisonville, MO

- -

PREP: 25 min. • **MAKES:** 8 servings (3¼ qt.)

1	Tbsp. canola oil
2	Anaheim or poblano peppers, finely chopped
1	medium onion, chopped
3	garlic cloves, minced
1	lb. boneless skinless chicken breasts
1	carton (48 oz.) chicken broth
1	can (14½ oz.) Mexican diced tomatoes, undrained
1	can (10 oz.) enchilada sauce
2	Tbsp. tomato paste
1	Tbsp. chili powder
2	tsp. ground cumin
½	tsp. pepper
½	to 1 tsp. chipotle hot pepper sauce, optional
⅓	cup minced fresh cilantro
	Optional: Shredded cheddar cheese, cubed avocado, sour cream and tortilla strips

CHICKEN ENCHILADA SOUP

TEST KITCHEN TIP

Canola oil is high in monounsaturated fat, a type that helps to decrease blood cholesterol levels, and low in saturated fat, which can increase blood cholesterol. Olive oil would also taste great in this recipe and has the same healthy-fat properties.

Fast Cook: **20 MIN. + RELEASING**

1. Select saute setting on a 6-qt. electric pressure cooker and adjust for high heat; add oil. When oil is hot, add peppers and onion; cook and stir until tender, 6-8 minutes. Add garlic; cook 1 minute longer.
2. Add chicken, broth, tomatoes, enchilada sauce, tomato paste, seasonings and, if desired, pepper sauce. Stir. Lock lid; close pressure-release valve. Adjust to pressure-cook on high for 8 minutes. Allow pressure to naturally release for 7 minutes; quick-release any remaining pressure.
3. Remove chicken from pressure cooker. Shred with 2 forks; return to pressure cooker. Stir in minced cilantro. Serve with toppings as desired.

Slow Cook: **6 HOURS**

1. In a large skillet, heat oil over medium heat. Add peppers and onion; cook and stir until tender, 6-8 minutes. Add garlic; cook 1 minute longer. Transfer pepper mixture and chicken to a 5- or 6-qt. slow cooker. Stir in broth, tomatoes, enchilada sauce, tomato paste, seasonings and, if desired, pepper sauce. Cook, covered, on low 6-8 hours or until chicken is tender (a thermometer should read at least 165°).
2. Remove chicken from slow cooker. Shred with 2 forks; return to slow cooker. Stir in cilantro. Serve with toppings as desired.

FREEZE OPTION: Freeze cooled soup in freezer containers. To use, partially thaw in refrigerator overnight. Heat through in a saucepan, stirring occasionally and adding a little water if necessary.

1½ **CUPS:** 132 cal., 4g fat (1g sat. fat), 35mg chol., 1117mg sod., 9g carb. (4g sugars, 2g fiber), 14g pro.

BURGUNDY BEEF

When my adult children come for dinner, this is the recipe I turn to first. They all just love it!
—Urilla Cheverie, Andover, MA

PREP: 10 min. • **MAKES:** 10 servings

- 4 lbs. beef top sirloin steak, cut into 1-in. cubes
- 3 large onions, sliced
- 1 cup water
- 1 cup burgundy wine or beef broth
- 1 cup ketchup
- ¼ cup quick-cooking tapioca
- ¼ cup packed brown sugar
- ¼ cup Worcestershire sauce
- 4 tsp. paprika
- 1½ tsp. salt
- 1 tsp. minced garlic
- 1 tsp. ground mustard
- 2 Tbsp. cornstarch
- 3 Tbsp. cold water
  Hot cooked noodles

BURGUNDY BEEF

Fast Cook: **20 MIN. + RELEASING**

1. Combine the first 12 ingredients in a 6-qt. electric pressure cooker. Lock lid; close pressure-release valve. Adjust to pressure-cook on high for 20 minutes. Let pressure release naturally for 10 minutes; quick-release any remaining pressure. Press cancel.
2. Combine cornstarch and water until smooth; stir into the pressure cooker. Select saute setting and adjust for low heat. Simmer, stirring constantly, until thickened, 1-2 minutes. Serve with noodles.

Slow Cook: **8¼ HOURS**

1. In a 5-qt. slow cooker, combine the first 12 ingredients. Cook, covered, on low 8-9 hours or until meat is tender.
2. Combine cornstarch and water until smooth; stir into pan juices. Cook, covered, on high until gravy is thickened, about 15 minutes. Serve with noodles.

FREEZE OPTION: Place beef in freezer containers; top with sauce. Cool and freeze. To use, partially thaw in refrigerator overnight. Heat through in a covered saucepan, stirring gently and adding a little water if necessary.

1 CUP: *347 cal., 8g fat (3g sat. fat), 74mg chol., 811mg sod., 24g carb. (15g sugars, 1g fiber), 40g pro.*

EASY PORK POSOLE

EASY PORK POSOLE

Looking for a meal in a bowl? Sit down to a Mexican classic full of cubed pork, sliced sausage. hominy and more. Whether you cook it fast or slow, you will be delighted with the results!
—Greg Fontenot, The Woodlands, TX

PREP: 30 min. • **MAKES:** 8 servings (2 qt.)

1	Tbsp. canola oil
½	lb. boneless pork shoulder butt roast, cubed
½	lb. fully cooked andouille sausage links, sliced
6	cups reduced-sodium chicken broth
2	medium tomatoes, seeded and chopped
1	can (15 oz.) hominy, rinsed and drained
1	cup minced fresh cilantro
1	medium onion, chopped
4	green onions, chopped
1	jalapeno pepper, seeded and chopped
2	garlic cloves, minced
1	Tbsp. chili powder
1	tsp. ground cumin
½	tsp. cayenne pepper
½	tsp. coarsely ground pepper
	Optional: Corn tortillas, chopped onion, minced fresh cilantro and lime wedges

TEST KITCHEN TIP

Canned hominy is dried corn that has been treated and soaked, resulting in a puffy, chewy texture. Look for hominy near the canned beans in the grocery store.

Fast Cook: **15 MIN. + RELEASING**

1. Select saute setting on a 6-qt. electric pressure cooker and adjust for medium heat; add oil. When oil is hot, cook and stir cubed pork and sausage until browned; drain. Return all to pressure cooker. Press cancel.
2. Add next 12 ingredients. Lock lid; close pressure-release valve. Adjust to pressure-cook on high for 10 minutes. Let pressure release naturally for 5 minutes; quick-release any remaining pressure. If desired, serve with tortillas, additional onion, cilantro and lime wedges.

Slow Cook: **6 HOURS**

1. In a large skillet, heat oil over medium-high heat. Brown pork and sausage; drain. Transfer to a 4-qt. slow cooker.
2. Stir in broth, tomatoes, hominy, cilantro, onion, green onions, jalapeno, garlic, chili powder, cumin, cayenne and pepper. Cook, covered, on low 6-8 hours or until meat is tender. If desired, serve with tortillas, additional onion, cilantro and lime wedges.

NOTE: *Wear disposable gloves when cutting hot peppers; the oils can burn skin. Avoid touching your face.*

1 CUP: *190 cal., 11g fat (3g sat. fat), 54mg chol., 957mg sod., 12g carb. (2g sugars, 3g fiber), 14g pro.*

HAM & CHEDDAR BREAKFAST CASSEROLE

This easy, cheesy casserole has made appearances at holiday breakfasts, potlucks and even my daughter's college apartment to feed her hungry roommates. This is also our family's go-to recipe for action-packed mornings.
—Patty Bernhard, Greenville, OH

PREP: 20 min. • **MAKES:** 6 servings

- 6 **large eggs**
- ½ **cup 2% milk**
- ½ **tsp. salt**
- ¼ **tsp. pepper**
- 4 **cups frozen shredded hash brown potatoes, thawed**
- 1 **cup cubed fully cooked ham**
- ½ **medium onion, chopped**
- 2 **cups shredded cheddar cheese**

Fast Cook: **35 MIN. + RELEASING**

1. Whisk together eggs, milk, salt and pepper. Combine the potatoes, ham, onion and cheese; transfer to a greased 1½-qt. baking dish; pour egg mixture over top. Cover dish with foil.
2. Place trivet insert and 1 cup water into a 6-qt. electric pressure cooker. Fold an 18x12-in. piece of foil lengthwise into thirds, making a sling. Use the sling to lower dish onto trivet. Lock lid; close pressure-release valve.
3. Adjust to pressure-cook on high for 35 minutes. Let pressure release naturally for 10 minutes; quick-release any remaining pressure. Using foil sling, carefully remove baking dish. Let stand 10 minutes.

Slow Cook: **4 HOURS + STANDING**

1. Whisk together first 4 ingredients. Place a third of the potatoes in a greased 5- or 6-qt. slow cooker insert; layer with a third of each of the following: ham, onion and cheese. Repeat layers twice. Pour egg mixture over top. Refrigerate, covered, overnight.
2. Cook, covered, on low 4-5 hours, until contents are set and edges begin to brown. Turn off slow cooker. Remove insert; let stand, uncovered, 30 minutes before serving.

1 SERVING: *324 cal., 19g fat (9g sat. fat), 239mg chol., 822mg sod., 17g carb. (3g sugars, 1g fiber), 22g pro.*

COOK IT FAST OR SLOW

ENGLISH PUB SPLIT PEA SOUP

This family-favorite recipe is the same one my grandmother used. Now with the magic of today's appliances, I can spend just a few minutes putting it together, and let my cooker do the rest. Finish it with more milk if you like your soup a bit thinner.
—Judy Batson, Tampa, FL

PREP: 15 min. • **MAKES:** 8 servings (2 qt.)

- 1 meaty ham bone
- 4 cups water
- 1 bottle (12 oz.) light beer
- 1⅓ cups dried green split peas, rinsed
- 2 celery ribs, chopped
- 1 large carrot, chopped
- 1 sweet onion, chopped
- 1 Tbsp. prepared English mustard
- ½ cup 2% milk
- ¼ cup minced fresh parsley
- ½ tsp. salt
- ¼ tsp. pepper
- ¼ tsp. ground nutmeg
  Additional minced fresh parsley, optional

Fast Cook: **15 MIN. + RELEASING**

1. Place ham bone in a 6-qt. electric pressure cooker. Add water, beer, peas, celery, carrot, onion and mustard. Lock lid; close pressure-release valve. Adjust to pressure-cook on high for 15 minutes. Let pressure release naturally.
2. Remove ham bone from soup. Cool slightly, trim away fat and remove meat from bone; discard fat and bone. Cut meat into bite-sized pieces; return to pressure cooker. Stir in remaining ingredients. If desired, top with additional minced parsley.

Slow Cook: **5 HOURS**

1. Place ham bone in a 4-qt. slow cooker. Add water, beer, peas, celery, carrot, onion and mustard. Cook, covered, on high 5-6 hours or until peas are tender.
2. Remove ham bone from soup. Cool slightly, trim away fat and remove meat from bone; discard fat and bone. Cut meat into bite-sized pieces; return to slow cooker. Stir in the remaining ingredients. If desired, top with minced parsley.

NOTE: We used Colman's prepared mustard when testing this recipe. If you can't find English mustard, horseradish mustard is a good substitute.

1 CUP: *141 cal., 1g fat (0 sat. fat), 1mg chol., 193mg sod., 25g carb. (6g sugars, 9g fiber), 9g pro.* **Diabetic exchanges:** *1½ starch, 1 lean meat.*

ITALIAN SHRIMP & PASTA

This dish will remind you a bit of classic shrimp Creole, but it has a surprise Italian twist. The hands-off ease of cooking makes it perfect for company.
—Karen Edwards, Sanford, ME

PREP: 20 min. • **MAKES:** 6 servings

- 2 Tbsp. canola oil
- 1 lb. boneless skinless chicken thighs, cut into 2x1-in. strips
- 1 can (28 oz.) crushed tomatoes
- 1½ cups water
- 2 celery ribs, chopped
- 1 medium green pepper, cut into 1-in. pieces
- 1 medium onion, coarsely chopped
- 2 garlic cloves, minced
- 1 Tbsp. sugar
- ½ tsp. salt
- ½ tsp. Italian seasoning
- ⅛ to ¼ tsp. cayenne pepper
- 1 bay leaf
- 1 cup uncooked orzo or other small pasta
- 1 lb. peeled and deveined cooked shrimp (31-40 per lb.)

ITALIAN SHRIMP & PASTA

Fast Cook: **20 MIN.**

1. Select saute setting on a 6-qt. electric pressure cooker and adjust for medium heat. Add 1 Tbsp. oil. When oil is hot, brown chicken in batches, adding oil as needed. Press cancel. Stir in next 11 ingredients. Lock lid; close pressure-release valve. Adjust to pressure-cook on high for 8 minutes. Quick-release pressure. Press cancel.

2. Discard bay leaf. Select saute setting and adjust for medium heat. Stir in orzo. Cook until al dente, stirring often. Stir in shrimp; cook until shrimp are heated through, about 2 minutes more. Press cancel.

Slow Cook: **7½ HOURS**

1. In a large skillet, heat oil; brown chicken. Transfer to a 3-qt. slow cooker. Stir in tomatoes, water, celery, pepper, onion, garlic, sugar and seasonings. Cook, covered, on low 7-8 hours or until chicken is just tender.

2. Discard bay leaf. Stir in pasta; cook, covered, on high until pasta is tender, about 15 minutes. Stir in shrimp; cook, covered, until heated through, about 5 minutes longer.

1½ **CUPS:** *418 cal., 12g fat (2g sat. fat), 165mg chol., 611mg sod., 40g carb. (10g sugars, 4g fiber), 36g pro.* **Diabetic exchanges:** *5 lean meat, 2½ starch, 1 fat.*

BEEF TIPS

BEEF TIPS

These beef tips remind me of a childhood favorite. I like to cook them with mushrooms and serve them over brown rice, noodles or mashed potatoes.
—*Amy Lents, Grand Forks, ND*

PREP: 20 min. • **MAKES:** 4 servings

- 3 tsp. olive oil
- 1 beef top sirloin steak (1 lb.), cubed
- ½ tsp. salt
- ¼ tsp. pepper
- ⅓ cup dry red wine or beef broth
- ½ lb. sliced baby portobello mushrooms
- 1 small onion, halved and sliced
- 2 cups beef broth
- 1 Tbsp. Worcestershire sauce
- 3 to 4 Tbsp. cornstarch
- ¼ cup cold water
  Hot cooked mashed potatoes

TEST KITCHEN TIP

The next day, stir a little heavy cream or sour cream into leftover sauce and serve over pasta for a dish that's different from the first meal, but every bit as tasty.

Fast Cook: **15 MIN.**

1. Select saute setting on a 6-qt. electric pressure cooker and adjust for medium heat. Add 2 tsp. oil. Sprinkle beef with salt and pepper. Brown meat in batches, adding oil as needed. Transfer meat to a bowl.

2. Add wine to cooker, stirring to loosen browned bits. Press cancel. Return beef to cooker; add the mushrooms, onion, broth and Worcestershire sauce. Lock lid; close the pressure-release valve. Adjust to pressure-cook on high for 15 minutes. Quick-release pressure.

3. Select saute setting and adjust for low heat; bring liquid to a boil. In a small bowl, mix cornstarch and water until smooth; gradually stir into beef mixture. Cook and stir until sauce is thickened, 1-2 minutes. Serve with mashed potatoes.

Slow Cook: **6¼ HOURS**

1. Place mushrooms and onion in a 3-qt. slow cooker. Sprinkle beef with salt and pepper. In a large skillet, heat 1 tsp. oil over medium-high heat; brown meat in batches, adding more oil as needed. Transfer meat to slow cooker.

2. Add wine to skillet, stirring to loosen browned bits from pan. Stir in broth and Worcestershire sauce; pour over meat. Cook, covered, on low 6-8 hours or until meat is tender.

3. In a small bowl, mix cornstarch and cold water until smooth; gradually stir into slow cooker. Cook, covered, on high until gravy is thickened, 15-30 minutes. Serve with mashed potatoes.

1 CUP: *212 cal., 7g fat (2g sat. fat), 46mg chol., 836mg sod., 8g carb. (2g sugars, 1g fiber), 27g pro.* **Diabetic exchanges:** *3 lean meat, ½ starch, ½ fat.*

TURKEY WITH BERRY COMPOTE

This delicious dish is a terrific way to get all that yummy turkey flavor without heating up the house, and the berries make the perfect summer chutney. For a browner turkey, just broil for a few minutes before serving.
—*Margaret Bracher, Robertsdale, AL*

- -

PREP: 15 min.
MAKES: 12 servings (3¼ cups compote)

- 1 tsp. salt
- ½ tsp. garlic powder
- ½ tsp. dried thyme
- ½ tsp. pepper
- 2 boneless skinless turkey breast halves (2 lbs. each)
- ⅓ cup water

COMPOTE

- 2 medium apples, peeled and finely chopped
- 2 cups fresh raspberries
- 2 cups fresh blueberries
- 1 cup white grape juice
- ¼ tsp. crushed red pepper flakes
- ¼ tsp. ground ginger

TURKEY WITH BERRY COMPOTE

Fast Cook: **45 MIN. + RELEASING**

1. Mix salt, garlic powder, thyme and pepper; rub over turkey breasts. Place in a 6-qt. electric pressure cooker. Pour water around turkey. Lock lid; close pressure-release valve. Adjust to pressure-cook on high for 30 minutes. Allow pressure to release naturally for 10 minutes; quick-release any remaining pressure. A thermometer inserted in turkey breast should read at least 165°.
2. Remove turkey and cooking juices from pressure cooker; tent with foil. Let stand before slicing.
3. Select saute setting and adjust for low heat. Add the compote ingredients; simmer, uncovered, until mixture is slightly thickened and apples are tender, 15-20 minutes, stirring occasionally. Serve turkey with compote.

Slow Cook: **3 HOURS + STANDING**

1. Mix salt, garlic powder, thyme and pepper; rub over turkey breasts. Place in a 5- or 6-qt. slow cooker. Pour water around turkey. Cook, covered, on low 3-4 hours (a thermometer inserted in turkey should read at least 165°).
2. Remove turkey from slow cooker; tent with foil. Let stand 10 minutes before slicing.
3. Meanwhile, in a large saucepan, combine compote ingredients. Bring to a boil. Reduce heat to medium; cook, uncovered, stirring occasionally, until mixture is slightly thickened and apples are tender, 15-20 minutes. Serve turkey with compote.

5 OZ. COOKED TURKEY WITH ¼ CUP COMPOTE: *215 cal., 1g fat (0 sat. fat), 94mg chol., 272mg sod., 12g carb. (8g sugars, 2g fiber), 38g pro.*
Diabetic exchanges: *5 lean meat, 1 starch.*

BEEF DAUBE PROVENCAL

BEEF DAUBE PROVENCAL

My meaty dish is perfect on chilly nights, especially after we have been out chopping wood. The melt-in-your-mouth goodness makes it a staple in my menu rotation.
—Brenda Ryan, Marshall, MO

PREP: 30 min. • **MAKES:** 8 servings

- 1 boneless beef chuck roast or venison roast (about 2 lbs.), cut into 1-in. cubes
- 1½ tsp. salt, divided
- ½ tsp. coarsely ground pepper, divided
- 2 tsp. olive oil
- 2 cups chopped carrots
- 1½ cups chopped onions
- 12 garlic cloves, crushed
- 1 Tbsp. tomato paste
- 1 cup dry red wine
- 1 can (14½ oz.) diced tomatoes, undrained
- ½ cup beef broth
- 1 tsp. chopped fresh rosemary
- 1 tsp. chopped fresh thyme
- 1 bay leaf
  Dash ground cloves
  Hot cooked pasta or mashed potatoes
  Additional chopped fresh thyme, optional

Fast Cook: **30 MIN. + RELEASING**

1. Sprinkle beef with ½ tsp. salt and ¼ tsp. pepper. Select saute setting on a 6-qt. electric pressure cooker. Adjust for medium heat; add oil. When oil is hot, brown beef in batches.

2. Add carrots, onions and garlic to pressure cooker; cook and stir until golden brown, 4-6 minutes. Add tomato paste; cook and stir until fragrant, about 1 minute. Add wine, stirring to loosen browned bits. Return beef to pressure cooker. Add tomatoes, broth, rosemary, thyme, bay leaf, cloves and remaining 1 tsp. salt and ¼ tsp. pepper. Press cancel.

3. Lock lid; close pressure-release valve. Adjust to pressure-cook on high for 30 minutes. Let pressure release naturally for 10 minutes; quick-release any remaining pressure. A thermometer inserted in beef should read at least 160°. Discard bay leaf. Serve with hot cooked pasta. If desired, sprinkle with additional thyme.

Slow Cook: **5 HOURS**

1. Sprinkle meat with ½ tsp. salt and ¼ tsp. pepper. In a large skillet, brown meat in olive oil in batches. Transfer beef to 4-qt. slow cooker.

2. Add carrots, onions, garlic and remaining salt and pepper to skillet; cook and stir until golden brown, 4-6 minutes. Add tomato paste; cook and stir until fragrant, about 1 minute. Add wine, stirring to loosen browned bits from pan; bring to a boil.

3. Transfer meat mixture, tomatoes, broth and seasonings to slow cooker. Cook, covered, on low 5-7 hours or until tender. Discard bay leaf. Serve with hot cooked pasta or mashed potatoes. If desired, sprinkle with additional thyme.

FREEZE OPTION: Place beef and vegetables in freezer containers; top with cooking juices. Cool and freeze. To use, partially thaw in refrigerator overnight. Heat through in a covered saucepan, stirring gently and adding a little broth if necessary.

1 CUP BEEF MIXTURE: *237 cal., 12g fat (4g sat. fat), 74mg chol., 651mg sod., 8g carb. (3g sugars, 2g fiber), 23g pro.* **Diabetic exchanges:** *3 lean meat, 1 vegetable.*

MINI TERIYAKI TURKEY SANDWICHES

Preparing pulled turkey in a delicious teriyaki sauce for these snack-size sandwiches is a breeze using a pressure cooker or slow cooker. Serving them on lightly toasted sweet dinner rolls is a nice finishing touch.
—Amanda Hoop, Seaman, OH

PREP: 20 min. • **MAKES:** 20 servings

- 2 boneless skinless turkey breast halves (2 lbs. each)
- ⅔ cup packed brown sugar
- ⅔ cup reduced-sodium soy sauce
- ¼ cup cider vinegar
- 3 garlic cloves, minced
- 1 Tbsp. minced fresh gingerroot
- ½ tsp. pepper
- 2 Tbsp. cornstarch
- 2 Tbsp. cold water
- 20 Hawaiian sweet rolls
- 2 Tbsp. butter, melted

TEST KITCHEN TIP

This recipe also works great with boneless skinless chicken breasts. To spice things up, add crushed red pepper flakes or sliced fresh jalapeno.

MINI TERIYAKI TURKEY SANDWICHES

Fast Cook: 25 MIN. + RELEASING

1. Place turkey in a 6-qt. electric pressure cooker. In a small bowl, combine next 6 ingredients; pour over turkey. Lock lid; close pressure-release valve. Adjust to pressure-cook on high for 25 minutes. Allow pressure to release naturally for 10 minutes; quick-release any remaining pressure.

2. Remove turkey from pressure cooker. Select saute setting and adjust for high heat; bring juices to a boil. In a small bowl, mix cornstarch and water until smooth; gradually stir into cooking juices. Bring to a boil; cook and stir until sauce is thickened, about 2 minutes. When cool enough to handle, shred meat with 2 forks; return meat to pressure cooker. Stir to heat through.

3. Preheat oven to 325°. Split rolls; brush cut sides with butter. Place on an ungreased baking sheet, cut side up. Bake until golden brown, 8-10 minutes. Spoon ⅓ cup turkey mixture on roll bottoms. Replace tops.

Slow Cook: 5½ HOURS

1. Place turkey in a 5- or 6-qt. slow cooker. In a small bowl, combine brown sugar, soy sauce, vinegar, garlic, ginger and pepper; pour over turkey. Cook, covered, on low 5-6 hours or until meat is tender.

2. Remove turkey from slow cooker. In a small bowl, mix the cornstarch and cold water until smooth; gradually stir into cooking liquid. When cool enough to handle, shred meat with 2 forks and return meat to slow cooker. Cook, covered, on high until sauce is thickened, 30-35 minutes.

3. Preheat oven to 325°. Split rolls; brush cut sides with butter. Place on an ungreased baking sheet, cut side up. Bake until golden brown, 8-10 minutes. Spoon ⅓ cup turkey mixture on roll bottoms. Replace tops.

1 SANDWICH: *252 cal., 5g fat (2g sat. fat), 70mg chol., 501mg sod., 25g carb. (13g sugars, 1g fiber), 26g pro.*

**CORN WITH
CILANTRO-LIME BUTTER
PAGE 143**

Side Dishes & Condiments

A memorable menu just isn't complete without tasty on-the-side sensations that perfectly complement the main course. Here you'll find mouthwatering medleys of veggies, pasta, potatoes and more. And you and your family will relish every bite when your favorite foods are served alongside any of these jams and condiments.

BERRY CURD

ACORN SQUASH SLICES

Acorn squash is a family favorite. This recipe gets a sweet maple flavor from syrup and an appealing nuttiness from pecans. It's easy, too, because you don't have to peel the squash.
—Richard Lamb, Williamsburg, IN

- -

PREP: 15 min. • **BAKE:** 40 min. • **MAKES:** 6 servings

2   medium acorn squash (about 1½ lbs. each)
½   tsp. salt
¾   cup maple syrup
2   Tbsp. butter, melted
⅓   cup chopped pecans, optional

1. Cut squash in half lengthwise; remove and discard seeds and membrane. Cut each half widthwise into ½-in. slices; discard ends.
2. Place slices in a greased 13x9-in. baking dish. Sprinkle with salt. Combine syrup and butter; pour over squash slices. Sprinkle with pecans if desired.
3. Cover and bake at 350° for 40-45 minutes or until tender.
3 SLICES: *170 cal., 7g fat (0 sat. fat), 0 chol., 98mg sod., 31g carb. (0 sugars, 0 fiber), 2g pro.* **Diabetic exchanges:** *1 starch, 1 fruit, 1 fat.*

BERRY CURD

I love strawberries. Each time they're in season, I think of new and interesting ways to use them. I spoon this strawberry curd over just about everything, from waffles and pancakes to cake and ice cream.
—Margo Zoerner, Pleasant Prairie, WI

- -

PREP: 5 min. • **COOK:** 10 min. + chilling • **MAKES:** ¾ cup

1   cup chopped fresh strawberries
1   cup fresh raspberries
⅓   cup sugar
1   Tbsp. cornstarch
3   large egg yolks
2   Tbsp. butter
1   tsp. vanilla extract

1. Place strawberries and raspberries in a blender; cover and process until almost smooth. Press through a fine-mesh strainer into a bowl; reserve ½ cup plus 1 Tbsp. juice. Discard seeds.
2. In a small heavy saucepan, mix sugar and cornstarch. Whisk in egg yolks and berry puree until blended. Add butter; cook over medium heat, whisking constantly, until the mixture is just thick enough to coat a metal spoon and a thermometer reads at least 170°. Do not allow to boil. Remove from heat immediately; stir in the vanilla.
3. Transfer to a bowl; cool. Press plastic wrap onto surface of curd; refrigerate until cold. Serve or transfer curd to covered jars and refrigerate up to 2 weeks.
2 TBSP.: *66 cal., 3g fat (2g sat. fat), 51mg chol., 18mg sod., 9g carb. (7g sugars, 1g fiber), 1g pro.*

ACORN SQUASH SLICES

RUSTIC TOMATO PIE

Perk up your plate with this humble tomato pie. We use fresh-from-the-garden tomatoes and herbs, but store-bought produce work in a pinch.
—Taste of Home *Test Kitchen*

PREP: 15 min. • **BAKE:** 30 min.
MAKES: 8 servings

        Pastry for single-crust pie
1¾ lbs. mixed tomatoes, cut into
        ½-in. slices, seeded
¼   cup thinly sliced green onions
½   cup mayonnaise
½   cup shredded cheddar cheese
2   Tbsp. minced fresh basil
¼   tsp. salt
¼   tsp. pepper
2   bacon strips, cooked and crumbled
2   Tbsp. grated Parmesan cheese

1. Preheat oven to 400°. On a lightly floured surface, roll dough to a ⅛-in.-thick circle; transfer to a 9-in. pie plate. Trim crust to ½ in. beyond rim of plate.
2. Place half of the tomatoes and half of the onions in crust. Combine mayonnaise, cheddar cheese, basil, salt and pepper; spread over tomatoes. Top with remaining onions and tomatoes. Fold crust edge over filling, pleating as you go and leaving an 8-in. opening in the center. Sprinkle with bacon and Parmesan cheese. Bake on a lower oven rack until until crust is golden and filling is bubbly, 30-35 minutes. Transfer pie to a wire rack to cool. If desired, sprinkle with additional basil.
1 PIECE: *325 cal., 25g fat (11g sat. fat), 41mg chol., 409mg sod., 19g carb. (3g sugars, 2g fiber), 6g pro.*
PASTRY FOR SINGLE-CRUST PIE (9 IN.) Combine 1¼ cups all-purpose flour and ¼ tsp. salt; cut in ½ cup cold butter until crumbly. Gradually add 3-5 Tbsp. ice water, tossing with a fork until dough holds together when pressed. Wrap and refrigerate 1 hour.

CHERRY ALMOND HAM GLAZE

CHERRY ALMOND HAM GLAZE

I was looking for an alternative to traditional sauces for Easter and other holiday meats. Mostly, I serve it with ham, and it goes over well—probably because it is such a change of taste. But the glaze should be fine with almost any meat...and its cheery color!
—Julie Sterchi, Campbellsville, KY

TAKES: 10 min. • **MAKES:** about 1½ cups glaze

1   jar (12 oz.) cherry preserves
¼   cup vinegar
2   Tbsp. corn syrup
¼   tsp. ground cinnamon
¼   tsp. ground cloves
¼   tsp. ground nutmeg
⅓   cup slivered almonds
3   Tbsp. water

1. In a saucepan, combine all ingredients except almonds and water. Bring to a boil. Reduce heat; simmer 2 minutes, stirring frequently. Stir in the almonds.
2. About 15 minutes before ham is done, spoon ¼ to ⅓ cup glaze over ham. Repeat if desired.
3. Stir water into remaining glaze; heat through and serve with ham.
2 TBSP.: *98 cal., 2g fat (0 sat. fat), 0 chol., 4mg sod., 22g carb. (19g sugars, 0 fiber), 1g pro.*

⑤i

HOMEMADE SAUERKRAUT

Put down that store-bought jar! You only need two ingredients (and a little patience) to make fresh, zippy sauerkraut at home. Get those brats ready!
—Josh Rink, Milwaukee, WI

- -

PREP: 45 min. + standing
MAKES: 40 servings (about 10 cups)

- 6 lbs. cabbage (about 2 heads)
- 3 Tbsp. canning salt
  Optional: 2 peeled and thinly sliced Granny Smith apples, 2 thinly sliced sweet onions, 2 tsp. caraway seeds and 1 tsp. ground coriander

1. Quarter cabbages and remove cores; slice ⅛ in. thick. In an extra large bowl, combine salt and cabbage. With clean hands, squeeze cabbage until wilted and has released liquid, about 10 minutes. If desired, add optional ingredients.

2. Firmly pack cabbage mixture into 4-qt. fermenting crock or large glass container, removing as many air bubbles as possible. If cabbage mixture is not covered by 1-2 in. of liquid, make enough brine to cover by 1-2 in.

3. To make brine, combine 4½ tsp. canning salt per 1 qt. of water in a saucepan; bring to a boil until salt is dissolved. Cool brine before adding to crock.

4. Place crock weight over cabbage; the weight should be submerged in the brine. Or, place an inverted dinner plate or glass pie plate over cabbage. The plate should be slightly smaller than the container opening, but large enough to cover most of the shredded cabbage mixture. Weigh down the plate with 2 or 3 sealed qt. jars filled with water. If using a glass container with a lid, cover the opening loosely so any gas produced by the fermenting cabbage can escape. Alternately, you can cover the opening with a clean, heavy towel. If using a crock, seal according to manufacturer's instructions.

5. Store crock, undisturbed, between 70° and 75° for 3-4 weeks (bubbles will form and aroma will change). Cabbage must be kept submerged below surface of the fermenting liquid throughout fermentation. Check crock 2-3 times each week; skim and remove any scum that may form on top of the liquid. Fermentation is complete when bubbling stops. Transfer the sauerkraut to individual containers. Cover and store in the refrigerator for up to 3 months.
¼ CUP: *11 cal., 0 fat (0 sat. fat), 0 chol., 344mg sod., 3g carb. (1g sugars, 1g fiber), 1g pro.*

TEST KITCHEN TIP

Canning salt must be used. It does not contain additives like anti-caking agents that might be present in table or Kosher salt.

⏱ ⑤i

LEMON SPAGHETTI

We love everything lemon and everything pasta. So when I came across this recipe, it was an instant favorite. The refreshing flavor is especially good when paired with seafood.
—Cori Cooper, Boise, ID

- -

TAKES: 25 min. • **MAKES:** 10 servings

- 1 pkg. (16 oz.) spaghetti
- ⅔ cup grated Parmesan cheese
- ⅓ cup lemon juice
- ⅓ cup olive oil
- 5 fresh basil leaves, thinly sliced
- 3 tsp. grated lemon zest

1. Cook spaghetti according to package directions.

2. In a small bowl, combine the cheese, lemon juice and oil. Drain spaghetti and transfer to a large bowl. Pour the cheese mixture over the spaghetti; toss to coat. Sprinkle with basil and lemon zest.
¾ CUP: *257 cal., 9g fat (2g sat. fat), 5mg chol., 85mg sod., 35g carb. (1g sugars, 2g fiber), 8g pro.* **Diabetic exchanges:** *2 starch, 2 fat.*

HOMEMADE SAUERKRAUT

GLAZED PARMESAN POTATOES

HABANERO STRAWBERRY JAM

I love recipes that boast both sweet and spicy flavors. This jam tastes amazing layered over a bar of cream cheese and served with crackers, or you can slather it on a toasted English muffin. Yum!
—Sarah Gilbert, Beaverton, OR

PREP: 40 min. • **PROCESS:** 10 min. • **MAKES:** 9 half-pints

4½ cups crushed strawberries
½ cup minced seeded habanero peppers
¼ cup lemon juice
1 pkg. (1¾ oz.) powdered fruit pectin
7 cups sugar

1. In a Dutch oven, combine strawberries, peppers and lemon juice. Stir in pectin. Bring to a full rolling boil over high heat, stirring constantly. Stir in sugar; return to a full rolling boil. Boil and stir 1 minute.
2. Remove from heat; skim off foam. Ladle hot mixture into nine hot half-pint jars, leaving ¼-in. headspace. Wipe rims. Center lids on jars; screw on bands until fingertip tight.
3. Place jars into canner with simmering water, ensuring that they are completely covered with water. Bring to a boil; process for 10 minutes. Remove jars and cool.
NOTE: Wear disposable gloves when cutting hot peppers; the oils can burn skin. Avoid touching your face. The processing time listed is for altitudes of 1,000 feet or less. Add 1 minute to the processing time for each 1,000 feet of additional altitude.
2 TBSP.: 84 cal., 0 fat (0 sat. fat), 0 chol., 1mg sod., 21g carb. (21g sugars, 0 fiber), 0 pro.

GLAZED PARMESAN POTATOES

Potatoes are the ultimate comfort food to me. If you haven't tried them with a touch of honey, you won't be disappointed with this savory-sweet combination.
—Stephanie Shay, Orwigsburg, PA

PREP: 10 min. • **BAKE:** 40 min. • **MAKES:** 6 servings

1¾ lbs. red potatoes, cut into 1-in. cubes
5 Tbsp. butter, melted
3 Tbsp. honey
¾ tsp. salt
½ tsp. garlic powder
¼ tsp. pepper
¼ cup grated Parmesan cheese

1. Place potatoes in a greased 13x9-in. baking dish. In a small bowl, combine the butter, honey, salt, garlic powder and pepper; drizzle over potatoes.
2. Bake at 375° for 35-40 minutes or until potatoes are tender. Stir potatoes and sprinkle with cheese. Bake 5-10 minutes longer or until cheese is lightly browned.
¾ CUP: 227 cal., 11g fat (7g sat. fat), 28mg chol., 440mg sod., 30g carb. (10g sugars, 2g fiber), 4g pro.

HABANERO STRAWBERRY JAM

ASIAGO MASHED CAULIFLOWER

ASIAGO MASHED CAULIFLOWER

Asiago cheese and fresh parsley help turn this mashed potato alternative into a flavorful and healthier side dish that won't leave you feeling guilty or overstuffed.
—*Colleen Delawder, Herndon, VA*

- -

TAKES: 30 min. • **MAKES:** 4 servings

- 1   medium head cauliflower, cut into 1-in. pieces
- 1   tsp. sea salt, divided
- 4   oz. cream cheese, softened
- ½   cup shredded Asiago cheese
- 2   Tbsp. unsalted butter
- 2   Tbsp. coarsely chopped fresh parsley
- ¼   tsp. pepper

1. Place cauliflower and ½ tsp. sea salt in a large saucepan; add water to cover. Bring to a boil. Cook, covered, until very tender, 12-15 minutes. Drain; cool slightly.

2. Transfer to a food processor. Add the cream cheese, Asiago cheese, butter, parsley, pepper and remaining sea salt. Process until blended.
½ CUP: *239 cal., 20g fat (12g sat. fat), 56mg chol., 530mg sod., 10g carb. (4g sugars, 3g fiber), 9g pro.*

WARM GARLICKY GRAPE TOMATOES

This recipe is one of my favorite quick ways to use up a bumper crop of grape tomatoes...or to take care of an overenthusiastic tomato-shopping spree! Either way, it's delicious!
—*Rose Gulledge, Crofton, MD*

- -

TAKES: 30 min. • **MAKES:** 4 servings

- 2   cups grape tomatoes
- 3   garlic cloves, minced
- 1½   tsp. minced fresh basil
- ½   tsp. salt-free garlic seasoning blend
- ¼   tsp. salt

- ⅛   tsp. pepper
- 1   tsp. olive oil, divided
- ¼   cup soft whole wheat bread crumbs
- ¼   cup crumbled feta cheese

1. In a small bowl, combine the tomatoes, garlic, basil, seasoning blend, salt and pepper. Add ½ tsp. oil; toss to coat. Transfer to a 3-cup baking dish coated with cooking spray.
2. Bake at 425° for 15 minutes. Combine bread crumbs and remaining oil; sprinkle over the top. Sprinkle with cheese. Bake 5-10 minutes longer or until cheese is softened and tomatoes are tender.
½ CUP: *64 cal., 3g fat (1g sat. fat), 4mg chol., 259mg sod., 8g carb. (2g sugars, 2g fiber), 3g pro.* **DIABETIC EXCHANGES:** *1 vegetable, ½ fat.*

STEWED ZUCCHINI & TOMATOES

Zucchini, tomatoes and green peppers star in this fresh take on a traditional vegetable side dish. Bubbly cheddar cheese adds a homey feel to this slow-cooked sensation.
—*Barbara Smith, Salem, OR*

- -

PREP: 20 min. • **COOK:** 3½ hours
MAKES: 6 servings

- 3   medium zucchini, cut into ¼-in. slices
- 1   tsp. salt, divided
- ½   tsp. pepper, divided
- 1   medium onion, thinly sliced
- 1   medium green pepper, thinly sliced
- 3   medium tomatoes, sliced
- ⅔   cup condensed tomato soup, undiluted
- 1   tsp. dried basil
- 1   cup shredded cheddar cheese
      Minced fresh basil, optional

1. Place zucchini in a greased 3-qt. slow cooker. Sprinkle with ½ tsp. salt and ¼ tsp. pepper. Layer with the onion, green pepper and tomatoes. In a small bowl, combine the soup, basil and remaining salt and pepper; spread over tomatoes.
2. Cover and cook on low for 3-4 hours or until vegetables are tender. Sprinkle with cheese. Cover and cook 30 minutes longer or until cheese is melted. If desired, top with fresh basil.
¾ CUP: *126 cal., 6g fat (4g sat. fat), 20mg chol., 678mg sod., 14g carb. (8g sugars, 3g fiber), 7g pro.* **Diabetic exchanges:** *1 vegetable, 1 fat, ½ starch.*

STEWED ZUCCHINI & TOMATOES

GOLDEN ZUCCHINI PANCAKES

GOLDEN ZUCCHINI PANCAKES

If your garden is overflowing with zucchini, make these incredible pancakes to use it up. We squeeze the zucchini well before using to remove excess moisture.
—*Terry Ann Dominguez, Silver City, NM*

PREP: 15 min. • **COOK:** 10 min./batch • **MAKES:** 8 pancakes

- 3 cups shredded zucchini
- 2 large eggs
- 2 garlic cloves, minced
- ¾ tsp. salt
- ½ tsp. pepper
- ¼ tsp. dried oregano
- ½ cup all-purpose flour
- ½ cup finely chopped sweet onion
- 1 Tbsp. butter
- Marinara sauce, warmed, optional

1. Place zucchini in a colander to drain; squeeze well to remove excess liquid. Pat dry.

2. In a large bowl, whisk eggs, minced garlic, salt, pepper and oregano until blended. Stir in flour just until moistened. Fold in zucchini and onion.

3. Lightly grease a griddle with butter; heat over medium heat. Drop zucchini mixture by ¼ cupfuls onto griddle; flatten to ½-in. thickness (3-in. diameter). Cook until golden brown, 4-5 minutes on each side. If desired, serve with marinara sauce.

2 PANCAKES: 145 cal., 6g fat (3g sat. fat), 101mg chol., 510mg sod., 18g carb. (3g sugars, 2g fiber), 6g pro. **Diabetic exchanges:** *1 starch, 1 fat.*

MUSHROOM-STUFFED TOMATOES

These stuffed tomatoes are inexpensive, quick to prepare and always a favorite. With plenty of mushrooms, the cheesy mixture has fresh flavor. Serve them with grilled steak or your favorite roast.
—*Florence Palmer, Marshall, IL*

PREP: 30 min. • **BAKE:** 10 min. • **MAKES:** 8 servings

- 4 large tomatoes
- Dash salt
- 1 lb. sliced fresh mushrooms
- ¼ cup butter
- 2 Tbsp. all-purpose flour
- 1 cup half-and-half cream
- 2 Tbsp. soft bread crumbs
- ¾ cup minced fresh parsley
- ⅔ cup shredded cheddar cheese, divided

1. Cut tomatoes in half; scoop out and discard pulp, leaving a thin shell. Sprinkle lightly with salt; invert on paper towels to drain for 15 minutes.

2. In a large skillet, saute mushrooms in butter until most of the liquid has evaporated, about 5 minutes. Sprinkle with flour; stir in cream. Bring to a boil; cook and stir until mixture thickens, about 2 minutes.

3. Remove from the heat. Stir in the bread crumbs, minced parsley and ⅓ cup cheese. Spoon into the tomato cups; sprinkle with remaining cheese.

4. Place in a greased 13x9-in. baking dish. Bake, uncovered, at 400° until cheese is melted, about 10 minutes.

1 SERVING: 165 cal., 12g fat (8g sat. fat), 40mg chol., 145mg sod., 9g carb. (4g sugars, 2g fiber), 6g pro.

MUSHROOM-STUFFED TOMATOES

CORN WITH CILANTRO-LIME BUTTER

(SHOWN ON PAGE 134)

I use fresh cilantro from my garden in this butter I created to spread on grilled corn.
—Andrea Reynolds, Westlake, OH

- -

PREP: 15 min. + chilling • **GRILL:** 15 min.
MAKES: 12 servings

- ½ cup butter, softened
- ¼ cup minced fresh cilantro
- 1 Tbsp. lime juice
- 1½ tsp. grated lime zest
- 12 medium ears sweet corn, husked
  Grated Cotija cheese, optional

1. In a bowl, mix butter, cilantro, lime juice and lime zest. Shape into a log; wrap in waxed paper. Refrigerate until firm, about 30 minutes. Wrap each ear of corn in a piece of heavy-duty foil about 14 in. square.
2. Grill corn, covered, over medium heat until tender, turning occasionally, 15-20 minutes. Meanwhile, cut lime butter into 12 slices. Remove corn from grill. Carefully open foil, allowing steam to escape. Serve corn with butter and, if desired, cheese.
1 EAR OF CORN WITH 2 TSP. BUTTER: *145 cal., 9g fat (5g sat. fat), 20mg chol., 67mg sod., 17g carb. (3g sugars, 2g fiber), 3g pro.*

GRILLED ASPARAGUS

Tender, with a delicious barbecue flavor, this grilled asparagus makes a perfect side dish for grilled meats. Say you're not sure how to grill asparagus? Just pierce the spears with a double skewer and place them on the grill.
—Taste of Home *Test Kitchen*

- -

TAKES: 20 min. • **MAKES:** 4 servings

- 1 cup water
- 1 lb. fresh asparagus, trimmed
- ¼ cup barbecue sauce

1. In a large skillet, bring water to a boil; add asparagus. Cover and cook until crisp-tender, 4-6 minutes; drain and pat dry. Cool slightly.
2. Thread several asparagus spears onto 2 parallel soaked wooden skewers. Repeat. Grill, uncovered, over medium heat for 2 minutes, turning once. Baste with barbecue sauce. Grill 2 minutes longer, turning and basting once.

1 SERVING: *43 cal., 0 fat (0 sat. fat), 0 chol., 181mg sod., 9g carb. (7g sugars, 1g fiber), 2g pro.* **Diabetic exchanges:** *1 vegetable.*

GREEN BEANS WITH CREAMY PISTACHIO SAUCE

I was asked to bring veggies to a party and wasn't feeling inspired until I remembered Mom made them with butter and evaporated milk. I love pistachios, so I tossed in a handful of those instead of almonds. Everyone asked for the recipe, and I was pleased—minimal work and lots of happy family and friends!
—Loretta Ouellette, Pompano Beach, FL

- -

TAKES: 30 min. • **MAKES:** 10 servings

- 2 lbs. fresh green beans, trimmed
- 1 tsp. salt
- ½ cup butter, cubed
- ½ cup pistachios, coarsely chopped
- 1 cup evaporated milk
  Salt and pepper to taste

1. Place green beans and salt in a Dutch oven; add water to cover. Bring to a boil. Cook, uncovered, until tender, stirring occasionally, 5-8 minutes. Drain and remove from pan.
2. In the same pan, melt the butter over medium heat. Add the pistachios; cook and stir until pistachios begin to brown, 1-2 minutes. Stir in evaporated milk; bring to a boil. Cook until the sauce is slightly thickened, 2-4 minutes. Add green beans; heat through, stirring to coat with sauce. Season with salt and pepper to taste.
¾ CUP: *177 cal., 14g fat (7g sat. fat), 32mg chol., 365mg sod., 11g carb. (5g sugars, 4g fiber), 5g pro.*

GREEN BEANS WITH CREAMY PISTACHIO SAUCE

FREEZER TO TABLE

Take plain frozen veggies and turn them into something fabulous. The *Taste of Home* Field Editors offer creative ways to think outside the bag.

1 OLD BAY CAULIFLOWER

Prepare a 16-oz. pkg. frozen **cauliflower** according to package directions; drain. Drizzle with 1-2 Tbsp. melted **butter;** sprinkle with 1-2 tsp. **seafood seasoning.**
—Elizabeth Bramkamp, Gig Harbor, WA

2 CREAMY SAUTEED SPINACH

In a large skillet, heat 1 Tbsp. **olive oil** over medium-high heat. Add 1 small chopped **onion;** cook and stir until tender, 5-7 minutes. Add two 10-oz. pkg. frozen **spinach** (thawed and squeezed dry) and 2 minced **garlic** cloves; cook 2 minutes longer. Stir in 8 oz. softened **cream cheese,** ¼ cup 2% **milk,** ½ tsp. **salt** and ½ tsp. **pepper;** cook until cream cheese is melted.
—Debbie Glasscock, Conway, AR

3 ROSEMARY & THYME CARROTS

Prepare 2 cups frozen sliced **carrots** according to package directions. Meanwhile, combine ¼ cup softened **butter,** ½ tsp. minced fresh **thyme,** ½ tsp. minced fresh **rosemary** and ⅛ tsp. **salt.** Drain carrots; top with herb butter.
—Jolene Martinelli, Fremont, NH

4 SAUTEED ASPARAGUS WITH MUSHROOMS

In a large skillet, heat 1 Tbsp. **bacon drippings** or **olive oil** over medium-high heat. Add a thawed 8-oz. pkg. frozen **asparagus spears,** ½ lb. sliced fresh **mushrooms** and 1 small chopped **onion;** cook and stir until tender, 10-12 minutes. Sprinkle with 2 Tbsp. sliced toasted **almonds** and 1-2 tsp. **Greek seasoning;** heat through.
—Shawn Barto, Winter Garden, FL

5 PROSCIUTTO & PEAS

In a large skillet, heat 1 Tbsp. **olive oil** over medium heat. Add 4 to 8 julienned thin slices of **prosciutto;** cook and stir until crisp, stirring occasionally. Remove with a slotted spoon; drain on paper towels. Cook and stir ½ cup sliced fresh **shiitake mushrooms,** 2 cups thawed frozen **peas** and 1 small chopped **onion** in drippings until tender, 5-7 minutes. Sprinkle with prosciutto.
—Ann Sheehy, Lawrence, MA

6 BALSAMIC SEA SALT BRUSSELS SPROUTS

In a large skillet, heat 3-4 Tbsp. **extra virgin olive oil** over medium-high heat. Add a thawed 16-oz. pkg. of frozen **Brussels sprouts** to the skillet and cook until heated through, 5-7 minutes. Transfer to a serving bowl. Drizzle sprouts with 2 Tbsp. **balsamic vinegar;** sprinkle with 2 Tbsp. torn **fresh basil leaves,** ½-1 tsp. flaky **sea salt** and ½ tsp. **coarsely ground pepper.**
—*Kallee Krong-McCreery, Escondido, CA*

7 SALSA CORN

Prepare 2 cups (about 10 oz.) frozen **corn** according to package directions; drain. Stir in ¼-½ cup **pico de gallo** or **salsa.**
—*Danielle Lee, Sewickley, PA*

8 BACON & GARLIC SUGAR SNAPS

In a large skillet, cook 2 coarsely chopped **bacon** strips over medium heat until crisp, stirring occasionally. Remove with a slotted spoon; drain on paper towels. Cook and stir a thawed 14-oz. pkg. frozen **sugar snap peas** in bacon drippings until heated through. Add 1 thinly sliced **shallot** and 2 thinly sliced **garlic cloves;** cook 1 minute longer. Sprinkle with reserved bacon.
—*Tami Kuehl, Loup City, NE*

9 CHEESY CRUMB-TOPPED BROCCOLI

Prepare a 16-oz. pkg. frozen **broccoli florets** according to package directions; drain. Combine ⅓ cup toasted **panko bread crumbs,** ⅓ cup **extra sharp cheddar cheese,** ½ tsp. **salt,** ¼ tsp. **ground black pepper** and ¼ tsp. **garlic powder;** sprinkle over broccoli.
—*Joan Hallford, North Richland Hills, TX*

10 SESAME & SOY GLAZED GREEN BEANS

In a large skillet, heat 1 Tbsp. **toasted sesame oil** over medium-high heat. Add 2 cups (about 8 oz.) thawed frozen **green beans;** cook and stir until heated through. Add 1 minced **garlic clove;** cook 1 minute longer. Stir in 2 Tbsp. **soy sauce** and 1-2 tsp. **sugar** or **honey** until the sugar is dissolved. If desired, sprinkle with **sesame seeds.**
—*Susan Bickta, Kutztown, PA*

**PANZANELLA
WITH OLIVES**

SIMPLE HARVARD BEETS

A colorful and nourishing addition to any autumn table, this quick and simple dish makes a classic side for many meat entrees.
—*Stella Quade, Carthage, MO*

- -

TAKES: 30 min. • **MAKES:** 2 servings

- 1 cup sliced fresh beets
- 2 Tbsp. sugar
- ¾ tsp. all-purpose flour
- 2 Tbsp. white vinegar
- ⅛ tsp. salt
- 2 tsp. butter

1. Place beets in a small saucepan; cover with water. Bring to a boil. Reduce heat; cover and cook until tender, 15-20 minutes. Drain, reserving 1 Tbsp. cooking liquid; set beets aside.
2. In the same pan, combine the sugar, flour, vinegar and reserved liquid. Cook over low heat until thickened. Stir in the beets, salt and butter. Bring to a boil. Reduce the heat; simmer, uncovered, for 5 minutes.
½ **CUP:** *115 cal., 4g fat (2g sat. fat), 10mg chol., 239mg sod., 20g carb. (16g sugars, 2g fiber), 1g pro.* **Diabetic exchanges:** *1 starch, 1 vegetable, ½ fat.*

ROASTED CAULIFLOWER

Seasoned with a blend of herbs, this side dish is easy enough for weeknight dinners.
—*Leslie Palmer, Swampscott, MA*

- -

TAKES: 30 min. • **MAKES:** 4 servings

- 3 cups fresh cauliflowerets
- 2 Tbsp. lemon juice
- 4½ tsp. olive oil
- 1 garlic clove, minced
- 1 tsp. dried parsley flakes
- ½ tsp. dried thyme
- ½ tsp. dried tarragon
- ¼ tsp. pepper
- ¼ cup grated Parmesan cheese

In a large bowl, combine first 8 ingredients; toss to coat. Transfer to an ungreased 15x10x1-in. baking pan. Bake at 425° until tender, 15-20 minutes, stirring occasionally. Sprinkle with cheese.
¾ **CUP:** *107 cal., 7g fat (2g sat. fat), 4mg chol., 120mg sod., 9g carb. (4g sugars, 4g fiber), 5g pro.* **Diabetic exchanges:** *2 vegetable, 1 fat.*

PANZANELLA
WITH OLIVES

This quick and flavorful bread salad always gets rave reviews from my friends and family. The panzanella-style dish is a timesaver, too, as it can be made in advance. Just keep the bread cubes separate and add them right before serving.
—*Angela Spengler, Niceville, FL*

- -

TAKES: 30 min. • **MAKES:** 9 servings

- 1 loaf (14 oz.) ciabatta bread, cut into ½-in. cubes (about 10 cups)
- ¾ cup olive oil
- 3 garlic cloves, minced
- ¼ tsp. pepper
- ¼ cup balsamic vinegar
- ¼ tsp. salt
- 2 large tomatoes, chopped
- ¼ cup sliced olives
- ⅓ cup coarsely chopped fresh basil
- 2 Tbsp. chopped fresh Italian parsley
- ¼ cup shredded Parmesan cheese

1. Preheat oven to 350°. Place bread cubes in a large bowl. In another bowl, mix oil, garlic and pepper; drizzle 3 Tbsp. over the bread and toss to coat. Reserve remaining oil mixture. Spread in a single layer on two 15x10x1-in. baking pans.
2. Bake until crisp and light brown, 12-18 minutes, stirring occasionally.
3. Meanwhile, whisk vinegar and salt into reserved oil mixture. Add tomatoes, olives and herbs; toss to coat.
4. Cool bread cubes slightly. Add to tomato mixture; toss to combine. Sprinkle with the cheese; serve immediately.
1 **CUP:** *316 cal., 21g fat (3g sat. fat), 2mg chol., 345mg sod., 31g carb. (5g sugars, 2g fiber), 5g pro.*

APRICOT-GINGER ACORN SQUASH

GRILLED VEGETABLE PLATTER

The best of summer in one dish! These pretty veggies are perfect for entertaining. Grilling brings out their natural sweetness, and the easy marinade really perks up the flavor.
—Heidi Hall, North St. Paul, MN

PREP: 20 min. + marinating • **GRILL:** 10 min. • **MAKES:** 6 servings

¼	cup olive oil
2	Tbsp. honey
4	tsp. balsamic vinegar
1	tsp. dried oregano
½	tsp. garlic powder
⅛	tsp. pepper
	Dash salt
1	lb. fresh asparagus, trimmed
3	small carrots, cut in half lengthwise
1	large sweet red pepper, cut into 1-in. strips
1	medium yellow summer squash, cut into ½-in. slices
1	medium red onion, cut into wedges

1. In a small bowl, whisk the first 7 ingredients. Place 3 Tbsp. marinade in a large bowl. Add vegetables; turn to coat. Cover; marinate 1½ hours at room temperature.
2. Transfer vegetables to a grilling grid; place grid on grill rack. Grill vegetables, covered, over medium heat until crisp-tender, 8-12 minutes, turning occasionally.
3. Place vegetables on a large serving plate. Drizzle with the remaining marinade.
1 SERVING: *144 cal., 9g fat (1g sat. fat), 0 chol., 50mg sod., 15g carb. (11g sugars, 3g fiber), 2g pro.* **Diabetic exchanges:** *2 vegetable, 2 fat.*

APRICOT-GINGER ACORN SQUASH

It's a real treat digging into tender baked squash with a buttery apricot sauce. Natural fruit preserves add sweetness, and the ginger makes it savory without loading on unwanted calories.
—Trisha Kruse, Eagle, ID

PREP: 10 min. • **BAKE:** 1 hour • **MAKES:** 2 servings

1	small acorn squash
2	Tbsp. apricot preserves
4	tsp. butter, melted
1½	tsp. reduced-sodium soy sauce
¼	tsp. ground ginger
¼	tsp. pepper

1. Preheat oven to 350°. Cut squash lengthwise in half; remove seeds. Cut a thin slice from bottoms to level if desired. Place in a greased 11x7-in. baking dish, cut side up.
2. Mix remaining ingredients; spoon over squash. Bake, covered, 45 minutes. Uncover; bake until tender, 15-20 minutes.
½ SQUASH: *234 cal., 8g fat (5g sat. fat), 20mg chol., 221mg sod., 43g carb. (15g sugars, 4g fiber), 3g pro.* **Diabetic exchanges:** *1 starch.*

GRILLED VEGETABLE PLATTER

MASHED CAULIFLOWER

CARROTS LYONNAISE

My sister Laurie brought home this recipe from her junior high home economics class. Our family liked it so much it became a part of our Christmas dinner tradition.
—Elizabeth Plants, Kirkwood, MO

TAKES: 30 min. • **MAKES:** 8 servings

- 2 lbs. fresh carrots, cut into 2-in. pieces
- 1 medium onion, thinly sliced
- ⅓ cup butter
- 2 Tbsp. all-purpose flour
- 2 tsp. chicken bouillon granules
- ¼ tsp. salt
- ⅛ tsp. pepper
- 1 cup water
   Minced fresh parsley

1. In a Dutch oven, bring 1 in. of water to a boil. Add carrots; cover and cook until crisp-tender, 5-8 minutes.

2. Meanwhile, in a large cast-iron or other heavy skillet, saute onion in butter until tender. Stir in the flour, bouillon, salt and pepper until blended; gradually add water. Bring to a boil; cook and stir until thickened, 2 minutes. Drain carrots; stir into sauce. Sprinkle with parsley.

¾ **CUP:** *129 cal., 8g fat (5g sat. fat), 20mg chol., 416mg sod., 14g carb. (7g sugars, 4g fiber), 2g pro.* **Diabetic exchanges:** *2 vegetable, 1½ fat.*

MASHED CAULIFLOWER

This side dish is lower in carbs than mashed potatoes but just as flavorful and satisfying. It makes an enticing addition to a holiday table. I add chopped green onions for a festive garnish.
—Tina Martini, Sparks, NV

TAKES: 25 min. • **MAKES:** 3 servings

- 1 medium head cauliflower, broken into florets
- ½ cup shredded Swiss cheese
- 1 Tbsp. butter
- ¾ tsp. salt
- ¼ tsp. pepper
- ⅛ tsp. garlic powder
- 2 to 3 Tbsp. 2% milk

1. In a large saucepan, bring 1 in. water to a boil. Add cauliflower; cook, covered, until very tender, 8-12 minutes. Drain.

2. Mash cauliflower, adding cheese, butter, seasonings and enough milk to reach desired consistency.

¾ **CUP:** *160 cal., 10g fat (6g sat. fat), 28mg chol., 718mg sod., 11g carb. (4g sugars, 4g fiber), 9g pro.*

CARROTS LYONNAISE

LOADED STUFFED POTATO PANCAKES

Whenever I make mashed potatoes, I always cook extra so I can use them for these over-the-top pancakes. Fill them with sour cream, ranch dressing, melted cheese—or all three.
—Jane Whittaker, Pensacola, FL

PREP: 25 min. • **COOK:** 5 min./batch
MAKES: 4 servings

- 2 cups mashed potatoes
  (with added milk and butter)
- ⅔ cup shredded cheddar cheese
- ⅓ cup all-purpose flour
- 1 large egg, lightly beaten
- 1 Tbsp. minced chives
- ½ tsp. salt
- ½ tsp. pepper
- ⅔ cup seasoned bread crumbs
- 1 tsp. garlic powder
- 1 tsp. onion powder
- ½ tsp. cayenne pepper
- ⅓ cup cream cheese, softened
  Oil for deep-fat frying

1. In a bowl, combine first 7 ingredients. In a shallow bowl, mix bread crumbs, garlic powder, onion powder and cayenne.
2. Shape 2 tsp. cream cheese into a ball. Wrap ¼ cup of potato mixture around cream cheese to cover completely. Drop into the crumb mixture. Gently coat and shape into a ½-in.-thick patty. Repeat with the remaining cream cheese and potato mixture.
3. In an electric skillet or deep-fat fryer, heat oil to 375°. Fry stuffed pancakes, a few at a time, until golden brown, 1-2 minutes on each side. Drain on paper towels.
2 PANCAKES: *491 cal., 34g fat (12g sat. fat), 96mg chol., 987mg sod., 35g carb. (3g sugars, 2g fiber), 12g pro.*

RHUBARB CHUTNEY

RHUBARB CHUTNEY

This tangy-sweet chutney is among our favorite condiments. We love it served with pork or chicken, but it brightens up almost anything!
—Jan Paterson, Anchorage, AK

TAKES: 20 min. • **MAKES:** about 3 cups

- ¾ cup sugar
- ⅓ cup cider vinegar
- 1 Tbsp. minced garlic
- ¾ tsp. ground ginger
- ½ tsp. ground cumin
- ½ tsp. ground cinnamon
- ¼ tsp. crushed red pepper flakes
- ⅛ to ¼ tsp. ground cloves
- 4 cups coarsely chopped fresh or
  frozen rhubarb, thawed
- ½ cup chopped red onion
- ⅓ cup golden raisins
- 1 tsp. red food coloring, optional

1. In a large saucepan, combine the sugar, vinegar, garlic, ginger, cumin, cinnamon, red pepper flakes and cloves. Bring to a boil. Reduce heat; simmer, uncovered, until sugar is dissolved, about 2 minutes.
2. Add the rhubarb, onion and raisins. Cook and stir over medium heat until rhubarb is tender and mixture is slightly thickened, 5-10 minutes. Stir in the food coloring if desired. Cool chutney completely. Store in the refrigerator.
¼ CUP: *75 cal., 0 fat (0 sat. fat), 0 chol., 3mg sod., 19g carb. (17g sugars, 1g fiber), 1g pro.*

TEST KITCHEN TIP

During the simmering process, the vinegar aroma will be very pungent. So do it in a well-ventilated area.

OLIVE OIL DIP

Combine a blend of herbs to create this mouthwatering mix. Plumping the herbs in water before stirring into olive oil enhances the flavor.
—Taste of Home *Test Kitchen*

TAKES: 5 min. • **MAKES:** ½ cup per batch

- 1 Tbsp. dried minced garlic
- 1 Tbsp. dried rosemary, crushed
- 1 Tbsp. dried oregano
- 2 tsp. dried basil
- 1 tsp. crushed red pepper flakes
- ½ tsp. salt
- ½ tsp. coarsely ground pepper

ADDITIONAL INGREDIENTS (FOR EACH BATCH)

- 1 Tbsp. water
- ½ cup olive oil
- 1 French bread baguette (10½ oz.)

1. In a small bowl, combine the first 7 dry ingredients. Store herb mix in an airtight container in a cool, dry place for up to 6 months. Yield: 3 batches (¼ cup total).
2. To prepare the dipping oil: In a small microwave-safe bowl, combine 4 tsp. herb mix with water. Microwave, uncovered, on high for 10-15 seconds. Drain excess water. Transfer to a shallow serving plate; add ½ cup oil and stir. Serve with bread.
1 TBSP.: *122 cal., 14g fat (2g sat. fat), 0 chol., 50mg sod., 1g carb. (0 sugars, 0 fiber), 0 pro.*

GIARDINIERA

Sweet, tangy and a little hot, this Italian condiment is packed with peppers, carrots, cauliflower and other crisp-tender veggies. It's perfect to offer alongside pickles or olives on a relish tray.
—Alicia Rooker, Milwaukee, WI

PREP: 1 hour • **PROCESS:** 10 min./batch
MAKES: 10 pints

- 6 cups white vinegar
- 3½ cups sugar
- 3 cups water
- 4½ tsp. canning salt
- 1 Tbsp. dried oregano
- 1 Tbsp. fennel seed
- 2 small heads cauliflower, broken into small florets (about 12 cups)
- 4 large carrots, sliced
- 4 celery ribs, cut into ½-in. slices
- 48 pearl onions, peeled and trimmed (about 1¼ lbs.)
- 4 large sweet red peppers, cut into ½-in. strips
- 4 serrano peppers, seeds removed and thinly sliced
- 10 bay leaves
- 20 whole peppercorns
- 10 garlic cloves, thinly sliced

1. In a large stockpot, combine vinegar, sugar, water, canning salt, oregano and fennel seed. Bring to a boil. Add cauliflower, carrots, celery and onions; return to a boil. Remove from heat; add peppers.
2. Carefully ladle hot mixture into 10 hot 1-pint jars, leaving ½- in. headspace. Add a bay leaf and 2 peppercorns to each jar; divide garlic slices among jars. Remove air bubbles and adjust headspace, if necessary, by adding more hot mixture. Wipe rims. Center lids on jars; screw on bands until fingertip tight.
3. Place jars into canner with simmering water, ensuring that they are completely covered with water. Bring to a boil; process for 10 minutes. Remove jars and cool.
NOTE: Wear disposable gloves when cutting hot peppers; the oils can burn skin. Avoid touching your face. The processing time listed is for altitudes of 1,000 feet or less. For altitudes up to 3,000 feet, add 5 minutes; 6,000 feet, add 10 minutes; 8,000 feet, add 15 minutes; 10,000 feet, add 20 minutes.
¼ CUP: *74 cal., 1g fat (0 sat. fat), 0 chol., 323mg sod., 16g carb. (15g sugars, 1g fiber), 1g pro.*

OLIVE OIL DIP

SPICY GARLIC BROCCOLI RABE

When it comes to carefree entertaining, you simply can't beat a four-ingredient recipe like this one! Red pepper flakes add just the right amount of spice to colorful broccoli rabe.
—Clara Coulson Minney, Washington Court House, OH

TAKES: 30 min. • **MAKES:** 12 servings

- 3½ lbs. broccoli rabe
- 6 garlic cloves, thinly sliced
- 2 Tbsp. olive oil
- ½ tsp. crushed red pepper flakes
- 1 tsp. salt

1. Fill a Dutch oven two-thirds full with water; bring to a boil. Trim ½ in. from broccoli rabe stems; discard any coarse or damaged leaves. Rinse broccoli rabe in cold water and cut into 2-in. pieces. Add to boiling water. Reduce heat; simmer, uncovered, until crisp-tender, 1-2 minutes. Drain.

2. In a large skillet over medium heat, cook the garlic in oil for 1 minute. Add pepper flakes; cook and stir 30 seconds longer. Add broccoli rabe and salt; heat through.

⅔ CUP: *51 cal., 3g fat (0 sat. fat), 0 chol., 241mg sod., 4g carb. (0 sugars, 3g fiber), 4g pro.* **Diabetic exchanges:** *1 vegetable, ½ fat.*

SPICY GARLIC
BROCCOLI RABE

PEPPERED CILANTRO RICE

PEPPERED CILANTRO RICE

This colorful confetti rice is a traditional dish in Puerto Rico. We enjoy it in the summer alongside grilled shrimp kabobs, but it's good with almost any entree.
—Laura Lunardi, West Chester, PA

PREP: 10 min. • **COOK:** 25 min. • **MAKES:** 6 servings

- 1 small onion, finely chopped
- 1 small sweet yellow pepper, finely chopped
- 1 small sweet red pepper, finely chopped
- 2 garlic cloves, minced
- 1 Tbsp. olive oil
- 2 cups water
- 1 cup uncooked long grain rice
- ¾ tsp. salt
- ¼ tsp. pepper
- 2 Tbsp. minced fresh cilantro

1. In a large saucepan, saute the onion, peppers and garlic in oil until crisp-tender. Add the water, rice, salt and pepper. Bring to a boil. Reduce heat; cover and simmer until the rice is tender, 18-22 minutes.

2. Remove from the heat; fluff with a fork. Stir in cilantro.

⅔ CUP: *156 cal., 3g fat (0 sat. fat), 0 chol., 298mg sod., 30g carb. (1g sugars, 1g fiber), 3g pro.* **Diabetic exchanges:** *2 starch, ½ fat.*

LIME & SESAME GRILLED EGGPLANT

LIME & SESAME GRILLED EGGPLANT

I fell in love with eggplant while living in Greece. The seasonings in my recipe have an Asian twist, but the dish still makes me think Greek.
—*Allyson Meyler, Greensboro, NC*

TAKES: 20 min. • **MAKES:** 6 servings

- 3 Tbsp. lime juice
- 1 Tbsp. sesame oil
- 1½ tsp. reduced-sodium soy sauce
- 1 garlic clove, minced
- ½ tsp. grated fresh gingerroot or ¼ tsp. ground ginger
- ½ tsp. salt
- ⅛ tsp. pepper
- 1 medium eggplant (1¼ lbs.), cut lengthwise into ½-in. slices
- 2 tsp. honey
- ⅛ tsp. crushed red pepper flakes
  Thinly sliced green onion and sesame seeds

1. In a small bowl, whisk the first 7 ingredients until blended; brush 2 Tbsp. juice mixture over both sides of eggplant slices. Grill, covered, over medium heat until tender, 4-6 minutes on each side.

2. Transfer eggplant to a serving plate. Stir honey and pepper flakes into remaining juice mixture; drizzle over eggplant. Sprinkle with green onion and sesame seeds.

1 SERVING: *50 cal., 2g fat (0 sat. fat), 0 chol., 246mg sod., 7g carb. (4g sugars, 2g fiber), 1g pro.* **Diabetic exchanges:** *1 vegetable, ½ fat.*

SLOW-COOKED MAC & CHEESE

Slow-cooked mac and cheese—the words alone are enough to make mouths water. This is comfort food at its best: rich and extra cheesy. And the slow cooker makes it so easy.
—*Shelby Molina, Whitewater, WI*

PREP: 25 min. • **COOK:** 2½ hours • **MAKES:** 9 servings

- 2 cups uncooked elbow macaroni
- 1 can (12 oz.) evaporated milk
- 1½ cups whole milk
- 2 large eggs
- ¼ cup butter, melted
- 1 tsp. salt
- 2½ cups shredded cheddar cheese
- 2½ cups shredded sharp cheddar cheese, divided

1. Cook macaroni according to package directions; drain and rinse in cold water. In a large bowl, combine the evaporated milk, milk, eggs, butter and salt. Stir in the cheddar cheese, 2 cups sharp cheddar cheese and macaroni.

2. Transfer to a greased 3-qt. slow cooker. Cover and cook on low for 2½-3 hours or until center is set, stirring once. Sprinkle with remaining sharp cheddar cheese.

¾ CUP: *415 cal., 28g fat (20g sat. fat), 143mg chol., 745mg sod., 20g carb. (6g sugars, 1g fiber), 21g pro.*

SLOW-COOKED MAC & CHEESE

SAN DIEGO SUCCOTASH

I brought home some summer squash from my job at a nursery, decided to put it in succotash, and this recipe was born. I named it after my hometown because the yellow and green colors of the dish remind me of the sunny days here in beautiful San Diego.
—Pat Sallume, San Diego, CA

TAKES: 20 min. • **MAKES:** 6 servings

- 2 Tbsp. butter
- 1 medium zucchini, halved and sliced
- 1 small yellow summer squash, halved and sliced
- 1 pkg. (10 oz.) frozen corn
- 1½ cups frozen lima beans
- 1 shallot, chopped
- 1 garlic clove, minced
- ¼ tsp. salt
- ¼ tsp. pepper

In a large skillet, heat butter over medium-high heat. Add zucchini, summer squash, corn, lima beans and shallot; cook and stir until the vegetables are crisp-tender, 6-8 minutes. Add garlic, salt and pepper; cook 1 minute longer.

¾ CUP: *140 cal., 5g fat (3g sat. fat), 10mg chol., 149mg sod., 22g carb. (4g sugars, 4g fiber), 5g pro.* **Diabetic exchanges:** *1½ starch, 1 fat.*

AIR-FRIED RADISHES

Radishes aren't just for salads. This veggie makes a colorful side for any meal.
—Taste of Home *Test Kitchen*

TAKES: 25 min. • **MAKES:** 6 servings

- 2¼ lbs. radishes, trimmed and quartered (about 6 cups)
- 3 Tbsp. olive oil
- 1 Tbsp. minced fresh oregano or 1 tsp. dried oregano
- ¼ tsp. salt
- ⅛ tsp. pepper

Preheat air fryer to 375°. Toss radishes with the remaining ingredients. Place radishes on greased tray in air-fryer basket. Cook until crisp-tender, 12-15 minutes, stirring occasionally.

⅔ CUP: *88 cal., 7g fat (1g sat. fat), 0 chol., 165mg sod., 6g carb. (3g sugars, 3g fiber), 1g pro.* **Diabetic exchanges:** *1½ fat, 1 vegetable.*

ROAST CAULIFLOWER WITH PEPPERONCINI

ROAST CAULIFLOWER WITH PEPPERONCINI

Cauliflower was never one of my favorites, but I was determined to like it. I tweaked this recipe for many years and finally found the perfect mix of flavors and ingredients.
—Hannah Hicks, Marina del Rey, CA

TAKES: 30 min. • **MAKES:** 6 servings

- 1 large head cauliflower, broken into florets (about 8 cups)
- 1 Tbsp. plus 1 tsp. olive oil, divided
- ¼ tsp. kosher salt
- ¼ tsp. pepper
- 1 jar (3½ oz.) capers, drained and patted dry
- 1 jar (16 oz.) pepperoncini, drained and coarsely chopped
- ½ cup sliced almonds, toasted
- 1 Tbsp. sherry vinegar

1. Preheat oven to 450°. Place cauliflower in a 15x10x1-in. baking pan. Drizzle with 1 Tbsp. oil; sprinkle with salt and pepper. Roast until tender, 15-20 minutes, stirring halfway through cooking.
2. Meanwhile, in a small skillet, heat the remaining 1 tsp. oil over medium-high heat. Add the capers; cook and stir until golden brown, 4-6 minutes. Drain on paper towels.
3. Stir pepperoncini, almonds and capers into cauliflower; drizzle with vinegar. Serve immediately.

¾ CUP: *122 cal., 7g fat (1g sat. fat), 0 chol., 962mg sod., 11g carb. (3g sugars, 4g fiber), 5g pro.*

TEST KITCHEN TIP

If you cannot find sherry vinegar, red wine vinegar works just as well.

MEDITERRANEAN CAULIFLOWER

MOM'S PICKLED CARROTS

My mom came up with the recipe for these pickled carrots. Once folks try them, they are hooked.
—Robin Koble, Fairview, PA

- -

PREP: 15 min. + chilling • **COOK:** 20 min.
MAKES: 6 cups

2	lbs. carrots, cut lengthwise into ¼-in.-thick strips
1½	cups sugar
1½	cups water
1½	cups cider vinegar
¼	cup mustard seed
3	cinnamon sticks (3 in.)
3	whole cloves

1. Place carrots in a large saucepan; add enough water to cover. Bring to a boil. Cook, covered, until crisp-tender, 3-5 minutes. Drain. Transfer to a large bowl. In another large saucepan, combine remaining ingredients. Bring to a boil. Reduce heat; simmer, uncovered, for 20 minutes. Pour mixture over carrots. Refrigerate, covered, overnight to allow flavors to blend.
2. Transfer mixture to jars. Cover and refrigerate up to 1 month.
¼ CUP: 30 cal., 0 fat (0 sat. fat), 0 chol., 170mg sod., 7g carb. (6g sugars, 1g fiber), 1g pro.

FRESH HERB BUTTER

I love impressing dinner guests with flavored butter. I mix up a big batch and then freeze it so when company comes, it's ready to go.
—Pam Duncan, Summers, AR

- -

PREP: 25 min. + freezing • **MAKES:** 24 servings

1	cup butter, softened
2	Tbsp. minced fresh chives
2	Tbsp. minced fresh parsley
2	Tbsp. minced fresh tarragon
1	Tbsp. lemon juice
¼	tsp. pepper

In a small bowl, beat all ingredients until blended. Spread onto baking sheet to ½-in. thickness. Freeze, covered, until firm. Cut butter with a 1-in. cookie cutter. Store, layered between waxed paper, in an airtight container in the refrigerator up to 1 week or in the freezer up to 3 months.
1 SERVING: 202 cal., 23g fat (14g sat. fat), 61mg chol., 232mg sod., 0 carb. (0 sugars, 0 fiber), 0 pro.

MEDITERRANEAN CAULIFLOWER

I adapted a recipe I received from a friend to make this tasty—and deliciously different— cauliflower dish. It's prepared quickly in a skillet and uses only a handful of ingredients. It's a great way to take ordinary cauliflower to a whole new level!
—Valerie Smith, Aston, PA

- -

TAKES: 25 min. • **MAKES:** 10 servings

1	large head cauliflower, broken into florets
2	cans (14½ oz. each) diced tomatoes with basil, oregano and garlic, drained
½	cup sliced green olives with pimientos
4	green onions, sliced
½	tsp. pepper
¼	tsp. salt
1	cup crumbled feta cheese

1. In a 6-qt. stockpot, place a steamer basket over 1 in. of water. Place cauliflower in basket. Bring to a boil. Reduce heat; steam, covered, until crisp-tender, 4-6 minutes. Drain and return to pan.
2. Stir in tomatoes, olives, onions, pepper and salt. Bring to a boil. Reduce heat; simmer, uncovered, until cauliflower is tender and tomatoes are heated through, 3-5 minutes. Sprinkle with feta cheese before serving.
¾ CUP: 86 cal., 3g fat (1g sat. fat), 6mg chol., 548mg sod., 10g carb. (4g sugars, 4g fiber), 4g pro. **Diabetic exchanges:** 1 vegetable, ½ fat.

BROCCOLI WITH GARLIC,
BACON & PARMESAN

NUT-FREE PESTO

NUT-FREE PESTO

This pesto recipe was handed down from my grandmother. You will notice it has no nuts, which were considered a filler in my Italian family. Everyone I serve this to says it's the best. Spread it on pizza crust, toss with hot pasta or use as a sandwich spread.
—Mary Jo Galick, Portland, OR

TAKES: 10 min. • **MAKES:** 1 cup

- 2 cups loosely packed basil leaves
- 1 cup grated Parmesan cheese
- 1 cup packed fresh parsley sprigs
- 3 Tbsp. butter, softened
- 2 garlic cloves, halved
- ¼ tsp. salt
- ½ cup extra virgin olive oil

Pulse the first 6 ingredients in a food processor until coarsely chopped. While processing, gradually add oil in a steady stream until mixture is smooth. Store in an airtight container in the refrigerator for up to 1 week.

2 TBSP.: *206 cal., 21g fat (6g sat. fat), 20mg chol., 293mg sod., 2g carb. (0 sugars, 0 fiber), 3g pro.*

BROCCOLI WITH GARLIC, BACON & PARMESAN

This simple yet sophisticated side dish uses just a few basic ingredients. The way the bold garlic flavor blends with the smoky bacon makes ordinary broccoli irresistible..
—Erin Chilcoat, Central Islip, NY

TAKES: 30 min. • **MAKES:** 8 servings

- 1 tsp. salt
- 2 bunches broccoli (about 3 lbs.), stems removed, cut into florets
- 6 thick-sliced bacon strips, chopped
- 2 Tbsp. olive oil
- 6 to 8 garlic cloves, thinly sliced
- ½ tsp. crushed red pepper flakes
- ¼ cup shredded Parmesan cheese

1. Fill a 6-qt. stockpot two-thirds full with water; add salt and bring to a boil over high heat. In batches, add broccoli and cook until bright green, 2-3 minutes; remove broccoli with a slotted spoon.
2. In a large skillet, cook the bacon over medium heat until crisp, stirring occasionally. Remove with a slotted spoon; drain on paper towels. Discard drippings, reserving 1 Tbsp. in pan.
3. Add oil to drippings; heat over medium heat. Add garlic and pepper flakes; cook and stir until garlic is fragrant, 2-3 minutes (do not allow to brown). Add broccoli; cook until broccoli is tender, stirring occasionally. Stir in bacon; sprinkle with cheese.
¾ CUP: *155 cal., 10g fat (3g sat. fat), 11mg chol., 371mg sod., 11g carb. (3g sugars, 4g fiber), 8g pro.* **Diabetic exchanges:** *2 fat, 1 vegetable.*

BEST EVER BANANA BREAD
PAGE 166

Breads, Rolls & Muffins

Few things say lovin' from the oven like freshly baked breads, biscuits and other buttery delights. Turn here for a heartwarming collection of golden greats.

CINNAMON APPLE CIDER MONKEY BREAD

I use cinnamon and apple cider to turn plain cinnamon rolls into monkey bread. It's a hit with my boys, who love the sticky sweetness.
—Kelly Walsh, Aviston, IL

PREP: 20 min. • **BAKE:** 45 min. + standing
MAKES: 16 servings

- 5 envelopes (0.74 oz. each) instant spiced cider mix
- 3 tubes (12.4 oz. each) refrigerated cinnamon rolls with icing
- 2 medium Granny Smith apples, peeled and chopped
- 1 cup chopped pecans or walnuts
- 6 Tbsp. butter, melted
- 2 tsp. ground cinnamon

1. Preheat oven to 350°. Combine cider mixes. Separate cinnamon rolls, setting aside icings; cut each roll into quarters. Add to cider mixture; toss to coat.

2. Arrange a third of the dough pieces in a well-greased 10-in. fluted tube pan; top with half of the apples and half of the pecans. Repeat layers once. Top with remaining dough.

3. Mix the melted butter, cinnamon and icing from 1 container until blended. Drizzle over top of rolls. Bake until golden brown, 45-50 minutes. (If needed, cover the top loosely with foil during last 5 minutes to prevent overbrowning.)

4. Immediately invert the monkey bread onto a serving plate; keep the pan inverted 10 minutes, allowing bread to release. Remove pan. Meanwhile, microwave remaining icing, uncovered, until softened, about 10 seconds. Drizzle over monkey bread. Serve warm.

1 SERVING: *329 cal., 17g fat (5g sat. fat), 11mg chol., 553mg sod., 41g carb. (5g sugars, 1g fiber), 4g pro.*

HOMEMADE TORTILLAS

I usually have to double this recipe because we go through these so quickly. The tortillas are so tender, chewy and simple, you'll never use store-bought again.
—Kristin Van Dyken, Kennewick, WA

TAKES: 30 min. • **MAKES:** 8 tortillas

- 2 cups all-purpose flour
- ½ tsp. salt
- ¾ cup water
- 3 Tbsp. olive oil

1. In a large bowl, combine flour and salt. Stir in water and oil. Turn onto a floured surface; knead 10-12 times, adding a little flour or water if needed to achieve a smooth dough. Let rest for 10 minutes.

2. Divide dough into 8 portions. On a lightly floured surface, roll each portion into a 7-in. circle.

3. In a greased cast-iron or other heavy skillet, cook tortillas over medium heat until lightly browned, 1 minute on each side. Serve warm.

1 TORTILLA: *159 cal., 5g fat (1g sat. fat), 0 chol., 148mg sod., 24g carb. (1g sugars, 1g fiber), 3g pro.* **Diabetic exchanges:** *1½ starch, 1 fat.*

READER REVIEW

"Never thought I would make homemade tortillas, but now that I have, I probably won't buy them again! These are delicious. Made flavorful chicken fajitas to use them, as well as breakfast burritos. They freeze well, too!"
—JUJUBEE1762, TASTEOFHOME.COM

CINNAMON APPLE CIDER MONKEY BREAD

SWEET CORN MUFFINS

I love to make cornbread and corn muffins, but often the results are not moist or sweet enough for my taste. So I experimented until I came up with these light, pleasantly sweet muffins. They ended up winning a blue ribbon at our county fair.
—*Patty Bourne, Owings, MD*

PREP: 10 min. • **BAKE:** 25 min. • **MAKES:** 1 dozen

1½ cups all-purpose flour
1 cup sugar
¾ cup cornmeal
1 Tbsp. baking powder
½ tsp. salt
2 large eggs, room temperature
½ cup shortening
1 cup 2% milk, divided

In a bowl, combine the dry ingredients. Add eggs, shortening and ½ cup of milk; beat for 1 minute. Add remaining milk; beat just until blended. Fill 12 paper-lined muffin cups three-fourths full. Bake at 350° until muffins test done, 25-30 minutes.

1 MUFFIN: *254 cal., 10g fat (3g sat. fat), 33mg chol., 241mg sod., 38g carb. (18g sugars, 1g fiber), 4g pro.*

SWEET CORN MUFFINS

MUSHROOM & ONION CRESCENTS

MUSHROOM & ONION CRESCENTS

I knew these stuffed crescents would be a hit when my husband ate most of the filling before I could roll it into the dough! I've learned to be sneaky when making them now.
—*Carrie Pommier, Farmington, MN*

PREP: 25 min. • **BAKE:** 10 min. • **MAKES:** 8 rolls

3 Tbsp. butter, divided
1 cup sliced baby portobello mushrooms
1 medium onion, halved and sliced
3 garlic cloves, minced
⅓ cup grated Parmesan cheese
1 Tbsp. minced fresh parsley
1 tube (8 oz.) refrigerated reduced-fat crescent rolls
½ cup shredded part-skim mozzarella cheese

1. Preheat oven to 375°. In a large skillet, heat 2 Tbsp. butter over medium-high heat. Add mushrooms and onion; cook and stir 2-3 minutes or until softened. Reduce heat to medium-low; cook and stir 10-12 minutes or until onion is golden. Add garlic; cook 1 minute longer. Remove from heat; stir in Parmesan cheese and parsley.
2. Unroll crescent dough; separate into triangles. Place 1 Tbsp. mushroom mixture at the wide end of each triangle; top with 1 Tbsp. mozzarella cheese and roll up. Place 2 in. apart on an ungreased baking sheet, point side down; curve ends to form a crescent. Melt remaining butter; brush over tops.
3. Bake 10-12 minutes or until golden brown. Refrigerate leftovers.

1 CRESCENT: *174 cal., 11g fat (6g sat. fat), 19mg chol., 367mg sod., 15g carb. (3g sugars, 0 fiber), 5g pro.*

LEMON POPOVERS WITH PECAN HONEY BUTTER

EASY CAST-IRON PEACH BISCUIT ROLLS

I used to love going to the local coffee shop and enjoying fresh peach cinnamon rolls, but being a busy mom of three, I don't have the time anymore. To re-create it at home, I developed this no-yeast recipe that is quick and simple to make!
—Heather Karow, Burnett, WI

- -

PREP: 25 min. • **BAKE:** 25 min. + cooling
MAKES: 1 dozen

1 cup packed brown sugar
¼ cup butter, softened
3 tsp. ground cinnamon
DOUGH
2 cups all-purpose flour
2 Tbsp. sugar
1 Tbsp. baking powder
1 tsp. salt
3 Tbsp. butter
¾ cup 2% milk
1 can (15 oz.) sliced peaches in juice, undrained
1 cup confectioners' sugar

1. Preheat oven to 350°. In a small bowl, mix the brown sugar, butter and cinnamon until crumbly. Reserve half for topping. Sprinkle remaining crumb mixture onto bottom of a 10-in. cast-iron or other ovenproof skillet.
2. For dough, in a large bowl, mix the flour, sugar, baking powder and salt. Cut in butter until crumbly. Add the milk; stir to form a soft dough (dough will be sticky). Roll into an 18x12-in. rectangle. Sprinkle reserved topping to within ½ in. of edges.
3. Drain peaches, reserving 2 Tbsp. juice for glaze. Chop peaches; place over topping. Roll up jelly-roll style, starting with a long side; pinch seam to seal. Cut into 12 slices. Place in prepared skillet, cut side down. Bake until lightly browned, 25-30 minutes. Cool on a wire rack 10 minutes.
4. For glaze, combine the confectioners' sugar and 1-2 Tbsp. reserved peach juice to reach desired consistency. Drizzle over the warm rolls.
1 ROLL: *279 cal., 7g fat (4g sat. fat), 19mg chol., 746mg sod., 52g carb. (35g sugars, 1g fiber), 3g pro.*

LEMON POPOVERS WITH PECAN HONEY BUTTER

My mom passed this recipe down to me many years ago. We love the delicate lemon flavor with the pecan honey butter. The popovers are a nice addition to any dinner, but they're especially delicious at breakfast with a bowl of fruit and yogurt.
—Joan Hallford, North Richland Hills, TX

- -

PREP: 10 min. • **BAKE:** 25 min.
MAKES: 6 servings

2 large eggs
1 cup 2% milk
1 cup all-purpose flour
½ tsp. salt
5 Tbsp. finely chopped toasted pecans, divided
¾ tsp. grated lemon zest
2 tsp. lemon juice
6 Tbsp. butter, softened
6 Tbsp. honey

1. Preheat oven to 450°. In a large bowl, whisk eggs and milk until blended. Whisk in the flour and salt until smooth (do not overbeat). Stir in 3 Tbsp. pecans, lemon zest and lemon juice.
2. Generously grease a 6-cup popover pan with nonstick spray; fill cups half full with batter. Bake 15 minutes. Reduce oven setting to 350° (do not open oven door). Bake until deep golden brown, 10-15 minutes longer (do not underbake).
3. Meanwhile, combine butter, honey and remaining 2 Tbsp. pecans. Immediately remove popovers from pan to a wire rack. Pierce side of each popover with a sharp knife to let steam escape. Serve popovers immediately with pecan honey butter.
1 POPOVER WITH ABOUT 2 TBSP. HONEY BUTTER: *325 cal., 18g fat (9g sat. fat), 96mg chol., 332mg sod., 36g carb. (20g sugars, 1g fiber), 6g pro.*

**EASY CAST-IRON
PEACH BISCUIT ROLLS**

BACON-PEANUT BUTTER CORNBREAD MUFFINS

BACON-PEANUT BUTTER CORNBREAD MUFFINS

My family just can't get enough bacon and peanut butter, so I created these quick and easy cornbread muffins using ingredients I regularly keep stocked in my pantry and fridge. The streusel topping adds a delicious sweet-salty crunch! No peanut butter baking chips on hand? For a different flavor twist, swap in chocolate chips, then drizzle the warm muffins with chocolate syrup instead of caramel topping.
—Shannon Kohn, Summerville, SC

PREP: 25 min. • **BAKE:** 20 min. • **MAKES:** 6 muffins

- 6 Tbsp. softened butter, divided
- ½ cup dry roasted peanuts, chopped
- 1 pkg. (2.1 oz.) ready-to-serve fully cooked bacon, finely chopped, divided
- 1 Tbsp. light brown sugar
- 1 pkg. (8½ oz.) cornbread/muffin mix
- ½ cup buttermilk
- 2 large eggs, room temperature
- ¼ cup creamy peanut butter
- ⅔ cup peanut butter chips
  Caramel ice cream topping, optional

1. Preheat oven to 375°. Grease six 6-oz. ramekins or jumbo muffin cups with 2 Tbsp. butter. For topping, in a small bowl combine 2 Tbsp. butter, peanuts, 3 Tbsp. bacon and brown sugar; set aside.

2. In a large bowl, beat the muffin mix, buttermilk and eggs. Microwave peanut butter and remaining 2 Tbsp. butter until melted; stir into batter. Fold in peanut butter chips and remaining ⅔ cup bacon. Pour into prepared ramekins; sprinkle with topping.

3. Bake until a toothpick inserted in center comes out clean, 20-25 minutes. Cool 5 minutes before removing from ramekins to a wire rack. Serve warm. If desired, drizzle muffins with caramel ice cream topping.

1 MUFFIN: *590 cal., 38g fat (15g sat. fat), 94mg chol., 818mg sod., 45g carb. (20g sugars, 5g fiber), 18g pro.*

CARAMEL-SCOTCH CREAM CHEESE COFFEE CAKE

I came up with this cream cheese coffee cake recipe so I could make a delicious brunch treat using convenient crescent dough for the base. Serving it when it's cold means that all the cozy filling stays with each slice.
—Sherry Little, Sherwood, AR

PREP: 25 min. • **BAKE:** 20 min. + chilling • **MAKES:** 8 servings

- 1 tube (12 oz.) large refrigerated buttery crescent rolls
- 1 carton (7½ oz.) spreadable brown sugar and cinnamon cream cheese
- ⅓ cup butterscotch-caramel ice cream topping
- ½ cup chopped pecans
- ⅓ cup packed brown sugar
- ¼ cup all-purpose flour
- 2 Tbsp. cold butter
- 1 large egg, beaten

1. Preheat oven to 375°. Unroll crescent dough into long rectangle; place on a parchment-lined baking sheet. Press perforations to seal. Spread cream cheese down center third of rectangle. Drizzle with ice cream topping; sprinkle with pecans. Combine brown sugar and flour; cut in butter until crumbly. Sprinkle half the mixture over pecans.

2. On each long side of dough, cut 8 strips at an angle, about 2 in. into the center. Fold 1 strip from each side over filling and pinch ends together; repeat. Brush with beaten egg. Sprinkle with remaining brown sugar mixture.

3. Bake until deep golden brown, 18-22 minutes. Cool 5 minutes before removing from pan to a wire rack. Refrigerate until cold.

1 SLICE: *381 cal., 19g fat (8g sat. fat), 16mg chol., 472mg sod., 47g carb. (25g sugars, 2g fiber), 5g pro.*

CARAMEL-SCOTCH CREAM CHEESE COFFEE CAKE

BAVARIAN CHOCOLATE-HAZELNUT BRAID

Mmm! This delectable loaf gives you a little taste of Bavaria, thanks to the chocolaty, creamy filling and flaky crust.
—Mary Louise Lever, Rome, GA

- -

PREP: 15 min. • **BAKE:** 20 min. + cooling
MAKES: 12 servings

- ¾ cup (6 oz.) vanilla yogurt
- ⅓ cup sweetened shredded coconut
- 1 large egg, separated
- ¼ tsp. almond extract
- 1 tube (8 oz.) refrigerated crescent rolls
- ⅓ cup Nutella
- 3 Tbsp. sliced almonds
- 2 Tbsp. confectioners' sugar

1. In a small bowl, combine the yogurt, coconut, egg yolk and extract.
2. Unroll crescent dough onto a lightly greased baking sheet into 1 long rectangle; seal seams and perforations. Roll out into a 14x9-in. rectangle.
3. Carefully spread Nutella in a 3-in.-wide strip down center of rectangle. Top with yogurt mixture. On each long side, cut 1-in.-wide strips to within ½ in. of filling. Starting at 1 end, fold alternating strips at an angle across filling.
4. Whisk egg white; brush over top and sides of dough. Sprinkle with almonds.
5. Bake at 350° for 20-25 minutes or until golden brown. Sprinkle with confectioners' sugar. Cool for 10 minutes before cutting into slices.
1 SLICE: *160 cal., 9g fat (2g sat. fat), 18mg chol., 174mg sod., 17g carb. (10g sugars, 1g fiber), 3g pro.*

EGG-FREE DOUBLE CHOCOLATE BANANA MUFFINS

EGG-FREE DOUBLE CHOCOLATE BANANA MUFFINS

I am always looking to use up the brown bananas on my counter. My usual go-to was banana nut bread, but when my youngest developed an egg allergy I had to come up with something different. Since bananas and chocolate are so good together, I decided to make these muffins. You would never be able to tell they are egg-free.
—Danielle Siero, Farmington, MI

- -

PREP: 20 min. • **BAKE:** 15 min.
MAKES: 1 dozen

- 1½ cups all-purpose flour
- ⅔ cup sugar
- ½ cup baking cocoa
- 1 tsp. baking powder
- ½ tsp. baking soda
- 1⅓ cups mashed ripe bananas (about 2 to 3 medium)
- ½ cup plain yogurt
- ⅓ cup canola oil
- 1½ tsp. vanilla extract
- ¾ cup semisweet chocolate chips
  Baking cocoa, optional

1. Preheat oven to 350°. In a large bowl, whisk the first 5 ingredients. In another bowl, whisk the bananas, yogurt, oil and vanilla until blended. Add to the flour mixture; stir just until moistened. Fold in the chocolate chips.
2. Fill 12 greased or foil-lined muffin cups three-fourths full. Bake until a toothpick inserted in the center comes out clean, 15-20 minutes. Cool for 5 minutes before removing to a wire rack. If desired, dust with baking cocoa. Serve warm.
1 MUFFIN: *246 cal., 10g fat (3g sat. fat), 1mg chol., 99mg sod., 38g carb. (21g sugars, 2g fiber), 3g pro.*

GOUDA & ROASTED
POTATO BREAD

GOUDA & ROASTED POTATO BREAD

Our family tried roasted potato bread at a bakery on a road trip, and I came up with my own recipe when we realized we lived much too far away to have it regularly. It's ideal with soups and for sandwiches.
—Elisabeth Larsen, Pleasant Grove, UT

PREP: 45 min. + rising • **BAKE:** 40 min.
MAKES: 1 loaf (16 slices)

- ½ lb. Yukon Gold potatoes, chopped (about ¾ cup)
- 1½ tsp. olive oil
- 1½ tsp. salt, divided
- 1 pkg. (¼ oz.) active dry yeast
- 2½ to 3 cups all-purpose flour
- 1 cup warm water (120° to 130°)
- ½ cup shredded smoked Gouda cheese

1. Arrange 1 oven rack at lowest rack setting; place second rack in middle of oven. Preheat oven to 425°. Place potatoes in a greased 15x10x1-in. baking pan. Drizzle with oil; sprinkle with ½ tsp. salt. Toss to coat. Roast until tender, 20-25 minutes, stirring occasionally.

2. In a large bowl, mix yeast, remaining 1 tsp. salt and 2 cups flour. Add warm water; beat on medium speed until smooth. Stir in enough remaining flour to form a soft dough (dough will be sticky). Turn dough onto a floured surface; knead until smooth and elastic, 6-8 minutes. Gently knead in roasted potatoes and cheese. Place in a greased bowl, turning once to grease the top. Cover and let rise in a warm place until doubled, about 1 hour.

3. Punch down dough. Shape into a 7-in. round loaf. Place on a parchment-lined baking sheet. Cover with a kitchen towel; let rise in a warm place until dough expands to a 9-in. loaf, about 45 minutes.

4. Place an oven-safe skillet on bottom oven rack. Meanwhile, in a teakettle, bring 2 cups water to a boil. Using a sharp knife, make a slash (¼ in. deep) across top of loaf. Place bread on top rack. Pull bottom rack out by 6-8 in.; add boiling water to skillet. (Work quickly and carefully, pouring water away from you. Don't worry if some water is left in the kettle.) Carefully slide bottom rack back into place; quickly close door to trap steam in oven.

5. Bake 10 minutes. Reduce oven setting to 375°. Bake until deep golden brown,

30-35 minutes longer. Remove loaf to a wire rack to cool.

1 SLICE: *101 cal., 2g fat (1g sat. fat), 4mg chol., 253mg sod., 18g carb. (0 sugars, 1g fiber), 3g pro.*

VANILLA-GLAZED GINGER SCONES

Gingerbread is a flavor that works with all sorts of delicious holiday baked goods. To glaze these ginger scones, just dip a fork or spoon into the glaze mixture and then drizzle over the tops.
—Colleen Delawder, Herndon, VA

PREP: 25 min. • **BAKE:** 15 min.
MAKES: 12 servings

- 2 cups all-purpose flour
- ¼ cup packed light brown sugar
- 2½ tsp. baking powder
- 1½ tsp. ground cinnamon
- 1 tsp. ground ginger
- ¼ tsp. salt
- 6 Tbsp. cold butter
- ¾ cup heavy whipping cream
- 1 large egg, room temperature
- ¼ cup molasses
- 1 Tbsp. maple syrup

GLAZE
- 1 cup confectioners' sugar
- ¼ cup heavy whipping cream
- 1 tsp. vanilla extract
  Dash salt
- ¼ cup finely chopped crystallized ginger

1. Preheat oven to 400°. In a large bowl, whisk the first 6 ingredients. Cut in butter until mixture resembles coarse crumbs. In another bowl, whisk cream, egg, molasses and syrup until blended; stir into crumb mixture just until moistened.

2. Drop the dough by ¼ cupfuls onto a parchment-lined baking sheet. Bake until golden brown, 12-15 minutes. In a small bowl, combine confectioners' sugar, cream, vanilla and salt; stir until smooth. Drizzle over the scones; sprinkle with ginger. Serve scones warm.

1 SCONE: *299 cal., 14g fat (8g sat. fat), 53mg chol., 226mg sod., 42g carb. (23g sugars, 1g fiber), 3g pro.*

VANILLA-GLAZED GINGER SCONES

BLUEBERRIES & CREAM COFFEE CAKE

3. Bake until a toothpick inserted near the center comes out clean, 55-60 minutes. Cool for 10 minutes before removing from pan to a wire rack to cool completely. Just before serving, dust cake with confectioners' sugar.

1 SLICE: *428 cal., 20g fat (12g sat. fat), 76mg chol., 233mg sod., 60g carb. (45g sugars, 1g fiber), 4g pro.*

BEST EVER BANANA BREAD

(SHOWN ON PAGE 156)

Whenever I pass a display of bananas in the grocery store, I can almost smell the wonderful aroma of this bread. It really is amazingly good!
—Gert Kaiser, Kenosha, WI

PREP: 15 min. • **BAKE:** 1¼ hours + cooling
MAKES: 1 loaf (16 slices)

- 1¾ cups all-purpose flour
- 1½ cups sugar
- 1 tsp. baking soda
- ½ tsp. salt
- 2 large eggs, room temperature
- 2 medium ripe bananas, mashed (1 cup)
- ½ cup canola oil
- ¼ cup plus 1 Tbsp. buttermilk
- 1 tsp. vanilla extract
- 1 cup chopped walnuts

1. Preheat oven to 350°. In a large bowl, stir together flour, sugar, baking soda and salt. In another bowl, combine the eggs, bananas, oil, buttermilk and vanilla; add to flour mixture, stirring just until combined. Fold in nuts.

2. Pour into a greased or parchment-lined 9x5-in. loaf pan. If desired, sprinkle with additional walnuts. Bake until a toothpick comes out clean, 1¼-1½ hours. Cool in pan for 15 minutes before removing to a wire rack.

1 SLICE: *255 cal., 12g fat (1g sat. fat), 27mg chol., 166mg sod., 34g carb. (21g sugars, 1g fiber), 4g pro.*

BLUEBERRIES & CREAM COFFEE CAKE

This blueberry coffee cake is a Saturday morning tradition my boys grew up with. It's also my go-to recipe for all of our holiday get-togethers because it's just perfect for breakfast, brunch or even dessert. It's easy to make, and it's the most delicious coffee cake I've ever had.
—Susan Ober, Franconia, NH

PREP: 20 min. • **BAKE:** 55 min. + cooling
MAKES: 12 servings

- 1 cup butter, softened
- 2 cups sugar
- 2 large eggs, room temperature
- 1 tsp. vanilla extract
- 1¾ cups all-purpose flour
- 1 tsp. baking powder
- ¼ tsp. salt
- 1 cup sour cream
- 1 cup fresh or frozen unsweetened blueberries
- ½ cup packed brown sugar
- ½ cup chopped pecans, optional
- 1 tsp. ground cinnamon
- 1 Tbsp. confectioners' sugar

1. Preheat oven to 350°. In a large bowl, cream butter and sugar until light and fluffy, 5-7 minutes. Add eggs, 1 at a time, beating well after each addition. Beat in vanilla. Combine the flour, baking powder and salt; add to the creamed mixture alternately with the sour cream, beating well after each addition. Fold in blueberries.

2. Spoon half of batter into a greased and floured 10-in. fluted tube pan. In a small bowl, combine the brown sugar, pecans if desired, and cinnamon. Sprinkle half over the batter. Top with remaining batter; sprinkle with remaining sugar mixture. Cut through batter with a knife to swirl.

GRANDMA'S ONION SQUARES

CARAWAY CHEESE BISCUITS

My grandchildren are always happy when I pull a pan of these cheesy biscuits from the oven. We all think that the golden brown goodies are just perfect for dipping into chili or stew.
—Lorraine Caland, Shuniah, ON

PREP: 10 min. • **BAKE:** 15 min. • **MAKES:** 10 biscuits

- 2 cups all-purpose flour
- 3 tsp. baking powder
- ¾ tsp. salt
- 6 Tbsp. cold butter, cubed
- 1 cup (4 oz.) finely shredded cheddar cheese, divided
- 1½ tsp. caraway seeds
- ¾ cup 2% milk

1. Preheat oven to 425°. In a large bowl, whisk the flour, baking powder and salt. Cut in butter until mixture resembles coarse crumbs. Stir in ¾ cup cheese and caraway seeds. Add milk; stir just until moistened.
2. Drop by ¼ cupfuls onto ungreased baking sheets. Sprinkle with the remaining cheese. Bake 12-15 minutes or until golden brown. Serve warm.
1 BISCUIT: *208 cal., 11g fat (7g sat. fat), 31mg chol., 459mg sod., 20g carb. (1g sugars, 1g fiber), 6g pro.*

GRANDMA'S ONION SQUARES

My grandma brought this recipe with her when she emigrated from Italy as a young wife and mother. It is still a family favorite.
—Janet Eddy, Stockton, CA

PREP: 40 min. • **BAKE:** 35 min. • **MAKES:** 9 servings

- 2 Tbsp. olive oil
- 2 cups sliced onions
- 1 tsp. salt, divided
- ¼ tsp. pepper
- 2 cups all-purpose flour
- 3 tsp. baking powder
- 5 Tbsp. shortening
- ⅔ cup 2% milk
- 1 large egg
- ¾ cup sour cream

1. Preheat the oven to 400°. In a large skillet, heat oil over medium heat. Add the onions; cook and stir until softened, 8-10 minutes. Reduce heat to medium-low; cook until onions are deep golden brown, 30-40 minutes, stirring occasionally. Stir in ½ tsp. salt and the pepper.
2. Meanwhile, in a large bowl, combine flour, baking powder and remaining ½ tsp. salt. Cut in shortening until mixture resembles coarse crumbs. Stir in the milk just until moistened. Press into a greased 9-in. square baking pan; top with onions.
3. Combine the egg and sour cream; spread over the onion layer. Bake until golden brown, 35-40 minutes. Cut into 9 squares. Serve warm.
1 PIECE: *256 cal., 15g fat (5g sat. fat), 27mg chol., 447mg sod., 25g carb. (3g sugars, 1g fiber), 5g pro.*

CARAWAY CHEESE BISCUITS

Simply Sourdough (Starter)
Baking bread is a snap with a handy starter on hand.

SOURDOUGH STARTER

Some 25 years ago, I received this recipe and some starter from a good friend who is now a neighbor. Use it to make all sorts of loaves, including the recipes that follow.
—Delila George, Junction City, OR

- -

PREP: 10 min. + standing
MAKES: about 3 cups

> 2 **cups all-purpose flour**
> 1 **pkg. (¼ oz.) active dry yeast**
> 2 **cups warm water (110° to 115°)**

1. In a covered 4-qt. glass or ceramic container, mix flour and yeast. Gradually stir in warm water until smooth. Cover loosely with a kitchen towel; let stand in a warm place 2-4 days or until mixture is bubbly and sour smelling and a clear liquid has formed on top. (The starter may darken, but if the starter turns another color or develops an offensive odor or mold, discard it and start over.)

2. Cover tightly and refrigerate starter until ready to use. Use and replenish starter, or nourish it, once every 1-2 weeks.

To use and replenish starter: Stir to blend in any liquid on top. Remove amount of starter needed; bring to room temperature before using. For each ½ cup starter removed, add ½ cup flour and ½ cup warm water to the remaining starter and stir until smooth. Cover loosely and let stand in a warm place 1-2 days or until light and bubbly. Stir; cover tightly and refrigerate.

To nourish starter: Remove half of the starter. Stir in equal parts of flour and warm water; cover loosely and let stand in a warm place 1-2 days or until light and bubbly. Stir; cover tightly and refrigerate.

1 TBSP.: *19 cal., 0 fat (0 sat. fat), 0 chol., 0 sod., 4g carb. (0 sugars, 0 fiber), 1g pro.*

HONEY WHOLE GRAIN SOURDOUGH

Honey adds a slightly sweet taste to this bread, which nicely complements the tangy sourdough. It's a great way to use the starter.
—Evelyn Newlands, Sun Lakes, AZ

- -

PREP: 20 min. + rising
BAKE: 25 min. + cooling
MAKES: 2 loaves (12 slices each)

> 1 **Tbsp. active dry yeast**
> 1 **cup warm water (110° to 115°)**
> 3 **Tbsp. butter, softened**
> 2 **Tbsp. honey**
> 2 **Tbsp. molasses**
> 2 **cups SOURDOUGH STARTER**
> 3 **Tbsp. toasted wheat germ**
> 1 **Tbsp. sugar**
> 1 **tsp. baking soda**
> 1 **tsp. salt**
> 1 **cup whole wheat flour**
> 3¼ **to 3¾ cups all-purpose flour**
>   **Canola oil**

1. In a large bowl, dissolve yeast in warm water. Add the butter, honey, molasses, Sourdough Starter, wheat germ, sugar, baking soda, salt, whole wheat flour and 2 cups all-purpose flour. Beat until smooth. Stir in enough remaining all-purpose flour to form a soft dough.

2. Turn onto a floured surface; knead until smooth and elastic, about 6-8 minutes. Place in a greased bowl, turning once to grease top. Cover and let rise in a warm place until doubled, about 1 hour.

3. Punch dough down. Turn onto a lightly floured surface; divide in half. Shape into loaves. Place in 2 greased 8x4-in. loaf pans. Cover and let rise until doubled, about 1 hour. Preheat oven to 375°.

4. Brush with oil. Bake 25-30 minutes or until browned. Remove from pans to wire racks to cool.

1 SLICE: *109 cal., 2g fat (1g sat. fat), 4mg chol., 164mg sod., 20g carb. (3g sugars, 1g fiber), 3g pro.*

SOURDOUGH STARTER

SAGE & GRUYERE SOURDOUGH BREAD

SAGE & GRUYERE SOURDOUGH BREAD

A sourdough starter gives loaves extra flavor and helps the rising process. This bread, with sage and Gruyere cheese, comes out so well that I'm thrilled to share it.
—*Debra Kramer, Boca Raton, FL*

- -

PREP: 35 min. + rising • **BAKE:** 25 min. • **MAKES:** 1 loaf (16 slices)

½   **cup SOURDOUGH STARTER**
1⅛   **tsp. active dry yeast**
⅓   **cup warm water (110° to 115°)**
½   **cup canned pumpkin**
½   **cup shredded Gruyere cheese, divided**
4   **tsp. butter, softened**
1   **Tbsp. sugar**
1   **Tbsp. minced fresh sage**
1   **tsp. salt**
2¼   **to 2¾ cups all-purpose flour**
1   **large egg, lightly beaten**

1. Let the Sourdough Starter come to room temperature before using.
2. In a small bowl, dissolve yeast in warm water. In a large bowl, combine Sourdough Starter, pumpkin, ¼ cup cheese, butter, sugar, sage, salt, yeast mixture and 1 cup flour; beat on medium speed until smooth. Stir in enough remaining flour to form a stiff dough (dough will be slightly sticky).
3. Turn dough onto a floured surface; knead until smooth and elastic, 6-8 minutes. Place in a greased bowl, turning once to grease the top. Cover and let rise in a warm place until doubled, about 1 hour.
4. Punch down dough. Turn onto a lightly floured surface; shape into a round loaf. Place on a greased baking sheet. Cover with a kitchen towel; let rise in a warm place until doubled, about 30 minutes. Preheat oven to 375°.
5. Brush egg over loaf; sprinkle with the remaining cheese. Bake 25-30 minutes or until golden brown. Remove from pan to a wire rack to cool.

1 SLICE: *98 cal., 3g fat (1g sat. fat), 18mg chol., 186mg sod., 15g carb. (1g sugars, 1g fiber), 3g pro.*

COUNTRY CRUST SOURDOUGH BREAD

For many years, I've been making 45 loaves of this bread for an annual Christmas bazaar, where we feed bread and soup to over 300 folks.
—*Beverley Whaley, Camano Island, WA*

- -

PREP: 20 min. + rising • **BAKE:** 30 min. • **MAKES:** 2 loaves

2   **pkg. (¼ oz. each) active dry yeast**
1¼   **cups warm water (110° to 115°)**
1   **cup SOURDOUGH STARTER**
2   **large eggs, room temperature**
¼   **cup sugar**
¼   **cup vegetable oil**
1   **tsp. salt**
6   **to 6½ cups all-purpose flour**
    Melted butter

1. In a large bowl, dissolve the yeast in warm water. Add the Sourdough Starter, eggs, sugar, oil, salt and 3 cups flour. Beat until smooth. Stir in enough remaining flour to form a soft dough.
2. Turn onto a floured surface; knead until smooth and elastic, 6-8 minutes. Place in a greased bowl, turning once to grease top. Cover and let rise in a warm place until doubled, about 1 hour.
3. Punch dough down. Turn onto a lightly floured surface; divide in half. Shape into loaves. Place in 2 greased 8x4-in. loaf pans. Cover and let rise until doubled, about 45 minutes. Preheat oven to 375°.
4. Bake 30-35 minutes or until golden brown. Remove from pans to wire racks to cool. Brush with butter.

1 SLICE: *113 cal., 2g fat (0 sat. fat), 12mg chol., 79mg sod., 20g carb. (2g sugars, 1g fiber), 3g pro.*

COUNTRY CRUST SOURDOUGH BREAD

SOURDOUGH FRENCH BREAD

CRANBERRY SOURDOUGH MUFFINS WITH STREUSEL TOPPING

Sourdough, tart dried fruit and crunchy hazelnuts take these muffins to a new level. We serve them warm or at room temperature.
—Patricia Quinn, Omaha, NE

- -

PREP: 30 min. • **BAKE:** 20 min.
MAKES: 1 dozen

- 1   cup SOURDOUGH STARTER
- ½   cup packed brown sugar
- ⅓   cup plus 1½ cups all-purpose flour, divided
- ½   tsp. ground cinnamon
- ¼   cup cold butter, cubed
- ¼   cup chopped hazelnuts
- ½   cup sugar
- 1   tsp. baking powder
- ½   tsp. baking soda
- ½   tsp. salt
- 1   large egg, room temperature
- ½   cup butter, melted
- 1½ tsp. grated orange zest
- 1   cup fresh or frozen cranberries, thawed
- ¼   cup chopped dried apricots

1. Let Sourdough Starter come to room temperature before using.
2. Preheat oven to 400°. In a small bowl, mix brown sugar, ⅓ cup flour and the cinnamon; cut in cold butter until crumbly. Stir in hazelnuts.
3. In a large bowl, whisk sugar, baking powder, baking soda, salt and remaining flour. In another bowl, whisk egg, melted butter and orange zest until blended; stir in Sourdough Starter. Add to flour mixture; stir just until moistened. Fold in cranberries and apricots.
4. Fill paper-lined muffin cups three-fourths full. Sprinkle with hazelnut mixture.
5. Bake 16-20 minutes or until a toothpick inserted in center comes out clean. Cool 5 minutes before removing from pan to a wire rack. Serve warm.
1 MUFFIN: *272 cal., 14g fat (8g sat. fat), 46mg chol., 293mg sod., 36g carb. (19g sugars, 1g fiber), 3g pro.*

SOURDOUGH FRENCH BREAD

These loaves rival any found in stores and can be made with relative ease.
—Delila George, Junction City, OR

- -

PREP: 15 min. + rising • **BAKE:** 20 min.
MAKES: 2 loaves (10 slices each)

- 1   pkg. (¼ oz.) active dry yeast
- 1¾ cups warm water (110° to 115°)
- ¼   cup SOURDOUGH STARTER
- 2   Tbsp. canola oil
- 2   Tbsp. sugar
- 2   tsp. salt
- 4¼ cups all-purpose flour

CORNSTARCH WASH
- ½   cup water
- 1½ tsp. cornstarch

1. In a large mixing bowl, dissolve yeast in warm water. Add the Sourdough Starter, oil, sugar, salt and 3 cups flour. Beat until smooth. Stir in enough additional flour to form a soft dough.
2. Turn onto a floured surface; knead gently 20-30 times (dough will be slightly sticky).

Place in a greased bowl, turning once to grease top. Cover and let rise in a warm place until doubled, 1-1½ hours.
3. Preheat oven to 400°. Punch dough down. Turn onto a lightly floured surface; divide in half. Roll each into a 12x8-in. rectangle. Roll up, jelly-roll style, starting with a long side; pinch ends to seal. Place seam side down on 2 greased baking sheets; tuck ends under. Cover and let rise until doubled, about 30 minutes.
4. With a sharp knife, make 4 shallow diagonal slashes across top of each loaf. In a small saucepan, combine water and cornstarch. Cook and stir over medium heat until thickened. Brush some of the cornstarch wash over the loaves.
5. Bake for 15 minutes. Brush loaves with remaining cornstarch wash. Bake until lightly browned, 5-10 minutes. Remove from pans to wire racks to cool.
1 SLICE: *116 cal., 2g fat (0 sat. fat), 0 chol., 237mg sod., 22g carb. (1g sugars, 1g fiber), 3g pro.*

PARMESAN SWEET CREAM BISCUITS

Sweet cream biscuits were the first kind I mastered. Since the ingredients are so simple, I can scale the recipe up or down. The recipe is so easy, in fact, that I've actually memorized it!
—Helen Nelander, Boulder Creek, CA

TAKES: 25 min. • **MAKES:** about 1 dozen

- 2 **cups all-purpose flour**
- ⅓ **cup grated Parmesan cheese**
- 2 **tsp. baking powder**
- ½ **tsp. salt**
- 1½ **cups heavy whipping cream**

1. Preheat oven to 400°. Whisk together the first 4 ingredients. Add cream; stir just until moistened.

2. Turn the dough onto a lightly floured surface; knead gently 6-8 times. Roll or pat the dough to ½-in. thickness; cut with a floured 2¾-in. biscuit cutter. Place 1 in. apart on an ungreased baking sheet.

3. Bake until light golden brown, 12-15 minutes. Serve warm.

1 BISCUIT: *187 cal., 12g fat (7g sat. fat), 36mg chol., 227mg sod., 17g carb. (1g sugars, 1g fiber), 4g pro.*

**PARMESAN
SWEET CREAM BISCUITS**

CARAMEL APPLE MUFFINS

CARAMEL APPLE MUFFINS

These muffins are perfect for anyone who loves caramel apples. They are particularly good with breakfast or during a coffee break.
—Therese Puckett, Shreveport, LA

PREP: 25 min. • **BAKE:** 20 min.
MAKES: 1 dozen

- 2 **cups all-purpose flour**
- ¾ **cup sugar**
- 2 **tsp. baking powder**
- 2½ **tsp. ground cinnamon**
- ½ **tsp. salt**
- 1 **large egg, room temperature**
- 1 **cup 2% milk**
- ¼ **cup butter, melted**
- 2 **tsp. vanilla extract**
- ½ **cup chopped peeled tart apple**
- 12 **caramels, chopped**

TOPPING

- ½ **cup packed brown sugar**
- ¼ **cup quick-cooking oats**
- 3 **Tbsp. butter, melted**
- 1 **tsp. ground cinnamon**

1. Preheat oven to 350°. In a large bowl, combine the flour, sugar, baking powder, cinnamon and salt. In another bowl, whisk the egg, milk, butter and vanilla. Stir into dry ingredients just until moistened. Fold in apple and caramels.

2. Fill 12 paper-lined muffin cups three-fourths full. Combine topping ingredients; sprinkle over batter.

3. Bake until a toothpick inserted in the cake portion comes out clean, 20-25 minutes. Cool for 5 minutes before removing from pan to a wire rack. Serve warm.

1 MUFFIN: *245 cal., 8g fat (4g sat. fat), 33mg chol., 219mg sod., 41g carb. (26g sugars, 1g fiber), 4g pro.*

BACON & EGG CHILAQUILES
PAGE 175

Breakfast & Brunch

Upgrade any morning when you turn to the eye-opening specialties in this chapter. Find overnight dishes perfect for holiday entertaining, great-for-you smoothies, savory takes on waffles, and so much more. Let the sunshine in!

THE BEST
EVER PANCAKES

THE BEST EVER PANCAKES

I'm not joking when I say I make pancakes every weekend. I love them in any form and variation, and this is one of my favorite pancake recipes.
—James Schend, Pleasant Prairie, WI

PREP: 15 min. • **COOK:** 5 min./batch • **MAKES:** 12 pancakes

- 1½ cups all-purpose flour
- 2 Tbsp. sugar
- 1 tsp. baking powder
- ½ tsp. baking soda
- ½ tsp. salt
- 1 cup buttermilk
- 2 large eggs, room temperature
- ¼ cup butter, melted
- 1 tsp. vanilla extract

1. In a large bowl, whisk together the first 5 ingredients. In another bowl, whisk remaining ingredients; stir into dry ingredients just until moistened.

2. Preheat griddle over medium heat. Lightly grease griddle. Pour batter by ¼ cupfuls onto griddle; cook until bubbles on top begin to pop and bottoms are golden brown. Turn; cook until second side is golden brown.

3 PANCAKES: 360 cal., 15g fat (8g sat. fat), 126mg chol., 817mg sod., 45g carb. (10g sugars, 1g fiber), 10g pro.

TEST KITCHEN TIP

To make these pancakes lactose-free, replace the buttermilk and butter with lactose-free 2% milk and lactose-free butter or dairy-free margarine. If you want to make them dairy-free, replace buttermilk with any plant-based milk, like soy or almond, and use melted shortening in place of the butter.

LIME COCONUT SMOOTHIE BOWL

This stylish smoothie bowl is the most refreshing thing on the planet!
—Madeline Butler, Denver, CO

TAKES: 15 min. • **MAKES:** 2 servings

- 1 medium banana, peeled and frozen
- 1 cup fresh baby spinach
- ½ cup ice cubes
- ½ cup cubed fresh pineapple
- ½ cup chopped peeled mango or frozen mango chunks
- ½ cup plain Greek yogurt
- ¼ cup sweetened shredded coconut
- 3 Tbsp. honey
- 2 tsp. grated lime zest
- 1 tsp. lime juice
- ½ tsp. vanilla extract
- 1 Tbsp. spreadable cream cheese, optional
  Optional: Lime wedges, sliced banana, sliced almonds, granola, dark chocolate chips and additional shredded coconut

Place the first 11 ingredients in a blender; if desired, add cream cheese. Cover and process until smooth. Pour into chilled bowls. Serve immediately, with optional toppings if desired.

1 CUP: 325 cal., 10g fat (7g sat. fat), 15mg chol., 80mg sod., 60g carb. (51g sugars, 4g fiber), 4g pro.

LIME COCONUT
SMOOTHIE BOWL

BACON & EGG CHILAQUILES

(SHOWN ON PAGE 172)

In Mexico and throughout the Southwest, chilaquiles are typically made for brunch, using tortillas and leftovers from the previous day's dinner. I love to bring this dish to family gatherings, as it gives the traditional eggs-and-bacon combination a unique twist. The empty pan proves that it's a family favorite!
—Naylet LaRochelle, Miami, FL

PREP: 15 min. • **BAKE:** 25 min.
MAKES: 6 servings

3½ cups salsa
½ cup sour cream
1 pkg. (9 oz.) tortilla chips
2 cups coarsely chopped fresh spinach
2 cups shredded taco cheese blend or Mexican cheese blend
12 bacon strips, cooked and crumbled
6 large eggs
⅓ cup crumbled Cotija or feta cheese
¼ cup minced fresh cilantro
Sliced avocado, optional

1. Preheat oven to 350°. In a small bowl, combine salsa and sour cream. Arrange half the tortilla chips in a greased 13x9-in. baking pan. Layer with half of the salsa mixture, all of the spinach, half of the shredded cheese and half the bacon. Top with remaining tortilla chips, salsa mixture, shredded cheese and bacon.
2. Bake until dish is heated through and the cheese is melted, 20-25 minutes. Meanwhile, heat a large nonstick skillet over medium-high heat. Break eggs, 1 at a time, into pan; reduce heat to low. Cook until whites are set and yolks begin to thicken, turning once if desired.
3. Top chilaquiles with cooked eggs, Cotija cheese, cilantro and, if desired, avocado.
1 SERVING: 623 cal., 38g fat (15g sat. fat), 247mg chol., 1426mg sod., 41g carb. (6g sugars, 2g fiber), 25g pro.

MIGAS BREAKFAST TACOS

MIGAS BREAKFAST TACOS

Unless you grew up in the Southwest or visit there often, you might be hearing of migas for the first time. Think of them as the best scrambled eggs ever. The secret ingredient: corn tortillas. They really make my migas tacos special!
—Stephen Exel, Des Moines, IA

TAKES: 30 min. • **MAKES:** 3 servings

¼ cup finely chopped onion
1 jalapeno pepper, seeded and chopped
1 Tbsp. canola oil
2 corn tortillas (6 in.), cut into thin strips
4 large eggs
¼ tsp. salt
⅛ tsp. pepper
½ cup crumbled queso fresco or shredded Monterey Jack cheese
¼ cup chopped seeded tomato
6 flour tortillas (6 in.), warmed
Optional toppings: Refried beans, sliced avocado, sour cream and minced fresh cilantro

1. In a large skillet, saute onion and jalapeno in oil until tender. Add tortilla strips; cook 3 minutes longer. In a small bowl, whisk the eggs, salt and pepper. Add to skillet; cook and stir until almost set. Stir in crumbled cheese and tomato.
2. Serve in flour tortillas with toppings of your choice.
NOTE: Wear disposable gloves when cutting hot peppers; the oils can burn skin. Avoid touching your face.
2 TACOS: 424 cal., 21g fat (5g sat. fat), 295mg chol., 821mg sod., 39g carb. (2g sugars, 1g fiber), 21g pro.

Morning Glory

A breakfast like this—simple classics with special flair—sets the tone for a weekend filled with family, fun, and any excuse to linger just a bit longer.

RECIPES BY **KAILEY THOMPSON**, PALM BAY, FL

Blueberry Pancake Smoothie

Cheesy Cajun Shrimp & Grits

Mom's Fluffy Scrambled Eggs

BLUEBERRY PANCAKE SMOOTHIE

Have your blueberry pancakes and drink them, too! A smoothie loaded with fruit, oatmeal, maple syrup and cinnamon is great in the morning or at any time of day. If your berries are fresh instead of frozen, freeze the banana ahead of time.

TAKES: 5 min. • **MAKES:** 2 servings

- 1   cup unsweetened almond milk
- 1   medium banana
- ½   cup frozen unsweetened blueberries
- ¼   cup instant plain oatmeal
- 1   tsp. maple syrup
- ½   tsp. ground cinnamon
       Dash sea salt

Place the first 6 ingredients in a blender; cover and process until smooth. Pour into 2 chilled glasses; sprinkle with sea salt. Serve immediately.

1 CUP: *153 cal., 3g fat (0 sat. fat), 0 chol., 191mg sod., 31g carb. (13g sugars, 5g fiber), 3g pro.* **Diabetic exchanges:** *2 starch.*

CHEESY CAJUN SHRIMP & GRITS

I was born and raised in the South. A few years ago I moved to Pennsylvania, where good Southern comfort food was hard to find. So I created these creamy, smoky Cajun shrimp and grits to remind me of home.

TAKES: 30 min. • **MAKES:** 8 servings

- 8   cups water
- ¾   tsp. salt
- 2   cups quick-cooking grits
- 2   cups shredded cheddar cheese
- ½   cup butter, cubed
- 8   bacon strips, chopped
- 2   lbs. uncooked shrimp (26-30 per lb.), peeled and deveined
- 4   garlic cloves, minced
- 1   Tbsp. Cajun seasoning
- 1   Tbsp. minced fresh parsley or 1 tsp. dried parsley flakes

1. In a large saucepan, bring water and salt to a boil. Slowly stir in grits. Reduce heat to medium-low; cook, covered, until thickened, about 5 minutes, stirring occasionally. Remove from the heat. Stir in the cheese and butter until melted; keep grits warm.

2. Meanwhile, in a large skillet, cook bacon over medium heat until crisp, stirring occasionally. Remove with a slotted spoon; drain on paper towels. Cook and stir the shrimp in bacon drippings until shrimp turn pink, 3-4 minutes. Add the garlic; cook 1 minute longer. Stir in Cajun seasoning and parsley.

3. Divide grits among 8 serving bowls; top with shrimp mixture and the bacon.

1 SERVING: *560 cal., 34g fat (17g sat. fat), 215mg chol., 968mg sod., 32g carb. (1g sugars, 2g fiber), 32g pro.*

MOM'S FLUFFY SCRAMBLED EGGS

I make these fluffy scrambled eggs when family comes for breakfast or when I just want to do something extra special for myself in the morning. My favorite cheese for this recipe is freshly grated white cheddar, but whatever you happen to have in the fridge will work!

TAKES: 30 min. • **MAKES:** 8 servings

- 8   bacon strips
- 12   large eggs, beaten
- 6   Tbsp. butter, divided
- 2   cups shredded white cheddar cheese
- ¼   cup minced fresh parsley
- ¼   cup snipped fresh dill
- ½   tsp. salt
- ¼   tsp. pepper
- 8   bread slices, toasted
       Hot pepper sauce

1. In a large nonstick skillet, cook bacon over medium heat until crisp, stirring occasionally. Remove; drain on paper towels and break into 1-in. pieces. Discard the bacon drippings. In the same pan, cook and stir eggs over medium heat until almost set. Stir in 2 Tbsp. butter; cook and stir until no liquid egg remains. Add cheese, parsley, dill, salt, pepper and remaining 4 Tbsp. butter; stir gently until the cheese is melted.

2. Top toast with eggs and bacon; drizzle with hot pepper sauce.

1 SERVING: *403 cal., 29g fat (14g sat. fat), 338mg chol., 772mg sod., 14g carb. (2g sugars, 1g fiber), 21g pro.*

OMELET WAFFLES WITH SAUSAGE CHEESE SAUCE

This waffle-omelet mashup is topped with sausage, onions and sweet peppers and finished with a chunky cheesy sauce. Morning or evening, the dish is fun and satisfying.
—Ronna Farley, Rockville, MD

PREP: 30 min. • **COOK:** 5 min./batch
MAKES: 4 servings

- 1 lb. bulk pork sausage
- ½ lb. whole fresh mushrooms, chopped
- ½ cup chopped onion
- ½ cup chopped sweet red pepper
- 2 Tbsp. all-purpose flour
- 2 cups half-and-half cream, divided
- 1 tsp. seasoned salt, divided
- 1 cup shredded sharp cheddar cheese
- 8 large eggs, room temperature
- 1 Tbsp. minced fresh parsley

1. Preheat waffle maker. In a large skillet, cook sausage, mushrooms, onion and red pepper over medium heat until sausage is no longer pink and vegetables are tender, 8-10 minutes, breaking up sausage into crumbles; drain. Remove from heat and keep warm.

2. Meanwhile, in a large saucepan, whisk flour, 1¾ cups cream and ½ tsp. seasoned salt until smooth. Bring to a boil, stirring constantly; cook and stir until thickened, 2-3 minutes. Stir in cheese and 1 cup sausage mixture until cheese is melted. Remove from heat and keep warm.

3. In a large bowl, whisk eggs and the remaining ¼ cup cream and ½ tsp. seasoned salt until blended. Bake in a well-greased waffle maker until golden brown, 2-3 minutes. Serve with sausage mixture and cheese sauce; sprinkle each serving with parsley.

2 WAFFLES: *734 cal., 56g fat (24g sat. fat), 521mg chol., 1461mg sod., 15g carb. (7g sugars, 1g fiber), 38g pro.*

GARLIC-HERB BAGEL SPREAD

This creamy spread is loaded with oregano, basil, garlic and feta. The flavorful, savory combination is perfect slathered on a toasted bagel. But don't stop there. Try it as a dip for crunchy breadsticks, too.
—Taste of Home *Test Kitchen*

TAKES: 10 min. • **MAKES:** 8 servings (1 cup)

- 3 oz. cream cheese, softened
- ⅓ cup sour cream
- ¼ cup crumbled feta cheese
- 2 garlic cloves, minced
- ½ tsp. each garlic powder, dried oregano and basil
  Bagels, split

In a small bowl, beat the cream cheese until smooth. Add the sour cream, feta cheese, minced garlic and seasonings; mix well. Toast bagels if desired; top with spread.

2 TBSP.: *68 cal., 6g fat (4g sat. fat), 15mg chol., 71mg sod., 2g carb. (1g sugars, 0 fiber), 2g pro.*

OMELET WAFFLES WITH SAUSAGE CHEESE SAUCE

**APPLE-CINNAMON
QUINOA PANCAKES**

APPLE-CINNAMON QUINOA PANCAKES

*My daughter and daughter-in-law got me hooked on quinoa.
I dressed up a regular pancake recipe to create these delicious
apple-cinnamon breakfast treats. The shredded apple remains
slightly crunchy with the short cooking time, and it complements
the chewy texture of the quinoa nicely.*
—Sue Gronholz, Beaver Dam, WI

PREP: 15 min. • **COOK:** 5 min./batch • **MAKES:** 10 pancakes

- ¾ cup all-purpose flour
- 2 tsp. baking powder
- 1 tsp. ground cinnamon
- ½ tsp. salt
- 1 large egg, room temperature
- 1 large egg white, room temperature
- ⅓ cup vanilla almond milk
- 2 Tbsp. maple syrup
- 1 Tbsp. canola oil
- 1 tsp. vanilla extract
- 1 medium Gala apple, shredded
- 1 cup ready-to-serve quinoa
- 1 Tbsp. butter or canola oil

1. Whisk together the flour, baking powder, cinnamon and salt. In
another bowl, whisk together egg, egg white, almond milk, syrup,
canola oil and vanilla extract. Add to flour mixture; stir just until
moistened. Stir in apple and quinoa.
2. In a large nonstick skillet, heat butter over medium heat. Pour
batter by ¼ cupfuls onto griddle; cook until bubbles on top begin
to pop and bottoms are golden brown. Turn; cook until second
side is golden brown.
2 PANCAKES: *222 cal., 8g fat (2g sat. fat), 43mg chol., 538mg sod., 32g
carb. (10g sugars, 3g fiber), 6g pro.* **Diabetic exchanges:** *2 starch,
1 fat.*

> **TEST KITCHEN TIP**
>
> If you can't find ready-to-serve quinoa, simply simmer
> 1 cup of quinoa with 2 cups of water until tender.

BRAIN FOOD SMOOTHIE

*My grandson refuses fruits and vegetables almost completely. After
he and our son moved home, I tried everything to improve his diet.
This smoothie was one of the only ways I could sneak him something
nutritious, and he loves it!*
—Sandra Roberts, Dexter, MO

TAKES: 15 min. • **MAKES:** 6 cups

- 1½ cups fat-free vanilla Greek yogurt
- ½ cup 2% milk
- 2 medium ripe avocados, peeled and pitted
- 2 cups halved fresh strawberries
- 1 cup sliced ripe banana
- 1 cup fresh raspberries or frozen unsweetened raspberries,
thawed
- 1 cup fresh baby spinach
- 1 cup fresh blueberries
- ½ cup fresh blackberries or frozen unsweetened blackberries,
thawed
- ¼ cup unflavored whey protein powder

Place all ingredients in a blender; cover and process until smooth.
1 CUP: *215 cal., 8g fat (1g sat. fat), 3mg chol., 65mg sod., 29g carb.
(17g sugars, 7g fiber), 10g pro.*

BRAIN FOOD SMOOTHIE

OPEN-FACED PROSCIUTTO & EGG SANDWICH

OPEN-FACED PROSCIUTTO & EGG SANDWICH

We love breakfast at any time of day in my house. I came up with this healthy egg sandwich as something new for brinner (aka breakfast for dinner), but it's fabulous no matter when you serve it.
—Casey Galloway, Columbia, MO

TAKES: 20 min. • **MAKES:** 4 servings

4 large eggs
4 Tbsp. mayonnaise
2 garlic cloves, minced
4 thick slices sourdough bread, toasted
1 cup fresh arugula
1 medium tomato, sliced
⅓ lb. thinly sliced prosciutto
⅛ tsp. salt
⅛ tsp. pepper

1. Heat a large nonstick skillet over medium-high heat. Break eggs, 1 at a time, into pan; reduce heat to low. Cook until whites are set and yolks begin to thicken, turning once if desired.
2. Meanwhile, combine mayonnaise and garlic; spread over toast slices. Top with arugula, tomato, prosciutto and fried eggs; sprinkle with salt and pepper.
1 OPEN-FACED SANDWICH: *531 cal., 22g fat (5g sat. fat), 221mg chol., 1563mg sod., 56g carb. (6g sugars, 3g fiber), 28g pro.*

EVERYTHING BREAKFAST SLIDERS

These breakfast sliders combine all of your favorite morning foods—like eggs, bacon and bagels—into one tasty package.
—Rashanda Cobbins, Milwaukee, WI

PREP: 30 min. • **BAKE:** 15 min.
MAKES: 8 servings

8 large eggs
¼ cup 2% milk
2 green onions, thinly sliced
¼ tsp. pepper
8 Tbsp. spreadable chive and onion cream cheese
8 miniature bagels, split
8 slices cheddar cheese, halved
8 slices Canadian bacon
8 cooked bacon strips, halved
GLAZE
2 Tbsp. butter, melted
1½ tsp. maple syrup
⅛ tsp. garlic powder
2 Tbsp. everything seasoning blend

1. Preheat oven to 375°. Heat a large nonstick skillet over medium heat. In a large bowl, whisk eggs, milk, green onions and pepper until blended; pour into skillet. Cook and stir until eggs are thickened and no liquid egg remains; remove from heat.
2. Spread cream cheese over bagel bottoms; place in a greased 13x9-in. baking dish. Layer each with half a slice of cheese and Canadian bacon. Spoon scrambled eggs over top. Layer with remaining halved cheese slices, Canadian bacon and bagel tops. Stir together butter, maple syrup and garlic powder; brush over bagel tops. Sprinkle with everything seasoning blend.
3. Bake until tops of bagels are golden brown and cheese is melted, 12-15 minutes.
1 SLIDER: *415 cal., 26g fat (13g sat. fat), 253mg chol., 1070mg sod., 18g carb. (4g sugars, 1g fiber), 24g pro.*

EVERYTHING BREAKFAST SLIDERS

PECAN BACON

Crispy, sweet bacon always dresses up any breakfast. When my girls see this, they call it "special breakfast." The big flavor punch may just surprise you.
—Catherine Ann Goza, Charlotte, NC

- -

PREP: 10 min. • **BAKE:** 25 min.
MAKES: 1 dozen

- 12 bacon strips
- ¼ cup packed brown sugar
- ¼ cup finely chopped pecans
- ⅛ tsp. ground cinnamon
- ⅛ tsp. pepper

1. Preheat oven to 375°. Place bacon in a single layer in a foil-lined 15x10x1-in. baking pan. Bake until bacon is lightly browned, 16-18 minutes.
2. Remove bacon strips from pan. Discard the drippings from pan, wiping clean if necessary.
3. In a shallow bowl, mix the remaining ingredients. Dip both sides of bacon in brown sugar mixture, patting to help coating adhere; return to pan.
4. Bake until bacon strips are caramelized, 8-10 minutes longer. Remove immediately from pan.
1 BACON STRIP: *142 cal., 12g fat (4g sat. fat), 18mg chol., 186mg sod., 4g carb. (4g sugars, 0 fiber), 4g pro.*

EGG-TOPPED SAUSAGE HERB PIZZA

My family loves homemade pizza, and I love to watch cooking shows. One day I saw the hosts of a show visit a pizza place that had fried eggs on top of pizza. That set me off on a quest to come up with my own perfect egg-topped pizza. I started with the herbed pizza dough that I make all the time and topped it with sausage, different types of cheese and, of course, eggs. This recipe is the one my family likes best.
—Kristen Caperila, Phoenixville, PA

- -

PREP: 45 min. + rising • **BAKE:** 20 min.
MAKES: 8 servings

- 1 Tbsp. sugar
- 2 tsp. quick-rise yeast
- ½ tsp. salt
- 1 to 1½ cups all-purpose flour
- ½ cup water
- 2 Tbsp. olive oil

EGG-TOPPED SAUSAGE HERB PIZZA

- 1¼ tsp. Italian seasoning
- 2 Tbsp. cornmeal
- 2 hot Italian sausage links (4 oz. each), casings removed
- ¾ cup pizza sauce
- 1½ cups shredded part-skim mozzarella cheese
- 4 large eggs
- ¼ tsp. pepper
- ¼ cup grated Parmesan cheese
- ¼ cup grated Romano cheese
- ½ cup fresh arugula or baby spinach
- ½ cup fresh baby spinach

1. In a small bowl, mix the sugar, yeast, salt and ¾ cup flour. In a small saucepan, heat water and oil to 120°-130°; stir into dry ingredients. Stir in Italian seasoning and enough remaining flour to form a soft dough (dough will be sticky).
2. Turn dough onto a floured surface; knead until smooth and elastic, 6-8 minutes. Place in a greased bowl, turning once to grease the top. Cover bowl and let dough rise in a warm place until doubled,

about 45 minutes. Grease a 12-in. pizza pan; sprinkle with cornmeal.
3. Meanwhile, in a small skillet, cook sausage links over medium heat until no longer pink, 4-5 minutes, breaking into crumbles; drain.
4. Preheat oven to 450°. Roll dough to fit pan. Pinch edge to form a rim. Spread with pizza sauce; top with cooked sausage and mozzarella cheese. Bake until crust is lightly browned, 8-10 minutes.
5. Using the back of a tablespoon, make 4 indentations in pizza at least 2 in. from edge. Carefully break an egg into each indentation; sprinkle with pepper and Parmesan and Romano cheeses.
6. Bake until egg whites are completely set and yolks begin to thicken but are not hard, 8-10 minutes longer. Just before serving, top with arugula and spinach.
1 SLICE: *339 cal., 21g fat (8g sat. fat), 131mg chol., 729mg sod., 20g carb. (3g sugars, 1g fiber), 17g pro.*

EGG BASKETS BENEDICT

BACON CORN PANCAKES

Stir in bacon and corn for pancake perfection! I always cook gluten-free, but you can easily use regular all-purpose flour to make these.
—Anne-Marie Nichols, Watkinsville, GA

PREP: 20 min. • **COOK:** 10 min./batch
MAKES: 18 pancakes

- 2 cups gluten-free all-purpose baking flour or all-purpose flour
- 1 Tbsp. sugar
- 2 tsp. baking powder
- ½ tsp. salt
- ⅛ tsp. pepper
- 2 large eggs, room temperature
- 1½ to 1¾ cups rice milk
- 2½ cups fresh or frozen corn
- 1 cup crumbled cooked bacon
- ⅓ cup chopped onion
- Maple syrup

1. Preheat griddle over medium heat. In a large bowl, combine the flour, sugar, baking powder, salt and pepper. In another bowl, whisk the eggs and rice milk; stir into dry ingredients just until moistened. Stir in corn, bacon and onion.

2. Lightly grease griddle. Pour batter by ¼ cupfuls onto griddle; cook until edges are dry and bottoms are golden brown. Turn; cook until the second side is golden brown. Serve with syrup.

FREEZE OPTION: Freeze cooled pancakes between layers of waxed paper in a freezer container. To use, place pancakes on an ungreased baking sheet, cover with foil and reheat in a preheated 375° oven until heated through, 5-10 minutes. Or, place 3 pancakes on a microwave-safe plate and microwave on high until heated through, 45-90 seconds.

3 PANCAKES: *318 cal., 8g fat (2g sat. fat), 67mg chol., 868mg sod., 50g carb. (10g sugars, 5g fiber), 16g pro.*

EGG BASKETS BENEDICT

A little puff pastry turns Canadian bacon and eggs into a tasty update on eggs Benedict. We use a packaged hollandaise or cheese sauce for the finish. It's delicious and easy.
—Sally Jackson, Fort Worth, TX

TAKES: 30 min.
MAKES: 1 dozen (1 cup sauce)

- 1 sheet frozen puff pastry, thawed
- 12 large eggs
- 6 slices Canadian bacon, finely chopped
- 1 envelope hollandaise sauce mix

1. Preheat oven to 400°. On a lightly floured surface, unfold puff pastry. Roll into a 16x12-in. rectangle; cut into twelve 4-in. squares. Place in greased muffin cups, pressing gently onto bottoms and up sides, allowing corners to point up.

2. Break and slip an egg into center of each pastry cup; sprinkle with Canadian bacon. Bake until pastry is golden brown, egg whites are completely set, and yolks begin to thicken but are not hard, 10-12 minutes. Meanwhile, prepare the hollandaise sauce according to package directions.

3. Remove pastry cups to wire racks. Serve warm with hollandaise sauce.

1 PASTRY CUP WITH ABOUT 1 TBSP. SAUCE: *237 cal., 15g fat (6g sat. fat), 201mg chol., 355mg sod., 14g carb. (1g sugars, 2g fiber), 10g pro.*

DID YOU KNOW?

Quebec Is King

North America's top maple syrup producer—by far—is the Canadian province of Quebec. Directly north and west of Vermont, Quebec produces an astounding amount of syrup each year: 6.5 million gallons. Vermont is runner-up, producing over half a million gallons of the sweet stuff.

BACON CORN PANCAKES

CINNAMON BLUEBERRY FRENCH TOAST

I like to prep this breakfast in the afternoon, let it chill, then put into the slow cooker before I go to bed. When we wake up in the morning, it's done just right.
—*Angela Lively, Conroe, TX*

PREP: 15 min. + chilling • **COOK:** 3 hours • **MAKES:** 6 servings

- 3 **large eggs**
- 2 **cups 2% milk**
- ¼ **cup sugar**
- 1 **tsp. ground cinnamon**
- 1 **tsp. vanilla extract**
- ¼ **tsp. salt**
- 9 **cups cubed French bread (about 9 oz.)**
- 1 **cup fresh or frozen blueberries, thawed**
  Maple syrup

1. Whisk together the first 6 ingredients. Place half of the bread in a greased 5-qt. slow cooker; top with ½ cup blueberries and half of the milk mixture. Repeat layers. Refrigerate, covered, for 4 hours or overnight.

2. Cook, covered, on low for 3-4 hours, until a knife inserted in the center comes out clean. Serve warm with syrup.

1 CUP: *265 cal., 6g fat (2g sat. fat), 100mg chol., 430mg sod., 42g carb. (18g sugars, 2g fiber), 11g pro.*

AIR-FRYER HAM & EGG POCKETS

CINNAMON BLUEBERRY FRENCH TOAST

AIR-FRYER HAM & EGG POCKETS

Refrigerated crescent roll dough makes these savory breakfast pockets a cinch to prepare.
—*Taste of Home Test Kitchen*

TAKES: 25 min. • **MAKES:** 2 servings

- 1 **large egg**
- 2 **tsp. 2% milk**
- 2 **tsp. butter**
- 1 **oz. thinly sliced deli ham, chopped**
- 2 **Tbsp. shredded cheddar cheese**
- 1 **tube (4 oz.) refrigerated crescent rolls**

1. Preheat air fryer to 300°. In a small bowl, combine egg and milk. In a small skillet, heat butter until hot. Add egg mixture; cook and stir over medium heat until eggs are completely set. Remove from the heat. Fold in ham and cheese.

2. Separate crescent dough into 2 rectangles. Seal perforations; spoon half the filling down the center of each rectangle. Fold dough over filling; pinch to seal. Place in a single layer on greased tray in air-fryer basket. Cook until golden brown, 8-10 minutes.

1 SERVING: *326 cal., 20g fat (5g sat. fat), 118mg chol., 735mg sod., 25g carb. (6g sugars, 0 fiber), 12g pro.*

GREEK SALAD-INSPIRED QUICHE

GREEK SALAD-INSPIRED QUICHE

I love using my cast-iron skillet to create this meatless, family-sized Greek quiche for a quick meal. Just throw together a green salad and add some pita bread, and dinner is on the table with little fuss and no extra dishes to wash!
—Donna M. Ryan, Topsfield, MA

PREP: 20 min. • **BAKE:** 20 min. + standing
MAKES: 6 servings

- 1 Tbsp. olive oil
- 1 cup cherry tomatoes, halved
- ⅔ cup finely chopped green pepper
- ½ cup thinly sliced red onion
- ⅔ cup chopped fresh spinach
- 2 garlic cloves, minced
- 1 cup crumbled feta cheese
- ½ cup pitted Greek olives, sliced
- 6 large eggs
- 1 cup 2% milk
- 1 Tbsp. minced fresh oregano or
  1 tsp. dried oregano
- ½ tsp. salt
- ⅛ to ¾ tsp. crushed red pepper flakes

1. In a 9-in. cast-iron or other ovenproof skillet, heat olive oil over medium-high heat. Add tomatoes, green peppers and onion; cook and stir until vegetables are tender, 6-7 minutes; drain. Add chopped spinach and garlic; cook and stir until spinach is wilted, 1-2 minutes. Remove from heat and stir in feta and olives.
2. In a large bowl, whisk eggs, milk, oregano, salt and pepper flakes until blended. Pour over vegetables.
3. Bake until a knife inserted in center of quiche comes out clean, 20-25 minutes. Let stand 10 minutes before serving.
1 PIECE: *354 cal., 22g fat (9g sat. fat), 175mg chol., 778mg sod., 25g carb. (5g sugars, 2g fiber), 12g pro.*

BERRY RICOTTA PUFF PANCAKE

This slightly sweet berry pancake is filled with berries and has a custardy texture that puffs up beautifully when baked. It makes an easy yet impressive breakfast.
—Jessi Smith, Fort Myers, FL

PREP: 20 min. • **BAKE:** 25 min.
MAKES: 8 slices

- 3 Tbsp. butter
- 5 large eggs, room temperature
- 1½ cups reduced-fat ricotta cheese
- ½ cup fat-free milk
- 1½ tsp. vanilla extract
- ½ tsp. grated lemon zest
- ¾ cup all-purpose flour
- ¼ cup sugar
- ½ tsp. baking powder
- ½ tsp. salt
- ½ cup sliced fresh strawberries
- ½ cup fresh raspberries
- ½ cup fresh blueberries
  Confectioners' sugar

1. Preheat oven to 400°. Place butter in a 12-in. cast-iron or other ovenproof skillet. Place in oven until butter is melted, 4-5 minutes; carefully swirl to coat evenly.
2. Meanwhile, in a blender, process eggs, ricotta, milk, vanilla and lemon zest until blended. Add flour, sugar, baking powder and salt and process until blended. Pour into hot skillet. Top with berries.
3. Bake until pancake is puffed and sides are golden brown and crisp, 25-30 minutes. Remove from oven; serve immediately with confectioners' sugar.
1 SLICE: *287 cal., 13g fat (6g sat. fat), 186mg chol., 406mg sod., 29g carb. (15g sugars, 2g fiber), 13g pro.*

BERRY RICOTTA PUFF PANCAKE

POACHED EGG BUDDHA BOWLS

CURRY SCRAMBLE

I have eggs every morning, and this is a great change from the classic scrambled egg meal. I like to add sliced peppers on top if I have them on hand.
—*Valerie Belley, St. Louis, MO*

TAKES: 15 min. • **MAKES:** 4 servings

- 8 **large eggs**
- ¼ **cup fat-free milk**
- ½ **tsp. curry powder**
- ¼ **tsp. salt**
- ⅛ **tsp. pepper**
- ⅛ **tsp. ground cardamom, optional**
- 2 **medium tomatoes, sliced or chopped**

1. In a large bowl, whisk eggs, milk, curry powder, salt, pepper and, if desired, cardamom until blended.
2. Place a lightly greased large nonstick skillet over medium heat. Pour in egg mixture; cook and stir until eggs are thickened and no liquid egg remains. Serve with tomatoes.
1 SERVING: *160 cal., 10g fat (3g sat. fat), 372mg chol., 299mg sod., 4g carb. (3g sugars, 1g fiber), 14g pro.* **Diabetic exchanges:** *2 medium-fat meat.*

POACHED EGG BUDDHA BOWLS

My husband and I celebrate the arrival of spring with this dish, enjoying it in the backyard. I often include fresh peas and other spring delights.
—*Amy McDonough, Carlton, OR*

PREP: 10 min. • **COOK:** 65 min. • **MAKES:** 2 servings

- ¾ **cup wheat berries**
- 3½ **cups water, divided**
- 2 **Tbsp. olive oil**
- 2 **Tbsp. lemon juice**
- 1 **Tbsp. thinly sliced fresh mint leaves**
- ¼ **tsp. salt**
- ⅛ **tsp. freshly ground pepper**
- ½ **cup quartered cherry tomatoes**
- ½ **cup reduced-fat ricotta cheese**
- 2 **Tbsp. sliced Greek olives**
- 2 **large eggs**
  Optional: Additional olive oil and pepper

1. Place wheat berries and 2½ cups water in a large saucepan; bring to a boil. Reduce heat; simmer, covered, until tender, about 1 hour. Drain; transfer to a bowl. Cool slightly.
2. Stir in oil, lemon juice, mint, salt and pepper; divide between 2 bowls. Top with tomatoes, ricotta cheese and olives.
3. To poach egg, place ½ cup water in a small microwave-safe bowl or glass measuring cup. Break an egg into water. Microwave, covered, on high 1 minute. Microwave in 10-second intervals until white is set and yolk begins to thicken; let stand 1 minute.
4. Using a slotted spoon, transfer egg to 1 of the bowls. Repeat. If desired, top with additional oil and pepper.
1 SERVING: *526 cal., 24g fat (5g sat. fat), 201mg chol., 563mg sod., 58g carb. (5g sugars, 10g fiber), 21g pro.*

> ### TEST KITCHEN TIP
> Wheat berries are whole kernels of wheat. They cook up to a chewy texture with a hint of buttery flavor. Look for wheat berries near other whole grains; they're usually in the baking aisle in small packages.

CURRY SCRAMBLE

**SLOW-COOKER
COCONUT GRANOLA**

BLUEBERRY CORNMEAL PANCAKES

These blueberry cornmeal pancakes are one of my family's favorite breakfasts. No time to make it from scratch? No problem! My grandmother's standby of store-bought corn muffin mix makes quick work of the job.
—Carolyn Eskew, Dayton, OH

- -

TAKES: 30 min. • **MAKES:** 10 corn cakes

- 1 pkg. (8½ oz.) cornbread/muffin mix
- 1 cup fresh or frozen blueberries
- ⅓ cup canned white or shoepeg corn
- Maple syrup

In a large bowl, prepare the muffin mix according to package directions. Gently stir in blueberries and corn. Lightly grease a griddle; heat over medium heat. Pour batter by ¼ cupfuls onto griddle; flatten slightly. Cook until bottoms are golden brown. Turn; cook until second side is golden brown. Serve with syrup.
2 CAKES: *251 cal., 7g fat (2g sat. fat), 39mg chol., 454mg sod., 41g carb. (14g sugars, 4g fiber), 6g pro.*

SLOW-COOKER COCONUT GRANOLA

Here's a versatile treat with a taste of the tropics. Mix it up, if you like, by subbing dried pineapple or tropical fruits for the cherries.
—Taste of Home *Test Kitchen*

- -

PREP: 15 min. • **COOK:** 3½ hours + cooling • **MAKES:** 6 cups

- 4 cups old-fashioned oats
- 1 cup sliced almonds
- 1 cup unsweetened coconut flakes
- 1 tsp. ground cinnamon
- 1 tsp. ground ginger
- ¼ tsp. salt
- ½ cup coconut oil, melted
- ½ cup maple syrup
- 1 cup dried cherries

1. Combine oats, almonds, coconut, cinnamon, ginger and salt in a 3-qt. slow cooker. In small bowl, whisk together oil and maple syrup. Pour into slow cooker; stir to combine. Cook, covered, on low, stirring occasionally, 3½-4 hours. Stir in cherries.
2. Transfer mixture to a baking sheet; let stand until cool.
½ CUP: *343 cal., 19g fat (12g sat. fat), 0 chol., 55mg sod., 41g carb. (18g sugars, 5g fiber), 6g pro.*

**BLUEBERRY CORNMEAL
PANCAKES**

MARMALADE CHEWS
PAGE 190

Cookies, Bars & Candies

There's no simpler, sweeter way to treat yourself than with a little hand-held sweet. You'll love discovering soon-to-be-favorite cookie-tin treats in this chapter. Find new no-bakes, irresistible candies and cookies galore.

51

GRANDMA'S SCOTTISH SHORTBREAD

My Scottish grandmother was renowned for her baking, and one of the highlights whenever we visited my grandparents was her bringing out the baking tin. Her shortbread was my favorite, and now, whenever I make it, I remember her. This is not a thin, crispy dessert shortbread. It's a deep bar that is best served with a cup of tea.
—Jane Kelly, Wayland, MA

PREP: 15 min. • **BAKE:** 45 min. + cooling
MAKES: 4 dozen

- 1 lb. butter, softened
- 8 oz. superfine sugar (about 1¼ cups)
- 1 lb. all-purpose flour (3⅔ cups)
- 8 oz. white rice flour (1⅓ cups)

1. Preheat the oven to 300°. Cream butter and sugar until light and fluffy, 5-7 minutes. Combine the flours; gradually beat into creamed mixture. Press dough into an ungreased 13x9-in. baking pan. Prick with a fork.

2. Bake until light brown, 45-50 minutes. Cut into 48 bars or triangles while warm. Cool completely on a wire rack.

1 BAR: *139 cal., 8g fat (5g sat. fat), 20mg chol., 61mg sod., 16g carb. (5g sugars, 0 fiber), 1g pro.*

MARMALADE CHEWS

(SHOWN ON PAGE 188)
I live in the heart of citrus country and think this cookie really captures the area's flavor. Orange marmalade, juice and zest give the cookie and frosting a delightful tropical taste.
—Shirleene Wilkins, Lake Placid, FL

PREP: 20 min. • **BAKE:** 10 min./batch + cooling
MAKES: about 4½ dozen

- ¼ cup shortening
- ½ cup sugar
- 1 large egg, room temperature
- 1½ cups all-purpose flour
- ¼ tsp. baking soda
- ¼ tsp. salt
- ½ cup orange marmalade
- ½ cup chopped pecans, optional

FROSTING
- 2 cups confectioners' sugar
- 2 Tbsp. butter, melted
- 1 tsp. grated orange zest
- 2 to 3 Tbsp. orange juice

1. In a large bowl, cream shortening and sugar until light and fluffy, 5-7 minutes. Beat in egg. Combine the flour, baking soda and salt; gradually add to the creamed mixture and mix well. Stir in marmalade and, if desired, pecans.

2. Drop by heaping teaspoonfuls 2 in. apart onto greased baking sheets. Bake at 350° for 10-15 minutes or until golden brown. Remove to wire racks to cool.

3. In a small bowl, combine confectioners' sugar, butter and orange zest until blended. Add enough orange juice to reach spreading consistency. Frost cooled cookies.

1 COOKIE: *58 cal., 1g fat (1g sat. fat), 5mg chol., 23mg sod., 11g carb. (8g sugars, 0 fiber), 0 pro.*

GRANDMA'S SCOTTISH SHORTBREAD

NO-GUILT BROWNIES

DARK CHOCOLATE PUMPKIN TRUFFLES

Here's an inviting way to bring fall flavors into the home—and the fact that these don't require baking provides a little lingering sense of summer.
—Monica Mooney, Roseville, CA

PREP: 30 min. + freezing • **MAKES:** 2½ dozen

- ⅔ cup reduced-fat cream cheese
- ½ cup confectioners' sugar
- ⅔ cup canned pumpkin
- 1 tsp. pumpkin pie spice
- 1 tsp. vanilla extract
- 2¼ cups crushed reduced-fat graham crackers
- 1 pkg. (10 oz.) dark chocolate chips

1. In a small bowl, beat cream cheese and confectioners' sugar until blended. Beat in the pumpkin, pie spice and vanilla. Stir in cracker crumbs. Freeze, covered, until firm enough to shape, about 20 minutes.

2. Shape the pumpkin mixture into 1-in. balls; place on waxed paper-lined baking sheets. Freeze 20 minutes or until firm.

3. In a microwave, melt chocolate; stir until smooth. Dip truffles in chocolate; allow excess to drip off. Return to baking sheets; refrigerate until set. Store in airtight containers in the refrigerator.

1 TRUFFLE: *97 cal., 5g fat (3g sat. fat), 4mg chol., 60mg sod., 13g carb. (8g sugars, 1g fiber), 2g pro.*

NO-GUILT BROWNIES

Yes, you can watch your diet and enjoy brownies, too! These light and luscious treats are the perfect cure for a serious chocolate craving.
—Rita Ross, Delta, OH

PREP: 10 min. • **BAKE:** 20 min. + cooling • **MAKES:** 16 brownies

- 3 large egg whites, room temperature
- ¾ cup 1% cottage cheese
- 1 tsp. vanilla extract
- 3 oz. unsweetened chocolate, melted and cooled
- 1 cup sugar
- ¾ cup all-purpose flour
- ½ tsp. baking powder
- ¼ tsp. salt
- 2 tsp. confectioners' sugar

1. Place the egg whites, cottage cheese and vanilla in a blender; cover and process until smooth. Add chocolate; cover and process just until blended, about 15 seconds. Combine the sugar, flour, baking powder and salt; add to cottage cheese mixture. Cover and pulse until just moistened.

2. Spread into an 8-in. square baking pan coated with cooking spray. Bake at 350° until a toothpick inserted in the center comes out clean, 20-25 minutes (do not overbake). Cool on a wire rack. Dust with confectioners' sugar. Cut into bars.

1 BROWNIE: *117 cal., 3g fat (2g sat. fat), 1mg chol., 107mg sod., 19g carb. (13g sugars, 1g fiber), 3g pro.* **Diabetic exchanges:** *1 starch, ½ fat.*

DARK CHOCOLATE PUMPKIN TRUFFLES

PEANUT BUTTER
BROWNIE MIX

PEANUT BUTTER BROWNIE MIX

I discovered this recipe in our local newspaper, and when I gave it a try, my family loved it. While you can pack the dry ingredients into any kind of quart-sized container, a glass jar lets the pretty layers show. Cover an ordinary canning-jar lid with printed fabric to customize the gift for the occasion or season.
—*Lynn Dowdall, Perth, ON*

- -

PREP: 15 min. • **BAKE:** 25 min. + cooling • **MAKES:** 16 brownies

- 1   **cup packed brown sugar**
- ½   **cup sugar**
- ⅓   **cup baking cocoa**
- 1   **cup peanut butter chips**
- 1   **cup all-purpose flour**
- ½   **tsp. baking powder**
- ¼   **tsp. salt**
- ½   **cup semisweet chocolate chips**
- ½   **cup chopped walnuts**

ADDITIONAL INGREDIENTS
- 2   **large eggs, room temperature**
- ½   **cup butter, melted**
- 1   **tsp. vanilla extract**

1. In a 1-qt. glass container, layer the first 9 ingredients in the order listed, packing well between each layer. Cover tightly. Store in a cool, dry place up to 6 months.
2. To prepare brownies: Preheat oven to 350°. In a bowl, combine eggs, butter, vanilla and brownie mix. Spread into a greased 8-in. square baking dish. Bake until set, 25-30 minutes (do not overbake). Cool on a wire rack. Cut into squares.
1 SERVING: *270 cal., 13g fat (6g sat. fat), 42mg chol., 148mg sod., 35g carb. (26g sugars, 2g fiber), 5g pro.*

CINNAMON TWIRL COOKIES

These rolled cookies are tasty and fun to make with your family. The sugary mixture of walnuts and cinnamon is a light, sweet filling that will leave everyone wanting another bite.
—*Phyllis Cappuccio, Boston, MA*

- -

PREP: 40 min. + chilling • **BAKE:** 20 min./batch + cooling
MAKES: 64 cookies

- 1   **cup margarine, softened**
- 1   **cup sour cream**
- 1   **large egg yolk, room temperature**
- 2½   **cups all-purpose flour**
-    **Dash salt**

FILLING
- 1   **cup finely chopped walnuts**
- 1   **cup sugar**
- 2½   **tsp. ground cinnamon**
-    **Confectioners' sugar**

1. In a large bowl, beat margarine and sour cream until blended. Add egg yolk; mix well. Combine flour and salt; add to margarine mixture and mix well (dough will be sticky). Cover and refrigerate for 4 hours or overnight.
2. Preheat the oven to 350°. Divide the dough into eighths. On a well-floured surface, roll each portion into a 10-in. circle. Cut each circle into 8 triangles. Combine the walnuts, sugar and cinnamon; sprinkle over each triangle.
3. Roll up triangles from the wide ends and place point side down 1 in. apart on parchment-lined baking sheets. Bake until lightly browned, 20-22 minutes. Remove to wire racks to cool. Dust with confectioners' sugar. Store in an airtight container.
1 COOKIE: *68 cal., 5g fat (1g sat. fat), 4mg chol., 37mg sod., 6g carb. (2g sugars, 0 fiber), 1g pro.*

CINNAMON
TWIRL COOKIES

MICROWAVE OATMEAL BARS

5i
MICROWAVE OATMEAL BARS

My mother shared this speedy recipe with me. There are not a lot of ingredients, making these microwave treats easy enough for kids to whip up.
—*Annette Self, Junction City, OH*

PREP: 20 min. + chilling • **MAKES:** 10 servings

- 2 cups quick-cooking oats
- ½ cup packed brown sugar
- ½ cup butter, melted
- ¼ cup corn syrup
- 1 cup semisweet chocolate chips

1. In a large bowl, combine oats and brown sugar. Stir in butter and corn syrup. Press mixture into a greased 9-in. square microwave-safe dish.
2. Microwave, uncovered, on high for 1½ minutes. Rotate a half turn; microwave 1½ minutes longer. Sprinkle with chocolate chips. Microwave at 30% power 4½ minutes or until chips are glossy; spread evenly over the top.
3. Refrigerate 15-20 minutes before cutting.
1 PIECE: *287 cal., 15g fat (9g sat. fat), 25mg chol., 109mg sod., 38g carb. (24g sugars, 3g fiber), 3g pro.*

READER REVIEW

"This was so easy to make, and everyone loved it! Half the dish was eaten right up. I cooked it for a little less and also added some peanut butter to the mix. It tasted like a chewy PB chocolate granola bar!"
—DEANA2431, TASTEOFHOME.COM

5i
CAN'T LEAVE ALONE BARS

I bring these quick-and-easy treats to church meetings, potlucks and housewarming parties. I often make a double batch so we can enjoy some at home.
—*Kimberly Biel, Java, SD*

PREP: 20 min. • **BAKE:** 20 min. + cooling • **MAKES:** 3 dozen

- 1 pkg. white cake mix (regular size)
- 2 large eggs, room temperature
- ⅓ cup canola oil
- 1 can (14 oz.) sweetened condensed milk
- 1 cup semisweet chocolate chips
- ¼ cup butter, cubed

1. Preheat oven to 350°. In a large bowl, combine the cake mix, eggs and oil. Press two-thirds of the mixture into a greased 13x9-in. baking pan. Set remaining cake mixture aside.
2. In a microwave-safe bowl, combine the milk, chocolate chips and butter. Microwave, uncovered, until chips and butter are melted; stir until smooth. Pour over crust.
3. Drop teaspoonfuls of remaining cake mixture over top. Bake until lightly browned, 20-25 minutes. Cool before cutting.
1 BAR: *152 cal., 7g fat (3g sat. fat), 19mg chol., 122mg sod., 20g carb. (15g sugars, 0 fiber), 2g pro.*

CAN'T LEAVE ALONE BARS

POWERED-UP MOLASSES COOKIES

POWERED-UP MOLASSES COOKIES

These tender cookies are so soft and flavorful. You would never guess that they're also lower in fat!
—Jean Ecos, Hartland, WI

PREP: 20 min. • **BAKE:** 10 min./batch + cooling
MAKES: 2 dozen

- ⅔ cup plus 2 Tbsp. sugar, divided
- ¼ cup sunflower oil
- 1 large egg, room temperature
- ¼ cup molasses
- 2 cups white whole wheat flour or whole wheat pastry flour
- 2 tsp. baking soda
- 1 tsp. ground cinnamon
- ½ tsp. salt
- ¼ tsp. ground ginger
- ¼ tsp. ground cloves
- 3 Tbsp. confectioners' sugar

1. Preheat oven to 375°. In a large bowl, beat ⅔ cup sugar and sunflower oil until blended. Beat in egg, then molasses. In another bowl, whisk flour, baking soda, cinnamon, salt, ginger and cloves; gradually beat into sugar mixture.
2. Combine confectioners' sugar and remaining sugar. Shape dough into 1-in. balls; roll in sugar mixture. Place 1 in. apart on greased baking sheets. Bake until edges are firm, 10-12 minutes. Cool on pans 5 minutes. Remove to wire racks to cool. Store in an airtight container.
1 COOKIE: *110 cal., 3g fat (0 sat. fat), 8mg chol., 158mg sod., 19g carb. (10g sugars, 2g fiber), 3g pro.*

CHOCOLATE PEANUT DROPS

I got this recipe from a friend. I was surprised to learn that these chocolaty candies came from a slow cooker. You'll get dozens of candies from each batch.
—Anita Bell, Hermitage, TN

PREP: 20 min. • **COOK:** 1½ hours + standing • **MAKES:** about 11 dozen

- 4 oz. German sweet chocolate, chopped
- 1 pkg. (12 oz.) semisweet chocolate chips
- 4 pkg. (10 to 12 oz. each) white baking chips
- 2 jars (16 oz. each) lightly salted dry roasted peanuts

1. In a 6-qt. slow cooker, layer ingredients in order listed (do not stir). Cover and cook on low for 1½ hours. Stir to combine. (If chocolate is not melted, cover and cook 15 minutes longer; stir. Repeat in 15-minute increments until chocolate is melted.)
2. Drop mixture by rounded tablespoonfuls onto waxed paper and let stand until set. Store candy in an airtight container at room temperature.
1 PIECE: *102 cal., 7g fat (3g sat. fat), 1mg chol., 31mg sod., 8g carb. (7g sugars, 1g fiber), 2g pro.*
Chocolate Peanut Bark: Cook chocolate mixture as directed; spread into two 15x10x1-in. waxed paper-lined baking pans. Refrigerate until firm, about 30 minutes. Cut or break into bite-sized pieces.

CHOCOLATE PEANUT DROPS

CARAMEL APPLE OATMEAL COOKIES

CARAMEL APPLE OATMEAL COOKIES

CARAMEL APPLE OATMEAL COOKIES

This recipe for caramel apple cookies is a fun twist on traditional oatmeal raisin. These treats are hard to resist!
—Rachel Lewis, Danville, VA

- -

PREP: 10 min. • **BAKE:** 15 min./batch
MAKES: 4 dozen

½ cup butter, softened
¾ cup packed brown sugar
¼ cup sugar
1 pkg. (3.4 oz.) instant caramel pudding mix
2 large eggs, room temperature
½ cup unsweetened applesauce
1¼ cups all-purpose flour
1 tsp. baking soda
3½ cups old-fashioned oats
1 medium apple, peeled and chopped

1. Preheat oven to 350°. In a large bowl, cream butter, sugars and pudding mix until light and fluffy. Add eggs; mix well. Beat in applesauce. In another bowl, whisk flour and baking soda; gradually beat into creamed mixture. Stir in oats and apple.
2. Drop dough by tablespoonfuls 2 in. apart onto greased baking sheets. Bake until golden brown, 15-18 minutes. Cool on pans for 3 minutes. Serve warm, or remove to wire racks to cool completely. Store in an airtight container.
FREEZE OPTION: Freeze cooled cookies in freezer containers, separating layers with waxed paper. To use, thaw before serving.
1 COOKIE: *80 cal., 3g fat (1g sat. fat), 13mg chol., 78mg sod., 13g carb. (7g sugars, 1g fiber), 1g pro.*

MACKINAC FUDGE

When I got married, a woman at my parents' church gave me this version of a popular Michigan treat. I sometimes pipe a bit of frosting onto each piece for decoration during the holidays.
—Kristen Ekhoff, Akron, IN

- -

PREP: 5 min. • **COOK:** 25 min. + chilling • **MAKES:** 3 lbs. (117 pieces)

2 tsp. plus 1 cup butter, divided
4 cups sugar
1 cup 2% milk
25 large marshmallows
1 pkg. (11½ oz.) milk chocolate chips
2 cups semisweet chocolate chips
2 oz. unsweetened chocolate, chopped
1 tsp. vanilla extract
Decorating icing and sprinkles, optional

1. Line a 13x9-in. pan with foil; grease the foil with 2 tsp. butter. In a large heavy saucepan, combine the sugar, milk and remaining 1 cup butter. Bring to a rapid boil over medium heat, stirring constantly. Cook, without stirring, for 2 minutes. Remove from the heat.
2. Stir in marshmallows until melted. Add all chocolate; stir until melted. Stir in vanilla. Immediately spread into prepared pan; cool for 1 hour.
3. Score into 1-in. squares. Refrigerate, covered, until firm, about 3 hours. Using foil, lift out fudge. Remove foil; cut fudge. Store between layers of waxed paper in airtight containers. Decorate as desired.
1 PIECE: *79 cal., 4g fat (2g sat. fat), 5mg chol., 18mg sod., 12g carb. (11g sugars, 0 fiber), 1g pro.*

MACKINAC FUDGE

GIANT BUCKEYE COOKIE

GIANT BUCKEYE COOKIE

I'm from Ohio, and we love our buckeye candy! Buckeyes are a delicious combination of peanut butter and chocolate, which is exactly what this cookie is.
—*Arianna Joy Harding, Cincinnati, OH*

PREP: 15 min. • **BAKE:** 20 min. + cooling
MAKES: 12 servings

- 1 pkg. chocolate cake mix (regular size)
- 2 large eggs, room temperature
- ½ cup canola oil
- 1 cup semisweet chocolate chips
- 1 cup creamy peanut butter
- ½ cup confectioners' sugar
  Optional: Hot fudge ice cream topping, vanilla ice cream, whipped cream and melted peanut butter

1. Preheat oven to 350°. In a large bowl, combine cake mix, eggs and oil until blended. Stir in chocolate chips. Press half the dough into a 10-in. cast-iron or other ovenproof skillet. Combine peanut butter and confectioners' sugar; spread over dough in skillet. Press remaining dough between sheets of parchment into a 10-in. circle; place over filling.
2. Bake until a toothpick inserted in center of cookie comes out with moist crumbs, 20-25 minutes. Serve warm, with optional ingredients as desired.
1 PIECE: *443 cal., 27g fat (6g sat. fat), 31mg chol., 372mg sod., 48g carb. (31g sugars, 3g fiber), 8g pro.*

HOW-TO

Warm Eggs for Better Baking

Many recipes benefit from room-temperature eggs, and it's an easy thing to do. Just place eggs in hot water while you prep your recipe. They'll be ready when it's time to get cracking.

HOMEMADE MANGO MARSHMALLOWS

HOMEMADE MANGO MARSHMALLOWS

Homemade marshmallows are much better than bagged ones. I had yummy results when I flavored my recipe with mango nectar. Look for it in your store's Mexican food section.
—*Deirdre Cox, Kansas City, MO*

PREP: 25 min. • **COOK:** 20 min. + cooling
MAKES: 1½ lbs.

- 2 envelopes unflavored gelatin
- 1¼ cups chilled mango nectar, divided
- 1½ cups sugar
- ¾ cup light corn syrup
- 1 tsp. almond extract
- 2 cups sweetened shredded coconut, toasted

1. Line an 8-in. square pan with foil, letting ends extend over sides by 1 in.; grease foil with cooking spray. In a heatproof bowl of a stand mixer, sprinkle gelatin over ½ cup of nectar.
2. In a large heavy saucepan, combine sugar, corn syrup and remaining nectar. Bring to a boil, stirring occasionally. Cook, without stirring, over medium heat until a candy thermometer reads 240° (soft-ball stage).
3. Remove from heat; slowly drizzle into gelatin, beating on high speed. Continue beating until very stiff and doubled in volume, about 10 minutes. Immediately beat in extract. Spread into prepared pan. Cover and let cool at room temperature 6 hours or overnight.
4. Place coconut in a food processor; process until finely chopped. Using foil, lift candy out of pan. Using lightly buttered kitchen scissors, cut into 1-in. pieces. Roll in coconut. Store in an airtight container in a cool, dry place.
1 MARSHMALLOW: *48 cal., 1g fat (1g sat. fat), 0 chol., 11mg sod., 10g carb. (10g sugars, 0 fiber), 0 pro.*

TRIPLE-CHOCOLATE CHEESECAKE BARS

What could be better than a brownie crust layered with chocolate cheesecake and chocolate ganache? These cheesecake bars will satisfy the biggest chocolate lovers.
—Andrea Price, Grafton, WI

PREP: 35 min. • **BAKE:** 25 min. + chilling
MAKES: 2½ dozen

- ¼ cup butter, cubed
- ½ cup sugar
- 3 Tbsp. baking cocoa
- ½ tsp. vanilla extract
- 1 large egg, room temperature
- ¼ cup all-purpose flour
- ⅛ tsp. baking powder
- ⅛ tsp. salt

CHEESECAKE LAYER
- 2 pkg. (8 oz. each) cream cheese, softened
- ½ cup sugar
- 1½ tsp. vanilla extract
- ¾ cup semisweet chocolate chips, melted and cooled
- 2 large eggs, room temperature, lightly beaten

GANACHE
- 1½ cups semisweet chocolate chips
- ½ cup heavy whipping cream
- 1 tsp. vanilla extract

1. Preheat oven to 350°. Line a 13x9-in. pan with foil, letting ends extend up sides; grease foil. In a microwave, melt butter in a large microwave-safe bowl. Stir in sugar, cocoa and vanilla. Add egg; blend well. Add flour, baking powder and salt; stir just until combined. Spread into a thin layer into prepared pan. Bake until top appears dry, 6-8 minutes.
2. Meanwhile, in a large bowl, beat cream cheese, sugar and vanilla until smooth. Beat in cooled chocolate chips. Add beaten eggs; beat on low speed just until combined. Spread over brownie layer. Bake until filling is set, 25-30 minutes. Cool 10 minutes on a wire rack.
3. For ganache, place chocolate chips in a small bowl. In a saucepan, bring cream just to a boil. Pour over chocolate; let stand 5 minutes. Stir with a whisk until smooth. Stir in the vanilla; cool slightly, stirring occasionally. Pour over the cheesecake layer; cool in pan on a wire rack 1 hour.

Refrigerate at least 2 hours. Lifting with foil, remove bars from pan. Cut into bars.
1 BAR: *180 cal., 13g fat (7g sat. fat), 42mg chol., 81mg sod., 17g carb. (14g sugars, 1g fiber), 2g pro.*

ALMOND CHOCOLATE BISCOTTI

My neighbors look forward to getting my gifts of these white chocolate-drizzled cookies. And I like that they're a cinch to make.
—Ginger Chatfield, Muscatine, IA

PREP: 20 min. • **BAKE:** 40 min. + cooling
MAKES: about 3½ dozen

- 1 pkg. chocolate cake mix (regular size)
- 1 cup all-purpose flour
- ½ cup butter, melted
- 2 large eggs, room temperature
- ¼ cup chocolate syrup
- 1 tsp. vanilla extract
- ½ tsp. almond extract
- ½ cup slivered almonds
- ½ cup miniature semisweet chocolate chips
- 1 cup white baking chips
- 1 Tbsp. shortening

1. Preheat oven to 350°. In a large bowl, beat cake mix, flour, butter, eggs, chocolate syrup and extracts until well blended. Stir in almonds and chocolate chips. Divide dough in half. On ungreased baking sheets, shape each portion into a 12x2-in. log.
2. Bake 30-35 minutes or until firm to the touch. Carefully remove to wire racks; cool 20 minutes.
3. Transfer baked logs to a cutting board. Using a serrated knife, cut diagonally into ½-in. slices. Place on ungreased baking sheets, cut side down. Bake 10-15 minutes or until firm. Remove from pans to wire racks to cool completely.
4. In a microwave, melt the baking chips and shortening; stir until smooth. Drizzle over biscotti; let stand until set. Store cookies between layers of waxed paper in airtight containers.
FREEZE OPTION: Freeze undrizzled cookies in freezer containers. To use, thaw in covered containers. Drizzle with baking chip mixture as directed.
1 COOKIE: *126 cal., 6g fat (3g sat. fat), 16mg chol., 117mg sod., 17g carb. (10g sugars, 1g fiber), 2g pro.*

TRIPLE-CHOCOLATE CHEESECAKE BARS

MELOMAKARONA

Growing up in Cyprus, we saw this cookie everywhere during the holidays. My mother, Thelma, made plate after plate of them every Christmas season. It's just not the holidays without them.
—Paris Paraskeva, San Francisco, CA

PREP: 15 min. • **BAKE:** 25 min./batch + cooling • **MAKES:** 4½ dozen

- 1 cup sugar
- 1 cup water
- ¾ cup honey

COOKIES
- 1 cup confectioners' sugar
- 2 cups olive oil
- ½ cup Cognac
- ½ cup orange juice
- 1 Tbsp. honey
- 7½ cups all-purpose flour
- 4 tsp. grated orange zest
- 3 tsp. baking powder
- 1 tsp. ground cinnamon
- ½ cup ground toasted walnuts

1. Preheat oven to 350°. In a saucepan, combine sugar, water and honey; bring to a boil. Reduce heat; simmer, uncovered, 10 minutes. Cool completely.

2. Meanwhile, for cookies, in a large bowl, beat confectioners' sugar and oil until blended. Beat in Cognac, orange juice and honey. In another bowl, whisk flour, orange zest, baking powder and cinnamon; gradually beat into sugar mixture.

3. Shape tablespoons of dough into 1-in.-thick ovals. Place 1 in. apart on parchment-lined baking sheets. Bake until lightly browned, 20-25 minutes. Cool on pans 5 minutes. Remove to wire racks.

4. Float and turn warm cookies in syrup about 10 seconds; allow excess to drip off. Place on waxed paper; sprinkle with walnuts. Let stand until set. Store between pieces of waxed paper in airtight containers.

1 COOKIE: *172 cal., 9g fat (1g sat. fat), 0 chol., 27mg sod., 20g carb. (7g sugars, 1g fiber), 2g pro.*

CRUNCHY CANDY CLUSTERS

Before I retired, I took these yummy peanut butter bites to work for special occasions. They're so simple! I still make them for holidays because my family looks forward to the clusters of coated cereal and marshmallows.
—Faye O'Bryan, Owensboro, KY

PREP: 15 min. • **COOK:** 1 hour + standing • **MAKES:** about 6½ dozen

- 2 lbs. white candy coating, coarsely chopped
- 1½ cups peanut butter
- ½ tsp. almond extract, optional
- 4 cups Cap'n Crunch cereal
- 4 cups crisp rice cereal
- 4 cups miniature marshmallows

1. Place candy coating in a 5-qt. slow cooker. Cover and cook on high for 1 hour. Add peanut butter. Stir in extract if desired.

2. In a large bowl, combine the cereals and marshmallows. Add the peanut butter mixture and stir until the cereal mixture is well coated. Drop by tablespoonfuls onto waxed paper. Let stand until set. Store at room temperature.

1 PIECE: *112 cal., 6g fat (4g sat. fat), 0 chol., 51mg sod., 14g carb. (11g sugars, 0 fiber), 1g pro.*

CRUNCHY CANDY CLUSTERS

MINE RUN CANDY

MINE RUN CANDY

This candy always brings back memories of my childhood in mining country. It is so easy to make, and you can choose whether you want the pieces coated in chocolate.
—Lisa Henshall, Wichita, KS

- -

PREP: 20 min. • **COOK:** 20 min. + cooling • **MAKES:** 2 lbs.

2 **tsp. butter**
1 **cup sugar**
1 **cup dark corn syrup**
1 **Tbsp. vinegar**
1 **Tbsp. baking soda**
1 **pkg. (11½ oz.) milk chocolate chips**
1 **Tbsp. shortening**

1. Line a 13x9-in. pan with foil and grease the foil with butter; set aside. In a large heavy saucepan, combine the sugar, corn syrup and vinegar. Cook and stir over medium heat until sugar is dissolved. Bring to a boil. Cook, without stirring, until a candy thermometer reads 300° (hard-crack stage).
2. Remove from the heat; stir in baking soda. Immediately pour into prepared pan. Do not spread candy. Cool. Using foil, lift candy out of pan. Gently peel off foil; break candy into pieces.
3. In a microwave, melt chips and shortening; stir until smooth. Dip candies into the chocolate mixture, allowing excess to drip off. Place on waxed paper; let stand until set. Store candies in an airtight container.
2 OZ.: 223 cal., 7g fat (3g sat. fat), 5mg chol., 284mg sod., 41g carb. (28g sugars, 1g fiber), 2g pro.

DID YOU KNOW?

A simple way to test your thermometer's accuracy is to place it in boiling water (it should measure 212° if you're at or near sea level). If your reading is different, simply recalibrate your thermometer or account for the number of degrees' difference in your recipes.

MARBLED MERINGUE HEARTS

Pretty pastel cookies are a fun way to brighten any special occasion. Replace the vanilla with a different extract for a change of flavor.
—Laurie Herr, Westford, VT

- -

PREP: 25 min. • **BAKE:** 20 min. + cooling • **MAKES:** about 2 dozen

3 **large egg whites**
½ **tsp. vanilla extract**
¼ **tsp. cream of tartar**
¾ **cup sugar**
   Red food coloring

1. Place egg whites in a large bowl; let stand at room temperature for 30 minutes. Line baking sheets with parchment.
2. Preheat oven to 200°. Add vanilla and cream of tartar to egg whites; beat on medium speed until soft peaks form. Gradually beat in sugar, 1 Tbsp. at a time, on high until stiff peaks form. Remove ¼ cup and tint pink. Lightly swirl pink mixture into the remaining meringue. Fill pastry bag with meringue. Pipe 2-in. heart shapes 2 in. apart onto prepared baking sheets.
3. Bake until set and dry, about 20 minutes. Turn oven off; leave meringues in oven until oven has completely cooled. Store in an airtight container.
1 MERINGUE: 27 cal., 0 fat (0 sat. fat), 0 chol., 7mg sod., 6g carb. (6g sugars, 0 fiber), 0 pro.

MARBLED MERINGUE HEARTS

PASSOVER RAINBOW COOKIES

---

⑤ MICROWAVE MARSHMALLOW FUDGE

This foolproof fudge takes just four ingredients and 15 minutes, so it's super when time is short. It's so easy, you can fix it anytime you're craving a sweet treat. Use different flavors of frosting and chips to create variety.
—*Sue Ross, Casa Grande, AZ*

- -

PREP: 15 min. + chilling • **MAKES:** about 2 lbs.

- 1 tsp. butter
- 1 can (16 oz.) chocolate frosting
- 2 cups semisweet chocolate chips
- ½ cup chopped walnuts
- ½ cup miniature marshmallows

1. Line a 9-in. square pan with foil and grease the foil with butter; set aside. In a microwave, melt frosting and chocolate chips; stir until smooth. Stir in walnuts; cool for 10 minutes. Stir in marshmallows. Transfer to prepared pan. Cover and refrigerate until firm.

2. Using foil, lift fudge out of pan. Discard foil; cut fudge into 1-in. squares. Store in an airtight container in the refrigerator.

1 PIECE: 51 cal., 3g fat (1g sat. fat), 0 chol., 17mg sod., 6g carb. (5g sugars, 0 fiber), 0 pro.

PASSOVER RAINBOW COOKIES

"Rainbow cookie" is actually a bit of a misnomer for this classic New York treat. To make the pretty layered confections, you'll bake three thin cakes, spread jam between them, and coat both sides with smooth melted chocolate.
—*Shannon Sarna, South Orange, NJ*

- -

PREP: 35 min. • **BAKE:** 10 min./batch + chilling
MAKES: about 3 dozen

- 4 large eggs, room temperature
- 1 cup sugar
- 4 oz. almond paste, cut into small pieces
- ½ cup stick margarine
- ½ cup almond flour
- ½ cup matzo cake meal
- ½ tsp. salt
- ½ tsp. vanilla extract
- 6 to 8 drops red food coloring
- 6 to 8 drops green food coloring
- ¼ cup seedless raspberry jam

GLAZE
- 1 cup dark chocolate chips
- 1 Tbsp. shortening
  Dash salt

1. Preheat oven to 375°. Line bottoms of 3 greased 8-in. square baking pans with parchment; grease parchment. In a large bowl, beat eggs and sugar until thick and lemon-colored, 2-3 minutes. Gradually add almond paste; mix well. Gradually add margarine, almond flour, cake meal, salt and vanilla.

2. Divide batter into thirds. Tint 1 portion red and 1 portion green; leave remaining portion plain. Spread each portion into a separate prepared pan.

3. Bake until a toothpick inserted in center comes out clean and edges begins to brown, 10-12 minutes. Cool 10 minutes before gently removing from pans to wire racks to cool completely.

4. Place red layer on waxed paper; spread with 2 Tbsp. jam. Top with plain layer and remaining jam. Add the green layer; press down gently.

5. For glaze, in a microwave, melt chocolate chips, shortening and salt; stir until smooth. Spread half over green layer. Refrigerate for 20 minutes or until set. Turn over onto another piece of waxed paper; spread remaining glaze over red layer. Refrigerate 20 minutes or until set.

6. With a sharp knife, trim edges. Cut into 4 rows; cut each row into 1-in. slices.

NOTE: This recipe was tested with Earth Balance Buttery Sticks to make a dairy-free cookie. But if you're not keeping kosher or avoiding dairy, you can easily substitute unsalted butter for the margarine.

1 COOKIE: 32 cal., 2g fat (1g sat. fat), 6mg chol., 21mg sod., 4g carb. (3g sugars, 0 fiber), 1g pro.

**CHERRY HAND PIES
PAGE 215**

Cakes & Pies

From hand-held bites to holiday showstoppers, few desserts steal the show quite like the must-try delights found here. Bake up a new family favorite today!

BEST VANILLA CAKE

There's a reason this vanilla cake recipe is the best. Adding creamy vanilla bean paste to this moist, rich cake batter creates a power-packed vanilla flavor that can't be bought in stores. Try spreading the Best Vanilla Buttercream frosting on top to finish it off; see my recipe at right.
—Margaret Knoebel, Milwaukee, WI

PREP: 20 min. + standing
BAKE: 30 min. + cooling • **MAKES:** 16 servings

1½ cups sour cream
1 Tbsp. vanilla bean paste
1 Tbsp. vanilla extract
4 cups cake flour
2½ cups sugar
4½ tsp. baking powder
2 tsp. salt
1 cup unsalted butter, softened
¼ cup canola oil
6 large egg whites, room temperature
2 large eggs, room temperature

1. Preheat oven to 350°. In a small bowl, mix sour cream, vanilla paste and vanilla extract until combined. Let stand 10 minutes. Line bottoms of 3 greased 9-in. round baking pans with parchment; grease paper.
2. Sift cake flour, sugar, baking powder and salt together twice into a large bowl. Add butter and canola oil; beat until mixture is crumbly. Add egg whites, 1 at a time, beating well after each addition. Add the eggs, 1 at a time, beating well after each addition. Beat in the sour cream mixture just until combined.
3. Transfer batter to prepared pans. Bake until a toothpick inserted in center comes out clean, 30-35 minutes. Cool in pans for 10 minutes before removing to wire racks; remove paper. Cool completely. Frost cake as desired.

1 SLICE: *399 cal., 16g fat (8g sat. fat), 54mg chol., 462mg sod., 59g carb. (32g sugars, 1g fiber), 5g pro.*

BEST VANILLA BUTTERCREAM

Why has this recipe been crowned the best vanilla buttercream frosting? With an intensely decadent vanilla bean flavor and delightfully creamy texture, the frosting will have your family and friends scraping every last bit off their plates.
—Margaret Knoebel, Milwaukee, WI

PREP: 30 min. + cooling • **MAKES:** 5 cups

6 oz. white baking chips
¼ cup heavy whipping cream
1 Tbsp. vanilla bean paste
1 Tbsp. vanilla extract
6 large egg whites, room temperature
1½ cups sugar
½ tsp. cream of tartar
½ tsp. salt
2 cups unsalted butter, cubed

1. In a microwave, melt the baking chips with cream until smooth, stirring every 30 seconds. Stir in vanilla paste and extract. Set aside to cool slightly. Meanwhile, in a heatproof bowl of a stand mixer, whisk egg whites, sugar, cream of tartar and salt until blended. Place over simmering water in a large saucepan over medium heat. Whisking constantly, heat mixture until a thermometer reads 160°, 8-10 minutes.
2. Remove from the heat. With whisk attachment of stand mixer, beat on high speed until cooled to 90°, about 7 minutes. Gradually beat in butter, a few tablespoons at a time, on medium speed until smooth. Beat in the cooled baking chip mixture until blended.

2 TBSP.: *144 cal., 11g fat (7g sat. fat), 27mg chol., 43mg sod., 10g carb. (10g sugars, 0 fiber), 1g pro.*

**BEST VANILLA CAKE &
BEST VANILLA BUTTERCREAM**

BLACK FOREST UPSIDE-DOWN CAKE

CREAMY BISCOFF PIE

I tasted Biscoff cookie butter at a grocery store one day, and it was so delicious I decided to create a no-bake pie with it. You can make it your own by substituting peanut butter or another kind of spread and matching toppings.
—Katrina Adams, Mount Olive, AL

PREP: 20 min. + freezing • **MAKES:** 2 pies (8 servings each)

- 1 pkg. (8 oz.) cream cheese, softened
- 1 cup Biscoff creamy cookie spread
- ¾ cup confectioners' sugar
- 2 cartons (8 oz. each) frozen whipped topping, thawed, divided
  Two 9-in. graham cracker crusts (about 6 oz. each)
- ¼ cup caramel sundae syrup
- 4 Biscoff cookies, crushed

In a large bowl, beat cream cheese, cookie spread and confectioners' sugar until combined. Fold in 1 carton whipped topping. Divide between crusts. Top with remaining container whipped topping. Drizzle with syrup; sprinkle with cookie crumbs. Freeze, covered, until firm, at least 4 hours.

1 SLICE: *367 cal., 21g fat (10g sat. fat), 14mg chol., 187mg sod., 40g carb. (31g sugars, 0 fiber), 3g pro.*

BLACK FOREST UPSIDE-DOWN CAKE

This is a simple, elegant and delicious dessert is bound to impress. Be prepared to give the recipe to guests!
—Kimberly Campbell, Wheeling, WV

PREP: 20 min. • **BAKE:** 40 min. + cooling • **MAKES:** 16 servings

- 1 can (21 oz.) cherry pie filling
- 1 pkg. (8 oz.) cream cheese, softened
- ¾ cup sugar
- 2 Tbsp. all-purpose flour
- 1 tsp. vanilla extract
- 2 large eggs, room temperature
- 1 pkg. devil's food cake mix
  Whipped cream

1. Preheat oven to 350°. Spoon pie filling into a greased 12-in. cast-iron or ovenproof skillet. In a large bowl, beat cream cheese, sugar, flour and vanilla until blended. Gently beat in eggs. Pour over pie filling. Prepare cake mix according to package directions; spoon over cream cheese layer.

2. Bake until a toothpick inserted in the center comes out clean, 40-45 minutes. Cool 10 minutes before inverting onto a serving plate. If needed, spoon cherries from pan over cake. Top with whipped cream.

1 SLICE: *321 cal., 14g fat (5g sat. fat), 72mg chol., 319mg sod., 44g carb. (30g sugars, 1g fiber), 4g pro.*

CREAMY BISCOFF PIE

CHERRY CHOCOLATE MARBLE CAKE

CHERRY CHOCOLATE MARBLE CAKE

Cherries and chocolate are natural partners that make desserts like this one simply scrumptious! The marbled effect is easily achieved by layering the two contrasting batters.
—Sandra Campbell, Chase Mills, NY

PREP: 20 min. • **BAKE:** 1¼ hours + cooling • **MAKES:** 12 servings

- 1 cup butter, softened
- 2 cups sugar
- 3 large eggs, room temperature
- 6 Tbsp. maraschino cherry juice
- 6 Tbsp. water
- 1 tsp. almond extract
- 3¾ cups all-purpose flour
- 2¼ tsp. baking soda
- ¾ tsp. salt
- 1½ cups sour cream
- ¾ cup chopped maraschino cherries, drained
- ¾ cup chopped walnuts, toasted
- 3 oz. unsweetened chocolate, melted
  Confectioners' sugar, optional

1. In a large bowl, cream butter and sugar until light and fluffy, 5-7 minutes. Add eggs, 1 at a time, beating well after each addition. Add the cherry juice, water and extract; mix well. Combine the flour, baking soda and salt; add to creamed mixture alternately with sour cream, beating well after each addition.
2. Divide batter in half. To 1 portion, add cherries and walnuts; mix well. To the second portion, add chocolate; mix well. Spoon half the cherry mixture into a greased and floured 10-in. fluted tube pan. Cover with half of the chocolate mixture. Repeat layers.
3. Bake at 350° until a toothpick inserted near center comes out clean, about 1¼ hours. Cool for 15 minutes; remove from pan to a wire rack to cool completely. Dust with confectioners' sugar if desired.
1 SLICE: *606 cal., 31g fat (16g sat. fat), 94mg chol., 544mg sod., 74g carb. (39g sugars, 3g fiber), 9g pro.*

BLOOD ORANGE CARAMEL TARTE TATIN

Blood orange season is pretty short, so I use them in everything that I possibly can. I'd never had blood oranges until moving to California and I've found that the perfect combination is the sweet orange flavor combined with brown sugar. Whenever I have to take a dish, my friends demand that I bring this dessert.
—Pamela Butkowski, Hermosa Beach, CA

PREP: 20 min. • **BAKE:** 20 min. + cooling • **MAKES:** 6 servings

- ½ cup butter, cubed
- ½ cup packed brown sugar
- 1 tsp. vanilla extract
- 1 medium blood orange, thinly sliced
- 1 sheet frozen puff pastry, thawed
  Vanilla ice cream, optional

1. Preheat oven to 400°. In an 8-in. cast-iron or other ovenproof skillet, melt butter over medium heat; stir in brown sugar and vanilla until dissolved. Arrange orange slices in a single layer over brown sugar.
2. On a lightly floured surface, unfold puff pastry. Roll to a 9-in. square; place over oranges, tucking in corners.
3. Bake until tart is golden brown and filling is heated through, 20-25 minutes. Cool 10 minutes before inverting onto a serving plate. Serve warm, with ice cream if desired.
1 SLICE: *416 cal., 26g fat (12g sat. fat), 41mg chol., 262mg sod., 43g carb. (19g sugars, 3g fiber), 3g pro.*

BLOOD ORANGE CARAMEL TARTE TATIN

BLACKBERRY APPLE PIE

My mother made this pie so often, she could do it with her eyes closed! We picked the berries ourselves, and the apples came from the trees in our orchard. I can still taste the delicious combination of fruits encased in Mother's flaky pie crust.
—Fran Stanfield, Wilmington, OH

PREP: 20 min. • **BAKE:** 50 min.
MAKES: 8 servings

Pastry for a double-crust pie (9 in.)
5 cups thinly sliced peeled tart apples (about 5 medium)
1 pint fresh blackberries, rinsed and drained
1 Tbsp. lemon juice
¾ cup sugar
2 Tbsp. cornstarch
2 Tbsp. butter
1 large egg, room temperature, lightly beaten
1 Tbsp. water or whole milk

1. On a lightly floured surface, roll out half the dough to fit a 9-in. pie plate; trim to 1 in. beyond rim of plate. Top with a thin layer of apples. In a large bowl, combine blackberries and the remaining apples; sprinkle with lemon juice. Combine sugar and cornstarch. Add to the fruit mixture; toss gently to coat. Spoon into crust; dot with butter.
2. Roll out the remaining dough; make a lattice crust. Trim, seal and flute edges. Beat egg with water; brush over lattice top and pie edges.
3. Bake at 375° for 50 minutes or until filling is bubbly and apples are tender. Cool on a wire rack. Serve pie warm or at room temperature.
1 SLICE: *415 cal., 18g fat (8g sat. fat), 44mg chol., 238mg sod., 62g carb. (32g sugars, 2g fiber), 3g pro.*

CONFETTI BIRTHDAY CAKE

CONFETTI BIRTHDAY CAKE

This is a moist vanilla cake featuring lots of sprinkles and a vanilla buttercream. It's impossible not to feel happy when you see it!
—Courtney Rich, Highland, UT

PREP: 30 min. • **BAKE:** 35 min. + cooling
MAKES: 16 servings

1 cup unsalted butter, room temperature
⅓ cup vegetable oil
1¾ cups sugar
3 large eggs, room temperature
3 large egg whites, room temperature
1 Tbsp. vanilla extract
3 cups cake flour
2 tsp. baking powder
1 tsp. salt
1 cup buttermilk, room temperature
¼ cup rainbow sprinkles
BUTTERCREAM
1½ cups unsalted butter, softened
4½ cups confectioners' sugar, sifted
3 Tbsp. heavy whipping cream
2 tsp. clear vanilla extract

Soft pink paste food coloring
Additional rainbow sprinkles, optional

1. Preheat oven to 325°. Grease a 13x9-in. baking dish. In a large bowl, cream butter, oil and sugar until light and fluffy, 5-7 minutes. Add eggs, then egg whites, 1 at a time, beating well after each addition. Beat in vanilla. In another bowl, whisk flour, baking powder and salt; add to creamed mixture alternately with buttermilk, beating well after each addition. Fold in sprinkles.
2. Transfer to prepared pan. Bake until a toothpick inserted in center comes out clean, 35-40 minutes. Cool completely on a wire rack.
3. For buttercream, in a large bowl, beat butter until creamy. Gradually beat in confectioners' sugar until smooth. Add cream, vanilla and food coloring. Beat until light and fluffy, 5-7 minutes. Frost top of cake with frosting, and top with additional sprinkles if desired.
1 PIECE: *823 cal., 47g fat (26g sat. fat), 138mg chol., 279mg sod., 97g carb. (75g sugars, 0 fiber), 6g pro.*

LEMON LOVER'S
POUND CAKE

ELEGANT FRESH BERRY TART

*This lovely tart was my first original creation.
If other fresh fruits are used, adjust the
simple syrup flavor to match.*
—Denise Nakamoto, Elk Grove, CA

PREP: 45 min. + chilling
BAKE: 10 min. + cooling • **MAKES:** 10 servings

½	cup butter, softened
⅓	cup sugar
½	tsp. grated orange zest
¼	tsp. orange extract
⅛	tsp. vanilla extract
1	cup all-purpose flour

FILLING
1	pkg. (8 oz.) cream cheese, softened
¼	cup sugar
½	tsp. lemon juice

SYRUP
2	Tbsp. water
1½	tsp. sugar
1½	tsp. red raspberry or strawberry preserves
⅛	tsp. lemon juice

TOPPING
¾	cup fresh strawberries, sliced
½	cup fresh raspberries
½	cup fresh blueberries
2	medium kiwifruit, peeled and sliced

LEMON LOVER'S POUND CAKE

*Everyone raves about this pretty dessert—
it sure doesn't last long in my family. It also
freezes beautifully, so why not make two and
pop one into the freezer for another day?*
—Annettia Mounger, Kansas City, MO

PREP: 20 min. • **BAKE:** 55 min. + cooling
MAKES: 12 servings

1	cup butter, softened
3	cups sugar
6	large eggs, room temperature
5	Tbsp. lemon juice
1	Tbsp. grated lemon zest
1	tsp. lemon extract
3	cups all-purpose flour
½	tsp. baking soda
¼	tsp. salt
1¼	cups sour cream

ICING
¼	cup sour cream, room temperature
2	Tbsp. butter, softened
2½	cups confectioners' sugar
2	to 3 Tbsp. lemon juice
2	tsp. grated lemon zest

1. In a large bowl, cream butter and sugar until light and fluffy, 5-7 minutes. Add eggs, 1 at a time, beating well after each addition. Stir in the lemon juice, zest and extract. Combine the flour, baking soda and salt; add to the creamed mixture alternately with sour cream. Beat just until combined.
2. Pour batter into a greased and floured 10-in. fluted tube pan. Bake at 350° until a toothpick inserted near the center comes out clean, 55-60 minutes. Cool for 10 minutes before removing from pan to a wire rack to cool completely.
3. For icing, in a small bowl, beat the sour cream and butter until smooth. Gradually add confectioners' sugar. Beat in lemon juice and zest. Drizzle over the cake. If desired, top with additional grated lemon zest. Store in the refrigerator.
1 SLICE: *658 cal., 26g fat (15g sat. fat), 146mg chol., 286mg sod., 101g carb. (76g sugars, 1g fiber), 8g pro.*

1. Preheat oven to 375°. Cream butter and sugar until light and fluffy, 5-7 minutes. Add orange zest and extracts; gradually add flour until mixture forms a ball. Press into a greased 9-in. fluted tart pan with a removable bottom. Bake until golden brown, 10-12 minutes. Cool on a wire rack.
2. For filling, beat cream cheese, sugar and lemon juice until smooth; spread over crust. Cover and refrigerate until set, about 30 minutes.
3. Meanwhile, for the syrup, bring water, sugar, preserves and lemon juice to a boil in a small saucepan. Reduce heat; simmer, uncovered, for 10 minutes. Set aside to cool.
4. Combine strawberries, raspberries, blueberries and kiwi; toss with syrup to glaze. Arrange fruit as desired over filling. Cover tart and refrigerate at least 1 hour before serving.
1 SLICE: *277 cal., 17g fat (10g sat. fat), 47mg chol., 145mg sod., 29g carb. (17g sugars, 2g fiber), 3g pro.*

> **TEST KITCHEN TIP**
>
> For the glaze, you can add more confectioners' sugar or lemon juice to get just the right consistency.

STRAWBERRY-RHUBARB UPSIDE-DOWN CAKE

I prepare this colorful dessert quite often in late spring or summer, when fresh rhubarb is abundant. When I take it to church potlucks, people literally line up for a piece.
—Bonnie Krogman, Thompson Falls, MT

- -

PREP: 15 min. • **BAKE:** 40 min. + cooling • **MAKES:** 12 servings

- 5 cups sliced fresh or frozen rhubarb, thawed and drained
- 1 pkg. (6 oz.) strawberry gelatin
- ½ cup sugar
- 2 cups miniature marshmallows
- 1 pkg. white or yellow cake mix (regular size)
  Whipped topping, optional

1. Place rhubarb in a greased 13x9-in. baking pan. Sprinkle with the gelatin, sugar and marshmallows. Prepare cake mix according to package directions; pour batter over marshmallows.
2. Bake at 350° until a toothpick inserted in the center comes out clean, 40-45 minutes. Cool for 10 minutes; invert cake onto a serving plate. Serve with whipped topping if desired.
1 PIECE: *353 cal., 9g fat (2g sat. fat), 47mg chol., 359mg sod., 65g carb. (44g sugars, 2g fiber), 5g pro.*

**STRAWBERRY-RHUBARB
UPSIDE-DOWN CAKE**

FLOURLESS CHOCOLATE TORTE

FLOURLESS CHOCOLATE TORTE

Here's the perfect dessert for chocoholics like me! I bake the melt-in-your-mouth torte all the time for special occasions. For an elegant finish, dust it with confectioners' sugar.
—Kayla Albrecht, Freeport, IL

- -

PREP: 20 min. • **BAKE:** 40 min. + cooling • **MAKES:** 12 servings

- 5 large eggs, separated
- 12 oz. semisweet chocolate, chopped
- ¾ cup butter, cubed
- ¼ tsp. cream of tartar
- ½ cup sugar
  Confectioners' sugar, optional

1. Place egg whites in a large bowl; let stand at room temperature 30 minutes. Preheat oven to 350°. In top of a double boiler or a metal bowl over barely simmering water, melt chocolate and butter; stir until smooth. Remove from heat; cool slightly.
2. In another large bowl, beat egg yolks until thick and lemon-colored. Beat in chocolate mixture. With clean beaters, beat egg whites and cream of tartar on medium speed until foamy.
3. Gradually add sugar, 1 Tbsp. at a time, beating on high after each addition until sugar is dissolved. Continue beating until stiff glossy peaks form. Fold a fourth of the egg whites into chocolate mixture, then fold in remaining whites.
4. Transfer to a greased 9-in. springform pan. Bake until a toothpick inserted near the center comes out with moist crumbs, 40-45 minutes (do not overbake). Cool completely on a wire rack.
5. Loosen sides from pan with a knife. Remove rim from pan. If desired, dust with confectioners' sugar.
1 SLICE: *326 cal., 24g fat (14g sat. fat), 108mg chol., 121mg sod., 15g carb. (14g sugars, 1g fiber), 5g pro.*

SHOOFLY CHOCOLATE PIE

If you like traditional shoofly pie, the chocolate version is even better! If you've never tried shoofly pie, here's a tasty reason to do so. I sometimes serve it with vanilla ice cream.
—Gwen Brounce Widdowson, Fleetwood, PA

PREP: 20 min. • **BAKE:** 45 min. + cooling • **MAKES:** 8 servings

Pastry for single-crust pie (9 in.)
- ½ cup semisweet chocolate chips
- 1½ cups all-purpose flour
- ½ cup packed brown sugar
- 3 Tbsp. butter-flavored shortening
- 1 tsp. baking soda
- 1½ cups water
- 1 large egg, lightly beaten
- 1 cup molasses

1. Roll out dough to fit a 9-in. deep-dish pie plate or cast-iron skillet. Trim to ½ in. beyond rim of plate; flute edges. Sprinkle chocolate chips into crust; set aside.

2. In a large bowl, combine flour and brown sugar; cut in the shortening until crumbly. Set aside 1 cup for topping. Add the baking soda, water, egg and molasses to remaining crumb mixture and mix well. Pour over the chips. Sprinkle with the reserved crumb mixture.

3. Bake at 350° until a knife inserted in the center comes out clean, 45-55 minutes. Let stand on a wire rack for 15 minutes before cutting. Serve warm.

1 SLICE: *526 cal., 20g fat (10g sat. fat), 53mg chol., 341mg sod., 83g carb. (49g sugars, 2g fiber), 6g pro.*

SHOOFLY CHOCOLATE PIE

APPLE PEAR CAKE

APPLE PEAR CAKE

When my sister Catherine made her apple cake for me, I knew I needed the recipe. For my version, I added some pears from the trees on our acreage. This cake is very moist and so good. Every time I make it, people ask for the recipe.
—Mary Ann Lees, Centreville, AL

PREP: 25 min. • **BAKE:** 1 hour + cooling • **MAKES:** 15 servings

- 2 cups shredded peeled tart apples
- 2 cups shredded peeled pears
- 2 cups sugar
- 1¼ cups canola oil
- 1 cup raisins
- 1 cup chopped pecans
- 2 large eggs, room temperature, lightly beaten
- 1 tsp. vanilla extract
- 3 cups all-purpose flour
- 2 tsp. baking soda
- 2 tsp. ground cinnamon
- ½ tsp. ground nutmeg
- ½ tsp. salt

CREAM CHEESE FROSTING
- 3 oz. cream cheese, softened
- 3 cups confectioners' sugar
- ¼ cup butter, softened
- 2 Tbsp. 2% milk
- ½ tsp. vanilla extract

1. In a large bowl, combine the first 8 ingredients. Combine dry ingredients; stir into the fruit mixture.

2. Pour into a greased 13x9-in. baking pan. Bake at 325° until a toothpick inserted in the center comes out clean, about 1 hour. Cool on a wire rack.

3. For frosting, in a large bowl, beat cream cheese, confectioners' sugar and butter until smooth. Beat in the milk and vanilla; frost cake. Store in the refrigerator.

1 PIECE: *613 cal., 30g fat (6g sat. fat), 43mg chol., 306mg sod., 84g carb. (60g sugars, 3g fiber), 5g pro.*

CREAMY STRAWBERRY PIE

I like to end a nice company meal with this easy make-ahead dessert. The eye-catching pie has a big strawberry flavor and extra richness from ice cream.
—Dixie Terry, Goreville, IL

PREP: 25 min. + chilling • **MAKES:** 6 servings

- 1 pkg. (10 oz.) frozen sweetened sliced strawberries, thawed
- 1 pkg. (3 oz.) strawberry gelatin
- 2 cups vanilla ice cream
- 1 pastry shell (9 in.), baked
  Sliced fresh strawberries, optional

1. Drain the strawberries into a 1-cup measuring cup and reserve the juice; set berries aside. Add enough water to juice to measure 1 cup; pour into a large saucepan. Bring to a boil over medium heat. Remove from the heat; stir in gelatin until dissolved. Add the ice cream; stir until blended. Refrigerate for 5-10 minutes or just until thickened (watch carefully).

2. Fold in reserved strawberries. Pour into crust. Refrigerate until firm, about 1 hour. Garnish with fresh strawberries if desired. Refrigerate leftovers.

1 SLICE: *345 cal., 14g fat (7g sat. fat), 26mg chol., 202mg sod., 52g carb. (33g sugars, 1g fiber), 4g pro.*

DOUBLE BUTTERSCOTCH COCONUT CAKE

I got this recipe for coconut cake from a co-worker years ago, then I changed it up a bit by adding a family favorite: butterscotch. It's easy to throw together, and it makes a perfect accompaniment to coffee or tea. Try it on a brunch buffet, too!
—Marina Castle Kelley, Canyon Country, CA

PREP: 20 min. • **BAKE:** 40 min. + cooling
MAKES: 16 servings

- 1 pkg. yellow cake mix (regular size)
- 1 pkg. (3.4 oz.) instant butterscotch pudding mix
- 4 large eggs, room temperature
- 1 cup canned coconut milk
- ¼ cup canola oil
- 1 cup sweetened shredded coconut
- ½ cup butterscotch chips

GLAZE
- ½ cup butterscotch chips
- 2 Tbsp. heavy whipping cream
- ⅓ cup sweetened shredded coconut, toasted

1. Preheat oven to 350°. Grease and flour a 10-in. fluted tube pan.

2. In a large bowl, combine cake mix, pudding mix, eggs, coconut milk and oil; beat on low speed 30 seconds. Beat on medium speed 2 minutes. Stir in coconut and butterscotch chips. Transfer to the prepared pan.

3. Bake until a toothpick inserted near center comes out clean, 40-45 minutes. Cool in pan 10 minutes before removing to a wire rack to cool completely. For glaze, in a microwave, melt butterscotch chips and cream; stir until smooth. Drizzle over cake; sprinkle with coconut.

1 SLICE: *327 cal., 15g fat (10g sat. fat), 49mg chol., 359mg sod., 42g carb. (30g sugars, 1g fiber), 4g pro.*

DOUBLE BUTTERSCOTCH COCONUT CAKE

JELLY DOUGHNUT CAKE

Cake. Doughnuts. Now you don't have to choose between the two. Impress your family with this easy jelly-filled doughnut cake. Try your best to center the jelly in the middle of the half-filled Bundt pan so the jelly will not leak out of the edges of the cake.
—Colleen Delawder, Herndon, VA

- -

PREP: 25 min. + chilling
BAKE: 45 min. + cooling • **MAKES:** 12 servings

 1   cup sugar
 2   tsp. ground cinnamon
 ½   tsp. salt
 ¼   tsp. ground nutmeg
 ¾   cup unsalted butter, melted
 2   large eggs, room temperature
 1   cup 2% milk
 2   Tbsp. sour cream
 1   Tbsp. vanilla extract
 2⅔ cups all-purpose flour
 2½ tsp. baking powder
 ¾   cup raspberry, strawberry
     or apple jelly
FROSTING
 1   pkg. (8 oz.) cream cheese, softened
 1½ cups confectioners' sugar
 1   tsp. ground cinnamon
 ½   tsp. vanilla extract

1. Preheat the oven to 350°. Grease and flour a 10-in. fluted tube pan. Place the sugar, cinnamon, salt and nutmeg in a food processor; process for 30 seconds. Transfer to a large bowl.
2. Beat in melted butter, eggs, milk, sour cream and vanilla until well blended. In another bowl, whisk flour and baking powder; gradually beat into sugar mixture.
3. Pour half of the batter into prepared pan. Spoon jelly over batter to within ½ in. of edges; top with remaining batter. Bake until a toothpick inserted near center comes out clean, 45-50 minutes. Cool in the pan for 10 minutes before removing to a wire rack to cool completely.
4. In a large bowl, combine all frosting ingredients; beat until smooth. Spread over cake; sprinkle with additional sugar and cinnamon. Refrigerate at least 1 hour before serving.
1 SLICE: *475 cal., 20g fat (12g sat. fat), 83mg chol., 283mg sod., 69g carb. (45g sugars, 1g fiber), 6g pro.*

SLOW-COOKER
APPLE PUDDING CAKE

A satisfying dessert like this is a superb treat on a chilly night. It has three layers—apples, cake and sauce—so I like to serve it in a clear glass bowl.
—Ellen Schroeder, Reedsburg, WI

- -

PREP: 15 min. • **COOK:** 2 hours
MAKES: 10 servings

 2   cups all-purpose flour
 ⅔   cup plus ¼ cup sugar, divided
 3   tsp. baking powder
 1   tsp. salt
 ½   cup cold butter
 1   cup 2% milk
 2   medium tart apples, peeled
     and chopped
 1½ cups orange juice
 ½   cup honey
 2   Tbsp. butter, melted
 1   tsp. ground cinnamon
 1⅓ cups sour cream
 ¼   cup confectioners' sugar

1. In a small bowl, combine the flour, ⅔ cup sugar, baking powder and salt. Cut in butter until mixture resembles coarse crumbs. Stir in milk just until moistened. Spread into the bottom of a greased 4- or 5-qt. slow cooker; sprinkle apples over batter.
2. In a small bowl, combine orange juice, honey, melted butter, cinnamon and remaining ¼ cup sugar; pour over apples. Cover and cook on high until apples are tender, 2-3 hours .
3. In a small bowl, combine sour cream and the confectioners' sugar. Serve with warm pudding cake.
1 CUP WITH 2 TBSP. TOPPING: *431 cal., 17g fat (11g sat. fat), 53mg chol., 461mg sod., 64g carb. (44g sugars, 1g fiber), 5g pro.*

JELLY DOUGHNUT CAKE

BANANA POUND CAKE

I adapted a basic pound cake recipe from my great-aunt for this treat. It makes a moist cake that pops out of the pan perfectly.

—Nancy Zimmerman, Cape May Court House, NJ

PREP: 20 min. • **BAKE:** 1¼ hours + cooling
MAKES: 12 servings

- 3 tsp. plus 3 cups sugar, divided
- 1 cup butter, softened
- 6 large eggs, room temperature
- 1 cup mashed ripe bananas (about 2 medium)
- 1½ tsp. vanilla extract
- ½ tsp. lemon extract
- 3 cups all-purpose flour
- ¼ tsp. baking soda
- 1 cup sour cream

GLAZE

- 1½ cups confectioners' sugar
- ½ tsp. vanilla extract
- 3 to 4 tsp. 2% milk

1. Grease a 10-in. fluted tube pan. Sprinkle with 3 tsp. sugar; set aside.
2. In a large bowl, cream butter and the remaining 3 cups sugar until light and fluffy, 5-7 minutes. Add eggs, 1 at a time, beating well after each addition. Stir in bananas and extracts. Combine flour and baking soda; add to the creamed mixture alternately with sour cream, beating just until combined.
3. Pour into prepared pan (pan will be full). Bake at 325° until a toothpick inserted near the center comes out clean, 75-85 minutes. Cool for 10 minutes before removing from pan to a wire rack to cool completely.
4. In a small bowl, whisk glaze ingredients until smooth; drizzle over cake. Store in the refrigerator.

1 SLICE: *600 cal., 22g fat (13g sat. fat), 138mg chol., 192mg sod., 96g carb. (69g sugars, 1g fiber), 7g pro.*

DUTCH CRAN-APPLE PIE

Fresh cranberries bring tongue-tingling tartness and festive Christmas color to classic apple pie. With orange peel, spices and a crumb topping, this is a warm and wintry favorite.

—Jerri Gradert, Lincoln, NE

PREP: 35 min. • **BAKE:** 50 min.
MAKES: 8 servings

- 3 large apples, peeled and thinly sliced
- 1 Tbsp. lemon juice
- 2 cups fresh cranberries
- ½ cup raisins
- ¼ cup chopped walnuts
- ¾ cup packed brown sugar
- ¼ cup cornstarch
- 1 Tbsp. grated orange zest
- 1 tsp. ground cinnamon
- ¼ tsp. ground nutmeg
  Pastry for single-crust pie
- 2 Tbsp. butter

TOPPING

- ½ cup all-purpose flour
- ¼ cup packed brown sugar
- 3 Tbsp. cold butter

1. In a large bowl, toss apples with lemon juice; add the cranberries, raisins and walnuts. Combine the brown sugar, cornstarch, orange zest, cinnamon and nutmeg; add to apple mixture and toss gently to coat.
2. Roll out dough to fit a 9-in. pie plate; transfer to pie plate. Trim crust to ½ in. beyond rim of plate; flute edges. Fill with apple mixture and dot with butter.
3. For topping, combine flour and brown sugar; cut in butter until crumbly. Sprinkle over filling. Bake at 350° for 50-60 minutes or until topping is golden brown and filling is bubbly. Cover edges with foil during the last 15 minutes to prevent overbrowning if necessary.

1 PIECE: *427 cal., 17g fat (8g sat. fat), 24mg chol., 163mg sod., 69g carb. (41g sugars, 3g fiber), 3g pro.*

BANANA POUND CAKE

CHERRY HAND PIES

(SHOWN ON PAGE 202)

There's nothing better than a sweet, from-scratch delight like traditional cherry pie. These precious little hand pies always go fast when I sell them at my bakery!
—Allison Cebulla, Milwaukee, WI

- -

PREP: 45 min. • **BAKE:** 25 min. + cooling
MAKES: 8 servings

- 6 Tbsp. water, divided
- 2 Tbsp. sugar
- 2 Tbsp. cherry brandy
- 4½ tsp. cornstarch
- 1½ tsp. lemon juice
- 1 tsp. quick-cooking tapioca
- ¼ tsp. grated lemon zest
    Dash salt
- 2 cups fresh or frozen pitted tart cherries, thawed and halved
- 1 cup fresh or frozen pitted dark sweet cherries, thawed and halved
    Pastry for double-crust pie
- 1 large egg

ICING
- 2⅔ cups confectioners' sugar
- 3 to 4 Tbsp. hot water
- 2 Tbsp. butter, melted
- ½ tsp. almond extract
- ¼ tsp. vanilla extract
    Dash salt
    Freeze-dried strawberries, crushed, optional

1. In a large saucepan, whisk 4 Tbsp. water, sugar, brandy, cornstarch, lemon juice, tapioca, lemon zest and salt until combined. Add cherries. Bring to a boil; cook and stir until thickened, 3-5 minutes. Remove from heat. Set aside to cool.

2. Preheat the oven to 400°. On a lightly floured surface, roll half the dough to a 14x9-in. rectangle. Cut eight 3½x4½-in. rectangles. Repeat with remaining dough.

3. Transfer 8 rectangles to parchment-lined baking sheets; spoon about 3 Tbsp. cherry mixture in center of each. Whisk egg and remaining 2 Tbsp. water. Brush edges of crust with egg wash. Top with remaining 8 rectangles; press edges with a fork to seal. Brush the tops with egg wash; cut slits in tops.

4. Bake until crust is golden brown and slightly puffed, 25-30 minutes. Remove from pans to wire racks to cool. Combine confectioners' sugar, hot water, butter, extracts and salt; drizzle over pies. Garnish

EASY KEY LIME PIE

with freeze-dried strawberries if desired. Let stand until set.

1 PIE: *589 cal., 27g fat (16g sat. fat), 91mg chol., 380mg sod., 83g carb. (49g sugars, 2g fiber), 6g pro.*

PASTRY FOR DOUBLE-CRUST PIE (9 IN.)
Combine 2½ cups all-purpose flour and ½ tsp. salt; cut in 1 cup cold butter until crumbly. Gradually add ⅓-⅔ cup ice water, tossing with a fork until the dough holds together when pressed. Divide dough in half. Shape each into a disk; wrap. Refrigerate 1 hour or up to overnight.

5i

EASY KEY LIME PIE

You need only five ingredients to create this refreshing pie. It's easy enough to make for a weeknight dessert, but special enough for weekend potlucks.
—Taste of Home *Test Kitchen*

- -

PREP: 20 min. + chilling • **MAKES:** 8 servings

- 1 pkg. (8 oz.) cream cheese, softened
- 1 can (14 oz.) sweetened condensed milk
- ½ cup Key lime juice or lime juice
    One 9-in. graham cracker crust (about 6 oz.)
- 2 cups whipped topping
    Lime slices, optional

In a large bowl, beat cream cheese until smooth. Beat in milk and lime juice until blended. Transfer to crust. Refrigerate, covered, at least 4 hours. Just before serving, garnish with whipped topping and, if desired, lime slices.

1 SLICE: *417 cal., 22g fat (13g sat. fat), 46mg chol., 274mg sod., 48g carb. (42g sugars, 0 fiber), 7g pro.*

**COASTAL
COCONUT CREAM CAKE**

COASTAL
COCONUT CREAM CAKE

*This is my son's county fair cake. He was
awarded a top-10 prize and auctioned his
coconut cream cake off for big bucks!*
—Amy Freeze, Avon Park, FL

- -

PREP: 45 min. + chilling
BAKE: 35 min. + cooling • **MAKES:** 16 servings

- 1   cup butter, softened
- 2   cups sugar
- 4   large eggs, room temperature
- 1½ tsp. coconut extract
- 3   cups all-purpose flour
- 1½ tsp. baking soda
- 1½ tsp. baking powder
- 1   tsp. salt
- 1   cup canned coconut milk
- ½   cup cream of coconut
- ¼   cup sweetened shredded coconut

FILLING
- 1   cup sugar
- 6   Tbsp. cornstarch
- 1   can (20 oz.) unsweetened crushed
      pineapple, undrained
- 2   Tbsp. butter

FROSTING
- 3¾ cups confectioners' sugar
- 1   cup shortening
- ½   cup butter, softened
- 1½ tsp. meringue powder
- ¾   tsp. coconut extract
- ¼   tsp. salt
- 2   to 3 Tbsp. canned coconut milk
- 2   cups sweetened shredded coconut,
      toasted

1. Preheat oven to 350°. Line bottoms
of 2 greased 9-in. round baking pans with
parchment; grease paper.
2. In a large bowl, cream butter and sugar
until light and fluffy, 5-7 minutes. Add eggs,
1 at a time, beating well after each. Beat in
extract. In another bowl, whisk flour, baking
soda, baking powder and the salt; add to
creamed mixture alternately with coconut
milk, beating well after each addition. Fold
in cream of coconut and shredded coconut.
3. Transfer to prepared pans. Bake until
a toothpick inserted in center comes out
clean, 35-40 minutes. Cool in pans for
10 minutes before removing to wire racks;
remove paper. Cool completely.

4. For filling, in a large saucepan, mix sugar
and cornstarch. Whisk in pineapple and
butter. Cook and stir over medium heat
until thickened and bubbly. Reduce heat to
low; cook and stir 2 minutes longer. Remove
from heat; cool completely.
5. For frosting, in a large bowl, beat the
confectioners' sugar, shortening, butter,
meringue powder, extract, salt and enough
coconut milk to reach desired consistency.
6. To assemble cake, using a long serrated
knife, cut each cake horizontally in half.
Place 1 cake layer on a serving plate; spread
with a third of the filling. Repeat twice. Top
with remaining cake layer. Frost top and
sides of cake with frosting. Gently press
toasted coconut into frosting on sides
of cake. Refrigerate cake at least 4 hours
before serving.
1 SLICE: *788 cal., 41g fat (23g sat. fat), 96mg
chol., 560mg sod., 103g carb. (81g sugars,
2g fiber), 5g pro.*

BLACKBERRY
BUTTERCREAM

*Juicy blackberry buttercream frosting has a
stunning color and sophisticated flavor. This
frosting works especially well when used on
rich, decadent chocolate cake.*
—Jocelyn Adams, GrandBaby-Cakes.com

- -

TAKES: 10 min. • **MAKES:** 5 cups

- 1   cup fresh blackberries
- 2   cups unsalted butter, softened
- 1   tsp. vanilla extract
      Dash salt
- 7   cups confectioners' sugar

1. Place blackberries in a blender; cover
and process until pureed. Press through a
fine-mesh strainer into a bowl; discard the
blackberry seeds.
2. In a large bowl, beat butter until creamy.
Beat in vanilla and salt. Gradually beat in
confectioners' sugar until smooth. Add
blackberry puree; beat until blended.
2 TBSP.: *165 cal., 9g fat (6g sat. fat), 24mg
chol., 5mg sod., 21g carb. (21g sugars,
0 fiber), 0 pro.*

DEPLOYMENT PUMPKIN PIES

When my husband, Randy, was deployed in Afghanistan, I sent him the ingredients to make this easy pumpkin pie recipe. He and his team were so happy to have the smell of homemade pie wafting through the base kitchen while they were away from home over the holidays.
—Rowenna Hamper, Mishawaka, IN

PREP: 20 min. • **BAKE:** 45 min. + cooling
MAKES: 2 pies (8 slices each)

2½ cups graham cracker crumbs
½ cup sugar
⅔ cup butter, melted
FILLING
2 large eggs, lightly beaten
1 can (15 oz.) pumpkin
1 can (12 oz.) evaporated milk
¾ cup sugar
1 tsp. ground cinnamon
½ tsp. salt
½ tsp. ground mace or nutmeg
½ tsp. ground cloves

1. Preheat oven to 425°. In a small bowl, mix graham cracker crumbs and sugar; stir in butter. Press onto bottom and up sides of 2 greased 9-in. metal pie plates. Bake until lightly browned, 5-7 minutes. Cool on a wire rack.

2. In a large bowl, beat filling ingredients until blended. Divide evenly between crusts. Bake on a middle oven rack for 15 minutes. Reduce oven setting to 350°. Bake until center is set, 25-30 minutes longer. Cool completely on a wire rack. Store in the refrigerator.

Toaster oven option: Preheat toaster oven to 425°. Prepare crusts as directed. Bake until lightly browned, 5-7 minutes. Cool on a wire rack. Combine filling ingredients; pour into crusts. Bake until center is set, 25-30 minutes.

NOTE: If desired, use prepared store-bought crusts but do not prebake them.

1 SLICE: *245 cal., 12g fat (6g sat. fat), 51mg chol., 239mg sod., 33g carb. (23g sugars, 1g fiber), 4g pro.*

BREAD PUDDING PIE

This change-of-pace dessert is a tasty bread pudding-pie combo. It was created by my paternal grandmother's family. They had a farm and made their own bread, which made this a low-cost dessert.
—Kelly Barnes, Lexington, IN

PREP: 15 min. • **BAKE:** 55 min. + chilling
MAKES: 8 servings

Pastry for single-crust pie
1 cup cubed bread
2 large eggs, room temperature
2 cups 2% milk
¾ cup sugar
½ tsp. vanilla extract
¼ tsp. ground nutmeg
2 tsp. butter

1. Preheat oven to 425°. On a floured surface, roll dough to fit a 9-in. pie plate. Trim and flute edge. Arrange bread in bottom of pie crust. In a large bowl, whisk eggs, milk, sugar and vanilla; pour over bread. Sprinkle with nutmeg and dot with butter. Bake 10 minutes. Reduce oven setting to 350°.

2. Bake until a knife inserted in the center comes out clean, 45-50 minutes longer. Cover the edges with foil during the last 15 minutes to prevent overbrowning if necessary. Cool on a wire rack for 1 hour. Refrigerate the pie for at least 3 hours before serving.

1 SLICE: *314 cal., 15g fat (9g sat. fat), 84mg chol., 230mg sod., 39g carb. (22g sugars, 1g fiber), 6g pro.*

PASTRY FOR SINGLE-CRUST PIE (9 IN.)
Combine 1¼ cups all-purpose flour and ¼ tsp. salt; cut in ½ cup cold butter until crumbly. Gradually add 3-5 Tbsp. ice water, tossing with a fork until dough holds together when pressed. Wrap and refrigerate 1 hour or up to overnight.

BREAD PUDDING PIE

RUSTIC CARAMEL APPLE TART

RUSTIC CARAMEL APPLE TART

Like an apple pie without the pan, this most scrumptious tart has a yummy topping and a crispy crust that cuts nicely.
—*Betty Fulks, Onia, AR*

PREP: 20 min. + chilling • **BAKE:** 25 min. • **MAKES:** 4 servings

- ⅔ cup all-purpose flour
- 1 Tbsp. sugar
- ⅛ tsp. salt
- ¼ cup cold butter, cubed
- 6½ tsp. cold water
- ⅛ tsp. vanilla extract

FILLING

- 1½ cups chopped peeled tart apples
- 3 Tbsp. sugar
- 1 Tbsp. all-purpose flour

TOPPING

- 1 tsp. sugar
- ¼ tsp. ground cinnamon
- 1 large egg
- 1 Tbsp. water
- 2 Tbsp. caramel ice cream topping, warmed

1. In a large bowl, combine flour, sugar and salt; cut in butter until crumbly. Gradually add water and vanilla, tossing with a fork until dough forms a ball. Cover and refrigerate until easy to handle, about 30 minutes.

2. Preheat oven to 400°. On a lightly floured surface, roll dough into a 10-in. circle. Transfer to a parchment-lined baking sheet. Combine the filling ingredients; spoon over crust to within 2 in. of edges. Fold up edges of crust over filling, leaving center uncovered. Combine sugar and cinnamon; sprinkle over filling. Whisk egg and water; brush over crust.

3. Bake until crust is golden and filling is bubbly, 25-30 minutes. Using parchment, slide tart onto a wire rack. Drizzle with caramel topping. Serve warm.

1 SLICE: *298 cal., 13g fat (8g sat. fat), 77mg chol., 8mg sod., 42g carb. (24g sugars, 1g fiber), 4g pro.*

MOM-MOM BESSIE'S COCONUT MOLASSES PIE

I'm the keeper of my husband's grandmother's handwritten recipe book. Mom-Mom Bessie was one of the best cooks I knew, and we think of her every time we make this pie. The flavor combination of coconut and molasses is a family favorite.
—*Susan Bickta, Kutztown, PA*

PREP: 10 min. • **BAKE:** 55 min. + cooling • **MAKES:** 8 servings

- 1 cup packed light brown sugar
- 1 cup sour cream
- ½ cup dark corn syrup
- ½ cup dark molasses
- 2 large eggs, room temperature, lightly beaten
- ¼ cup 2% milk
- 2 Tbsp. all-purpose flour
- ¼ tsp. baking soda
- 1½ cups sweetened shredded coconut
- 1 frozen deep-dish pie crust
  Whipped cream, optional

Preheat the oven to 350°. In a large bowl, combine the first 8 ingredients. Stir in coconut. Pour into crust. Cover edges loosely with foil. Bake until center is set, 45-55 minutes. Remove foil. Cool on a wire rack. If desired, serve with whipped cream.

1 PIECE: *486 cal., 19g fat (10g sat. fat), 54mg chol., 243mg sod., 80g carb. (66g sugars, 1g fiber), 5g pro.*

TEST KITCHEN TIP

For less molasses flavor, substitute ½ cup additional dark Karo syrup in place of the molasses.

MOM-MOM BESSIE'S COCONUT MOLASSES PIE

MAPLE PECAN PIE

Our Vermont maple syrup can't be beat, and this is one of my favorite pies. It's also quick and easy to make.
—Mildred Wescom, Belvidere, VT

PREP: 10 min. • **BAKE:** 40 min. + cooling
MAKES: 8 servings

Pastry for single-crust pie
3 large eggs, room temperature
½ cup sugar
1 cup maple syrup
3 Tbsp. butter, melted
½ tsp. vanilla extract
¼ tsp. salt
2 cups pecan halves
Whipped cream, optional

1. Preheat oven to 375°. On a lightly floured surface, roll out dough to fit a 9-in. pie plate; transfer to pie plate. Trim to 1 in. beyond rim of plate; flute edges.
2. In a bowl, whisk eggs and sugar until smooth. Add maple syrup, butter, vanilla, salt and pecans. Pour into crust.
3. Bake until a knife inserted in the center comes out clean, 30-40 minutes. Cool on a wire rack for 1 hour. If desired, top with whipped cream to serve. Store in the refrigerator.
1 SLICE: *561 cal., 35g fat (12g sat. fat), 111mg chol., 294mg sod., 58g carb. (38g sugars, 3g fiber), 7g pro.*

RASPBERRY MOSCOW MULE CAKE

This Moscow mule cake is the best cake I've ever made from scratch. It's so moist and flavorful, and it reminds me of my all-time favorite cocktail.
—Becky Hardin, St. Peters, MO

PREP: 25 min. • **BAKE:** 70 min. + cooling
MAKES: 16 servings

1½ cups unsalted butter, softened
2¾ cups sugar
5 large eggs, room temperature
1 Tbsp. vanilla extract
3 cups cake flour
½ tsp. salt
1 cup alcoholic raspberry ginger beer or nonalcoholic plain ginger beer
2 cups fresh raspberries

RASPBERRY MOSCOW MULE CAKE

SYRUP
½ cup alcoholic raspberry ginger beer or nonalcoholic plain ginger beer
½ cup sugar
¼ cup lime juice
GLAZE
1½ cups confectioners' sugar
2 to 3 Tbsp. lime juice

1. Preheat oven to 325°. Grease and flour a 10-in. fluted tube pan.
2. In a large bowl, cream butter and sugar until light and fluffy, 5-7 minutes. Add eggs, 1 at a time, beating well after each addition. Beat in vanilla. In another bowl, whisk cake flour and salt; add to creamed mixture alternately with ginger beer, beating well after each addition (mixture may appear slightly curdled).
3. Gently fold the raspberries into the batter; pour into prepared pan. Bake until a toothpick inserted in center comes out clean, 70-80 minutes. Meanwhile, for syrup, in a small saucepan, bring sugar, ginger beer and lime juice to a boil. Reduce heat; simmer 10 minutes. Cool slightly.
4. Poke holes in warm cake using a fork or wooden skewer. Spoon syrup over the cake. Cool 15 minutes before removing from pan to a wire rack; cool completely. For glaze, in a small bowl, mix the confectioners' sugar and enough lime juice to reach desired consistency; pour over the cake. Let stand until set. If desired, top with additional fresh raspberries.
1 SLICE: *488 cal., 19g fat (11g sat. fat), 104mg chol., 100mg sod., 75g carb. (53g sugars, 1g fiber), 5g pro.*

RUSTIC HONEY CAKE

CREAMY COCONUT PEPPERMINT PIE

Garnished with toasted coconut and peppermint candy, this creamy dessert welcomes the holidays! Look for premade shortbread crusts in the baking aisle of the grocery store.
—*Cheryl Perry, Hertford, NC*

PREP: 15 min. + chilling • **MAKES:** 8 servings

1   envelope unflavored gelatin
½   cup coconut milk
2½ cups peppermint ice cream, melted
¼   cup crushed peppermint candies, divided
¼   tsp. coconut extract
1   cup flaked coconut, toasted, divided
1   shortbread crust (9 in.)

1. In a large microwave-safe bowl, sprinkle gelatin over coconut milk; let stand 1 minute. Microwave on high for 30-40 seconds. Stir until gelatin is completely dissolved, 1 minute.
2. Stir ice cream, 2 Tbsp. crushed candies and extract into gelatin mixture; fold in ½ cup coconut. Pour into crust. Sprinkle with remaining coconut. Refrigerate at least 2 hours before serving.
3. Just before serving, top with remaining crushed candies.
1 SLICE: *281 cal., 15g fat (10g sat. fat), 18mg chol., 165mg sod., 33g carb. (22g sugars, 1g fiber), 4g pro.*

RUSTIC HONEY CAKE

When my boys were young, they couldn't drink milk but they could have yogurt. This was a cake they could eat. And it's one dessert that doesn't taste overly sweet, which is always a nice change of pace.
—*Linda Leuer, Hamel, MN*

PREP: 15 min. • **BAKE:** 30 min. + cooling • **MAKES:** 12 servings

½   cup butter, softened
1   cup honey
2   large eggs, room temperature
½   cup plain yogurt
1   tsp. vanilla extract
2   cups all-purpose flour
2   tsp. baking powder
½   tsp. salt
    Assorted fresh fruit and additional honey
    Chopped pistachios, optional

1. Preheat oven to 350°. Grease a 9-in. cast-iron skillet.
2. In a large bowl, beat butter and honey until blended. Add eggs, 1 at a time, beating well after each addition. Beat in yogurt and vanilla. In another bowl, whisk flour, baking powder and salt; add to butter mixture. Transfer batter to prepared skillet.
3. Bake until a toothpick inserted in the center comes out clean, 30-35 minutes. Cool completely in pan on a wire rack. Serve with fruit, additional honey and, if desired, chopped pistachios.
FREEZE OPTION: Securely wrap cooled cake in foil; freeze. To use, thaw at room temperature and top as directed.
1 SLICE: *248 cal., 9g fat (5g sat. fat), 53mg chol., 257mg sod., 40g carb. (24g sugars, 1g fiber), 4g pro.*

TEST KITCHEN TIP

The beauty of this cake is how delicious it is all on its own, but we do recognize that some folks just can't imagine having a cake without frosting. If you're in that camp, just spread some cream cheese frosting on the cooled cake.

CREAMY COCONUT PEPPERMINT PIE

MINCE PIES

Most people use canned mincemeat, but this is the old-fashioned way to make quite a few mini mince pies.
—Diane Selich, Vassar, MI

- -

PREP: 20 min. + chilling
BAKE: 20 min./batch + cooling
MAKES: 20 mini pies

- 4   cups all-purpose flour
- 2   tsp. salt
- 1⅓ cups shortening
- ½   cup plus 2 Tbsp. ice water

FILLING
- ¼   lb. ground beef
- 3   medium apples, peeled and chopped
- 1   medium apricot, peeled and chopped
- ¾   cup packed light brown sugar
- ½   cup golden raisins
- ½   cup unsweetened apple juice
- 1   Tbsp. cider vinegar
- 1½ tsp. grated orange zest
- 1½ tsp. ground cinnamon
- ½   tsp. salt
- ½   tsp. ground cloves
- ¼   cup rum
- 1   large egg, beaten
- 1   to 2 Tbsp. coarse sugar

1. In a large bowl, mix flour and salt; cut in shortening until crumbly. Gradually add ice water, tossing with a fork until dough forms a ball. Divide dough in half. Shape each into a disk; wrap and refrigerate 1 hour or overnight.
2. For filling, in a Dutch oven, cook beef over medium heat until no longer pink, breaking into crumbles; drain. Add apples, apricot, brown sugar, raisins, juice, vinegar, orange zest and seasonings. Bring to a boil. Reduce heat; simmer until the apples are tender, 15-17 minutes. Remove from heat; stir in rum.
3. Preheat oven to 375°. On a lightly floured surface, roll half of the dough to ⅛-in. thickness. Cut 20 circles with a floured 2¾-in. round biscuit cutter. Top half the circles with 1 Tbsp. filling. Top with the remaining circles; press edges with a fork to seal. Cut slits in top. Brush tops with egg; sprinkle with coarse sugar. Repeat.
4. Bake until crust is golden brown and filling is bubbly, 20-25 minutes. Cool on a wire rack.
1 MINI PIE: *280 cal., 14g fat (4g sat. fat), 4mg chol., 302mg sod., 34g carb. (14g sugars, 1g fiber), 4g pro.*

APRICOT MUD HEN CAKE BARS

These mud hen bars have been in my family for generations. My maternal grandmother gave this recipe to my mother, who shared it with me. I've been told the name comes from the speckled meringue topping that resembles the coloring of hens.
—Kristine Chayes, Smithtown, NY

- -

PREP: 20 min. • **BAKE:** 30 min. + cooling
MAKES: 24 servings

- ¾   cup butter, softened
- ⅓   cup sugar
- 2   large egg yolks, room temperature
- 1   tsp. vanilla extract
- 1½ cups all-purpose flour
- ⅛   tsp. salt

MERINGUE
- 2   large egg whites, room temperature
- ⅛   tsp. cream of tartar
- ⅓   cup sugar
- ¾   cup finely chopped pecans
- 1   cup apricot preserves

1. Preheat oven to 350°. In a large bowl, cream butter and sugar until light and fluffy, 5-7 minutes. Add egg yolks, 1 at a time, beating well after each addition. Beat in vanilla. In another bowl, whisk flour and salt; beat into creamed mixture. Spread into a greased 13x9-in. baking pan. Bake until a toothpick inserted in center comes out clean, 12-15 minutes.
2. Meanwhile for meringue, with clean beaters, beat egg whites with cream of tartar on medium speed until foamy. Gradually add sugar, 1 Tbsp. at a time, beating on high after each addition until the sugar is dissolved. Continue beating until stiff glossy peaks form; gently fold in the pecans.
3. Gently spread preserves over the hot cake. Gently spread the meringue over preserves, sealing meringue to edges of pan. Bake until meringue is golden brown, 15-20 minutes. Cool completely on a wire rack. Refrigerate leftovers.
1 PIECE: *163 cal., 9g fat (4g sat. fat), 31mg chol., 69mg sod., 21g carb. (12g sugars, 1g fiber), 2g pro.*

APRICOT MUD HEN CAKE BARS

LONDON FOG ICE CREAM
PAGE 224

Just Desserts

No dinner is complete without a final sweet treat! With options ranging from cool and light to rich and decadent, you'll find exactly the dessert to finish your meal in style!

APPLE BETTY WITH ALMOND CREAM

I love making this treat for friends during the peak of apple season. I plan a quick and simple soup and bread meal so we can get right to the dessert!
—Elizabeth Godecke, Chicago, IL

PREP: 15 min. • **COOK:** 3 hours
MAKES: 8 servings

- 3 lbs. tart apples, peeled and sliced
- 10 slices cinnamon-raisin bread, cubed
- ¾ cup packed brown sugar
- ½ cup butter, melted
- 1 tsp. almond extract
- ½ tsp. ground cinnamon
- ¼ tsp. ground cardamom
- ⅛ tsp. salt

ALMOND CREAM
- 1 cup heavy whipping cream
- 2 Tbsp. sugar
- 1 tsp. grated lemon zest
- ½ tsp. almond extract

1. Place apples in an ungreased 4- or 5-qt. slow cooker. In a large bowl, combine the bread, brown sugar, butter, extract, cinnamon, cardamom and salt; spoon over apples. Cover and cook on low until the apples are tender, 3-4 hours.
2. In a small bowl, beat cream until it begins to thicken. Add the sugar, lemon zest and extract; beat until soft peaks form. Serve with the apple mixture.

1 CUP WITH ¼ CUP ALMOND CREAM: *468 cal., 23g fat (14g sat. fat), 71mg chol., 224mg sod., 65g carb. (45g sugars, 5g fiber), 5g pro.*

LONDON FOG ICE CREAM

(*SHOWN ON PAGE 222*)
One of my favorite coffee shop beverages is the London Fog (made with Earl Grey tea). I turned it into a decadent treat that turns up the elegance factor of simple ice cream. Serve with lemon sandwich cookies or lemon sugar wafers, or in frosted glasses with sugar, lavender and lemon zest on the rims for an extra punch of high-class fun.
—Noelle Myers, Grand Forks, ND

PREP: 1¼ hours + chilling
PROCESS: 20 min./batch + freezing
MAKES: 5 cups

- 2 cups whole milk
- 2 cups half-and-half cream
- 6 Earl Grey tea bags
- 1 vanilla bean
- 1 can (14 oz.) sweetened condensed milk
- ¼ tsp. salt
- 4 large eggs, lightly beaten

1. In a small saucepan, heat whole milk and cream to 175°. Remove from the heat; add the tea bags. Split vanilla bean lengthwise. Using the tip of a sharp knife, scrape seeds from the center into pan; add bean. Cover and steep 1 hour. Discard tea bags.
2. Reheat cream mixture just to a boil; stir in sweetened condensed milk and salt until dissolved. Whisk a small amount of the hot mixture into eggs. Return all to the pan, whisking constantly. Cook and stir over low heat until mixture is just thick enough to coat a metal spoon and a thermometer reads at least 160°, stirring constantly. Do not allow to boil. Remove from heat immediately.
3. Strain through a fine-mesh strainer into a large bowl; place bowl in a pan of ice water. Stir gently and occasionally until cool, about 5 minutes. Press plastic wrap onto the surface of custard. Refrigerate for several hours or overnight.
4. Fill cylinder of ice cream maker no more than two-thirds full; freeze according to manufacturer's directions. (Refrigerate any remaining mixture until ready to freeze.)
5. Transfer ice cream to freezer containers, allowing headspace for expansion. Freeze until firm, 2-4 hours.

½ CUP: *250 cal., 12g fat (7g sat. fat), 117mg chol., 183mg sod., 26g carb. (26g sugars, 0 fiber), 9g pro.*

JUST DESSERTS

APPLE BETTY WITH ALMOND CREAM

MAPLE-APPLE CLAFOUTI

APRICOT ICE CREAM SODA

This ginger ale float recipe came from my husband's aunt, who was born in the early 1900s. It's a delightful drink for hot Texas summers.
—*Joan Hallford, North Richland Hills, TX*

PREP: 20 min. + freezing • **MAKES:** 4 servings

- 2 cans (15 oz. each) apricot halves, drained
- ⅔ cup sugar
- 2 Tbsp. lemon juice
- 1 cup heavy whipping cream, whipped
- 2 cups chilled ginger ale

Press apricots through a fine-mesh strainer into a bowl; discard skins and pulp. Stir sugar and lemon juice into the apricot puree. Gently fold in whipped cream. Transfer to a 8-in. square dish. Freeze until firm, about 6 hours or overnight. Divide ice cream among 4 glasses; top with ginger ale. Serve immediately.
1 SERVING: *554 cal., 22g fat (14g sat. fat), 68mg chol., 34mg sod., 92g carb. (88g sugars, 3g fiber), 3g pro.*

MAPLE-APPLE CLAFOUTI

This fruit pudding could not be easier to make! A traditional comfort food in France, it is often made with cherries. I use apples and maple syrup to give it a midwestern flair.
—*Bridget Klusman, Otsego, MI*

PREP: 20 min. • **BAKE:** 40 min. • **MAKES:** 8 servings

- 4 medium tart apples, thinly sliced
- 2 Tbsp. lemon juice
- 4 large eggs, room temperature
- 1¼ cups 2% milk
- ½ cup maple syrup
- 1 tsp. vanilla extract
- ½ cup all-purpose flour
- ½ tsp. ground cinnamon
  Dash salt
  Additional maple syrup, optional

1. Preheat oven to 375°. Toss apples with lemon juice; place in a greased 2-qt. baking dish. In a large bowl, whisk eggs, milk, syrup and vanilla until combined. In another bowl, combine flour, cinnamon and salt; add to egg mixture. Pour batter over apples.
2. Bake until puffed and lightly browned, 40-50 minutes. Serve warm, or cool on a wire rack first. If desired, serve with additional maple syrup.
1 PIECE: *177 cal., 3g fat (1g sat. fat), 96mg chol., 75mg sod., 32g carb. (22g sugars, 2g fiber), 5g pro.* **Diabetic exchanges:** *1½ starch, ½ fruit, ½ fat.*

TEST KITCHEN TIP

When it's pulled right out of the oven, this is a showstopping masterpiece, all puffed up and golden brown. However, when it sits, it will deflate a bit. So if you're looking to impress folks, serve it hot out of the oven.

APRICOT ICE CREAM SODA

SCOOP DREAMS

Vanilla ice cream makes the coolest canvas for these tricked-out topping ideas we're all screaming for.

Ritz Crackers & Chocolate Sauce

Hershey's chocolate sauce and Ritz crackers!
—Brooklyn Reynolds, Anderson, IN

Bacon & Maple Syrup

I top mine with maple syrup and crispy thick-cut bacon.
—Carol Feldmann, Sheboygan Falls, WI

Cornflakes & Cinnamon

From my sister's brain: Cornflakes and cinnamon. It tastes like apple pie—you don't even need the apples!
—Sabrina Eileen Stebbins Brown, Saratoga Springs, UT

Jam & Chocolate

I load mine up with strawberry jam, mini chocolate chips and chopped pecans.
—Donna Paprocki, Des Plaines, IL

Cooled Espresso

Pour on some cooled Cuban coffee or espresso. It's just plain awesome.
—Cathy Killinger Lopez, Charlotte, NC

French Fries & Fudge
Fresh-baked french fries and hot fudge sauce. So good.
—Tracy Strickland, Shipshewana, IN

Nerds Candy
I like to top mine with rainbow Nerds candy. I love the fun color and crunch!
—Rachel Bernhard Seis, Taste of Home *Senior Editor*

Melted Peanut Butter
I drizzle mine with melted peanut butter.
—Rd Stendel-Freels, Albuquerque, NM

Balsamic & Fruit
Whatever the flavor, balsamic vinegar has served me well as an ice cream topping. It adds just the right amount of tang.
—Allison Ochoa, Hays, KS

Crushed Potato Chips
The flavor combo gives you both sweet and salty. Yum!
—Pam Slack, Freeburg, IL

YOGURT-RICOTTA CHEESECAKE

FROZEN GRAND MARNIER SOUFFLES

This delicious no-bake frozen souffle is perfect for summer and will impress just about everyone. It's a fantastic make-ahead dessert!
—Andrea Potischman, Menlo Park, CA

- -

PREP: 30 min. + freezing • **MAKES:** 8 servings

6	large egg yolks
½	cup sugar
¼	cup orange liqueur
2	Tbsp. water
2	tsp. orange juice
1	tsp. grated orange zest
1½	cups heavy whipping cream
1	Tbsp. confectioners' sugar

1. In top of a double boiler or a metal bowl over simmering water whisk egg yolks and sugar until blended. Stir in liqueur, water, orange juice and zest. Cook over low heat until mixture is just thick enough to coat a metal spoon and a thermometer reads at least 160°, about 10 minutes, stirring constantly but gently. Do not allow to boil. Immediately transfer to a bowl.
2. Place bowl in an ice-water bath for a few minutes, stirring occasionally. Cool to room temperature. In a large bowl, beat cream until it begins to thicken. Add confectioners' sugar; beat until stiff peaks form. Gently fold into cooled custard mixture.
3. Transfer to eight 4-oz. ramekins; smooth tops. Freeze until firm, at least 4 hours or overnight. Garnish with additional orange zest.
1 SOUFFLE: *258 cal., 20g fat (12g sat. fat), 189mg chol., 18mg sod., 17g carb. (16g sugars, 0 fiber), 3g pro.*

YOGURT-RICOTTA CHEESECAKE

I have always liked Italian ricotta cheesecakes, but they have too much sugar for me. I made a diabetic version and my family couldn't even tell! I serve mine with sugar-free strawberry ice cream topping and fresh strawberries.
—Diane Shipley, Mentor, OH

- -

PREP: 35 min. • **BAKE:** 80 min. + chilling • **MAKES:** 16 servings

2	pkg. (8 oz. each) reduced-fat cream cheese
2	cups reduced-fat ricotta cheese
	Sugar substitute blend (made with sucralose) equivalent to 1½ cups sugar
2	cups vanilla yogurt
½	cup butter, melted
¼	cup cornstarch
3	Tbsp. all-purpose flour
2	Tbsp. lemon juice
1	tsp. vanilla extract
4	large eggs, room temperature, lightly beaten
	Halved fresh strawberries, optional

1. Preheat oven to 325°. In a large bowl, beat cream cheese, ricotta and sugar blend until smooth. Beat in yogurt, butter, cornstarch, flour, lemon juice and vanilla. Add eggs; beat on low speed just until blended. Pour into a greased 9-in. springform pan. Place pan on a baking sheet.
2. Bake until center is almost set, 80-85 minutes. Cool on a wire rack 10 minutes. Loosen sides from pan with a knife. Cool 1 hour longer. Refrigerate overnight, covering when completely cooled.
3. Remove rim from pan. If desired, serve the cheesecake with fresh strawberries.
1 SLICE: *246 cal., 15g fat (9g sat. fat), 91mg chol., 231mg sod., 19g carb. (16g sugars, 0 fiber), 9g pro.*

FROZEN GRAND MARNIER SOUFFLES

CHOCOLATE MINT SOUFFLES

These delectable little desserts are fancy, utterly foolproof and a family favorite recipe for decades. Give them a try!
—Ruth Lee, Troy, ON

PREP: 20 min. • **BAKE:** 20 min.
MAKES: 2 servings

- 2 large eggs, separated
- 1 tsp. plus 4 Tbsp. sugar, divided
- 2 Tbsp. baking cocoa
- 1 tsp. cornstarch
   Dash salt
- ⅓ cup fat-free milk
- 2 Tbsp. semisweet chocolate chips
- ⅛ tsp. mint extract
   Confectioners' sugar

1. Place egg whites in a small bowl; let stand at room temperature for 30 minutes. Place yolks in another bowl; set aside.
2. Coat two 10-oz. ramekins or custard cups with cooking spray and lightly sprinkle with 1 tsp. sugar; place on a baking sheet and set aside.
3. In a small saucepan over medium heat, combine 2 Tbsp. sugar, the cocoa, cornstarch and salt. Gradually stir in milk. Bring to a boil, stirring constantly. Cook and stir 1-2 minutes or until thickened.
4. Remove from the heat; stir in chocolate chips and extract until the chips are melted. Transfer to a small bowl. Stir a small amount of the hot mixture into egg yolks; return all to the bowl, stirring constantly. Cool slightly.
5. Beat the egg whites on medium speed until soft peaks form. Gradually beat in the remaining sugar, 1 Tbsp. at a time, on high until stiff peaks form. With a spatula, fold a fourth of the egg whites into chocolate mixture until no white streaks remain. Fold in the remaining egg whites until combined.
6. Transfer to the prepared ramekins. Bake at 375° for 18-22 minutes or until the tops are puffed and the centers are almost set. Sprinkle with confectioners' sugar. Serve immediately.
1 SERVING: *265 cal., 9g fat (3g sat. fat), 213mg chol., 159mg sod., 40g carb. (35g sugars, 2g fiber), 9g pro.*
CHOCOLATE SOUFFLES: Substitute ¼ tsp. vanilla extract for the mint extract.

VERY BLUEBERRY CLAFOUTI

VERY BLUEBERRY CLAFOUTI

Traditionally a French dessert using cherries, a clafouti [Klah-foo-tea] is something between a fruit-filled pancake and a fruity egg custard. It is a quick and easy alternative to pie, and adapts easily to any berry or cut fruit. Even children can make clafoutis if they have help moving the pan to and from the oven. Wrong season for fresh berries? Use frozen berries thawed in a colander and discard the juice.
—Ken Hulme, Venice, FL

PREP: 10 min. • **BAKE:** 30 min. + standing
MAKES: 8 servings

- 2 tsp. butter
- 16 oz. fresh or frozen unsweetened blueberries
- 3 large eggs
- ¾ cup all-purpose flour
- ¾ cup whole milk
- ⅓ cup sugar
- 1 tsp. vanilla extract
- ½ tsp. ground cinnamon

1. Preheat oven to 400°. Place butter in a 12-in. cast-iron or other ovenproof skillet. Place skillet in oven until butter is melted, 1-2 minutes. Carefully tilt pan to coat bottom and sides with butter. Spread blueberries in bottom of pan. In a large bowl, whisk eggs, flour, milk, sugar, vanilla and cinnamon. Pour egg mixture over blueberries.
2. Bake until center is puffed and edges are browned, 30-35 minutes. Sprinkle with additional cinnamon if desired. Let stand 15 minutes before cutting.
1 PIECE: *188 cal., 4g fat (2g sat. fat), 75mg chol., 46mg sod., 34g carb. (20g sugars, 3g fiber), 5g pro.* **Diabetic exchanges:** *2 starch, 1 fat.*

CHERRY FUDGE TRUFFLE COCONUT CHEESECAKE

Cherries and chocolate come together in this dazzling coconut cheesecake. It's a holiday showstopper!
—Jeanne Holt, Mendota Heights, MN

PREP: 40 min. • **BAKE:** 1 hour 20 min. + chilling
MAKES: 16 servings

- 1⅔ cups crushed Oreo cookies (about 17 cookies)
- ⅔ cup sweetened shredded coconut, toasted
- ¼ cup butter, melted

FILLING
- 4 pkg. (8 oz. each) cream cheese, softened, divided
- 1 cup sugar
- ¾ cup cream of coconut
- 1 tsp. coconut extract
- 3 large eggs, room temperature, lightly beaten
- ¼ cup chopped maraschino cherries
- 1 cup 60% cacao bittersweet chocolate baking chips, melted and cooled
- ⅓ cup cherry preserves, finely chopped

TOPPING
- ½ cup 60% cacao bittersweet chocolate baking chips, melted and cooled
- 1 cup sweetened whipped cream
- ⅓ cup sweetened shredded coconut, toasted
- 16 maraschino cherries with stems, patted dry

1. Preheat oven to 375°. Place a greased 10-in. springform pan on a double thickness of heavy-duty foil (about 18 in. square). Wrap foil securely around pan. Place on a baking sheet.

2. In a small bowl, mix crushed cookies and coconut; stir in butter. Press onto bottom and ½ in. up sides of prepared pan. Bake 10 minutes. Cool on a wire rack. Reduce oven setting to 325°.

3. In a large bowl, beat 3 pkg. cream cheese and sugar until smooth. Beat in cream of coconut and extract. Add eggs; beat on low speed just until blended. Stir in chopped cherries. Pour 3 cups batter into crust, reserving the rest.

4. In another bowl, beat the remaining 8 oz. cream cheese until smooth. Beat in cooled chocolate and cherry preserves. Drop by tablespoonfuls over the coconut batter. Carefully spoon the remaining coconut batter over top. Place springform pan in a larger baking pan; add 1 in. hot water to larger pan.

5. Bake until center is just set and top appears dull, 80-85 minutes. Remove springform pan from water bath. Cool on a wire rack 10 minutes. Loosen sides from pan with a knife; remove foil. Cool 1 hour longer. Refrigerate overnight, covering when completely cooled.

6. Remove rim from pan. Top cheesecake with chocolate, whipped cream, toasted coconut and cherries.

1 PIECE: *545 cal., 37g fat (22g sat. fat), 108mg chol., 290mg sod., 52g carb. (44g sugars, 2g fiber), 6g pro.*

LYCHEE GREEN TEA MILKSHAKES

My family can't get enough of milkshakes. Everyone is happy when I prepare this vibrant-colored version and pass a plate of fortune cookies.
—Amy Dodson, Durango, CO

TAKES: 15 min. • **MAKES:** 6 servings

- 1 can (15 oz.) lychees
- 1 cup 2% milk
- 4 cups vanilla ice cream
- 1 can (8½ oz.) cream of coconut
- 2 Tbsp. matcha (green tea powder)
- ¾ cup whipped topping
- 1 Tbsp. finely chopped crystallized ginger

1. Drain lychees, reserving ½ cup syrup. Divide lychees among 6 chilled glasses.

2. In a blender, combine half of the milk, ice cream, cream of coconut, matcha and reserved lychee syrup; cover and process until smooth. Pour into 3 of the prepared glasses; top with whipped topping and ginger. Repeat with remaining ingredients and glasses. Serve immediately.

¾ CUP: *437 cal., 19g fat (14g sat. fat), 42mg chol., 132mg sod., 63g carb. (55g sugars, 0 fiber), 5g pro.*

CHERRY FUDGE TRUFFLE COCONUT CHEESECAKE

ORANGE CARAMEL
ICE CREAM SAUCE

⑤ⁱ

CHOCOLATE-AVOCADO MOUSSE

I have rheumatoid arthritis and follow a special diet to help manage the symptoms. This pudding is simple to make, tastes heavenly and helps reduce inflammation. I like it frozen, too.
—Kelly Kirby, Mill Bay, BC

- -

PREP: 5 min. + chilling • **MAKES:** 4 servings

- ¼ cup refrigerated sweetened coconut milk
- ¼ cup maple syrup
- ¼ tsp. vanilla extract
- 2 medium ripe avocados, peeled and pitted
- ¼ cup baking cocoa

Place all ingredients in a blender; cover and process until smooth. Transfer to 4 dessert dishes. Refrigerate until serving, at least 2 hours.

⅓ **CUP:** *181 cal., 11g fat (1g sat. fat), 0 chol., 8mg sod., 22g carb. (12g sugars, 6g fiber), 2g pro.*

TEST KITCHEN TIP

Feel free to swap in honey or agave syrup for the maple syrup. Just don't use granulated sugar or you'll end up with a slightly gritty texture.

CHOCOLATE-AVOCADO MOUSSE

---

⑤ⁱ

ORANGE CARAMEL ICE CREAM SAUCE

We added a touch of orange extract to a creamy caramel sauce to make a rich homemade ice cream topping you won't find in stores. Try it drizzled over butter pecan, vanilla or chocolate ice cream.
—Taste of Home *Test Kitchen*

- -

PREP: 10 min. • **COOK:** 10 min. + chilling • **MAKES:** 1⅓ cups

- 1 cup packed brown sugar
- 1 cup heavy whipping cream
- ½ cup sweetened condensed milk
- ½ tsp. orange extract
  Ice cream or dessert of choice

1. In a large saucepan, cook and stir brown sugar and cream over medium heat until sugar is dissolved. Bring to a boil; cook until mixture is reduced by half, about 5 minutes. Remove from the heat. Stir in milk and orange extract. Cover and refrigerate.

2. Just before serving, warm over low heat. Serve with ice cream or dessert of choice.

2 **TBSP.:** *215 cal., 10g fat (6g sat. fat), 38mg chol., 37mg sod., 30g carb. (30g sugars, 0 fiber), 2g pro.*

INDIAN KULFI ICE CREAM

BERRY COOL CREAM & PRETZEL PIE

This cool no-bake strawberry pie is the perfect antidote for your sweet tooth this summer. Made with pantry staples and as easy as pie to make, it's become one of my family's favorite warm-weather treats.
—Shauna Havey, Roy, UT

PREP: 45 min. + chilling • **MAKES:** 16 servings

- 4   cups miniature pretzels
- 6   Tbsp. butter, melted
- ¼   cup sugar
- ¾   cup boiling water
- 1   pkg. (6 oz.) strawberry gelatin
- ¼   cup lemon juice
- 1   lb. fresh strawberries, hulled, divided
- 2   cups heavy whipping cream, divided
- 1   jar (7 oz.) marshmallow creme
- ⅔   cup whipped cream cheese
- ⅔   cup sweetened condensed milk

1. Place pretzels in a food processor; pulse until chopped. Add butter and sugar; pulse until combined. Reserve ⅓ cup pretzel mixture for topping. Press the remaining mixture onto bottom of a greased 9-in. springform pan. Refrigerate 30 minutes.
2. Meanwhile, in a bowl, add boiling water to gelatin; stir 2 minutes to completely dissolve. Stir in lemon juice. Refrigerate 30 minutes, stirring occasionally.
3. Chop half the strawberries; cut the remaining berries as desired and reserve for topping.
4. In a large bowl, beat 1 cup heavy cream until stiff peaks form. Beat marshmallow cream, cream cheese and sweetened condensed milk into cooled gelatin mixture until blended. Gently fold in chopped strawberries and whipped cream. Pour into the crust.
5. Refrigerate, covered, until pie is firm, 4-6 hours. Beat the remaining 1 cup heavy cream until stiff peaks form; spread over pie. Top with the reserved strawberries and pretzel mixture.
1 PIECE: *350 cal., 19g fat (12g sat. fat), 56mg chol., 284mg sod., 39g carb. (30g sugars, 1g fiber), 4g pro.*

INDIAN KULFI ICE CREAM

I grew up near Little India in California, and I loved the baked goods and desserts from Indian sweets shops. One of them sold kulfi, similar to a sort of spiced and nutty frozen custard in cone molds. Here I use a shortcut method to make kulfi quickly and without special equipment. To make mango kulfi, replace the whole milk with mango pulp.
—Justine Kmiecik, Crestview, FL

PREP: 30 min. + freezing • **MAKES:** 6 servings

- 1   can (14 oz.) sweetened condensed milk
- 1   cup whole milk
- 1   cup heavy whipping cream
- ¼   cup nonfat dry milk powder
- ½   tsp. ground cardamom
- ¼   tsp. sea salt
- 1   pinch saffron threads or ¼ tsp. ground turmeric, optional
- ¼   cup chopped cashews, toasted
- ¼   cup chopped shelled pistachios
- ¼   tsp. almond extract

1. In a large heavy saucepan, whisk milks, cream, milk powder, cardamom, sea salt and, if desired, saffron until blended. Cook over low heat until mixture thickens slightly, about 15 minutes, stirring constantly. Do not allow to boil. Remove from heat. Strain through a fine-mesh strainer into a small bowl; cool.
2. Stir in cashews, pistachios and extract. Transfer to four 4-oz. ramekins. Cover and freeze for 8 hours or overnight. If desired, serve with additional nuts.
½ **CUP:** *446 cal., 27g fat (14g sat. fat), 72mg chol., 266mg sod., 44g carb. (41g sugars, 1g fiber), 11g pro.*

BERRY COOL
CREAM & PRETZEL PIE

RHUBARB CRUMBLE

RHUBARB CRUMBLE

To tell you the truth, I'm not sure how well my crumble keeps...we usually eat it all in a day! You can make this with all rhubarb, but the apples and strawberries make this dessert extra good.
—Linda Enslen, Schuler, AB

PREP: 20 min. • **BAKE:** 40 min. • **MAKES:** 8 servings

- 3 cups sliced fresh or frozen rhubarb (½-in. pieces)
- 1 cup diced peeled apples
- ½ to 1 cup sliced strawberries
- ⅓ cup sugar
- ½ tsp. ground cinnamon
- ½ cup all-purpose flour
- 1 tsp. baking powder
- ¼ tsp. salt
- 4 Tbsp. cold butter
- ⅔ cup packed brown sugar
- ⅔ cup quick-cooking oats
  Vanilla ice cream, optional

1. Combine rhubarb, apples and strawberries; spoon into a greased 8-in. square baking dish. Combine sugar and cinnamon; sprinkle over the rhubarb mixture. Set aside.
2. In a bowl, combine flour, baking powder and salt. Cut in butter until mixture resembles coarse crumbs. Stir in brown sugar and oats. Sprinkle over the rhubarb mixture.
3. Bake at 350° for 40-50 minutes or until lightly browned. Serve warm or cold, with a scoop of ice cream if desired.
1 SERVING: *227 cal., 6g fat (4g sat. fat), 15mg chol., 191mg sod., 41g carb. (29g sugars, 2g fiber), 2g pro.*

CREAMY COCONUT RICE PUDDING PARFAITS

When my daughter's friends come over for lunch, she treats them to her signature tropical parfaits made with brown rice and coconut milk. They're fresh, creamy and comforting.
—Suzanne Clark, Phoenix, AZ

PREP: 15 min. • **COOK:** 45 min. • **MAKES:** 6 servings

- 2 cups 2% milk
- 1½ cups coconut milk
- 1½ cups cooked cold brown rice
- ¼ cup maple syrup
- ¼ tsp. salt
- 2 tsp. vanilla extract
- ¼ tsp. almond extract
- 2 medium oranges, peeled and sectioned
- 2 medium kiwifruit, peeled and sliced
- ¼ cup sliced almonds, toasted
  Toasted sweetened shredded coconut

1. In a large heavy saucepan, combine the first 5 ingredients; bring to a boil over medium heat. Reduce heat to maintain a low simmer. Cook, uncovered, 35-45 minutes or until the rice is soft and the milk is almost absorbed, stirring occasionally.
2. Remove from heat; stir in extracts. Cool slightly. Serve warm or refrigerate, covered, and serve cold. To serve, spoon pudding into dishes. Top with fruit; sprinkle with almonds and coconut.
1 SERVING: *291 cal., 13g fat (10g sat. fat), 7mg chol., 157mg sod., 37g carb. (19g sugars, 3g fiber), 7g pro.*

CREAMY COCONUT RICE PUDDING PARFAITS

LEMON NOODLE KUGEL

Comforting kugel is a traditional dessert at our family's Polish Christmas Eve supper. Rich with butter, sugar, sour cream and cinnamon, it suits any special-occasion meal.
—Romaine Smith, Garden Grove, IA

PREP: 25 min. • **BAKE:** 55 min. + standing
MAKES: 12 servings

- 5   cups uncooked egg noodles
- 2   Tbsp. butter
- 4   large eggs
- 2   cups sour cream
- 2   cups 4% cottage cheese
- 1   cup whole milk
- ¾   cup plus 1½ tsp. sugar, divided
- 1½ tsp. lemon extract
- 1   tsp. vanilla extract
- ½   tsp. ground cinnamon

1. Preheat oven to 350°. Cook noodles according to package directions; drain and return to pan. Toss with butter; set aside.
2. Beat eggs, sour cream, cottage cheese, milk, ¾ cup sugar and extracts until well blended. Stir in noodles. Transfer to a 13x9-in. baking dish coated with cooking spray. Combine cinnamon and remaining sugar; sprinkle over noodles.
3. Bake, uncovered, until a thermometer reads 160°, 55-60 minutes. Let stand for 10 minutes before cutting. Serve warm or cold. Refrigerate leftovers.
1 PIECE: *321 cal., 15g fat (9g sat. fat), 133mg chol., 330mg sod., 30g carb. (19g sugars, 1g fiber), 14g pro.*

CINNAMON-BASIL ICE CREAM

I started experimenting with herbal ice creams while teaching herb classes at our local technical college. My students and my family both loved the results! A favorite is made with cinnamon basil, but unless you grow the variety yourself, it can be difficult to find. For this delicious recipe, I re-created the flavor with regular basil and a cinnamon stick!
—Sue Gronholz, Beaver Dam, WI

PREP: 45 min. + chilling
PROCESS: 10 min. + freezing • **MAKES:** 2 cups

- 1¼ cups whole milk
- 12   fresh basil leaves
- 1   cinnamon stick (3 in.)
- ½   cup sugar
- 4   large egg yolks, lightly beaten

CINNAMON-BASIL ICE CREAM

- ¾   cup heavy whipping cream
- ¼   tsp. vanilla extract
     Ground cinnamon, optional

1. In a small saucepan, heat milk to 175°. Remove from heat; add basil and cinnamon stick. Cover and steep for 30 minutes. Strain, discarding basil and cinnamon stick.
2. Return to the heat; stir in sugar until dissolved. Whisk a small amount of the hot mixture into egg yolks. Return all to the pan, whisking constantly. Cook and stir over low heat until mixture is just thick enough to coat a metal spoon and a thermometer reads at least 160°, stirring constantly. Do not allow to boil. Remove from heat immediately.
3. Quickly transfer to a large bowl; place bowl in a pan of ice water. Stir gently and occasionally until cool, about 5 minutes. Stir in cream and vanilla. Press plastic wrap onto surface of custard. Refrigerate several hours or overnight.

4. Fill cylinder of ice cream maker no more than two-thirds full; freeze according to the manufacturer's directions. (Refrigerate any remaining mixture until ready to freeze.)
5. Transfer ice cream to freezer containers, allowing headspace for expansion. Freeze until firm, 2-4 hours.
6. If desired, sprinkle individual servings with ground cinnamon.
½ CUP: *353 cal., 23g fat (13g sat. fat), 243mg chol., 53mg sod., 31g carb. (30g sugars, 0 fiber), 6g pro.*

LEMON COCONUT STREUSEL
ICE CREAM CAKE

LEMON COCONUT STREUSEL ICE CREAM CAKE

Sweet cream of coconut and tart lemon juice make a delicious combo in this cool treat, and the streusel adds a nice crunch. This recipe came about through my desire to find a new use for cream of coconut. (You'll find it in the cocktail mixer section of many grocery stores.) You can use any crunchy sugar, lemon or coconut cookie you'd like, as long as it measures about 2 inches.
—Janet Gill, Canton, OH

- -

PREP: 30 min. + freezing • **MAKES:** 16 servings

- 1   pkg. (11.2 oz.) shortbread cookies
- ½   cup sweetened shredded coconut, toasted
- ¼   cup macadamia nuts, coarsely chopped and toasted
- 1   tsp. grated lemon zest
- 1   can (15 oz.) cream of coconut
- ½   cup lemon juice
- 1½ qt. vanilla ice cream, softened
- 1   carton (8 oz.) frozen whipped topping, thawed, divided
    Optional: Fresh blueberries, raspberries and strawberries

1. Reserve 10 cookies. Crush the remaining cookies; transfer to a bowl. Stir in the coconut, macadamia nuts and lemon zest. Reserve 2 Tbsp. crumb mixture for topping.
2. In a large bowl, whisk cream of coconut and lemon juice until combined. Stir in softened ice cream until smooth. Fold in 1 cup whipped topping.
3. Sprinkle 1 cup of the crumb mixture onto bottom of a greased 9-in. springform pan. Top with half the ice cream mixture. Layer with remaining 1 cup crumbs and ice cream mixture. Place reserved whole cookies around edge of pan. Top with remaining 2½ cups whipped topping; sprinkle with reserved 2 Tbsp. crumb mixture. Freeze, covered, until firm, at least 8 hours or overnight. If desired, serve with berries.
1 PIECE: *384 cal., 21g fat (13g sat. fat), 29mg chol., 149mg sod., 45g carb. (35g sugars, 1g fiber), 4g pro.*

APPLE PIE OATMEAL DESSERT

This warm and comforting dessert brings back memories of time spent with my family around the kitchen table. I serve the dish with sweetened whipped cream or vanilla ice cream on top.
—Carol Greer, Earlville, IL

- -

PREP: 15 min. • **COOK:** 4 hours
MAKES: 6 servings

- 1   cup quick-cooking oats
- ½   cup all-purpose flour
- ⅓   cup packed brown sugar
- 2   tsp. baking powder
- 1½   tsp. apple pie spice
- ¼   tsp. salt
- 3   large eggs
- 1⅔   cups 2% milk, divided
- 1½   tsp. vanilla extract
- 3   medium apples, peeled and finely chopped
       Vanilla ice cream, optional

1. In a large bowl, whisk oats, flour, brown sugar, baking powder, pie spice and salt. In a small bowl, whisk eggs, 1 cup milk and the vanilla until blended. Add to the oat mixture, stirring just until moistened. Fold in apples.
2. Transfer to a greased 3-qt. slow cooker. Cook, covered, on low until the apples are tender and top is set, 4-5 hours.
3. Stir in the remaining milk. Serve warm or cold, with ice cream if desired.
¾ CUP: *238 cal., 5g fat (2g sat. fat), 111mg chol., 306mg sod., 41g carb. (22g sugars, 3g fiber), 8g pro.*

APPLE PIE
OATMEAL DESSERT

QUICK MANGO SORBET

5i

MOM'S FRIED APPLES

Mom often made these rich cinnamon-sugar apples when I was growing up. It's a trip down memory lane whenever I make them. The recipe is very dear to me.
—Margie Tappe, Prague, OK

PREP: 15 min. • **COOK:** 30 min. • **MAKES:** 8 servings

½ cup butter, cubed
6 medium unpeeled tart red apples, sliced
¾ cup sugar, divided
¾ tsp. ground cinnamon

1. Melt butter in a large cast-iron or other ovenproof skillet. Add apples and ½ cup sugar; stir to mix well. Cover and cook over low heat for 20 minutes or until apples are tender, stirring frequently.
2. Add cinnamon and the remaining sugar. Cook and stir over medium-high heat 5-10 minutes longer.
1 SERVING: *235 cal., 12g fat (7g sat. fat), 31mg chol., 116mg sod., 35g carb. (31g sugars, 3g fiber), 0 pro.*

QUICK MANGO SORBET

Last summer, I decided to try my hand at making a passion fruit and mango sorbet. But fresh fruits require more prep and are difficult to find ripe at the same time. So I experimented using frozen fruit and juice, and voila! Both are readily available and inexpensive, too.
—Carol Klein, Franklin Square, NY

TAKES: 5 min. • **MAKES:** 2½ cups

1 pkg. (16 oz.) frozen mango chunks, slightly thawed
½ cup passion fruit juice
2 Tbsp. sugar

Place all ingredients in a blender; cover and process until smooth. Serve immediately. If desired, for a firmer texture, cover and freeze for at least 3 hours.
½ CUP: *91 cal., 0 fat (0 sat. fat), 0 chol., 2mg sod., 24g carb. (21g sugars, 2g fiber), 1g pro.*

MOM'S FRIED APPLES

CHOCOLATE PECAN FONDUE

CHOCOLATE PECAN FONDUE

When our kids have friends sleep over, I like to surprise them with this chocolate treat. Our favorite dippers include fruit, marshmallows, cookies and pound cake.
—Suzanne McKinley, Lyons, GA

TAKES: 15 min. • **MAKES:** 1⅓ cups

- ½ cup half-and-half cream
- 2 Tbsp. honey
- 9 oz. semisweet chocolate, broken into small pieces
- ¼ cup finely chopped pecans
- 1 tsp. vanilla extract
   Fresh fruit and shortbread cookies

1. In a heavy saucepan over low heat, combine cream and honey; heat until warm. Add chocolate; stir until melted. Stir in pecans and vanilla.
2. Transfer to a fondue pot or a 1½-qt. slow cooker and keep warm. Serve with fruit and cookies.
2 TBSP.: 178 cal., 12g fat (6g sat. fat), 6mg chol., 6mg sod., 19g carb. (17g sugars, 2g fiber), 3g pro.

SUMMER STRAWBERRY SHORTCAKE SOUP

When the sun is beating down in the summer and folks are longing for something cool and refreshing, this soup hits the spot. To serve with dinner as an appetizer, omit the shortcake.
—Joan Hallford, North Richland Hills, TX

PREP: 15 min. + chilling • **MAKES:** 4 cups

- 2 cups fresh or frozen strawberries, hulled
- 1½ cups unsweetened pineapple juice
- ½ cup white grape juice
- ⅓ cup confectioners' sugar
- ½ cup moscato wine or additional white grape juice
- ½ cup sour cream
- 6 individual round sponge cakes
   Whipped cream and additional strawberries

1. Place strawberries in a blender; cover and process until pureed. Add juices and confectioners' sugar; cover and process until smooth. Transfer to a bowl; whisk in wine and sour cream. Refrigerate, covered, until chilled, 1-2 hours. Stir.
2. Serve with sponge cakes, whipped cream and additional strawberries.
¾ CUP: 227 cal., 6g fat (3g sat. fat), 32mg chol., 191mg sod., 37g carb. (27g sugars, 1g fiber), 3g pro.

SUMMER STRAWBERRY SHORTCAKE SOUP

NECTARINE PLUM COBBLER

I live in northern Manitoba, where fresh nectarines and plums are usually available only at summer's end. So I make up the fruit filling and freeze it for use all winter. This cobbler is wonderful topped with vanilla ice cream.
—Darlene Jackson, The Pas, MB

- -

PREP: 30 min. • **BAKE:** 30 min.
MAKES: 12 servings

1¼ cups sugar, divided
2 Tbsp. cornstarch
¾ cup unsweetened apple juice
5 cups sliced peeled fresh plums
5 cups sliced peeled nectarines or peaches
2½ cups all-purpose flour
3 tsp. baking powder
½ tsp. baking soda
½ tsp. salt
½ cup cold butter
1½ cups buttermilk
Vanilla ice cream, optional

1. Preheat the oven to 375°. In a large saucepan, combine ¾ cup sugar and the cornstarch. Gradually stir in apple juice until smooth. Stir in plums and nectarines. Cook and stir until mixture comes to a boil; cook 1-2 minutes longer or until thickened and bubbly. Reduce the heat; simmer, uncovered, for 5 minutes.

2. Remove from the heat; cool 10 minutes. Pour into a greased 13x9-in. baking dish.

3. In a large bowl, whisk flour, baking powder, baking soda, salt and the remaining ½ cup sugar. Cut in butter until crumbly. Make a well in the center; stir in buttermilk just until a soft dough forms. Drop by tablespoonfuls over the fruit mixture. Bake until golden brown, 30-35 minutes. Serve warm, with ice cream if desired.

1 SERVING: *333 cal., 9g fat (5g sat. fat), 22mg chol., 361mg sod., 61g carb. (36g sugars, 3g fiber), 5g pro.*

AIR-FRYER APPLE PIE EGG ROLLS

AIR-FRYER APPLE PIE EGG ROLLS

These easy egg rolls can be prepared as needed, using egg roll wrappers rather than pie crust to hold the fruit. Air-frying results in a crispy, crunchy crust with a tender, juicy filling. Flavored cream cheese spread may be used instead of plain, if you prefer.
—Sheila Joan Suhan, Scottdale, PA

- -

PREP: 25 min. • **COOK:** 15 min./batch
MAKES: 8 servings

3 cups chopped peeled tart apples
½ cup packed light brown sugar
2½ tsp. ground cinnamon, divided
1 tsp. cornstarch
8 egg roll wrappers
½ cup spreadable cream cheese
Butter-flavored cooking spray
1 Tbsp. sugar
⅔ cup hot caramel ice cream topping

1. Preheat air fryer to 400°. In a small bowl, combine apples, brown sugar, 2 tsp. cinnamon and cornstarch. With a corner of an egg roll wrapper facing you, spread 1 scant Tbsp. cream cheese to within 1 in. of edges. Place ⅓ cup apple mixture just below the center of the wrapper. (Cover the remaining wrappers with a damp paper towel until ready to use.)

2. Fold bottom corner over filling; moisten the remaining wrapper edges with water. Fold side corners toward the center over filling. Roll egg roll up tightly, pressing at tip to seal. Repeat.

3. In batches, arrange egg rolls in a single layer on greased tray in air-fryer basket; spritz with cooking spray. Cook until golden brown, 5-6 minutes. Turn; spritz with cooking spray. Cook until golden brown and crisp, 5-6 minutes longer.

4. Combine sugar and the remaining ½ tsp. cinnamon; roll hot egg rolls in mixture. Serve with caramel sauce.

1 ROLL: *273 cal., 4g fat (2g sat. fat), 13mg chol., 343mg sod., 56g carb. (35g sugars, 2g fiber), 5g pro.*

PECAN STRAWBERRY
RHUBARB COBBLER

SWEET FRUIT SLUSH

Whenever we're having company, I try to do all that I can before the guests arrive. This citrus slush is easy to make ahead and tastes so refreshing. I often add red seedless grapes.
—Martha Miller, Fredericksburg, OH

PREP: 20 min. + freezing
MAKES: 8 servings

- 3 cups water
- 1 cup sugar
- 1 can (20 oz.) crushed pineapple, undrained
- 1 can (6 oz.) frozen orange juice concentrate, thawed
- 1 medium ripe peach, chopped or ⅔ cup sliced frozen peaches, thawed and chopped

1. In a large saucepan over medium heat, bring water and sugar to a boil. Remove from the heat. Cool for 10 minutes.
2. Add the pineapple, orange juice concentrate and peach; stir well. Pour into a freezer container and freeze for at least 12 hours or overnight (may be frozen for up to 3 months). Remove from the freezer 1 hour before serving.
¾ CUP: *191 cal., 0 fat (0 sat. fat), 0 chol., 2mg sod., 49g carb. (47g sugars, 1g fiber), 1g pro.*

STRAWBERRIES ROMANOFF

Your clan will surely save room for dessert when they see this colorful concoction. It also makes a nice anytime snack.
—Denise Blackman, Port Cartier, QC

TAKES: 25 min. • **MAKES:** 6 servings

- 1 qt. fresh strawberries, hulled
- ½ cup confectioners' sugar
- 1 cup heavy whipping cream
- ¼ cup orange juice

1. Sprinkle strawberries with sugar. Cover and refrigerate 15-20 minutes.
2. Just before serving, whip cream until stiff. Gently stir in orange juice. Fold berries into cream mixture, or divide the berries among small bowls and top servings with the flavored cream.
1 SERVING: *209 cal., 15g fat (9g sat. fat), 54mg chol., 16mg sod., 19g carb. (16g sugars, 2g fiber), 1g pro.*

PECAN STRAWBERRY RHUBARB COBBLER

Brimming with berries and rhubarb, this pretty cobbler is the perfect finale for a dinner for two. Pecans in the topping and the delicious dessert sauce make it extra special.
—Lily Julow, Lawrenceville, GA

PREP: 20 min. + standing • **BAKE:** 25 min.
MAKES: 2 servings

- 1 cup sliced fresh or frozen rhubarb
- 1 cup sliced fresh strawberries
- ¼ cup sugar
- 1 Tbsp. quick-cooking tapioca
- 1 tsp. lemon juice
  Dash salt

TOPPING
- ⅓ cup all-purpose flour
- ¼ cup chopped pecans
- 3 Tbsp. sugar
- ⅛ tsp. baking powder
  Dash salt
- 2 Tbsp. cold butter
- 1 large egg

SAUCE
- ½ cup vanilla ice cream
- 2¼ tsp. Marsala wine

1. Preheat oven to 375°. Combine the first 6 ingredients; divide between 2 greased 8-oz. ramekins or custard cups. Let stand for 15 minutes.
2. In a small bowl, combine the flour, pecans, sugar, baking powder and salt; cut in butter until the mixture resembles coarse crumbs. Stir in egg. Drop by spoonfuls over fruit mixture; spread evenly.
3. Bake until the filling is bubbly and a toothpick inserted in topping comes out clean, 25-30 minutes.
4. In a microwave-safe bowl, combine ice cream and wine. Cook, uncovered, at 50% power for 1-2 minutes or until heated through; stir until blended. Serve with warm cobbler.
1 SERVING: *619 cal., 29g fat (11g sat. fat), 150mg chol., 318mg sod., 85g carb. (56g sugars, 5g fiber), 9g pro.*

GRASSHOPPER COOKIES & CREAM CHEESECAKE

I created this mint chocolate cheesecake for our high school's annual fundraiser. It brought a hefty price and was one of the first desserts to go! If you like, you can stir the cookie pieces into the batter instead of adding them in a layer. Keep the pieces fairly small; otherwise they have a tendency to rise to the top.

—Sue Gronholz, Beaver Dam, WI

- -

PREP: 20 min. • **BAKE:** 1¼ hours + chilling
MAKES: 16 servings

- 1 cup Oreo cookie crumbs
- 3 Tbsp. sugar
- 2 Tbsp. butter, melted

FILLING
- 4 pkg. (8 oz. each) cream cheese, softened
- 1 cup sugar
- 1 cup white baking chips, melted and cooled
- 6 Tbsp. creme de menthe
- ¼ cup all-purpose flour
- 2 Tbsp. creme de cacao
- ½ tsp. peppermint extract
- 4 large eggs, room temperature, lightly beaten
- 1 cup coarsely crushed Oreo cookies (about 10 cookies)

GANACHE
- ¾ cup semisweet chocolate chips
- 6 Tbsp. heavy whipping cream

1. Preheat oven to 325°. Place a greased 9-in. springform pan on a double thickness of heavy-duty foil (about 18 in. square). Wrap foil securely around pan. In a small bowl, mix cookie crumbs and sugar; stir in butter. Press onto bottom of prepared pan.
2. In a large bowl, beat cream cheese and sugar until smooth. Beat in cooled chips, creme de menthe, flour, creme de cacao and extract. Add eggs; beat on low speed just until blended. Pour half the batter over crust; sprinkle with crushed Oreos. Carefully spoon the remaining batter over top. Place springform pan in a larger baking pan; add 1 in. hot water to larger pan.
3. Bake until the center is just set and the top appears dull, 75-80 minutes. Remove springform pan from water bath. Cool cheesecake on a wire rack for 10 minutes. Loosen sides from pan with a knife; remove foil. Cool 1 hour longer. Refrigerate overnight, covering when completely cooled.
4. Remove rim from pan. Place chocolate chips in a small bowl. In a small saucepan, bring cream just to a boil. Pour over chocolate; stir with a whisk until smooth. Spread over cheesecake.

1 SLICE: *518 cal., 33g fat (18g sat. fat), 116mg chol., 296mg sod., 46g carb. (38g sugars, 1g fiber), 7g pro.*

GRASSHOPPER COOKIES & CREAM CHEESECAKE

BACON BUFFALO CHICKEN DIP
PAGE 244

Potluck Pleasers

These party-time greats include familiar classics, plus new and crowd-pleasing spins on dishes folks love. Get ready for sliders, sweets and snacks that steal the show.

BACON BUFFALO CHICKEN DIP

(*SHOWN ON PAGE 242*)

This Buffalo dip is a must-have dish at our annual Fourth of July barbecue. It celebrates America's love for Buffalo chicken dipped in creamy, tangy blue cheese dressing. And the bacon? That's just a bonus!
—Katie O'Keeffe, Derry, NH

- -

PREP: 15 min. • **BAKE:** 25 min.
MAKES: 6 cups

- 1 lb. ground chicken
- 2 cups sour cream
- 2 cups shredded mild cheddar cheese, divided
- 2 cups crumbled blue cheese, divided
- ¼ cup Buffalo wing sauce
- 2 Tbsp. butter
- ¼ tsp. pepper
- 1½ cups crushed tortilla chips
- 4 green onions, chopped
- 8 thick-sliced peppered bacon strips, cooked and chopped
  Celery sticks
  Tortilla chips

CHEESY MEATBALL SLIDERS

These sliders are a fun way to serve up meatballs at your party without using a slow cooker. Made on mini Hawaiian rolls, they have a hint of sweetness to balance out all the aromatic Italian seasonings.
—Taste of Home *Test Kitchen*

- -

PREP: 1 hour • **BAKE:** 30 min.
MAKES: 12 servings

- 2 lbs. lean ground beef (90% lean)
- 1 cup Italian-style bread crumbs
- 3 Tbsp. prepared pesto
- 1 large egg, lightly beaten
- 1 jar (24 oz.) pasta sauce
- 1 pkg. (18 oz.) Hawaiian sweet rolls
- 12 slices part-skim mozzarella cheese
- ½ tsp. dried oregano
- ¼ cup melted butter
- 1 Tbsp. olive oil
- 3 garlic cloves, minced
- 1 tsp. Italian seasoning
- ½ tsp. crushed red pepper flakes
- 2 Tbsp. grated Parmesan cheese
- 1 cup shredded part-skim mozzarella cheese or shredded Italian cheese blend
  Minced fresh basil

1. Preheat oven to 350°. Combine ground beef, bread crumbs, pesto and egg; mix lightly. Shape into 12 meatballs; place on a greased rack in a 15x10x1-in. baking pan. Bake until browned and a thermometer reads 160°, about 35 minutes. Toss meatballs with sauce; set aside.

2. Meanwhile, keeping rolls connected, cut them horizontally in half; arrange bottom halves in a greased 13x9-in. baking dish. Place half the cheese slices over the roll bottoms; sprinkle with oregano. Add meatballs and sauce. Top with remaining cheese slices and roll tops.

3. Combine butter, olive oil, garlic, Italian seasoning and red pepper flakes; brush over rolls. Bake, covered 20 minutes. Uncover; sprinkle with Parmesan and shredded mozzarella.

4. Bake, uncovered, until cheese is melted, 10-15 minutes longer. Sprinkle with basil before serving.

1 SLIDER: *514 cal., 25g fat (12g sat. fat), 120mg chol., 856mg sod., 39g carb. (15g sugars, 3g fiber), 33g pro.*

1. Preheat oven to 350°. In a large skillet, cook chicken over medium heat until no longer pink, 5-7 minutes, breaking into crumbles; drain. Transfer chicken to a large bowl; stir in sour cream, 1 cup cheddar cheese, 1 cup blue cheese, wing sauce, butter and pepper.

2. Transfer chicken mixture to a greased 8-in. square baking dish. Top with remaining cheeses and the crushed chips. Bake until cheese is melted, 10-12 minutes. Top with green onions and bacon. Serve with celery sticks and chips.

½ CUP: *381 cal., 31g fat (16g sat. fat), 82mg chol., 779mg sod., 8g carb. (2g sugars, 0 fiber), 20g pro.*

READER REVIEW

"One of the tastiest dips ever. I replaced the blue cheese with gruyere, only because I find blue cheese overpowering. But if you enjoy it, go ahead and make the recipe as is."
—FROMBRAZILTOYOU, TASTEOFHOME.COM

EASY KEY LIME PIE TRIFLE

I came up with this easy Key lime pie trifle because I adore Key lime pie in all its forms. It's a refreshing treat on a hot summer day, and since it can be made ahead, it's ideal for entertaining, too. The pie is easier to cut when still a little frozen, but be sure to let the pieces finish thawing before starting the recipe.
—Barbara Moorhead, Gaffney, SC

PREP: 20 min. + chilling • **MAKES:** 10 servings

- 1 pkg. (8 oz.) cream cheese, softened
- 1½ cups heavy whipping cream
- ¼ cup sugar
- 1½ tsp. vanilla extract
- 1 frozen key lime pie (36 oz.), cut into 1-in. cubes, thawed
- 1 cup sweetened shredded coconut, toasted
- 1 cup chopped pecans, toasted

In a large bowl, beat cream cheese, cream, sugar and vanilla until soft peaks form. Place half of the pie pieces in a 3-qt. trifle bowl or glass bowl. Spread with half the cream cheese mixture; top with ½ cup coconut and ½ cup pecans. Repeat layers. Refrigerate, covered, at least 1 hour before serving.

1 CUP: 685 cal., 48g fat (24g sat. fat), 79mg chol., 255mg sod., 58g carb. (46g sugars, 1g fiber), 9g pro.

MEXICAN PORK

MEXICAN PORK

My first time making this dish was a hit with all my family both young and old. Serve with black beans or white rice, or use as filling for tacos, enchiladas or tamales!
—Amy Vazquez, Brandon, MS

PREP: 20 min. • **COOK:** 8 hours • **MAKES:** 18 servings

- 1 bone-in pork shoulder roast (4 to 5 lbs.)
- 1 can (28 oz.) enchilada sauce
- 1 large green pepper, chopped
- 1 medium onion, finely chopped
- 2 garlic cloves, minced
- ¼ cup minced fresh cilantro
- 1 Tbsp. lime juice
- 1½ tsp. grated lime zest
  Flour tortillas (8 in.), optional
  Toppings of your choice

1. Cut roast in half; place in a 4- or 5-qt. slow cooker. Top with enchilada sauce, green pepper, onion and garlic. Cover and cook on low for 8-10 hours or until meat is tender.
2. Remove roast; cool slightly. Skim fat from cooking juices. Remove meat from bone; discard bone. Shred pork with 2 forks and return to slow cooker.
3. Stir in the cilantro, lime juice and lime zest; heat through. Serve with a slotted spoon, on tortillas if desired, with the toppings of your choice.

½ CUP PORK: 162 cal., 9g fat (3g sat. fat), 51mg chol., 280mg sod., 4g carb. (1g sugars, 1g fiber), 17g pro.

EASY KEY LIME PIE TRIFLE

WHAT'S CRACKIN'?

Bring these twists on a classic and get ready for a devilishly good time.

Italian Deviled Eggs

Stir together 3 Tbsp. mayo, ¼ tsp. each dried basil and oregano, and ⅛ tsp. each salt and pepper. Top with Parmesan and fresh oregano leaves.

Asian Deviled Eggs

Mix up 3 Tbsp. mayo, ¼ tsp. soy sauce, ¼ tsp. ginger, ⅛ tsp. each salt and pepper, and ⅛ tsp. chili sauce. Top with chopped green onion and black sesame seeds.

BUILD THESE BITES!

Hard-boil 6 large eggs. Cut in half. Remove yolks; set aside egg whites and 4 yolks (save remaining 2 yolks for another use). Mash the 4 yolks; add mix-ins. Stuff into egg whites.

Curried Deviled Eggs

Stir up 3 Tbsp. mayo, 2 Tbsp. hummus, ½ tsp. curry powder, ⅛ tsp. each salt and pepper, and a dash cayenne. Top with toasted pine nuts, cayenne and curry powder.

◄ Buffalo Deviled Eggs

Combine 3 Tbsp. mayo, 2 Tbsp. blue cheese, 1 Tbsp. chopped celery, 1 tsp. Louisiana-style hot sauce, and ⅛ tsp. each salt and pepper. Garnish with celery, blue cheese bits and hot sauce.

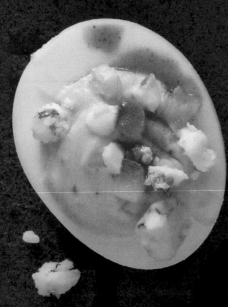

Chutney Deviled Eggs

Mix 3 Tbsp. mayo, 2 Tbsp. mango chutney, 1 Tbsp. chopped green onion, and ⅛ tsp. each salt and pepper. Sprinkle with chopped cashews and paprika.

Bloody Mary Deviled Eggs

Combine 3 Tbsp. mayo, 1 Tbsp. tomato juice, ¾ tsp. horseradish, ¼ tsp. hot pepper sauce, and ⅛ tsp. each salt and pepper. Crumble bacon on top.

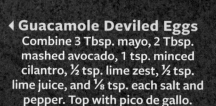

◀ Guacamole Deviled Eggs

Combine 3 Tbsp. mayo, 2 Tbsp. mashed avocado, 1 tsp. minced cilantro, ½ tsp. lime zest, ½ tsp. lime juice, and ⅛ tsp. each salt and pepper. Top with pico de gallo.

◀ Southwest Deviled Eggs

Mix up 3 Tbsp. mayo, 1 Tbsp. salsa, ½ tsp. chili powder, ¼ tsp. cumin, and ⅛ tsp. each salt and pepper. On top, layer jalapeno slices and grilled corn cut off the cob.

Herbed Deviled Eggs

Mix up 3 Tbsp. mayo, 2 tsp. minced chives, 1 tsp. dried parsley, ¼ tsp. dried tarragon, and ⅛ tsp. each salt and pepper. Add fresh dill and minced chives on top.

Crab Cake Deviled Eggs ▶

Combine 3 Tbsp. mayo, 2 Tbsp. crabmeat, 1 Tbsp. minced red pepper, 2 tsp. sweet pickle relish, ½ tsp. seafood seasoning, and ⅛ tsp. each salt, pepper and celery seed. Garnish with red pepper.

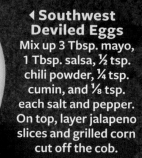

SAVORY CRACKER SNACK MIX

A Taste of Home recipe inspired this one! Because I love everything bagel seasoning, I decided to give this a try. A friend later suggested that I make the mix more versatile with something other than oyster crackers, and now it's a deliciously addictive snack!
—Cyndy Gerken, Naples, FL

PREP: 15 min. • **BAKE:** 15 min. + cooling • **MAKES:** 4½ cups

- 1½ cups potato sticks
- 1½ cups cheddar-flavored snack crackers
- 1½ cups sourdough pretzel nuggets
- 3 Tbsp. butter
- ¼ cup grated Parmesan cheese
- 3 Tbsp. olive oil
- 1½ tsp. sesame seeds
- 1½ tsp. dried minced garlic
- 1½ tsp. dried minced onion
- 1½ tsp. poppy seeds
- ¼ tsp. kosher salt

1. Preheat oven to 350°. In a large bowl, combine potato sticks, crackers and pretzels. In a small saucepan, melt butter; stir in remaining ingredients. Drizzle over pretzel mixture; toss to coat.
2. Spread in a greased 15x10x1-in. baking pan. Bake until crisp and lightly browned, 12-15 minutes, stirring every 4 minutes. Cool completely in pan on a wire rack. Store in an airtight container.
¾ CUP: *306 cal., 20g fat (7g sat. fat), 20mg chol., 468mg sod., 26g carb. (1g sugars, 1g fiber), 5g pro.*

SAVORY CRACKER SNACK MIX

TURKEY SHRIMP GUMBO

TURKEY SHRIMP GUMBO

This slimmed-down version of gumbo tastes just as hearty as the classic version.
—Michael Williams, Westfield, NY

PREP: 20 min. • **COOK:** 2 hours • **MAKES:** 10 servings

- 1 tsp. salt
- 1 tsp. pepper
- 1 tsp. cayenne pepper
- 2 lbs. uncooked skinless turkey breast, cubed
- ½ cup vegetable oil, divided
- ½ cup all-purpose flour
- 1 large onion, chopped
- 1 cup chopped celery
- 1 cup chopped sweet red pepper
- 4 garlic cloves, minced
- 4 cups chicken broth
- 2 cups sliced okra
- 4 green onions, sliced
- 10 oz. uncooked medium shrimp, peeled and deveined
- 5 cups hot cooked rice

1. In a small bowl, combine salt and peppers; sprinkle over turkey. In a Dutch oven, brown turkey in 2 Tbsp. oil; remove with a slotted spoon. Add remaining oil and flour, scraping pan bottom to loosen browned bits. Cook over medium-low heat for 25-30 minutes until dark brown in color, stirring occasionally.
2. Add the onion, celery, red pepper and garlic. Cook over medium heat until vegetables are crisp-tender, 4-5 minutes. Gradually stir in the broth. Bring to a boil. Reduce heat; cover and simmer for 30 minutes. Return turkey to pan; cover and simmer until turkey is tender, 30-45 minutes. Add okra and green onions; simmer for 10 minutes. Add the shrimp; simmer until shrimp turn pink, 4-5 minutes. Serve over rice.
1 CUP GUMBO WITH ½ CUP RICE: *381 cal., 13g fat (2g sat. fat), 88mg chol., 777mg sod., 33g carb. (3g sugars, 2g fiber), 30g pro.*

TACO BOWLS

We love this dish for the super simple prep. And it's so easy to customize with toppings.
—Hope Wasylenki, Gahanna, OH

PREP: 15 min. • COOK: 7 hours
MAKES: 10 servings

- 1   boneless beef chuck roast (2½ lbs.)
- ¼   cup beef broth
- 1   Tbsp. canola oil
- 1   small onion, finely chopped
- 1   jalapeno pepper, seeded and finely chopped
- 1   garlic clove, minced
- 3   tsp. chili powder
- 1½ tsp. ground cumin
       Dash salt
- 2   cups canned crushed tomatoes in puree
- 1   cup salsa verde
- 5   cups hot cooked brown rice
- 1   can (15 oz.) black beans, rinsed, drained and warmed
- 1   cup pico de gallo
       Optional: Reduced-fat sour cream, shredded cheddar cheese, sliced avocado, lime wedges and warmed corn tortillas

1. Place beef and broth in a 5-qt. slow cooker. Cook, covered, on low 6-8 hours or until meat is tender.
2. Remove beef; discard juices. Return beef to slow cooker; shred with 2 forks.
3. In a large skillet, heat oil over medium heat; saute onion and jalapeno until softened, 3-4 minutes. Add garlic and seasonings; cook and stir 1 minute. Stir in tomatoes and salsa; bring to a boil. Add to beef, stirring to combine. Cook, covered, on high for 1 hour or until flavors are blended.
4. For each serving, place ½ cup rice in a soup bowl. Top with beef mixture, beans and pico de gallo. Serve with optional ingredients as desired.
FREEZE OPTION: Freeze cooled meat mixture in freezer containers. To use, partially thaw in refrigerator overnight. Heat through in a saucepan, stirring occasionally.
NOTE: Wear disposable gloves when cutting hot peppers; the oils can burn skin. Avoid touching your face.
1 SERVING: 389 cal., 13g fat (5g sat. fat), 74mg chol., 550mg sod., 38g carb. (4g sugars, 5g fiber), 28g pro. **Diabetic exchanges:** *3 lean meat, 2½ starch, ½ fat.*

ALL VEGGIE LASAGNA

People often tell me you can't call something lasagna if it doesn't have meat. Then they try this dish and ask for the recipe!
—Kim Bender, Aurora, CO

PREP: 20 min. • BAKE: 1 hour + standing
MAKES: 12 servings

- 2   cups 1% cottage cheese
- 1   carton (15 oz.) reduced-fat ricotta cheese
- 2   Tbsp. minced fresh parsley
- 1   jar (26 oz.) meatless spaghetti sauce
- 9   uncooked lasagna noodles
- 2   medium carrots, shredded
- 1½ cups broccoli florets
- 4   oz. fresh mushrooms, sliced
- 1   small zucchini, thinly sliced
- 1   small yellow summer squash, thinly sliced
- 2   cups fresh spinach
- 2   cups shredded part-skim mozzarella cheese

1. Preheat oven to 350°. In a bowl, combine the cottage cheese, ricotta and parsley. Spread ½ cup spaghetti sauce in a 13x9-in. baking dish coated with cooking spray. Top with 3 noodles and a third of the cheese mixture. Sprinkle with half the carrots, broccoli, mushrooms, zucchini and squash. Top with a third of the remaining sauce.
2. Place half the spinach over spaghetti sauce; sprinkle with a third of the mozzarella cheese. Repeat layers of noodles, cheese mixture, vegetables, sauce, spinach and mozzarella. Top with the remaining noodles, cheese mixture, sauce and mozzarella.
3. Cover tightly and bake 45 minutes. Uncover; bake until noodles are tender, about 15 minutes longer. Let stand for 15 minutes before cutting.
1 PIECE: 252 cal., 6g fat (4g sat. fat), 24mg chol., 759mg sod., 27g carb. (10g sugars, 2g fiber), 21g pro. **Diabetic exchanges:** *2 lean meat, 1½ starch, 1 vegetable.*

ALL VEGGIE LASAGNA

DR PEPPER SHEET CAKE

DR PEPPER SHEET CAKE

When we visited the Dr Pepper museum in Dublin, Texas, I bought a Dr Pepper cake mix. It was so delicious I decided to try to come up with my own version.
—Karen Daigle, Burleson, TX

- -

PREP: 10 min. • **BAKE:** 20 min. + cooling
MAKES: 24 servings

2	cups all-purpose flour
2	cups sugar
1	tsp. baking soda
1	tsp. ground cinnamon
2	cups Dr Pepper
1	cup butter, cubed
¼	cup baking cocoa
2	large eggs, room temperature, lightly beaten

ICING

½	cup butter, cubed
⅓	cup Dr Pepper
¼	cup baking cocoa
3¾	cups confectioners' sugar
1	tsp. vanilla extract
1	tsp. ground cinnamon
1	cup chopped pecans, toasted

1. Preheat the oven to 350°. Grease a 15x10x1-in. baking pan. In a large bowl, whisk the flour, sugar, baking soda and cinnamon. In a small saucepan, combine Dr Pepper, butter and cocoa; bring just to a boil, stirring occasionally. Add to flour mixture, stirring just until moistened. Add eggs, whisking constantly.
2. Transfer to prepared pan, spreading evenly. Bake until a toothpick inserted in center comes out clean, 18-22 minutes.
3. Meanwhile, for icing, combine butter, Dr Pepper and cocoa in a small saucepan; stir over medium heat until smooth. Transfer to a bowl. Beat in confectioners' sugar, vanilla and cinnamon until smooth.
4. Remove cake from oven; place on a wire rack and let cool completely. Spread frosting evenly over cake; sprinkle with chopped pecans.
1 PIECE: 331 cal., 15g fat (8g sat. fat), 46mg chol., 154mg sod., 48g carb. (38g sugars, 1g fiber), 2g pro.

CAKE EYEBALLS

Customize these cake balls to your liking with the flavors of your choice.
—Taste of Home *Test Kitchen*

- -

PREP: 1 hour • **BAKE:** 35 min. + freezing
MAKES: 2 dozen

1	pkg. cake mix of your choice (regular size)
1	cup prepared frosting of your choice
1	pkg. (12 oz.) each orange, pink, blue, purple, vibrant green, black and white Wilton candy melts Decorations of your choice: Candy coating disks, jumbo sprinkles, candy-coated sunflower kernels, candy eyeballs, Life Savers, colored sugar, Twizzlers Rainbow Twists and assorted sprinkles

1. Prepare and bake cake mix according to package directions, using a greased 13x9-in. baking pan. Cool completely on a wire rack.
2. Crumble cake into a large bowl. Add frosting and mix well. Shape into 1½-in. balls. Place on baking sheets. Chill cake balls until firm, at least 2 hours in freezer or at least 3 hours in refrigerator.
3. In separate bowls, heat candy melts in the microwave until melted; stir until smooth. Dip each cake ball in coating; allow excess to drip off. Decorate as desired. Let stand until set.
1 CAKE BALL: 182 cal., 8g fat (2g sat. fat), 23mg chol., 208mg sod., 25g carb. (15g sugars, 1g fiber), 2g pro.

POLISH PIEROGI

I'm from a small town in New Jersey where a number of Polish immigrants settled, including my parents. My mother was a skilled cook who taught me lots of Polish recipes like this one, which I have adapted to use in my catering business. Also called Polish lasagna, it's a real crowd-pleaser!
—Adeline Piscitelli, Sayreville, NJ

PREP: 1 hour • **COOK:** 15 min./batch
MAKES: 4½ dozen

DOUGH
- 4 cups all-purpose flour
- 2 large eggs, room temperature
- ½ cup sour cream
- 1 tsp. salt
- ⅔ cup warm water

POTATO FILLING
- ½ lb. potatoes, peeled, cooked, drained and mashed, about 2 medium
- ¼ medium onion, chopped
- 2 Tbsp. butter, softened
- ¼ tsp. salt
- ¼ tsp. pepper

CHEESE FILLING
- 1 cup 4% cottage cheese, drained and patted dry
- 1 large egg yolk, beaten
- ¼ tsp. salt
- 2 Tbsp. butter, melted

COOKING LIQUID
- 3 chicken bouillon cubes
- 8 cups water
- 1 tsp. canola oil

TOPPING
- ½ cup butter
- 1 large onion, chopped
- 2 cups sliced mushrooms

1. To make dough, mix flour, eggs, sour cream, salt and water (a little at a time). Knead dough until firm and elastic; cover and let rest 10 minutes.

2. For potato filling, combine ingredients; set aside. For cheese filling, combine ingredients; set aside.

3. Divide dough into 3 parts. On floured surface, roll dough to ⅛-in. thickness; cut into 3-in. rounds with cutter, rerolling dough as needed. Place 1 tsp. filling in center of each round; fold and press edges together firmly to seal.

4. Dissolve bouillon cubes in water in a large saucepan; add oil. Heat to a simmer over medium heat. Working in batches, drop pierogi into simmering water. Do not crowd. Simmer until tender, about 15 minutes, stirring gently with a wooden spoon to prevent sticking. Remove with a slotted spoon; drain well.

5. Melt butter in a large skillet over medium heat; add onion. Cook until lightly browned, 2-3 minutes. Add the mushrooms; cook until tender, stirring occasionally, about 5 minutes. Place drained pierogi on serving platter. Top evenly with mushroom mixture.
3 PIECES: *223 cal., 11g fat (6g sat. fat), 54mg chol., 366mg sod., 26g carb. (2g sugars, 1g fiber), 6g pro.*

CHILLED CHRISTMAS PUNCH

A blend of juices gives this punch a little pizazz. For a more tart flavor, substitute cranberry juice for the cran-apple juice.
—Edna Hoffman, Hebron, IN

PREP: 10 min. + chilling
MAKES: 20 servings (3¾ qt.)

- 2 cups water
- ¾ cup sugar
- ½ tsp. ground cinnamon
- 1 can (46 oz.) pineapple juice, chilled
- 4 cups cranberry-apple juice, chilled
- 1 liter ginger ale, chilled

In a large saucepan, bring the water, sugar and cinnamon to a boil; stir until sugar is dissolved. Chill. Just before serving, combine the syrup mixture, juices and ginger ale in a punch bowl or large pitcher. Serve over ice.
¾ CUP: *112 cal., 0 fat (0 sat. fat), 0 chol., 6mg sod., 28g carb. (26g sugars, 0 fiber), 0 pro.*

POLISH PIEROGI

TOUCHDOWN BRAT SLIDERS

MARGARITA CAKE

This margarita cake is perfect for a picnic on a warm day. You'll be surprised at how closely its flavor resembles the real thing.
—Dawn E. Lowenstein, Huntingdon Valley, PA

PREP: 15 min. • **BAKE:** 45 min. + cooling • **MAKES:** 16 servings

- 1 pkg. lemon cake mix (regular size)
- 1 pkg. (3.4 oz.) instant lemon pudding mix
- 1 can (10 oz.) frozen nonalcoholic margarita mix, thawed
- 4 large eggs, room temperature
- ½ cup butter, softened
- 2 Tbsp. lime juice
- 3 tsp. grated lime zest

GLAZE
- 1½ cups confectioners' sugar
- 3 Tbsp. lime juice

1. Preheat oven to 350°. Grease and flour a 10-in. fluted tube pan. In a large bowl, combine cake mix, pudding mix, margarita mix, eggs, butter, lime juice and zest; beat on low speed for 30 seconds. Beat on medium for 2 minutes.
2. Transfer batter to prepared pan. Bake 45-50 minutes or until a toothpick inserted near the center comes out clean. Cool in pan 10 minutes before removing to a wire rack to cool completely.
3. Meanwhile, combine glaze ingredients. Drizzle over cake.
1 SLICE: *284 cal., 8g fat (5g sat. fat), 62mg chol., 379mg sod., 51g carb. (37g sugars, 1g fiber), 2g pro.*

TOUCHDOWN BRAT SLIDERS

It's game time when these minis make an appearance. Two things my husband loves—beer and brats—get stepped up a notch with crunchy flavored chips.
—Kirsten Shabaz, Lakeville, MN

TAKES: 50 min. • **MAKES:** 16 sliders

- 5 thick-sliced bacon strips, chopped
- 1 lb. uncooked bratwurst links, casings removed
- 1 large onion, finely chopped
- 2 garlic cloves, minced
- 1 pkg. (8 oz.) cream cheese, cubed
- 1 cup dark beer or nonalcoholic beer
- 1 Tbsp. Dijon mustard
- ¼ tsp. pepper
- 16 dinner rolls, split and toasted
- 2 cups cheddar and sour cream potato chips, crushed

1. In a large cast-iron or other heavy skillet, cook bacon over medium heat until crisp. Remove to paper towels with a slotted spoon; drain, reserving drippings. Cook bratwurst and onion in drippings over medium heat, breaking into crumbles, until meat is no longer pink. Add garlic; cook 1 minute longer. Drain well.
2. Stir in the cream cheese, beer, mustard and pepper. Bring to a boil. Reduce heat; simmer, uncovered, until thickened, 15-20 minutes, stirring occasionally. Stir in bacon. Spoon ¼ cup onto each roll; sprinkle with chips. Replace tops.
1 SLIDER: *354 cal., 24g fat (10g sat. fat), 62mg chol., 617mg sod., 23g carb. (2g sugars, 2g fiber), 10g pro.*

MARGARITA CAKE

CREAMY RANCH PASTA

MAKEOVER CREAMY MAC & CHEESE

Macaroni and cheese just may be the king of comfort foods. This sensational version is bubbling with creamy goodness—but is lower in calories.
—*April Taylor, Holcomb, KS*

PREP: 30 min. • **BAKE:** 25 min.
MAKES: 10 servings

- 1 pkg. (16 oz.) elbow macaroni
- ⅓ cup all-purpose flour
- ½ tsp. garlic powder
- ½ tsp. pepper
- ¼ tsp. salt
- 2 cups fat-free half-and-half
- 2 Tbsp. butter
- 2 cups fat-free milk
- 3 cups shredded reduced-fat sharp cheddar cheese

OPTIONAL TOPPING

- 2 Tbsp. butter
- 1 medium onion, chopped
- 3 cups soft bread crumbs
- ½ cup shredded reduced-fat cheddar cheese
  Optional garnish: Sliced cherry tomatoes and minced chives

1. Preheat the oven to 350°. Cook macaroni according to package directions; drain.
2. Meanwhile, in a small bowl, whisk flour, seasonings and half-and-half until smooth. In a large saucepan, melt butter over medium heat. Stir in half-and-half mixture. Add milk. Bring mixture to a gentle boil, stirring constantly; remove from heat. Add cheese; stir until melted.
3. Stir in macaroni. Transfer to a 13x9-in. baking dish coated with cooking spray.
4. For optional topping, in a large skillet, heat butter over medium-high heat. Add onion; cook and stir until tender. Add the bread crumbs; cook and stir 2 minutes longer. Sprinkle over macaroni mixture; top with cheese.
5. Bake, uncovered, until heated through, 25-30 minutes. Garnish if desired.
1 CUP: *343 cal., 11g fat (6g sat. fat), 31mg chol., 354mg sod., 45g carb. (8g sugars, 2g fiber), 18g pro.*

CREAMY RANCH PASTA

I came up with this after making recipes for a bridal shower. It was party day and I needed to take some shortcuts! Everyone loves the simple Parmesan ranch white sauce, and it's easy to throw in veggies you have on hand.
—*Merry Graham, Newhall, CA*

PREP: 25 min. • **BAKE:** 30 min.
MAKES: 8 servings

- 2½ cups uncooked bow tie pasta
- 2 cups (8 oz.) shredded Italian cheese blend
- 1¼ cups grated Parmesan cheese, divided
- 1 cup (8 oz.) sour cream
- 1 cup ranch salad dressing
- 1 pkg. (10 oz.) frozen chopped spinach, thawed and squeezed dry or 2 cups chopped fresh spinach
- 2 slices day-old French bread (½ in. thick)
- 1 Tbsp. olive oil
- 1 tsp. grated lemon zest
- 1 tsp. dried parsley flakes
- ¼ tsp. garlic salt

1. Preheat oven to 350°. Cook pasta according to package directions. In a large bowl, mix Italian cheese blend, 1 cup Parmesan cheese, sour cream and salad dressing. Drain pasta; add to cheese mixture. Fold in spinach. Transfer to a greased 13x9-in. baking dish.
2. Tear French bread into pieces; place in a food processor. Cover and pulse until crumbs form. Toss bread crumbs with oil, lemon zest, parsley, garlic salt and remaining Parmesan cheese. Sprinkle over pasta mixture.
3. Bake, covered, 25 minutes. Uncover; bake until golden brown and bubbly, 5-10 minutes.
¾ CUP: *436 cal., 30g fat (12g sat. fat), 40mg chol., 841mg sod., 25g carb. (3g sugars, 2g fiber), 15g pro.*

DID YOU KNOW?

Ranch dressing was created by Nebraska cowboy-turned-cook Steve Henson more than 70 years ago. While cooking for a work crew in Alaska in the late 1940s, Steve perfected his recipe for buttermilk salad dressing. It later became the house dressing at Hidden Valley Ranch, a dude ranch he bought with his wife, Gayle, outside Santa Barbara, California.

THE BEST PIZZA DOUGH

This easy dough is the key to making an extraordinary home made pizza. We use all-purpose flour because double zero is hard to find. But if you're lucky enough to live near an Italian market or you're willing to purchase double zero flour online, using this flour will take your crust to the next level. You won't be disappointed with the results!
—Josh Rink, Milwaukee, WI

- -

PREP: 30 min. + chilling
MAKES: 2 crusts (8 servings each)

1¼ cups warm water (110° to 115°)
2 tsp. sugar, divided
1 pkg. (¼ oz.) active dry yeast
3½ to 4 cups all-purpose or 00 flour
1 tsp. sea salt
1 tsp. each dried basil, oregano and
  marjoram, optional
⅓ cup vegetable or olive oil

1. In a small bowl, mix warm water and 1 tsp. sugar; add yeast and whisk until dissolved. Let stand until bubbles form on surface. In a large bowl, whisk 3 cups flour, salt, remaining 1 tsp. sugar and, if desired, dried herbs. Make a well in center; add yeast mixture and oil. Stir until smooth. Add enough remaining flour to form a soft dough.
2. Turn onto a floured surface; knead, adding more flour to surface as needed until no longer sticky and dough is smooth and elastic, 6-8 minutes. Place in a large greased bowl; turn once to grease top. Cover and let rise in a warm place for 30 minutes; transfer bowl to refrigerator and chill overnight. Allow dough to come to room temperature before rolling, about 30 minutes.
1 PIECE PLAIN CRUST: *144 cal., 5g fat (1g sat. fat), 0 chol., 121mg sod., 22g carb. (1g sugars, 1g fiber), 3g pro.*

THE BEST SAUSAGE PIZZAS

What makes this recipe unique is the slow overnight fermentation of the dough. The flour has time to hydrate and relax, which makes the dough so much easier to roll out.
—Josh Rink, Milwaukee, WI

- -

PREP: 30 min. • **BAKE:** 15 min.
MAKES: 2 pizzas (8 slices each)

1 batch Best Pizza Dough (recipe at left)
1 cup pizza sauce
1 lb. bulk Italian sausage
4 cups shredded part-skim mozzarella
  cheese
1 medium red onion, sliced
1 medium green pepper, chopped
2 cups sliced fresh mushrooms
  Grated Parmesan cheese, crushed
  red pepper flakes and fresh oregano
  leaves, optional

1. Divide dough in half. With greased fingers, pat each half onto an ungreased 12-in. pizza pan. Prick crust thoroughly with a fork. Bake at 400° until lightly browned, 10-12 minutes. Meanwhile, in a large skillet, cook the sausage over medium heat until sausage is no longer pink; drain.
2. Spread pizza sauce over crusts. Top with the cheese, onion, green pepper, mushrooms and sausage. Bake at 400° until golden brown and cheese is bubbling, 12-15 minutes. If desired, top with grated Parmesan cheese, crushed red pepper flakes and fresh oregano leaves.
FREEZE OPTION: After adding sausage, wrap pizzas and freeze for up to 2 months. To use, unwrap pizzas and place on pizza pans; thaw in refrigerator. Bake at 400° until golden brown, 18-22 minutes. Add desired toppings.
1 SLICE: *344 cal., 20g fat (7g sat. fat), 41mg chol., 651mg sod., 26g carb. (2g sugars, 1g fiber), 15g pro.*

THE BEST SAUSAGE PIZZAS

STRAWBERRY BUTTERMILK SKILLET SHORTCAKE

This scratch-made buttermilk shortcake is a family favorite. My grandma even carries on this summer tradition by making this old-fashioned recipe.
—Claudia Lamascolo, Melbourne, FL

PREP: 25 min. • **BAKE:** 50 min.
MAKES: 10 servings

- 10 Tbsp. shortening
- ¼ cup butter, softened
- 1 cup sugar
- 2 large eggs, room temperature
- 2½ cups all-purpose flour
- 3 tsp. baking powder
- ½ tsp. salt
- ⅔ cup buttermilk

STREUSEL TOPPING
- ⅔ cup all-purpose flour
- ½ cup sugar
- 1 tsp. ground cinnamon
- ¼ tsp. ground allspice
- ½ cup butter, softened
- 2 cups sliced fresh strawberries
  Whipped cream

1. Preheat oven to 350°. In a large bowl, cream shortening, butter and sugar until light and fluffy, 5-7 minutes. Add eggs, 1 at a time, beating well after each addition. In another bowl, whisk flour, baking powder and salt; add to the creamed mixture alternately with buttermilk, beating well after each addition. Transfer to a 12-in. cast-iron or other ovenproof skillet.
2. For streusel topping, in a small bowl, mix flour, sugar, cinnamon and allspice; cut in butter until crumbly. Sprinkle over batter. Top with strawberries. Bake until center is puffed and edges are golden brown, 50-60 minutes. Serve warm, with whipped cream.
1 SLICE: 526 cal., 27g fat (12g sat. fat), 74mg chol., 418mg sod., 64g carb. (33g sugars, 2g fiber), 6g pro.

TEST KITCHEN TIP

To create a glistening appearance, try sprinkling additional sugar and cinnamon over the top while the shortcake bakes.

SWEET & SPICY ASIAN CHICKEN PETITES

❄ SWEET & SPICY ASIAN CHICKEN PETITES

Using crescent roll dough, Sriracha and sweet chili sauce, I came up with these irresistible chicken bites. Freeze a batch to reheat when you have drop-in guests.
—Jeanette Nelson, Bridgeport, WV

PREP: 25 min. • **BAKE:** 10 min.
MAKES: 16 appetizers

- 4 tsp. olive oil, divided
- ⅓ cup finely chopped sweet red pepper
- 3 green onions, finely chopped
- 2 garlic cloves, minced
- 1 cup finely chopped cooked chicken breast
- 2 Tbsp. island teriyaki sauce
- 1 Tbsp. white grapefruit juice or water
- 1 Tbsp. sesame oil
- 1 tsp. Sriracha chili sauce
- 1 tube (8 oz.) refrigerated crescent rolls
- 2 tsp. sesame seeds
  Sweet chili sauce

1. Preheat oven to 375°. In a large skillet, heat 2 tsp. olive oil over medium-high heat. Add red pepper, green onions and garlic; cook and stir until vegetables are tender, 3-5 minutes. Stir in chicken, teriyaki sauce, grapefruit juice, sesame oil and Sriracha chili sauce. Remove from heat; cool slightly.
2. Unroll dough into 1 long rectangle; press perforations to seal. Roll dough into a 12-in. square; cut into sixteen 3-in. squares. Place 1 Tbsp. chicken mixture in center of each square. Bring edges of dough over filling, pinching seams to seal; shape into a ball.
3. Place on ungreased baking sheets, seam side down. Brush tops with remaining olive oil; sprinkle with sesame seeds. Bake for 10-12 minutes or until golden brown. Serve warm with sweet chili sauce.
FREEZE OPTION: Freeze cooled appetizers in freezer containers. To use, reheat on a baking sheet in a preheated 375° oven until heated through.
NOTE: This recipe was tested with Soy Vay brand teriyaki sauce.
1 APPETIZER: 97 cal., 5g fat (1g sat. fat), 7mg chol., 199mg sod., 8g carb. (2g sugars, 0 fiber), 4g pro.

BUFFALO CHICKEN ENCHILADAS

BUFFALO CHICKEN ENCHILADAS

These amazing enchiladas—filled with tender rotisserie chicken, lots of cheese and, of course, Buffalo sauce—are a crave-worthy, easy and delicious meal. The whole family will ask for these again and again.
—Becky Hardin, St. Peters, MO

PREP: 15 min. • BAKE: 25 min.
MAKES: 10 servings

- 3 cups shredded rotisserie chicken
- 2 cups shredded cheddar cheese, divided
- 1 can (10 oz.) diced tomatoes and green chiles, drained
- 1 can (10 oz.) enchilada sauce
- ½ cup Buffalo wing sauce
- 1 can (10½ oz.) condensed cream of celery soup, undiluted
- 4 oz. reduced-fat cream cheese, cubed
- ½ cup blue cheese salad dressing
- 10 flour tortillas (8 in.)
- ⅓ cup crumbled blue cheese
  Optional: Chopped tomatoes, sliced celery, shredded lettuce, sliced green onions, minced fresh cilantro and additional cheddar cheese

1. Preheat oven to 350°. In a large bowl, combine chicken, 1¾ cups shredded cheese, diced tomatoes and green chiles, enchilada sauce and wing sauce. In a small saucepan, heat soup, cream cheese, dressing and remaining ¼ cup shredded cheese over low heat until cheeses are melted, 5-10 minutes. Remove from heat.
2. Place ½ cup chicken mixture off center on each tortilla. Roll up and place in a greased 13x9-in. baking dish, seam side down. Top with sauce.
3. Bake, uncovered, until enchiladas are heated through and the cheese is melted, 25-30 minutes. Sprinkle with blue cheese and additional toppings of your choice.
1 ENCHILADA: *472 cal., 26g fat (10g sat. fat), 76mg chol., 1387mg sod., 34g carb. (2g sugars, 3g fiber), 25g pro.*

HAM & SWISS LAYERED SALAD

Layered salads rank among the classics in the potluck hall of fame. In this one, the combination of ham, cheese, egg and bacon is like a deconstructed sandwich, making it hearty enough for a main course.
—Stacy Huggins, Valley Center, CA

TAKES: 30 min. • MAKES: 12 servings

- 2 cups mayonnaise
- 1 cup sour cream
- ½ tsp. sugar
- ⅛ tsp. salt
- ⅛ tsp. pepper
- 8 cups fresh baby spinach (about 6 oz.)
- 6 hard-boiled large eggs, chopped
- ½ lb. sliced fully cooked ham, cut into strips
- 4 cups torn iceberg lettuce (about ½ head)
- 2½ cups frozen petite peas (about 10 oz.), thawed, optional
- 1 small red onion, halved and thinly sliced
- 8 oz. sliced Swiss cheese, cut into strips
- ½ lb. bacon strips, cooked and crumbled

For dressing, mix the first 5 ingredients. In a 3-qt. or larger glass bowl, layer spinach, eggs, ham, lettuce, peas if desired, and onion. Spread with dressing. Sprinkle with cheese and bacon. Refrigerate, covered, until serving.
1 CUP: *501 cal., 43g fat (12g sat. fat), 137mg chol., 665mg sod., 11g carb. (5g sugars, 3g fiber), 19g pro.*

HAM & SWISS LAYERED SALAD

CARAMEL HAVARTI

Havarti cheese is wonderful, and combined with pecans, caramel topping and apples, it's even better. This makes a simple but elegant snack.
—Tia Thomas, Mountain City, TN

TAKES: 15 min. • **MAKES:** 10 servings

- 10 oz. Havarti cheese
- ¼ cup chopped pecans
- 1 Tbsp. butter
- ⅓ to ½ cup caramel ice cream topping, warmed
- 2 medium tart apples, cut into small wedges

1. Place cheese in a small ungreased cast-iron skillet or shallow 1-qt. baking dish. Bake at 375° until edges of cheese just begin to melt, 5-7 minutes.

2. Meanwhile, in a small skillet, saute pecans in butter until toasted. Drizzle caramel over cheese; sprinkle with pecans. Serve with apple wedges.

1 SERVING: *173 cal., 12g fat (6g sat. fat), 30mg chol., 205mg sod., 12g carb. (10g sugars, 1g fiber), 7g pro.*

CHOCOLATE BABKA

I love this chocolate babka. It's a rewarding recipe for taking the next step in your bread baking. Even if it's slightly imperfect going into the oven, it turns out gorgeous. Look at those swirls!
—Lisa Kaminski, Wauwatosa, WI

PREP: 20 min. + chilling
BAKE: 35 min. + cooling
MAKES: 2 loaves (16 slices each)

- 4¼ to 4¾ cups all-purpose flour
- ½ cup sugar
- 2½ tsp. quick-rise yeast
- ¾ tsp. salt
- ⅔ cup butter
- ½ cup water
- 3 large eggs plus 1 large egg yolk, room temperature, beaten
- 2 Tbsp. grated orange zest

FILLING
- ½ cup butter, cubed
- 5 oz. dark chocolate chips
- ½ cup confectioners' sugar
- ⅓ cup baking cocoa
- ¼ tsp. salt

GLAZE
- ¼ cup sugar
- ¼ cup water

CHOCOLATE BABKA

1. In a large bowl, mix 2 cups flour, sugar, yeast and salt. Cut in butter until crumbly. In a small saucepan, heat water to 120°-130°; stir into dry ingredients. Stir in the eggs and yolk, orange zest and enough remaining flour to form a soft dough (dough will be sticky).

2. Turn dough onto a floured surface; knead until smooth and elastic, 6-8 minutes. Place in a greased bowl, turning once to grease the top. Cover and refrigerate for 8 hours or overnight.

3. Turn out dough onto a lightly floured surface; divide in half. Roll each half into a 12x10-in. rectangle. For filling, in a microwave, melt butter and chocolate chips; stir until smooth. Stir in the confectioners' sugar, cocoa and salt.

Spread filling to within ½ in. of edges. Roll up jelly-roll style, starting with a long side; pinch seam and ends to seal.

4. Using a sharp knife, cut each roll lengthwise in half; carefully turn each half cut side up. Loosely twist strips around each other, keeping cut surfaces facing up; pinch ends together to seal. Place in 2 greased 9x5-in. loaf pans, cut side up. Cover with kitchen towels; let rise in a warm place until almost doubled, about 1 hour.

5. Preheat oven to 375°. Bake until golden brown, 35-45 minutes, tenting with foil halfway through baking. Meanwhile, in a saucepan, combine sugar and water; bring to a boil. Reduce heat; simmer, uncovered, for 10 minutes. Brush over warm babka. Cool 10 minutes before removing from pans to wire racks.

1 SLICE: *181 cal., 9g fat (5g sat. fat), 41mg chol., 136mg sod., 23g carb. (10g sugars, 1g fiber), 3g pro.*

CHAMPAGNE WISHES
PAGE 300

Holiday & Seasonal Celebrations

*There's something all good cooks have in common—
they love a great celebration. What does it take?
Fun themes, bountiful foods, tried-and-true recipes,
and those you hold dear.*

GUINNESS
FLOAT

Emerald Style

Everyone's Irish on St. Patrick's Day! Celebrate with a classic
dinner that leaves your whole clan feeling lucky.

GUINNESS FLOAT

That very first sip of a Guinness is what inspired this quick and easy dessert. The rich, creamy foam that gathers on the top of a freshly poured draft made me think of vanilla ice cream. At that point, I knew I had to combine the two in a Guinness float.
—James Schend, Pleasant Prairie, WI

TAKES: 5 min. • **MAKES:** 2 floats

- 1 cup vanilla ice cream, softened if necessary
- 2 cups Guinness or other stout beer
- 2 Tbsp. chocolate syrup

Divide ice cream between 2 glasses. Slowly top with beer; drizzle with chocolate syrup. Serve immediately.

1 FLOAT: *286 cal., 7g fat (4g sat. fat), 29mg chol., 68mg sod., 36g carb. (31g sugars, 1g fiber), 4g pro.*

EASY IRISH CREAM

Stir up this fast and easy recipe for a potluck brunch. There's plenty of coffee flavor in every cozy cup.
—Anna Hansen, Park City, UT

TAKES: 15 min. • **MAKES:** 5 cups

- 2 cups half-and-half cream
- 1 can (13.4 oz.) dulce de leche or sweetened condensed milk
- 1¼ cups Irish whiskey
- ¼ cup chocolate syrup
- 2 Tbsp. instant coffee granules
- 2 tsp. vanilla extract
      Hot brewed coffee or
      cooled brewed coffee and ice cubes

Pulse first 6 ingredients in a blender until smooth. Stir 1-2 Tbsp. into a mug of hot coffee, or pour cooled coffee and cream over ice.

½ CUP: *415 cal., 21g fat (13g sat. fat), 79mg chol., 116mg sod., 35g carb. (34g sugars, 0 fiber), 4g pro.*

IRISH STEW PIE
(SHOWN ON PAGE 264)

The only thing more comforting than a hearty bowl of Irish lamb stew is when it's baked into a pie! The flavors blend well with lamb, but you can use cuts of beef instead if you wish.
—Nicolas Hortense, Perth, Australia

PREP: 1 hour • **BAKE:** 35 min. + standing
MAKES: 6 servings

- ½ cup plus 1 Tbsp. all-purpose flour, divided
- ¾ tsp. salt, divided
- ¾ tsp. pepper, divided
- 1 lb. boneless lamb shoulder roast, cubed
- 2 Tbsp. canola oil
- 2 medium carrots, finely chopped
- 1 medium onion, halved and sliced
- 1¼ cups beef stock
- 2 medium Yukon Gold potatoes, peeled and cubed
- 1 fresh thyme sprig
- 1 bay leaf
- 1 tsp. Worcestershire sauce
- 1 tsp. tomato paste
- 3 Tbsp. chopped fresh mint
- 1 large egg yolk
- 2 Tbsp. heavy whipping cream
- 1 pkg. (17.3 oz.) frozen puff pastry, thawed

1. Preheat oven to 350°. In a shallow bowl, mix ½ cup flour, ½ tsp. salt and ½ tsp. pepper. Add lamb, a few pieces at a time, and toss to coat; shake off excess. In a Dutch oven, heat oil over medium-high heat. Brown lamb in batches. Remove from pan. Add carrots and onion to same pan; cook and stir until crisp-tender, 6-8 minutes. Stir in remaining 1 Tbsp. flour until blended; gradually whisk in the stock. Bring to a boil, stirring to loosen browned bits from pan.
2. Add potatoes, thyme, bay leaf, Worcestershire sauce, tomato paste, the remaining ¼ tsp. salt and ¼ tsp. pepper, and lamb; return to a boil. Reduce heat. Simmer, uncovered, until sauce is thickened and lamb is tender, 25-30 minutes. Discard thyme sprig and bay leaf. Stir in mint. Transfer to a greased 9-in. deep-dish pie plate. Whisk egg yolk and cream; brush around edge of pie plate to help the pastry adhere.

3. On a lightly floured surface, unfold 1 sheet puff pastry; top with remaining sheet. Roll to fit over pie plate. Carefully place over filling; trim to fit. Using a fork, press crust firmly onto rim of pie plate to seal edge. Brush with the remaining egg mixture; cut slits in top. Place on a rimmed baking sheet. Bake until golden brown, 35-40 minutes. Let stand for 10 minutes before serving.

1 SERVING: *731 cal., 40g fat (11g sat. fat), 75mg chol., 608mg sod., 71g carb. (4g sugars, 8g fiber), 24g pro.*

IRISH SODA BREAD MUFFINS
(SHOWN ON PAGE 265)

Irish soda bread is traditionally prepared in a loaf shape, but these muffins have the same terrific flavor.
—Lorraine Ballsieper, Deep River, CT

TAKES: 30 min. • **MAKES:** 1 dozen

- 2¼ cups all-purpose flour
- ½ cup plus 1 Tbsp. sugar, divided
- 2 tsp. baking powder
- ½ tsp. salt
- ¼ tsp. baking soda
- 1 tsp. caraway seeds
- 1 large egg, room temperature
- 1 cup buttermilk
- ¼ cup butter, melted
- ¼ cup canola oil
- ¾ cup dried currants or raisins

1. In a large bowl, combine the flour, ½ cup sugar, baking powder, salt, baking soda and caraway seeds. In another bowl, beat the egg, buttermilk, butter and oil. Stir into dry ingredients just until moistened. Fold in currants.
2. Fill 12 greased muffin cups three-fourths full. Sprinkle with remaining sugar. Bake at 400° for 15 minutes or until a toothpick inserted in the center comes out clean. Cool for 5 minutes before removing from pan to wire rack. Serve warm.

1 MUFFIN: *235 cal., 9g fat (3g sat. fat), 28mg chol., 247mg sod., 35g carb. (17g sugars, 1g fiber), 4g pro.*

PUB IN A PINCH

Transform your kitchen into an Irish tavern with dark wood surfaces and rustic tableware. Add glimmering accents like green crystal and a pot full of coins.

Irish
Stew
Pie

Irish
Soda Bread
Muffins

The Breakfast Club

Fresh smoothies and fun toppers to mix and match make morning meals something to celebrate. Gather the gang and start the day with a smile.

Keep the smoothie in a pitcher for easy serving. In a pinch, even your blender's pitcher works!

Get experimental with spices such as cinnamon, turmeric and even ground peppercorn.

Corral similar toppings on separate serving trays. Think one for crunchers and one for sweet stuff.

FRUIT SMOOTHIE BOWLS

What's not to love about these bowls? They're easy, gorgeous, customizable and healthy. Blend up a big batch and invite your friends over for a feel-good brunch.
—Taste of Home *Test Kitchen*

TAKES: 15 min. • **MAKES:** 6 servings

2½ cups 2% milk
2 cups frozen unsweetened sliced peaches
2 cups frozen unsweetened strawberries
½ cup orange juice
¼ cup honey
 Optional toppings: Fresh berries, chia seeds, pumpkin seeds, flax seeds or toasted chopped nuts

In a blender, combine half of the milk, peaches, strawberries, orange juice and honey; cover and process until smooth. Transfer to a pitcher. Repeat, adding second batch to the same pitcher; stir to combine. Serve immediately. Top as desired.
1 CUP: *140 cal., 2g fat (1g sat. fat), 8mg chol., 49mg sod., 27g carb. (24g sugars, 2g fiber), 4g pro.*

HOW-TO

Power Up Your Smoothie with Healthy Add-Ins

• Berries can't be beat for flavor, fiber and healthy antioxidants. Frozen cranberries add zing!

• Avocados make a rich and creamy smoothie.

• Baby spinach is a smart way to sneak in a serving of veggies.

• Kefir (a cultured milk in the dairy case) has even more belly-friendly bugs than yogurt.

COCONUT COLD BREW LATTE

COCONUT COLD BREW LATTE

Cold brew lattes are all the rage at coffee shops, but they're so easy to make at home. This coconut cold brew latte is ridiculously refreshing and is even vegan!
—Natalie Larsen, Columbia, MD

PREP: 20 min. + chilling • **MAKES:** 4 servings

½ cup coarsely ground medium-roast coffee
½ cup hot water (205°)
3½ cups cold water
COCONUT SIMPLE SYRUP
1 cup water
½ cup sugar
½ cup sweetened shredded coconut
EACH SERVING
 Ice cubes
2 Tbsp. coconut milk

1. Place coffee grounds in a clean glass container. Pour hot water over grounds; let stand 10 minutes. Stir in cold water. Cover and refrigerate for 12-24 hours. (The longer the coffee sits, the stronger the flavor.)
2. Meanwhile, for coconut simple syrup, in a small saucepan, bring water, sugar and coconut to a boil. Reduce heat; simmer 10 minutes. Strain and discard coconut. Cool completely.
3. Strain coffee through a fine mesh sieve; discard grounds. Strain the coffee again through a coffee filter; discard grounds. Store coffee in the refrigerator for up to 2 weeks. For each serving, fill a large glass with ice. Add 1 cup cold brewed coffee and 4 Tbsp. coconut syrup; stir. Top with coconut milk.
1 CUP: *145 cal., 5g fat (5g sat. fat), 0 chol., 12mg sod., 26g carb. (26g sugars, 0 fiber), 1g pro.*

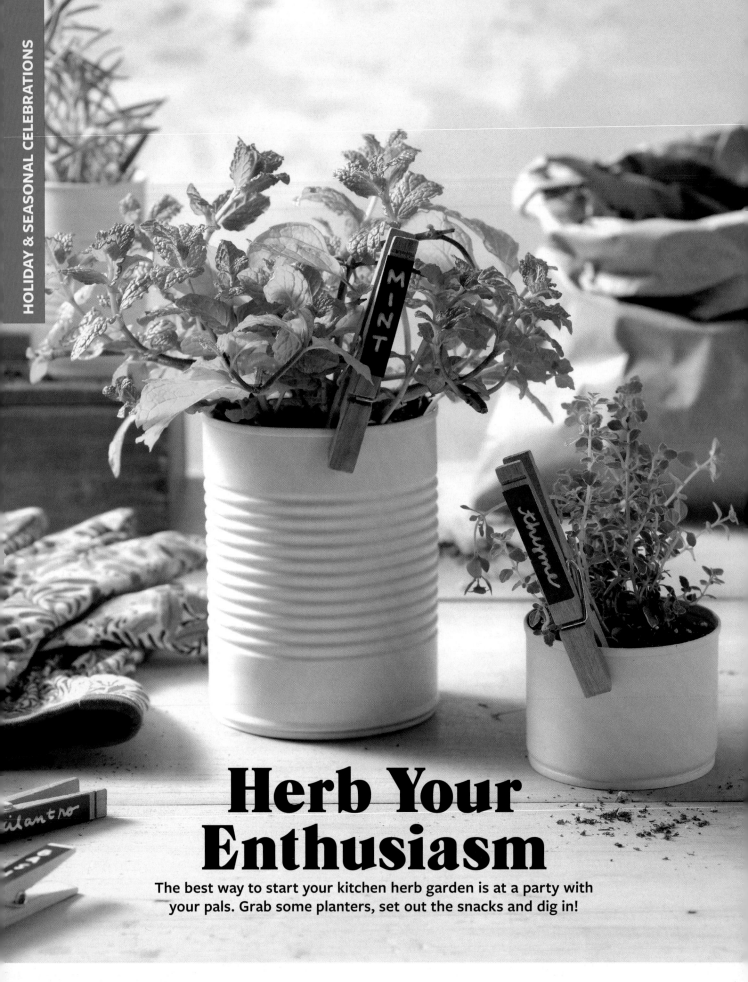

Herb Your Enthusiasm

The best way to start your kitchen herb garden is at a party with your pals. Grab some planters, set out the snacks and dig in!

LIME & DILL CHIMICHURRI SHRIMP

Chimichurri is a very popular condiment in Argentina and Uruguay and is most often used as a dipping sauce or a marinade for meats. My chimichurri shrimp version incorporates dill and lime, which give it a brighter flavor and make it ideal for spring and summer entertaining.
—Bonnie Landy, Castro Valley, CA

- -

PREP: 25 min. + standing • **GRILL:** 10 min.
MAKES: 4 servings

- ½ cup extra virgin olive oil
- ½ cup packed fresh parsley sprigs
- ¼ cup snipped fresh dill
- ¼ cup fresh cilantro leaves
- 3 Tbsp. lime juice
- 3 garlic cloves, halved
- ½ tsp. salt
- ¼ tsp. pepper
- 1 lb. uncooked shrimp (26-30 per lb.), peeled and deveined
- 1 medium red onion, cut into thick wedges
- 1 medium zucchini, cut into ½-in. pieces
- 1 medium yellow summer squash, cut into ½-in. pieces
- 8 cherry tomatoes
  Crusty bread

1. Place the first 8 ingredients in a food processor; process until pureed. Reserve 6 Tbsp. mixture for serving. Place the remaining mixture in a bowl; toss with shrimp and vegetables. Let stand for 15 minutes.

2. Alternately thread shrimp and vegetables onto 8 metal or soaked wooden skewers. Grill, covered, over medium heat or broil 4 in. from heat until shrimp turn pink, 3-4 minutes per side. Serve on a bed of additional herbs with crusty bread and reserved sauce.

2 KABOBS: 316 cal., 22g fat (3g sat. fat), 138mg chol., 371mg sod., 10g carb. (4g sugars, 2g fiber), 21g pro.

CILANTRO DIP

Stir together ½ cup sour cream, ¾ cup mayonnaise, 4 tsp. minced fresh cilantro, 2 tsp. lemon juice, 1 tsp. hot sauce, ½ tsp. salt and ¼ tsp. pepper. Serve with fresh veggies or pretzels for dipping, or spread over corn.

Lavender & Lemon Biscochitos

Press culinary lavender or fresh thyme into the dough before baking for extra-pretty treats.

Lime & Dill Chimichurri Shrimp

Rosemary Strawberry Daiquiri

"A portable bar cart doubles as a holder for finished planters, clearing up table space. When the party's over, roll it to guests' cars for easy transferring."
—ANNAMARIE HIGLEY, ASSISTANT EDITOR

HOW TO:

Store Fresh Herbs

Wrap fresh herbs in a slightly damp paper towel, place in a resealable bag and press out most of the air. Store in the refrigerator for 5-7 days.

Freeze Fresh Herbs

Chop fresh herbs and fill the empty sections of an ice cube tray with them. Carefully pour water into each herb-filled compartment and freeze.

Dry Fresh Herbs

Snip off healthy branches and remove the leaves from the bottom inch of each stem. Bundle several stems together with string or a rubber band, and hang upside down in a warm, airy room. Check the herbs weekly until they're completely dry. Crumble the leaves into spice jars.

The Basics for Your Herb Swap

Assign your fellow green thumbs a type of herb to bring along, let 'em swap and pot as they please, then send them on their way with a lush kitchen garden. From there, just add water!

Roll down brown paper bags and fill them with soil to contain the mess and add rustic flair to your table.

Spray-paint used veggie cans for simple pots. Be sure to poke holes in the bottom for drainage!

Label clothespins with herb names and clip 'em to your new windowsill friends.

① BASIL

Flavor: Depending on the variety, you'll notice hints of pepper, mint and anise.

How to use it: Pair it with mild cheeses, fresh tomatoes and spicy flavors. It's most commonly used in Mediterranean, Asian and Indian dishes. For best results, add it at the end of cooking.

② CILANTRO
(AKA CORIANDER LEAF)

Flavor: Some find this herb bright and refreshing with a zesty flavor. Some could find it "soapy" for reasons that might be genetic.

How to use it: You can eat cilantro raw or cooked, and it has the ability to bring dull sauces to life with its invigorating flavor. It's a Latin American and Asian staple.

③ DILL

Flavor: Delicate strands boast a strong flavor of clean, fresh earthiness, or a subtle licorice- or fennel-like flavor.

How to use it: Dill is best used in small quantities—too much can overwhelm a dish. It works well in spring salads and pairs well with vegetables like asparagus and peas. It's also a delicious addition to homemade salad dressings.

④ THYME

Flavor: This is a pungent herb with a slightly sweet and woodsy flavor. The leaves are aromatic and floral with a strong yet understated taste.

How to use it: A staple in French cooking, thyme works well with poultry dishes and strong cheeses. Or use it in breads, desserts and drinks.

LAVENDER & LEMON BISCOCHITOS

(SHOWN ON PAGE 269)

Biscochitos are the state cookie for our home state of New Mexico. They are traditionally made with anise seeds, but for this recipe I substituted lavender and lemon. The result is intriguing and delicious! I have also made these with thyme instead of lavender, and they are scrumptious.
—*Marla Clark, Albuquerque, NM*

PREP: 30 min. + chilling
BAKE: 10 min./batch + cooling
MAKES: 6 dozen

½	cup unsalted butter, softened
⅔	cup sugar
1	large egg, room temperature
1	Tbsp. dried lavender flowers
1	Tbsp. grated lemon zest
1½	cups all-purpose flour
1	tsp. baking powder
¼	tsp. salt

1. In a large bowl, cream butter and sugar until light and fluffy, 5-7 minutes. Beat in egg, lavender and lemon zest. In another bowl, whisk flour, baking powder and salt; gradually beat into creamed mixture. Divide dough in half. Shape each into a disk; cover and refrigerate 30 minutes or until firm enough to roll.

2. Preheat oven to 350°. On a lightly floured surface, roll each portion of dough to ¼-in. thickness. Cut with a floured 1-in. round cookie cutter. Place 1 in. apart on parchment-lined baking sheets. Sprinkle with additional sugar.

3. Bake until bottoms are light brown, 9-11 minutes. Remove from pans to wire racks to cool. Store in airtight containers.

FREEZE OPTION: Freeze cookies in freezer containers, separating layers with waxed paper. To use, thaw before serving.

1 COOKIE: *29 cal., 1g fat (1g sat. fat), 6mg chol., 16mg sod., 4g carb. (2g sugars, 0 fiber), 0 pro.*

ROSEMARY STRAWBERRY DAIQUIRI

ROSEMARY STRAWBERRY DAIQUIRI

This strawberry daiquiri recipe is a standout with its herbal twist! I used to teach herb classes at our local technical college and everyone enjoyed my segment on herbal cocktails like this one.
—*Sue Gronholz, Beaver Dam, WI*

PREP: 20 min. + cooling • **MAKES:** 8 servings

1	cup sugar
1	cup water
4	fresh rosemary sprigs

EACH SERVING

1	cup frozen unsweetened sliced strawberries
1½	oz. white rum
2	Tbsp. lime juice
	Whole fresh strawberries and additional rosemary sprigs

1. In a small saucepan, bring sugar and water to a boil. Reduce heat; simmer 10 minutes. Remove from heat; add rosemary. Steep, covered, 10-15 minutes according to taste. Discard rosemary. Cool completely. Store in an airtight container in the refrigerator up to 1 month.

2. For each serving, in a blender, combine frozen strawberries, rum, lime juice and 2 Tbsp. rosemary syrup; cover and process until smooth. Pour into a chilled glass; garnish with a whole strawberry and an additional rosemary sprig.

1 SERVING: *251 cal., 0 fat (0 sat. fat), 0 chol., 1mg sod., 41g carb. (32g sugars, 3g fiber), 0 pro.*

Summer Nights & Bright Lights

Oh, my stars! Set out this festive, fun spread to watch fireworks, and you just might forget to look up.

A dash of patriotic sprinkles makes snacks feel festive.

Once the sun goes down, snag a blanket to stay cozy.

Summer Fresh Pasta Salad

Cute food trays keep spillage to a minimum, even on the grass.

Rest your head on plush pillows when the display kicks off.

A convenient carrier corrals napkins and utensils when you're on the go. Pop in a mini flag for some extra fun!

Chocolate-Covered Strawberry Snack Mix

**WATERMELON &
BLACKBERRY SANGRIA**

WATERMELON & BLACKBERRY SANGRIA

This recipe is deliciously pink! Living in wine country of northern California, I use our local fare in my recipes often. Our scorching summer months of July and August inspired this refreshing, light style of sangria. I like to garnish it with sprigs of mint or basil for a bit of fresh flair. This easy recipe is perfect for entertaining, and it's especially nice for brunch.
—Carolyn Kumpe, El Dorado, CA

- -

PREP: 5 min. + chilling • **MAKES:** 8 servings

- 1 bottle (750 ml) white zinfandel or rose wine, chilled
- ¼ cup watermelon schnapps liqueur
- 1½ cups cubed seedless watermelon (½-in. cubes)
- 1 medium lime, thinly sliced
- ½ to 1 cup fresh blackberries, halved
- 1 can (12 oz.) lemon-lime soda, chilled
  Ice cubes
  Fresh basil or mint leaves

In a pitcher, stir together the wine and schnapps; add watermelon, lime and blackberries. Chill at least 2 hours. Just before serving, stir in soda. Serve over ice. Garnish with basil or mint.

¾ CUP: 119 cal., 0 fat (0 sat. fat), 0 chol., 10mg sod., 12g carb. (8g sugars, 1g fiber), 0 pro.

CHOCOLATE-COVERED STRAWBERRY SNACK MIX

(SHOWN ON PAGE 273)

I love chocolate-covered strawberries, but it's a treat you want to make only on special occasions. With a little experimenting, I've captured the same incredible flavor in a snack I can take anywhere. Everyone is always amazed when I pull these out at a picnic or tailgate, or on a car trip.
—TerryAnn Moore, Vineland, NJ

- -

PREP: 15 min. + standing • **MAKES:** 2 qt.

- 6 cups Rice Chex
- 2 cups Chocolate Chex
- 1 cup semisweet chocolate chips
- ½ cup seedless strawberry jam
- 3 Tbsp. butter
- 1 tsp. almond extract
- 2 cups ground almonds
- 1 cup white baking chips
  Sprinkles, optional

1. In a large bowl, combine the cereals. In a microwave, melt the chocolate chips, jam and butter; stir until smooth. Add almond extract. Pour over cereal mixture and toss to coat. Sprinkle with almonds; toss to coat.
2. Immediately spread onto waxed paper. In a microwave, melt white chips; stir until smooth. Drizzle over cereal mixture. If desired, add sprinkles. Let stand until set. Break into pieces.
3. Store snack mix in an airtight container.

¾ CUP: 443 cal., 24g fat (9g sat. fat), 11mg chol., 231mg sod., 55g carb. (33g sugars, 3g fiber), 7g pro.

SUMMER FRESH PASTA SALAD

(SHOWN ON PAGE 273)

We love to enjoy fresh fruits and veggies in season. I first made this fast and easy salad for dinner one day while preparing lunch. I served the salad with almond crackers and sharp cheddar cheese slices. So tasty!
—Cathy Orban, Chandler, AZ

- -

PREP: 20 min. + chilling • **MAKES:** 12 servings

- 4 cups uncooked campanelle or spiral pasta
- 2 medium carrots, finely chopped
- 2 medium peaches, chopped
- 1 pouch (11 oz.) light tuna in water
- ½ cup sliced celery
- ½ cup julienned cucumber
- ½ cup julienned zucchini
- ½ cup fresh broccoli florets, chopped
- ½ cup grated red cabbage
- ½ tsp. salt
- ½ tsp. pepper
- 2 cups Caesar salad dressing

1. Cook pasta according to the package directions for al dente. Drain; rinse with cold water and drain well. Transfer to a large bowl. Add carrots, peaches, tuna, celery, cucumber, zucchini, broccoli, cabbage, salt and pepper. Drizzle with dressing; toss to coat.
2. Refrigerated, covered, at least 3 hours before serving.

¾ CUP: 357 cal., 23g fat (4g sat. fat), 25mg chol., 651mg sod., 26g carb. (5g sugars, 2g fiber), 10g pro.

HOW-TO

Let Fun Times Ring!

To pass time until the main event, line up bottles (full or empty) of your favorite sipper in a wooden crate, and get to tossing!

Mason jar rings wrapped with yarn are an easy craft—and perfect for making soft landings. Fire away.

FRIGHT NIGHT FLICKS

GRAB A SECURITY
BLANKET AND STOCK
UP ON SNACKS. IT'S A
FEARSOME FILM FEST
FOR YOUR BRAVEST
MOVIE BUFFS.

Vampire Killer
Martini

Garlic Pizza Wedges

VAMPIRE KILLER MARTINI

If you're going to hang with vampires, you're going to need a strong drink. A little garlic helps, too!
—Taste of Home *Test Kitchen*

PREP: 5 min. + standing • **MAKES:** 8 servings

- 1 serrano pepper, seeded and quartered
- 2 garlic cloves, crushed
- 1 lemon zest strip (2 in.)
- 1½ cups vodka
- Ice

GARNISH
- Pickled baby beets

1. Place pepper, garlic, lemon zest strip and vodka in a large glass or plastic container. Cover and let stand at room temperature for 1 week.
2. For each serving, fill a shaker three-fourths full with ice. Add 1½ oz. infused vodka to shaker; cover and shake until condensation forms on outside of shaker, 10-15 seconds. Strain into a chilled martini glass. Garnish with a beet.

1½ OZ.: 96 cal., 0 fat (0 sat. fat), 0 chol., 0 sod., 0 carb. (0 sugars, 0 fiber), 0 pro.

GARLIC PIZZA WEDGES

Our pastor made this for a get-together, and my husband and I just couldn't stay away from the hors d'oeuvres table. The cheesy slices taste great served warm.
—Krysten Johnson, Simi Valley, CA

TAKES: 25 min. • **MAKES:** 2 dozen

- 1 prebaked 12-in. pizza crust
- 1 cup grated Parmesan cheese
- 1 cup mayonnaise
- 1 small red onion, chopped
- 3½ tsp. minced garlic
- 1 Tbsp. dried oregano
- Alfredo sauce, optional

Place crust on an ungreased 14-in. pizza pan. In a small bowl, combine Parmesan cheese, mayonnaise, onion, garlic and oregano; spread over crust. Bake at 450° until edges are lightly browned, 8-10 minutes. Cut into wedges. If desired, serve with Alfredo sauce.

1 PIECE: 119 cal., 8g fat (2g sat. fat), 4mg chol., 193mg sod., 8g carb. (0 sugars, 0 fiber), 3g pro.

Apple-Brined Turkey

A GLORIOUS THANKSGIVING

On the biggest feasting day of all, you want tried-and-true favorites that make guests extra grateful. These are the back-for-seconds recipes our readers can't get enough of.

Triple Cranberry Sauce

Sunday Dinner
Mashed Potatoes

**SUNDAY DINNER
MASHED POTATOES**

MAPLE & BACON GLAZED BRUSSELS SPROUTS

Here's a fantastic side dish even children will love. The sweet maple syrup and smoky bacon are Brussels sprouts' best friends.
—Jan Valdez, Chicago, IL

PREP: 15 min. • **COOK:** 20 min.
MAKES: 4 servings

5	bacon strips, chopped
1	lb. fresh Brussels sprouts, trimmed
3	Tbsp. butter
½	cup chicken broth
¼	cup chopped pecans
¼	cup maple syrup
¼	tsp. salt
¼	tsp. pepper

1. In a small skillet, cook bacon over medium heat until crisp. Remove to paper towels with a slotted spoon; drain.
2. Meanwhile, cut an X in the core of each Brussels sprout. In a large skillet, saute sprouts in butter until lightly browned, 4-5 minutes.
3. Stir in the broth, pecans, maple syrup, salt and pepper. Bring to a boil. Reduce heat; cover and simmer for 5 minutes. Uncover; cook and stir until Brussels sprouts are tender, 8-10 minutes longer. Sprinkle with bacon.
¾ CUP: *273 cal., 18g fat (7g sat. fat), 32mg chol., 544mg sod., 25g carb. (15g sugars, 5g fiber), 8g pro.*

READER REVIEW

"The best recipe for Brussels sprouts I have ever tasted, and everybody loves them!"
—MINDYPAULSON, TASTEOFHOME.COM

SUNDAY DINNER MASHED POTATOES

Sour cream and cream cheese give these potatoes their delicious flavor. The dish can be prepped in advance and is special enough to serve guests.
—Melody Mellinger, Myerstown, PA

PREP: 35 min. • **BAKE:** 20 min.
MAKES: 8 servings

5	lbs. potatoes, peeled and cubed
1	cup sour cream
1	pkg. (8 oz.) cream cheese, softened
3	Tbsp. butter, divided
1	tsp. salt
1	tsp. onion salt
¼	tsp. pepper

1. Place potatoes in a Dutch oven; cover with water. Cover and bring to a boil. Cook until very tender, 20-25 minutes; drain well.
2. In a large bowl, mash potatoes. Add the sour cream, cream cheese, 2 Tbsp. butter, salt, onion salt and pepper; beat until fluffy.
3. Transfer to a greased 2-qt. baking dish. Dot with the remaining butter. Bake, uncovered, at 350° until heated through, 20-25 minutes.
¾ CUP: *300 cal., 13g fat (9g sat. fat), 43mg chol., 617mg sod., 40g carb. (4g sugars, 3g fiber), 5g pro.*

MAPLE & BACON GLAZED BRUSSELS SPROUTS

YUMMY TEXAS PECAN PIE

YUMMY TEXAS PECAN PIE

This ooey-gooey pie's luscious and creamy filling offers that good old familiar flavor so many of us love!
—*Laurel Leslie, Sonora, CA*

PREP: 20 min. • **BAKE:** 70 min.
MAKES: 8 servings

- ½ cup sugar
- 3 Tbsp. all-purpose flour
- 1 cup light corn syrup
- 1 cup dark corn syrup
- 3 large eggs
- 1 tsp. white vinegar
- ½ tsp. vanilla extract
- 1 cup chopped pecans
     Pastry for single-crust pie

1. In a large bowl, whisk the sugar, flour, corn syrups, eggs, vinegar and vanilla until smooth. Stir in pecans. On a floured surface, roll out dough to fit a 9-in. pie plate; trim and flute edges. Pour filling into crust. Cover edges with foil.

2. Bake at 350° for 35 minutes. Remove foil; bake until puffed and golden (center will still wobble), 35-45 minutes. Cool on a wire rack. Refrigerate leftovers.

1 PIECE: *543 cal., 20g fat (5g sat. fat), 84mg chol., 215mg sod., 93g carb. (36g sugars, 2g fiber), 5g pro.*

HOW-TO

Make a Pie Shield

To avoid burning, fold a foil square in half twice (into a smaller square) and cut a ring. Gently drape it over pie edges before you begin to bake.

SLOW-COOKED SAUSAGE DRESSING

SLOW-COOKED SAUSAGE DRESSING

This savory dressing gets amped up with apples and pecans. It cooks easily in a slow cooker, so the stove and oven are free for all of your other dishes!
—*Raquel Haggard, Edmond, OK*

PREP: 20 min. • **COOK:** 3 hours
MAKES: 12 servings

- 7 cups seasoned stuffing cubes or croutons
- 1 medium tart apple, chopped
- ⅓ cup chopped pecans
- 1½ tsp. rubbed sage
- ½ tsp. pepper
- ½ lb. reduced-fat bulk pork sausage
- 1 large onion, chopped
- 2 celery ribs, chopped
- 1 can (14½ oz.) reduced-sodium chicken broth
- 2 Tbsp. reduced-fat butter, melted

1. Combine the first 5 ingredients. In a nonstick skillet, cook and crumble sausage with onion and celery over medium-high heat until no longer pink, 4-5 minutes; drain. Add to stuffing mixture; stir in the broth and butter. Transfer to a greased 5-qt. slow cooker.

2. Cook, covered, on low 3-4 hours, until apple is tender, stirring once.

⅔ CUP: *201 cal., 8g fat (2g sat. fat), 17mg chol., 640mg sod., 26g carb. (4g sugars, 3g fiber), 7g pro.*

TRIPLE CRANBERRY SAUCE

SWEET & TANGY CARROTS

With a brown sugar-mustard sauce, these simple simmered carrots bring bright flavor and color to the table.
—Paula Zsiray, Logan, UT

TAKES: 20 min. • **MAKES:** 8 servings

- 2 lbs. carrots, sliced
- ¼ tsp. salt
- ½ cup packed brown sugar
- 3 Tbsp. butter
- 2 Tbsp. Dijon mustard
- ¼ tsp. white pepper
- 2 Tbsp. minced fresh parsley

1. Place 1 in. of water, carrots and salt in a large saucepan; bring to a boil. Reduce heat; cover and simmer until tender, 15-20 minutes. Drain.

2. Return carrots to pan; add the brown sugar, butter, mustard and pepper. Cook and stir over low heat until coated. Sprinkle with parsley. Serve with a slotted spoon.

½ **CUP:** *143 cal., 5g fat (3g sat. fat), 11mg chol., 257mg sod., 25g carb. (21g sugars, 3g fiber), 1g pro.*

TRIPLE CRANBERRY SAUCE

This keepsake sauce recipe—with cranberry goodness in three forms, plus orange and allspice—is the only one you will ever need.
—Arlene Smulski, Lyons, IL

PREP: 10 min. • **COOK:** 15 min. + chilling • **MAKES:** 3 cups

- 1 pkg. (12 oz.) fresh or frozen cranberries
- 1 cup thawed cranberry juice concentrate
- ½ cup dried cranberries
- ⅓ cup sugar
- 3 Tbsp. orange juice
- 3 Tbsp. orange marmalade
- 2 tsp. grated orange zest
- ¼ tsp. ground allspice

1. In a small saucepan, combine the cranberries, cranberry juice concentrate, dried cranberries and sugar. Cook over medium heat until the berries pop, about 15 minutes.

2. Remove from the heat; stir in the orange juice, marmalade, orange zest and allspice. Transfer to a small bowl; refrigerate until chilled.

¼ **CUP:** *113 cal., 0 fat (0 sat. fat), 0 chol., 4mg sod., 29g carb. (24g sugars, 2g fiber), 0 pro.*

SWEET & TANGY CARROTS

APPLE-BRINED TURKEY

(SHOWN ON PAGE 278)
The sweet apple juice-based brine helps produce a juicy, amber-colored turkey that's bursting with flavor. You won't regret planning for the long brine time—this tasty grilled turkey is worth every minute.
—Trudy Williams, Shannonville, ON

PREP: 30 min. + brining
GRILL: 3 hours + standing
MAKES: 14 servings

2 qt. unsweetened apple juice
2½ cups packed brown sugar
1 cup kosher salt
4 oz. fresh gingerroot, peeled and thinly sliced
15 whole cloves
6 garlic cloves, crushed
3 bay leaves
3 medium oranges, quartered
3 qt. cold water
1 turkey (12 to 14 lbs.)
2 turkey-size oven roasting bags
2 Tbsp. canola oil

1. To make the brine, in a large kettle, combine the first 7 ingredients. Bring to a boil; cook and stir until salt and sugar are dissolved. Stir in oranges. Remove from the heat. Add cold water to cool the brine to room temperature.
2. Remove giblets from turkey (discard or save for another use). Place 1 oven roasting bag inside the second roasting bag; place turkey in inner bag. Carefully pour cooled brine into inner bag. Squeeze out as much air as possible; seal bags and turn to coat. Place in a roasting pan or other large container. Refrigerate for 18-24 hours, turning occasionally.
3. Prepare the grill for indirect heat. Drain turkey, discarding brine. Rinse turkey under cold water; pat dry. Rub oil over skin. Skewer turkey openings; tie drumsticks together.
4. Place breast side up on a rack in a disposable foil roasting pan. Grill, covered, over indirect medium heat 30-40 minutes. Tent turkey with foil; grill, covered, until a thermometer reads 165°, 2½-3 hours longer. Cover and let stand for 15 minutes before carving.
8 OZ. COOKED TURKEY: *473 cal., 23g fat (6g sat. fat), 210mg chol., 213mg sod., 1g carb. (1g sugars, 0 fiber), 62g pro.*

HERBED TURKEY GRAVY

HERBED TURKEY GRAVY

This traditional gravy recipe works for any roasted meat or poultry. You'll get eight ¼-cup servings in 2 cups of gravy.
—Taste of Home Test Kitchen

TAKES: 20 min. • **MAKES:** 2 cups

Turkey drippings
1 to 1½ cups chicken broth
¼ cup all-purpose flour
¼ tsp. dried thyme
¼ tsp. rubbed sage
¼ tsp. pepper

1. Pour drippings and loosened browned bits into a 2-cup measuring cup. Skim fat, reserving ¼ cup. Add enough broth to the drippings to measure 2 cups.
2. In a small saucepan, combine flour and reserved fat until smooth. Gradually stir in the drippings mixture. Stir in the thyme, sage and pepper. Bring to a boil; cook and stir until thickened, about 2 minutes.
¼ CUP: *74 cal., 7g fat (3g sat. fat), 7mg chol., 132mg sod., 3g carb. (0 sugars, 0 fiber), 1g pro.*

READER REVIEW

"Instead of thyme and sage, I used the Herbes de Provence I used on the turkey. It came out great!"
— COACHTOM, TASTEOFHOME.COM

GRANDMA'S HOLIDAY HANDBOOK

She knows the secrets to making Christmas feel effortlessly special. From the dishes you look forward to all year to the traditions that become lasting memories, here's how Grandma creates holiday magic time and time again.

Herbed Rib Roast

Mashed
Potatoes with Horseradish

Greens with
Hot Bacon Dressing

HERBED RIB ROAST

The aromatic mixture of herbs and garlic turns this tender roast into a real treat. Our children and grandchildren look forward to feasting on it at Christmastime and other special family occasions.
—Carol Jackson, South Berwick, ME

PREP: 10 min. • **BAKE:** 2 hours + standing
MAKES: 10 servings

- 1 beef ribeye roast (4 to 5 lbs.)
- 2 to 3 garlic cloves, thinly sliced
- 1 tsp. salt
- ½ tsp. pepper
- ½ tsp. dried basil
- ½ tsp. dried parsley flakes
- ½ tsp. dried marjoram

Cut 15-20 slits in the roast; insert garlic. Tie the roast at 1½-in. to 2-in. intervals with kitchen string. Combine salt, pepper, basil, parsley and marjoram; rub over roast. Place fat side up on a rack in a roasting pan. Bake, uncovered at 325° until meat reaches the desired doneness (for medium-rare, a thermometer should read 135°; medium, 140°; medium-well, 145°), 2-2½ hours. Let stand 15 minutes before slicing.

4 OZ. COOKED BEEF: *397 cal., 29g fat (12g sat. fat), 107mg chol., 319mg sod., 0 carb. (0 sugars, 0 fiber), 32g pro.*

GREENS WITH HOT BACON DRESSING

Growing up in a German community, I ate this salad often. It's an old traditional dish—I recall my grandmother talking about her mother making this recipe. As a variation, the old-timers in my family cut up some boiled potatoes on dinner plates, then serve the warm salad mixture over the top.
—Robert Enigk, Canastota, NY

TAKES: 20 min. • **MAKES:** 8 servings

- 4 cups torn fresh spinach
- 4 cups torn iceberg lettuce
- 3 celery ribs, sliced
- ½ cup chopped red onion
- 4 bacon strips, diced
- 1 large egg
- ⅔ cup water
- ⅓ cup cider vinegar
- 2 tsp. sugar
- 2 tsp. cornstarch
- ½ tsp. salt
- ¼ tsp. pepper

In a salad bowl, toss spinach, lettuce, celery and onion; set aside. In a large skillet, cook bacon until crisp; remove with a slotted spoon to paper towels to drain. Discard all but 2 Tbsp. drippings. In a small bowl, beat egg; add water and mix well. Add to the drippings. Combine vinegar, sugar, cornstarch, salt and pepper; add to skillet. Bring to a boil; stirring constantly. Remove from the heat; pour over salad. Add bacon. Toss and serve immediately.

1 SERVING: *93 cal., 7g fat (3g sat. fat), 34mg chol., 266mg sod., 5g carb. (3g sugars, 1g fiber), 3g pro.*

MASHED POTATOES WITH HORSERADISH

Instead of the ordinary garlic mashed potatoes, this unusual but delicious recipe calls for prepared horseradish. The side dish, which my family requests every Thanksgiving, is also fantastic with roast beef.
—Cynthia Gobeli, Norton, OH

TAKES: 25 min. • **MAKES:** 8 servings

- 6 medium potatoes, peeled and cubed
- ¼ cup butter, melted
- ¾ tsp. salt
- ⅛ tsp. pepper
- ½ cup sour cream
- 2 Tbsp. prepared horseradish

Place potatoes in a large saucepan and cover with water. Bring to a boil. Reduce heat and cook for 10 minutes or until tender; drain. Add butter, salt and pepper. Mash potatoes. Beat in the sour cream and horseradish.

1 CUP: *175 cal., 8g fat (5g sat. fat), 25mg chol., 301mg sod., 23g carb. (2g sugars, 2g fiber), 3g pro.*

**MASHED POTATOES
WITH HORSERADISH**

PARTY CHEESE BALLS

CRAN-RASPBERRY GELATIN SALAD

Just like Mom's, this pretty gelatin salad has full berry flavor without being too tart. It's perfect for any holiday dinner.
—Rosemary Burch, Phoenix, AZ

PREP: 15 min. + chilling • **MAKES:** 10 servings

- 2 pkg. (3 oz. each) raspberry gelatin
- 1 cup boiling water
- 1 can (14 oz.) whole-berry cranberry sauce
- 1 can (8 oz.) crushed pineapple, undrained
- 1 cup orange juice
  Sugared cranberries, optional

1. In a large bowl, dissolve gelatin in boiling water. Stir in the cranberry sauce, pineapple and orange juice. Pour into a 6-cup ring mold coated with cooking spray.
2. Cover and refrigerate until set, about 4 hours. Unmold onto a serving platter. If desired, garnish with sugared cranberries.
1 SERVING: 155 cal., 0 fat (0 sat. fat), 0 chol., 49mg sod., 39g carb. (32g sugars, 1g fiber), 2g pro.

PARTY CHEESE BALLS

These tangy cheese balls are guaranteed to spread cheer at your next gathering. The ingredients create a colorful presentation and a savory combination of flavors. As a grandmother who loves to cook, I send many pantry presents off to college.
—Shirley Hoerman, Nekoosa, WI

PREP: 20 min. + chilling
MAKES: 2 cheese balls (1¾ cups each)

- 1 pkg. (8 oz.) cream cheese, softened
- 2 cups shredded cheddar cheese
- 1 jar (5 oz.) sharp American cheese spread
- 1 jar (5 oz.) pimiento cheese spread
- 3 Tbsp. finely chopped onion
- 1 Tbsp. lemon juice
- 1 tsp. Worcestershire sauce
  Dash garlic salt
- ½ cup minced fresh parsley
- ½ cup chopped pecans, toasted
  Assorted crackers

1. In a large bowl, beat the first 8 ingredients until blended. Cover and refrigerate until easily handled, about 45 minutes.
2. Shape into 2 balls; roll in parsley and pecans. Cover and refrigerate. Remove from the refrigerator 15 minutes before serving with crackers.
2 TBSP.: 99 cal., 9g fat (5g sat. fat), 25mg chol., 188mg sod., 2g carb. (1g sugars, 0 fiber), 4g pro.

CRAN-RASPBERRY GELATIN SALAD

Plan Ahead with this Handy Timeline

The holidays will go off without a hitch thanks to this get-ready checklist.

2-3 Weeks Before:

• Plan the menu and create a grocery list from it.

1 Week Before:

• Stock up on nonperishables and beverages at the store.

• Start using up bulky items in your fridge and freezer to create space.

5 Days Before:

• If the turkey, ham or roast is frozen, determine how long it will take to thaw, and place in refrigerator when it's time.

3 Days Before:

• Buy the remaining groceries.

• Devise a warming strategy to ensure that dishes will be warm and ready to serve when needed.

1 Day Before:

• Set the table or buffet. (Label each serving dish with its respective recipe to make staying organized easy.)

• Prepare all the make-ahead dishes, and chop and measure as many ingredients as possible for the dishes that can't be made ahead.

• Put beverages in the fridge (or in the garage) to chill.

Morning of:

• Place the turkey, ham or roast in the oven.

• Finish preparing the remaining dishes.

Just Before Dinner:

• Arrange a bar so guests can pour themselves drinks.

• Set out any appetizers.

Pat yourself on the back and celebrate!

GRANDMA'S YEAST ROLLS

GRANDMA'S YEAST ROLLS

My grandmother used to make these rolls for family get-togethers and holidays. The applesauce may be an unexpected ingredient, but it adds so much flavor.
—Nancy Spoth, Festus, MO

- -

PREP: 20 min. + rising
BAKE: 15 min. + cooling
MAKES: 2 dozen

1   pkg. (¼ oz.) active dry yeast
1   cup 2% milk (110° to 115°)
¼   cup sugar
¼   cup unsweetened applesauce
2   large egg whites, room temperature, beaten
1   tsp. salt
3½ to 4 cups all-purpose flour

1. In a large bowl, dissolve yeast in warm milk. Add the sugar, applesauce, egg whites, salt and 2 cups flour; beat until smooth. Stir in enough remaining flour to form a soft dough.

2. Turn onto a lightly floured surface; knead until smooth and elastic, 6-8 minutes (dough will be slightly sticky). Place in a bowl coated with cooking spray, turning once to coat top. Cover and let rise in a warm place until doubled, about 1 hour.

3. Turn dough onto a lightly floured surface; divide into 24 pieces. Shape each portion into an 8-in. rope; tie into a knot. Place on 2 baking sheets coated with cooking spray.

4. Cover and let rise until doubled, about 30 minutes. Bake at 375° until golden brown, 12-16 minutes. Remove from pans to wire racks to cool.

1 ROLL: *83 cal., 1g fat (1g sat. fat), 1mg chol., 109mg sod., 17g carb. (0 sugars, 1g fiber), 3g pro.* **Diabetic exchanges:** *1 starch.*

Peppermint
Stick Dessert

Gingerbread

GINGERBREAD

My grandmother first made this over a century ago. As a child, I thought the kitchen smelled like heaven when Grandmother baked her gingerbread. The only thing better was when she took it out of the oven and served it with a generous topping of fresh whipped cream!
—Ellouise Halstead, Union Grove, WI

- -

PREP: 15 min. • **BAKE:** 20 min.
MAKES: 9 servings

- 1 large egg, room temperature, beaten
- ½ cup sugar
- ½ cup molasses
- 5 Tbsp. butter, melted
- ⅔ cup cold water
- 1½ cups all-purpose flour
- 1 tsp. baking soda
- 1 tsp. ground ginger
- ½ tsp. salt
  Whipped cream

Combine egg, sugar, molasses, butter and water; mix well. In a large bowl, stir together flour, baking soda, ginger and salt; add molasses mixture. Beat until well mixed. Pour into a greased 8-in. square baking pan. Bake at 350° until cake tests done, 20-25 minutes. Cut into squares; serve warm with whipped cream.

1 PIECE: 232 cal., 7g fat (4g sat. fat), 41mg chol., 350mg sod., 40g carb. (22g sugars, 1g fiber), 3g pro.

PEPPERMINT STICK DESSERT

With every spoonful of this cool and creamy trifle, my family goes back in time to when our Grandma Dagmar made it each Christmas. The minty, refreshing flavor can't be beat.
—Dianne Oertel, Racine, WI

- -

PREP: 20 min. + chilling • **MAKES:** 12 servings

- 8 oz. peppermint candy, crushed
- ½ cup half-and-half cream
- 1¼ tsp. unflavored gelatin
- 1 Tbsp. cold water
- 1½ cups heavy whipping cream, whipped
- 27 chocolate wafers

1. In a small saucepan, combine crushed candy and cream. Cook over low heat until candy is melted, stirring occasionally.

2. In a small bowl, sprinkle gelatin over water; let stand for 1 minute. Stir into hot peppermint mixture until dissolved. Refrigerate until mixture begins to set, about 20 minutes. Fold in whipped cream.

3. Crush 3 chocolate wafers; reserve for garnish. Line a 1½-qt. serving bowl with 12 wafers. Top with half of the peppermint mixture. Repeat layers. Sprinkle with the reserved chocolate crumbs. Refrigerate for at least 8 hours. If desired, sprinkle with additional crushed peppermint candy just before serving.

1 SERVING: 250 cal., 14g fat (8g sat. fat), 46mg chol., 103mg sod., 29g carb. (13g sugars, 0 fiber), 2g pro.

GRAM'S PLAN

It didn't matter if 30 people showed up for Christmas dinner: Grandma knew how to get everything on the table right on time and delicious as ever. How'd she do it all? These Field Editors share Grandma's simple secrets for a memory-making holiday.

"My grandmother used to keep her gravy in two large thermoses. That way it stayed hot but didn't take up extra stove space. She'd pour it into her gravy boat to serve."
—Susan Seymour, Valatie, NY

"If you're making a roast, cook, cool and slice it the day before (it's much easier to slice when cold), and arrange it in an oven-safe serving dish, drizzled with pan juices. The host can visit with guests while the roast warms at 325° in the oven."
**—Helen Nelander
Boulder Creek, CA**

"She would write out and post the menu for holiday meals on the refrigerator, always noting prep time needed, baking time and temperature. The menu list was written in order of time to start prep so everyone knew in what order things needed done."
—Julie Peterson, Crofton, MD

"My grandmother made cookie decorating an event. She had every Christmasy color of frosting imaginable, along with pretty sprinkles and sparkles— you couldn't help but be in the Christmas spirit!"
**—Gina Doieslager
Conway Springs, KS**

"One of her secrets was born of necessity, as kitchen real estate was at a premium: She stored all the desserts in the mudroom/ laundry room just off the kitchen to free up space on the kitchen table and counter. We had cookies, pies, cakes and more on top of the washer, dryer and deep freezer! A bonus: It kept everything a little cooler."
—Allison Ochoa, Hays, KS

"My grandma's secret was to let the kids open up gifts right away. That way the kids played away while she was able to finish cooking our meal."
—Anna Miller, Churdan, IA

Holiday Sweets & Treats

The best way to spread Christmas cheer is by making treats for all to share. These sweets of the season make spirits bright.

FESTIVE MERINGUE CHRISTMAS TREES

FESTIVE MERINGUE CHRISTMAS TREES

These whimsical meringues are eye-catching on the dessert table at a holiday party, and they taste heavenly! Look no further for the perfect treat to get you into the Christmas spirit.
—Jenni Sharp, Milwaukee, WI

- -

PREP: 20 min. • **BAKE:** 3 hours + standing
MAKES: about 26 meringues

- 3 **large egg whites**
- 1½ **tsp. clear or regular vanilla extract**
- ¼ **tsp. cream of tartar**
  Dash salt
- ⅔ **cup sugar**
  Green food coloring
  Assorted sprinkles
  Star nonpareils
  Confectioners' sugar, optional

1. Place egg whites in a large bowl; let stand at room temperature 30 minutes.
2. Preheat oven to 200°. Add vanilla, cream of tartar and salt to egg whites; beat on medium speed until foamy. Gradually add sugar, 1 Tbsp. at a time, beating on high after each addition until sugar is dissolved. Continue beating until stiff glossy peaks form, about 7 minutes. Tint with green food coloring and mix thoroughly.
3. Cut a small hole in the tip of a pastry bag; insert a large #828 open star tip. Transfer meringue to bag. Pipe 2-in.-diameter tree shapes 2 in. apart onto parchment-lined baking sheets; top with sprinkles and a star nonpareil.
4. Bake until firm to the touch, about 3 hours. Turn off oven and open door all the way; leave meringues in oven until cool. Remove meringues from parchment. If desired, sprinkle lightly with confectioners' sugar. Store in an airtight container at room temperature.
1 MERINGUE: *23 cal., 0 fat (0 sat. fat), 0 chol., 12mg sod., 5g carb. (5g sugars, 0 fiber), 0 pro.*

CHOCOLATE ANGEL FOOD CANDY

CHOCOLATE ANGEL FOOD CANDY

You might want to hide this candy until Christmas. Also called fairy food or sponge candy, it's crunchy, honeycombed, chocolate-covered and irresistible.
—Geralyn Emmerich, Hubertus, WI

- -

PREP: 20 min. • **COOK:** 20 min. + cooling
MAKES: about 1¼ lbs.

- 1 **tsp. butter**
- 1 **cup sugar**
- 1 **cup dark corn syrup**
- 1 **Tbsp. white vinegar**
- 1 **Tbsp. baking soda**
- ½ **lb. dark chocolate candy coating, coarsely chopped**
- 1 **tsp. shortening, divided**
- ½ **lb. milk chocolate candy coating, coarsely chopped**

1. Line a 9-in. square pan with foil and grease foil with butter; set aside. In a large heavy saucepan, combine the sugar, corn syrup and vinegar. Cook and stir over medium heat until sugar is dissolved. Bring to a boil. Cook, without stirring, until a candy thermometer reads 300° (hard-crack stage).
2. Remove from heat; stir in baking soda. Immediately pour into prepared pan; do not spread candy. Cool. Using foil, lift candy out of the pan. Gently peel off foil; break candy into pieces.
3. In a microwave, melt dark chocolate coating and ½ tsp. shortening; stir until smooth. Dip half the candies into the melted dark chocolate mixture, allowing excess to drip off. Place on waxed paper; let stand until set. Repeat with milk chocolate coating and remaining ½ tsp. shortening and candies. Store in an airtight container.
2 OZ.: *413 cal., 14g fat (12g sat. fat), 1mg chol., 431mg sod., 76g carb. (57g sugars, 1g fiber), 1g pro.*

LIME-IN-THE-COCONUT
ALMOND BARK

2 cups butter, softened
1 cup confectioners' sugar
1 tsp. vanilla extract
3½ cups all-purpose flour
1 cup chopped toasted pecans
8 oz. white candy coating, melted
⅓ to ½ cup crushed candy canes

1. Cream butter, sugar and vanilla until fluffy. Gradually beat in flour. Stir in pecans. Chill, covered, until firm enough to shape, 3-4 hours.

2. Preheat oven to 350°. Shape dough into 1-in. balls. Place 2 in. apart on ungreased baking sheets.

3. Bake until lightly browned, about 15 minutes. Remove from pans to wire racks; cool completely.

4. Dip tops of cookies into melted candy coating; dip into crushed candy. Let stand until set.

1 COOKIE: 123 cal., 9g fat (5g sat. fat), 16mg chol., 49mg sod., 11g carb. (5g sugars, 0 fiber), 1g pro.

 REINDEER MUNCH

This crunchy, salty-sweet mix disappears in a hurry from snack tables.
—Mary Newsom, Grand Ridge, FL

TAKES: 15 min. • **MAKES:** 25 cups

1 pkg. (24 oz.) roasted peanuts
1 pkg. (19.6 oz.) Golden Grahams cereal
1 pkg. (15 oz.) raisins
½ cup butter, cubed
12 oz. white candy coating, coarsely chopped
2 cups creamy peanut butter
1 pkg. (2 lbs.) confectioners' sugar
2½ cups red and green milk chocolate M&M's

1. In a large bowl, combine the peanuts, cereal and raisins. In a microwave, melt the butter, candy coating and peanut butter; stir until smooth. Pour over cereal mixture and toss to coat.

2. Working in batches, place sugar in a large bag; add coated mixture. Close bag and shake to coat. Spread onto baking sheets; sprinkle with M&M's. When cool, store in airtight containers.

¾ CUP: 594 cal., 29g fat (10g sat. fat), 10mg chol., 443mg sod., 79g carb. (60g sugars, 4g fiber), 11g pro.

LIME-IN-THE-COCONUT ALMOND BARK

I love the combination of flavors in this tropical treat, and it takes mere minutes to make.
—Julie Beckwith, Crete, IL

TAKES: 25 min. • **MAKES:** about 1 lb.

1 pkg. (10 to 12 oz.) white baking chips
4 tsp. shortening
2 to 4 drops green food coloring, optional
½ cup sweetened shredded coconut, toasted
½ cup chopped almonds, toasted
4 tsp. grated lime zest

1. Line a 9-in. square baking pan with foil; set aside. In a microwave, melt chips and shortening; stir until smooth. Stir in green food coloring if desired. Stir in the coconut, almonds and lime zest. Spread into prepared pan. Chill until firm, 10-15 minutes.

2. Break into small pieces. Store in an airtight container at room temperature.

1 OZ.: 143 cal., 10g fat (5g sat. fat), 2mg chol., 24mg sod., 13g carb. (12g sugars, 1g fiber), 2g pro.

CANDY CANE SNOWBALLS

Leftover candy canes inspired this festive Christmas cookie recipe.
—Debby Anderson, Stockbridge, GA

PREP: 30 min. + chilling
BAKE: 15 min. + cooling
MAKES: about 5 dozen

OLD-FASHIONED STOLLEN

Stollen is a traditional German Christmas bread. The fruit-filled loaf topped with confectioners' sugar icing and candied fruit has a shape like a giant Parker House roll.
—Linda Hinners, Brookfield, WI

PREP: 30 min. + rising
BAKE: 25 min. + cooling
MAKES: 3 loaves (12 slices each)

- 2 pkg. (¼ oz. each) active dry yeast
- ½ tsp. plus ½ cup sugar, divided
- ½ cup warm water (110° to 115°)
- 1 cup warm milk (110° to 115°)
- ¾ cup butter, softened
- 1½ tsp. salt
- ½ tsp. ground cardamom
- 2 large eggs plus 2 egg yolks, room temperature
- 6¼ to 6¾ cups all-purpose flour
- ½ cup raisins
- ½ cup diced citron or mixed candied fruit and peel
- ½ cup sliced candied cherries
  Melted butter

ICING
- 1 cup confectioners' sugar
- 5 to 6 tsp. whole milk
  Blanched whole almonds, coarsely chopped, and additional candied fruit

1. In a large bowl, dissolve the yeast and ½ tsp. sugar in warm water; let stand for 5 minutes. Add the milk, butter, salt, cardamom, eggs, egg yolks, remaining ½ cup sugar and 2 cups flour; beat until smooth. Stir in the raisins, citron, candied cherries and enough remaining flour to form a soft dough.

2. Turn out onto a lightly floured surface; knead until smooth and elastic, 6-8 minutes. Place in a greased bowl, turning once to grease top. Cover and let rise in a warm place until doubled, about 1¼ hours.

3. Punch down; divide into thirds. Roll each piece on a floured surface into a 10x6-in. oval. Brush with melted butter. Fold 1 long side over to within 1 in. of the opposite side. Press edges to seal. Place on greased baking sheets. Brush with melted butter. Cover and let rise until doubled, about 45 minutes.

4. Bake at 375° until lightly browned, about 25 minutes. For icing, combine confectioners' sugar and milk; spread over cooled bread. Decorate with almonds and additional fruit.

1 SLICE: *172 cal., 5g fat (3g sat. fat), 35mg chol., 156mg sod., 29g carb. (12g sugars, 1g fiber), 3g pro.*

OLD-FASHIONED STOLLEN

GINGER BUDDIES

Classic gingerbread men get a fresh batch of
new friends that are anything but cookie-cutter.

They're Wilton daisy sprinkles!

Use white sprinkles for fur!

It's a starburst candy!

GINGERBREAD COOKIE CUTOUTS

My kids linger around the kitchen when these aromatic cookies are baking. I make them throughout the year using a variety of cookie cutters. Decorating them with the family can be so much fun.
—Christy Thelen, Kellogg, IA

PREP: 30 min. + chilling
BAKE: 10 min./batch + cooling
MAKES: 5 dozen

- ¾ cup butter, softened
- 1 cup packed brown sugar
- 1 large egg, room temperature
- ¾ cup molasses
- 4 cups all-purpose flour
- 1½ tsp. baking soda
- ¼ tsp. salt
- 2 tsp. ground ginger
- 1½ tsp. ground cinnamon
- ¾ tsp. ground cloves
  Icing and decorations of choice
  (we used Royal Icing, at right)

1. Cream butter and brown sugar until light and fluffy, 5-7 minutes. Beat in egg and molasses. In another bowl, whisk together flour, baking soda, salt and spices; gradually beat into creamed mixture. Divide dough in half; shape each into a disk. Wrap and refrigerate, covered, until firm enough to roll, 4 hours or overnight.
2. Preheat oven to 350°. On a lightly floured surface, roll dough to ⅛-in. thickness. Cut 60 gingerbread men using a floured 3½-in. cookie cutter. Place 2 in. apart on ungreased baking sheets. If desired, cut sixty 1¼-in. triangles for hats; attach to gingerbread cutouts, pressing edges to seal. If desired, cut sixty ¼-in. circles; attach to hats for pompoms.
3. Bake cookies until edges are firm, 8-10 minutes. Remove to wire racks; cool completely.
4. Ice and decorate cookies as desired. Store between layers of waxed paper in an airtight container.
1 COOKIE: *78 cal., 2g fat (2g sat. fat), 9mg chol., 64mg sod., 13g carb. (7g sugars, 0 fiber), 1g pro.*

ROYAL ICING

This classic decorating icing sets up and dries quickly. It's nice to use when cookies will be stacked on a plate.
—Taste of Home *Test Kitchen*

TAKES: 10 min. • **MAKES:** about 1 cup

- 2 cups confectioners' sugar
- 2 Tbsp. plus 2 tsp. water
- 4½ tsp. meringue powder
- ¼ tsp. cream of tartar
  Food coloring, optional

1. In a small bowl, combine the confectioners' sugar, water, meringue powder and cream of tartar; beat on low speed just until combined. Beat on high for 4-5 minutes or until stiff peaks form. Tint with food coloring if desired. Keep unused icing covered at all times with a damp cloth. If necessary, beat again on high speed to restore texture.
2. Color icing and decorate cookies as desired.
1 TSP.: *24 cal., 0 fat (0 sat. fat), 0 chol., 3mg sod., 6g carb. (6g sugars, 0 fiber), 0 pro.*

OMA'S MARZIPAN STOLLEN

My German grandma made this stollen for us when we were young. I love its homey taste and how it reminds me of her and the German food she made. I often freeze the dough once it's shaped into a braid—then I can pull it out the night before, let it rise on the counter overnight, and bake it in the morning.
—Abigail Leszczynski, Beaufort, SC

PREP: 30 min. + rising
BAKE: 30 min. + cooling
MAKES: 1 loaf (16 slices)

- 3 to 3½ cups all-purpose flour
- ⅓ cup sugar
- 1 pkg. (¼ oz.) active dry yeast
- 1¼ cups 2% milk
- 6 Tbsp. butter, cubed
- 2 tsp. grated lemon zest

FILLING

- 1 can (12½ oz.) almond cake and pastry filling
- 1 cup finely ground almonds
- 1 Tbsp. 2% milk
- 1 tsp. rum extract

GLAZE

- ¼ cup confectioners' sugar
- ½ to 1 tsp. 2% milk

OMA'S MARZIPAN STOLLEN

1. In a large bowl, combine 2 cups flour, sugar and yeast. In a small saucepan, heat milk and butter to 120°-130°. Add to dry ingredients; beat just until moistened. Add lemon zest; beat until smooth. Stir in enough remaining flour to form a soft dough (dough will be sticky).
2. Turn onto a floured surface; knead until smooth and elastic, 6-8 minutes. Place in a greased bowl, turning once to grease the top. Cover and let rise in a warm place until doubled, about 1 hour.
3. For filling, in a large bowl, beat almond pastry filling, almonds, milk and extract. Punch dough down; turn onto a floured surface. Divide into thirds. Roll each portion into a 15x6-in. rectangle. Spread each portion with a third of the filling to within ¼ in. of edges. Roll up jelly-roll style, starting with a long slide; pinch seam to seal. Place ropes on a parchment-lined baking sheet. Using a sharp knife, make a ½-in.-deep cut lengthwise down the center of each rope, stopping ½ in. from ends. Keeping cut surfaces facing up, braid ropes. Pinch ends to seal; tuck under.
4. Cover with a kitchen towel; let rise in a warm place until almost doubled, about 30 minutes. Preheat oven to 375°. Bake until golden brown, 30-35 minutes. Remove to a wire rack to cool. Combine the glaze ingredients to desired consistency; drizzle over stollen.
1 SLICE: *270 cal., 10g fat (4g sat. fat), 13mg chol., 73mg sod., 41g carb. (16g sugars, 2g fiber), 5g pro.*

CHAMPAGNE WISHES

It's a roaring-good time at this New Year's Eve bash that's big on bubbles, bling and all the best bites.

Honey Champagne Fondue

Champagne
Blondies

Mango
Bellini

HONEY CHAMPAGNE FONDUE

This special champagne fondue has wonderful flavor from Swiss cheese and a hint of sweetness from honey. It clings well to any kind of dipper.
—*Shannon Copley, Upper Arlington, OH*

TAKES: 30 min. • **MAKES:** 4 cups

- 1 Tbsp. cornstarch
- 1 tsp. ground mustard
- ¼ tsp. white pepper
- 1¼ cups champagne
- 1 tsp. lemon juice
- 2 Tbsp. finely chopped shallot
- 1 garlic clove, minced
- 1½ lbs. Swiss cheese, shredded
- 2 Tbsp. honey
  Pinch ground nutmeg
  Toasted French bread, asparagus, tart apple slices, endive spears or cooked shrimp

1. In a large saucepan, combine cornstarch, ground mustard and white pepper. Whisk in champagne and lemon juice until smooth. Add shallot and garlic; bring to a boil. Reduce heat to medium-low; cook and stir until thickened, about 1 minute. Gradually stir in cheese until melted. Stir in honey. Sprinkle with nutmeg.
2. Keep warm in a fondue pot or small slow cooker. Serve fondue with toasted bread, asparagus, apple slices, endive or cooked shrimp as desired.
¼ **CUP:** *256 cal., 18g fat (10g sat. fat), 53mg chol., 107mg sod., 5g carb. (3g sugars, 0 fiber), 15g pro.*

HONEY CHAMPAGNE FONDUE

MANGO BELLINI

MANGO BELLINI

Simple yet delicious, this mango Bellini is made with fresh mango puree and your favorite sparkling wine—I usually choose Prosecco for mine. You can easily turn it into a mocktail by using sparkling water in place of the wine.
—*Ellen Folkman, Crystal Beach, FL*

TAKES: 5 min. • **MAKES:** 6 servings

- ¾ cup mango nectar or fresh mango puree, chilled
- 1 bottle (750 ml) champagne or other sparkling wine, chilled

Add 2 Tbsp. mango nectar to each of 6 champagne flutes. Top with champagne; gently stir to combine.
1 BELLINI: *101 cal., 0 fat (0 sat. fat), 0 chol., 1mg sod., 6g carb. (4g sugars, 0 fiber), 0 pro.*

ROASTED CURRY CHICKPEAS

For a low-fat snacking sensation, try toasting chickpeas with simple seasonings. This rivals calorie-laden snacks you'd find in the store.
—Taste of Home *Test Kitchen*

TAKES: 30 min. • **MAKES:** 1 cup

- 1 can (15 oz.) chickpeas or garbanzo beans
- 2 Tbsp. olive oil
- 1 tsp. salt
- ¼ tsp. pepper
- 2 tsp. curry powder
- ½ tsp. crushed red pepper flakes

Rinse and drain chickpeas; place on paper towels and pat dry. Place in a greased 15x10x1-in. baking pan; drizzle with oil and sprinkle with seasonings. Toss to coat. Bake at 450° until crispy and golden brown, 25-30 minutes.

¼ CUP: *162 cal., 9g fat (1g sat. fat), 0 chol., 728mg sod., 17g carb. (3g sugars, 5g fiber), 4g pro.*

READER REVIEW

"My family loved this. We like spicy food, so this snack had just the right amount of heat for us!"
— ANGEL182009, TASTEOFHOME.COM

ROASTED CURRY CHICKPEAS

CHAMPAGNE BLONDIES

CHAMPAGNE BLONDIES

I was looking for a fun champagne recipe to take to a friend's bridal shower, but I couldn't find one. That's when I came up with this twist on blondies. The recipe calls for white chocolate chips, but sometimes I like to use butterscotch or even chocolate instead.
—Heather Karow, Burnett, WI

PREP: 25 min. • **BAKE:** 25 min. + cooling • **MAKES:** 16 servings

- ½ cup butter, softened
- 1 cup packed light brown sugar
- 1 large egg, room temperature
- ¼ cup champagne
- 1¼ cups all-purpose flour
- 1 tsp. baking powder
- ¼ tsp. salt
- ½ cup white baking chips
- ½ cup chopped hazelnuts, optional

GLAZE
- 1 cup confectioners' sugar
- 2 Tbsp. champagne

1. Preheat oven to 350°. Line an 8-in. square baking pan with parchment, letting ends extend up sides. In a large bowl, beat butter and brown sugar until crumbly, about 2 minutes. Beat in egg and champagne (batter may appear curdled). In another bowl, whisk flour, baking powder and salt; gradually add to butter mixture. Fold in baking chips and, if desired, nuts.
2. Spread into prepared pan. Bake until edges are brown and center is set (do not overbake), 25-30 minutes. Cool completely in pan on a wire rack.
3. Combine glaze ingredients; drizzle over blondies. Lifting with parchment, remove blondies from pan. Cut into bars. Store in an airtight container.

1 BLONDIE: *203 cal., 8g fat (5g sat. fat), 28mg chol., 126mg sod., 32g carb. (24g sugars, 0 fiber), 2g pro.*

Substitutions & Equivalents

EQUIVALENT MEASURES

3 TEASPOONS	= 1 tablespoon		16 TABLESPOONS	= 1 cup
4 TABLESPOONS	= ¼ cup		2 CUPS	= 1 pint
5⅓ TABLESPOONS	= ⅓ cup		4 CUPS	= 1 quart
8 TABLESPOONS	= ½ cup		4 QUARTS	= 1 gallon

FOOD EQUIVALENTS

EGG NOODLES	4 ounces (3 cups) uncooked	= 4 cups cooked
MACARONI	4 ounces (1 cup) uncooked	= 2½ cups cooked
POPCORN	⅓ to ½ cup unpopped	= 8 cups popped
RICE, LONG GRAIN	1 cup uncooked	= 3 cups cooked
RICE, QUICK-COOKING	1 cup uncooked	= 2 cups cooked
SPAGHETTI	2 ounces uncooked	= 1 cup cooked
BREAD	1 slice	= ¾ cup soft crumbs, ¼ cup fine dry crumbs
GRAHAM CRACKERS	7 squares	= ½ cup finely crushed
BUTTERY ROUND CRACKERS	12 crackers	= ½ cup finely crushed
SALTINE CRACKERS	14 crackers	= ½ cup finely crushed
BANANA	1 medium	= ⅓ cup mashed
LEMON	1 medium	= 3 tablespoons juice, 2 teaspoons grated zest
LIME	1 medium	= 2 tablespoons juice, 1½ teaspoons grated zest
ORANGE	1 medium	= ¼–⅓ cup juice, 4 teaspoons grated zest

CABBAGE	1 head = 5 cups shredded		GREEN PEPPER	1 large = 1 cup chopped
CARROTS	1 pound = 3 cups shredded		MUSHROOMS	½ pound = 3 cups sliced
CELERY	1 rib = ½ cup chopped		ONION	1 medium = ½ cup chopped
CORN	1 ear fresh = ⅔ cup kernels		POTATOES	3 medium = 2 cups cubed
ALMONDS	1 pound = 3 cups chopped		PECANS	1 pound = 3¾ cups chopped
GROUND NUTS	3¾ ounces = 1 cup		WALNUTS	1 pound = 4½ cups chopped

EASY SUBSTITUTIONS

WHEN YOU NEED...		USE...
BAKING POWDER	1 teaspoon	½ teaspoon cream of tartar + ¼ teaspoon baking soda
BUTTERMILK	1 cup	1 tablespoon lemon juice or vinegar + enough milk to measure 1 cup (let stand 5 minutes before using)
CORNSTARCH	1 tablespoon	2 tablespoons all-purpose flour
HONEY	1 cup	1¼ cups sugar + ¼ cup water
HALF-AND-HALF CREAM	1 cup	1 tablespoon melted butter + enough whole milk to measure 1 cup
ONION	1 small, chopped (⅓ cup)	1 teaspoon onion powder or 1 tablespoon dried minced onion
TOMATO JUICE	1 cup	½ cup tomato sauce + ½ cup water
TOMATO SAUCE	2 cups	¾ cup tomato paste + 1 cup water
UNSWEETENED CHOCOLATE	1 square (1 ounce)	3 tablespoons baking cocoa + 1 tablespoon shortening or oil
WHOLE MILK	1 cup	½ cup evaporated milk + ½ cup water

Cooking Terms

AL DENTE An Italian term meaning "to the tooth." Used to describe pasta that is cooked but still firm.

BASTE To moisten food with melted butter, pan drippings, marinade or other liquid to add flavor and juiciness.

BEAT To mix rapidly with a spoon, fork, wire whisk or electric mixer.

BLEND To combine ingredients until just mixed.

BOIL To heat liquids until bubbles that cannot be stirred down are formed. In the case of water, the temperature will reach 212 degrees at sea level.

BONE To remove all bones from meat, poultry or fish.

BROIL To cook food 4 to 6 inches from a direct, radiant heat source.

CREAM To blend ingredients to a smooth consistency by beating; frequently done with butter and sugar for baking.

CUT IN To break down and distribute cold butter, margarine or shortening into a flour mixture with a pastry blender or two knives.

DASH A measurement less than ⅛ teaspoon that is used for herbs, spices and hot pepper sauce. This is not a precise measurement.

DREDGE To coat foods with flour or other dry ingredients. Most often done with pot roasts and stew meat before browning.

FLUTE To make a V shape or scalloped edge on pie crust with your thumb and fingers.

FOLD To blend dissimilar ingredients by careful and gentle turning with a spatula. Used most commonly to incorporate whipped cream, beaten egg whites, fruit, candy or nuts into a thick, heavy batter.

JULIENNE To cut foods into long thin strips much like matchsticks. Used often for salads and stir-fries.

KNEAD To work dough by using a pressing and folding action to make it smooth and elastic.

MARINATE To tenderize and/or flavor foods, usually vegetables or uncooked meat, by placing them in a mixture that may contain oil, vinegar, wine, lime or lemon juice, and herbs and spices.

MINCE To cut into very fine pieces. Often used for garlic, hot peppers and fresh herbs.

PARBOIL To boil foods, usually vegetables, until partially cooked. Most often used when vegetables are to be finished using another cooking method or chilled for marinated salads or dips.

PINCH A measurement less than ⅛ teaspoon that is easily held between the thumb and index finger. This is not a precise measurement.

PULSE To process foods in a food processor or blender with short bursts of power.

PUREE To mash solid foods into a smooth mixture with a food processor, mill, blender or sieve.

SAUTE To fry quickly in a small amount of fat, stirring almost constantly. Most often done with onions, mushrooms and other chopped vegetables.

SCORE To cut slits partway through the outer surface of foods. Often required for ham or flank steak.

SIMMER To cook liquids, or a combination of ingredients with liquid, at just under the boiling point (180-200°). The surface of the liquid will have some movement and there may be small bubbles around the sides of the pan.

STEAM To cook foods covered on a rack or in a steamer basket over a small amount of boiling water. Most often used for vegetables.

STIR-FRY To cook meats, grains and/or vegetables with a constant stirring motion, in a small amount of oil, in a wok or skillet over high heat.

General Index

This handy index lists every recipe by food category, major ingredient and/or cooking method, so you can easily locate recipes that suit your needs.

✓ Indicates an Eat Smart recipe

RECIPE INDEXES

RECIPE INDEXES

✓Guacamole Deviled Eggs, 247
Honey Champagne Fondue, 302
✓Italian Deviled Eggs, 246
Marinated Olives, 9
Party Cheese Balls, 290
✓Southwest Deviled Eggs, 247

Breakfast & Brunch
✓Apple-Cinnamon Quinoa
  Pancakes, 179
Carrot Cake Oatmeal, 122
✓Cinnamon Blueberry French
  Toast, 184
✓Curry Scramble, 186
Migas Breakfast Tacos, 175

Main Dishes
✓All Veggie Lasagna, 249
✓Black Bean Tortilla Pie, 90
✓Cauliflower Alfredo, 70
✓Makeover Creamy Mac &
  Cheese, 254
✓Portobello & Chickpea Sheet-Pan
  Supper, 70

Quick & Easy Vegetable Potpie, 82
✓Roasted Vegetable Sauce, 105
Skillet Pasta Florentine, 83
✓Tuscan Portobello Stew, 85
Vegetarian Skillet Enchiladas, 65
✓Veggie-Cashew Stir-Fry, 77

Sandwiches
✓Avocado Egg Salad Toast, 39
Garbanzo Bean Burgers, 36
✓Lentil Sloppy Joes, 42

Soups
✓Golden Butternut Squash
  Soup, 39
Mexican Street Corn Chowder, 48
Slow-Cooker Minestrone, 40

WHITE CHOCOLATE
Champagne Blondies, 303
Chocolate-Covered Strawberry
  Snack Mix, 275
Chocolate Peanut Drops, 194

Lime-in-the-Coconut Almond
  Bark, 296

WINTER SQUASH
✓Acorn Squash Slices, 136
✓Apricot-Ginger Acorn Squash, 147
✓Golden Butternut Squash Soup, 39

ZUCCHINI & SUMMER SQUASH
Golden Zucchini Pancakes, 142
✓Lime & Dill Chimichurri
  Shrimp, 269
✓One-Pan Sweet Chili Shrimp &
  Veggies, 61
✓Pork Grapefruit Stir-Fry, 63
✓Quick & Healthy Turkey Veggie
  Soup, 37
San Diego Succotash, 153
Stewed Zucchini & Tomatoes, 140
✓Zippy Turkey Zoodles, 9

Alphabetical Index

This convenient index lists every recipe in alphabetical order, so you can easily find your all-time favorite dishes.

✓ Indicates an Eat Smart recipe

RECIPE INDEXES